MULTICULTURAL
& PRACTICE EVALUATION

A Case Approach
To Evidence-Based
Practice

Monit Cheung & Patrick Leung

University of Houston

LOVE PUBLISHING COMPANY®
Denver • London • Sydney

To our parents
for their encouragement;
To our children, Carol & Marie,
for their multicultural understanding,
with thanks and love

Published by Love Publishing Company
P.O. Box 22353
Denver, Colorado 80222
www.lovepublishing.com

Library of Congress Control Number: 2007938792

Copyright © 2008 by Love Publishing Company
Printed in the United States of America
ISBN 978-0-89108-333-7

CONTENTS

Chapter 6: Family Systems Theory   135

Chapter 7: Structural Theory   157

Chapter 8: Client-Centered Theory   181

        An Adoptive Family   203
    Experts Say   204
    Best Practice Evaluation Stage 5:
        Assess Changes and Impacts   206
    Multicultural Practice Exercises   209
    Topics for Discussion   209

Chapter 9:   Gestalt Theory   211

    Perls's View of Gestalt   211
    On the Multicultural Stage: Family with Adolescents   214
    The Case Approach   215
    Multicultural Practice Applications   218
    Multicultural Practice Exercises   219
    Variations From the Standardized Case:
        A Family Dealing with Drug Problems   228
    Experts Say   230
    Best Practice Evaluation Stage 6:
        Assess Problems Within the Family   231
    Topics for Discussion   234

Chapter 10:   Strategic Theory   235

    Strategy as the Intervention Focus   237
    On the Multicultural Stage: Children Leaving Home   237
    The Case Approach   238
    Multicultural Practice Applications   246
    Variations From the Standardized Case:
        A Single-Parent Family   247
    Experts Say   248
    Best Practice Evaluation Stage 7:
        Measure Intergenerational Values   250
    Multicultural Practice Exercises   253
    Topics for Discussion   256

Chapter 11:   Behavioral Theory   257

    From Social Learning to Behavioral Action   258
    On the Multicultural Stage:
        Family with Adult Children   259
    The Case Approach   261
    Multicultural Practice Applications   266
    Variations From the Standardized Case:
        A Family Experiencing Domestic Violence   268

PREFACE

Multicultural practice has become an undeniable necessity in a variety of professional helping fields as a result of the ever increasing ethnic diversity throughout the world. In the United States, the Council on Social Work Education (2001; revised 2004), the national accrediting body for schools of social work, requires that all social work programs include curriculum content addressing nondiscrimination and human diversity. Similarly, the American Psychological Association (APA, 2002) provides accreditation guidelines to encourage student and faculty diversity in academic programs as well as increased cultural competency among practitioners in the field of psychology.

The National Council for the Accreditation of Teacher Education (2002) requires that all member schools implement multicultural education in their curricula. It encourages teachers to collaborate and interact with families from diverse ethnic backgrounds in an effort to better appreciate the distinct learning styles and unique learning difficulties faced by modern youth. Within the medical field, the standards concerning cultural diversity are enforced by the Liaison Committee on Medical Education (2007), the accreditation body of medical schools in the United States and Canada. Medical professionals are becoming part of interdisciplinary teams that seek multicultural consultation to ensure the effectiveness of quality treatment and discharge plans.

Specifically, according to the National Association of Social Workers (NASW, 2007b), developing multicultural sensitivity requires more than attention to race and ethnicity. Culturally competent social workers "address issues of gender and help persons with disabilities, older adults, gays, lesbians, bisexuals, and transgender people" (para. 6), and they seek to understand cultures and values related to their clients' needs. NASW (2007b) further strives to ensure that social work practice is conducted and evaluated within the parameters of protecting rights for all clients without any cultural biases or discriminatory actions:

> It can be persuasively argued that effective care is impossible without a working knowledge and understanding of a person's or group's culture and background. As we move into an ever more pluralistic and multicultural society, social workers are among those best-equipped to deliver that care and to empower people from all backgrounds to lead connected, healthy lives. (para. 7)

According to the APA (2002), cultural diversity is the expected environment for practice. Under "Principle E: Respect for People's Rights and Dignity," its code of ethics (2002) states:

> psychologists are aware of and respect cultural, individual, and role differences, including those based on age, gender, gender identity, race, ethnicity, culture, national origin, religion, sexual orientation, disability, language, and socioeconomic status and consider these factors when working with members of such groups. Psychologists try to eliminate the effect on their work of biases based on those factors, and they do not knowingly participate in or condone activities of others based upon such prejudices. (para. 1)

According to the American Counseling Association (ACA, 2005) code of ethics, the emphasis of practice should be the client, not the differences between client and practitioner. In addition, professional counselors must be culturally sensitive and accept the client's definition of a problem, based on the client's values. The ACA stresses that

> counselors do not condone or engage in discrimination based on age, culture, disability, ethnicity, race, religion/ spirituality, gender, gender identity, sexual orientation, marital status/partnership, language preference, socioeconomic status, or any basis proscribed by law. (para. C5)

In addition,

> counselors actively attempt to understand the diverse cultural backgrounds of the clients they serve. Counselors also explore their own cultural identities and how these affect their values and beliefs about the counseling process. (p.4)

Throughout the course of training, students in the fields of social work, psychology, counseling, education, and medicine are required to study, analyze, and develop their own theoretical frameworks while evaluating their learning through practice in the field. An important development in all of these fields of study is in evaluating practice and integrating evidence-based research in areas in which students and practitioners must demonstrate the integration of practice and evaluation (Blender & Sanathara, 2003; Briggs, Feyerherm, & Gingerich, 2004; Cone, 2001).

Many students are legitimately cautious about the limitations of practice theories when applying them within a multicultural context. On the one hand, mounting evidence indicates that the majority of educators and practitioners believe that incorporating a variety of theories is crucial for serving a culturally diverse population and for evaluating practice effectiveness. On the other, current literature regarding the development and implementation of an integrated perspective is scarce. To fill this need, this textbook provides innovative ways to assimilate practice theories and to facilitate practice evaluation based on various stages of integration in multicultural applications. These practice theories include: psychoanalytic, Adlerian, family systems, structural, client-centered, gestalt, strategic, behavioral, cognitive–behavioral, feminist/empowerment, and solution-focused. Our intent in addressing each of these theories is not to encourage the application of only one single theory to a given situation but, instead, to integrate multiple approaches in practice.

Each theoretical approach is demonstrated through single-system design examples with a hypothetical family and treated as a "standardized" case example. The hypothetical family consists of a couple with two children. Through information drawn from real practice experiences with diverse families, this standardized family presents a wide range of cultural, ethnic, gender, and human diversity issues. We discuss the strengths and limitations of each theory or approach relative to the cultural or ethnic identity of the case, whether the family is African American, Asian American, Latino American, Native American, multiracial, or of a nontraditional structure. Through specific examples, we apply these approaches to work with various family structures including, but not limited to, gay and lesbian couples, single-headed families, families with adopted children, recent immigrant families, families of interracial marriage, blended families, and families in poverty.

The practice–evaluation integration framework presented in this book is unique. Its application of multiple theories to a single practice example facilitates a holistic practice–evaluation perspective. We do not attempt to describe each theory in detail. Instead, we highlight the applicable techniques in brief in each chapter for a basic understanding of how theories are put into action. Upon review of these theories, case examples, and various practice scenarios, students and practitioners will become more aware of the limitations of using a single-theory approach when working with multiple cultural and family issues. The book is technique and application oriented; its intent is to provide readers with a tool for practical application by combining underlying theoretical orientations with evidence-based data linking theory with practice and evaluation.

Another distinct characteristic of this book is its emphasis on working with families *specifically*, through the variations of the case example, counseling dialogues for role-play, evaluation methods, and topics for discussion. This innovative approach allows learners to evaluate theories in different situations as they develop or augment their own practice style.

This text is ideal for undergraduate students who are studying behavioral theories, as well as social work and psychology graduate students, educators, and medical students who are seeking to integrate theories and evaluation methods into their own personal style of practice in our multifaceted and diverse modern environment. In addition, this text can be utilized as a reference guide for practitioners who work closely with diverse individuals and families, allowing these professionals to develop the necessary skills for integrating a variety of practice and evaluation approaches into their practice.

This book is organized into three main parts. Part One (chapters 1, 2, and 3) describes practice–evaluation within a framework of multiculturalism. It begins by describing the trend toward global migration as a rationale for working with multicultural families. The definition of globalization and indigenization will facilitate work with powerless, mobile, and culturally diverse populations based on their core beliefs and value systems. Integrating culture and diversity into evaluation and practice is important to uniquely design each intervention for culturally diverse clientele. Chapter 3 provides an overview of the evaluation process. Evaluation is necessary to ascertain whether selected interventions and specific techniques effectively reach their treatment goals. A multicultural self-assessment instrument is included, and a strong sense of self-awareness and continuous self-evaluation are recommended to help practitioners apply this practice–evaluation framework.

Part Two (chapters 4–14) presents a series of distinct theoretical approaches with an emphasis on using the cases to show how to apply theories to practice. The standardized case demonstrates and highlights practice applications along with theoretical assumptions and techniques. A narrative technique is applied, in the form of dialogues between clients and the practitioner. A reflective examination of these stories, relayed by people of various cultures, provides a framework for understanding patterns of meaning in their diverse day-to-day experiences (Holland & Kilpatrick, 1993).

To present realistic professional applications, each chapter also contains comments from national experts in social work education, practice, and evaluation. Each case scenario, modified with multicultural information, was sent to experts in the field. These experts were selected based on their contributions in practice, their research expertise in the selected area of the case review, and their willingness to participate in evaluating the case example presented to them. The experts offered comments based on their knowledge and professional experience with specific assessment and intervention approaches with multicultural families. This information is invaluable to students and practitioners alike. Each chapter concludes with a suggested evaluation for the client system discussed, as well as additional multicultural practice exercises.

Part Three (chapter 15) presents research-based principles for multicultural practice, integrates the practice–evaluation framework with practice philosophy, and includes a comprehensive literature review regarding validation of professional competency in social work and psychology. It provides an individual, family, and systems analysis of the strengths and limitations of each theoretical approach when applied to working with diverse cultures. The chapter concludes with a glimpse into the future of multicultural practice.

To ensure that practitioners respect clients' *individual* diversity, this text encourages flexibility and creativity in working with diverse populations. The specific techniques are presented as an aid to enhance learning and should not be considered as an exclusive medium to achieve a predefined goal for every client. The case approach utilized in this book provides a means to help practitioners assess the importance of each of the diverse therapeutic methods and techniques and develop an eclectic, integrated application to clients within our multifaceted world.

Acknowledgment

This book about human diversity could not have been completed without input from culturally diverse and nationally renowned experts and assistance from a team of dedicated research assistants. After receiving extensive input and gracious assistance from a team of individuals, we want to extend a wholehearted acknowledgment. We wish to take this opportunity to thank the following individuals for their expertise comments: Dr. Dale Alexander, University of Houston; Dr. Stephen Arch Erich, University of Houston, Clear Lake; Dr. Christine Lowery, University of Wisconsin at Milwaukee; Ms. Ann McFarland, Office of Community Projects, University of Houston; Dr. Peter Nguyen, Virginia Commonwealth University; Mr. Joe Papick, Child Welfare Education Project; Dr. Maria Puig, Colorado State University; Dr. Cheryl Waites, North Carolina State University; Dr. Joe Rubio, Catholic Charities, Archdiocese of Galveston-Houston; Mrs. Anne Rubio, Galveston Interfaith; Nada Miosevic, a private practitioner in Melbourne, Australia; Dr. Camille Hall, University of Tennessee; and Dr. Kay Stevenson, Rocky Mountain Survivors Center. In addition, we would like to thank Dr. Kathryn Briar-Lawson, Dean of the School of Social Welfare at the State University of New York at Albany and Dr. Rowena Fong, Ruby Lee Piester Centennial Professor in Services to Children and Families and BSW Program Director at the University of Texas-Austin, for their thorough and thoughtful review comments. Our sincere thanks also go to our graduate assistants, Ms. Jessica Carnesi, Ms. Demori Currid Driver, Ms. Yuanyuan Feng, Ms. Shetal Vohra-Gupta, Ms. Anny Kit-Yung Ma and Ms. Melanie Barr Fitzpatrick, all of the University of Houston, for their continuous administrative support and endless editorial efforts. Without the endeavors and contributions from all of these individuals, as well as from the graduate students who assisted in testing the use of the practice dialogues, this book would not have attained successful fruition.

Meet the Authors

Dr. Monit Cheung, MA, MSW, PhD, LCSW, is Professor and Chair of Children and Families Concentration at the Graduate College of Social Work, University of Houston. She is Principal Investigator of the Child Welfare Education Project, a state partnership program funded federally by Title IV-E for training child welfare social workers. She has been a social worker for 31 years and is currently a Licensed Clinical Social Worker specializing in family counseling, child/adolescent counseling, child protection, sexual and domestic violence, and incest survivor treatment. She has practiced as a volunteer clinician by providing counseling and case consultation at the Asian American Family Services, and served as a consultant trainer for the Hong Kong Social Welfare Department and the Hong Kong Police Force. She has presented 157 papers in workshops or conferences and written 265 articles and books on child protection and parenting issues in English and Chinese languages. Her research interests are related to treatment effectiveness in areas of child sexual abuse, creative therapy, therapeutic touch, and immigrant adjustment. Dr. Cheung currently serves on several boards of directors and has received numerous awards.

Dr. Patrick Leung is a professor and former Doctoral Program Director at the University of Houston Graduate College of Social Work (UH-GCSW). Currently, he is the President of the Asian & Pacific Islander Social Work Educators Association and the chair of the Texas Title IV-E Child Welfare Roundtable Evaluation Committee. His research areas include cultural sensitivity training, Asian mental health issues, children and families, immigrant issues, domestic violence and gerontology. He received his Ph.D., M.S.W., M.A. (Public Administration) and B.S.S.W. from Ohio State University. He has served as principal investigator and evaluator on numerous projects at the federal, state and local levels; has been a grant reviewer for ACYF (Administration for Children and Family, DDHS) and CSAP (Center for Substance Abuse Prevention, SAMSHA) and is currently coordinating the Social Work Research Center at the UH-GCSW. He has published over 80 articles, book chapters, and reports and has made numerous presentations at international, national, and local conferences. He has served on many boards of directors, and was the President and one of the founders of the Asian American Family Services (AAFS) in Houston, Texas. He is co-author of a book entitled *Child Protection Training and Evaluation*.

The Practice–Evaluation Framework

T his book provides a connection between a case approach and multicultural materials, presenting an integrated practice–evaluation theoretical framework as it applies to the stage–process approach of designing family interventions. Its aim is not to explain each theory in detail but, rather, to provide practice opportunities for integration purposes. The stage-process approach takes two routes:

1. *Stages of cultural understanding*: client-worker interactions from multicultural awareness of the practitioner to the attainment of solutions and treatment outcomes
2. *Process of working with a family:* based on the nonlinear family development stages, from the formation of a family to the separation of family members

Based on this stage–process approach (Figure 1.1), we outline 11 practice–evaluation integrative stages for the helping professional to walk through in working with a standardized case of a couple and their two children. These stages are as follows:

1. Assess the practitioner's own self, skills, and commitment to multicultural sensitivity.
2. Evaluate the client's family relationships.
3. Evaluate the family as a system.
4. Assess problems within the family.
5. Assess changes and impacts of family interactions.
6. Communicate with children and adolescents.
7. Measure intergenerational values.
8. Measure family stress.
9. Identify faulty thinking patterns.
10. Measure perception of power.
11. Map out solutions and alternatives.

Each stage corresponds to a method of building family relationships according to a case provided in this book that we will refer to as the *standardized case.* Variations of this case are presented in each chapter to enrich the clinical learning to expand the skills application and evaluation of practice.

The outcome of this learning process involves gaining a multicultural perspective from a case approach. Using the stage–process approach, we introduce major concepts, assumptions, assessments, and intervention techniques for each of the major therapeutic approaches and illustrate appropriate applications of each approach to the standardized case, studied through its psychosocial histories. Because this standardized case is based on composite clinical observations from our work with multicultural families, each chapter illustrates skills and techniques with this family, then present modifications to the family characteristics that correspond to prior experiences of various ethnic groups and various family compositions.

As an evidence-based procedure, the case with cultural and compositional variations has been supported by research data (presented in chapter 2) and then reviewed by nationally renowned experts in each chapter. The assessment–treatment information has been incorporated into the case dialogues for practice purposes. In addition, readers should design their own client–worker dialogues with the varied (or alternative) cases stemming from the standardized case to achieve their learning outcomes and to continue self-evaluation.

Another purpose of the stage–process approach is to provide an intimate and practical experience of theory in action. Application of human behavioral theories is discussed as it relates to culturally and compositionally diverse families. We hope the reader will understand how the various theoretical approaches, although sound in their underlying concepts, can be applied flexibly or restructured to fit the work in a multicultural system. We believe that a single case can demonstrate both disparities and parallels among the different multicultural groups, as well as clarify theoretical models and practice techniques.

To connect the stage–process approach to multicultural practices, a groundwork for analyzing intervention effectiveness is highlighted in chapter 1, which also addresses the purpose and process of working with culturally diverse families.

Chapter 2 explains how to use the case approach and family stage–process approach to address family issues. Although the narrative of the case is based on the experiences of mental health professionals in the United States, specific characteristics can be added to facilitate application to other cultural backgrounds. Through this learning process, mental health practices focus on assessing clients from a biopsychosocial perspective, treating them from a holistic body–mind–environmental perspective and evaluating the treatment effectiveness with a single-system research perspective centered exclusively on the individual, family, or system and its surrounding environment. This multifaceted perspective is helpful because, in reality, our clients come from widely diverse cultural backgrounds. Depending on the issues that each client presents in the standardized case, the choice of approach to these problems may be more effective in certain situations than in others. This effectiveness demonstration identifies an important premise in practice: No one approach can be considered a "cure-all." We also must take our clients' expectations and cultural influences into consideration without imposing any of our own assumptions. Multicultural practice is uniquely suited to this type of learning process, in that it reflects reality and identifies multiplicity in practice methods, even as the methods are examined through a single lens of the practitioner with one approach at a time.

Prior to the case presentation and application of theoretical approaches, chapter 3 discusses the practice–evaluation integrated framework. This framework identifies the importance of addressing culture and human diversity in counseling and social work practice based on two major trends: globalization and indigenization. These trends have created additional cultural changes that impact every individual in the world. This chapter also addresses immigrant and refugee issues.

CHAPTER ONE

Working With Multicultural Families

Because helping professionals often work with clients from diverse cultural backgrounds, the practitioner has to maintain an open-minded and unbiased attitude. This is a *time* perspective, in that past events in the practitioner's own life can be intertwined with his or her current practice and the client–worker relationship.

Second, from a *personal involvement* perspective, the practitioner has to become knowledgeable about how a client's culture may influence the practitioner's own perspectives on how problems will be defined and managed within the client's cultural context. In this regard, theories based on the experiential nature of human behavior that involve both the client's and the practitioner's perspectives are applicable in analyzing interrelationship issues.

Third, from a *social justice* perspective, the practitioner should encourage positive outcomes that influence the client's life meaning, a family's self-sufficiency in managing problems, and a community's collaborative efforts to support equality of service provision and equilibrium of system interactions.

Balancing the Three Perspectives

To balance these three perspectives, the practitioner will learn to integrate theories with past, present, and future orientations; theories with experiential, existential and equilibrium foci; and theories promoting justice, equality, and respect.

Figure 1.1 illustrates the stage-process approach.

1. *Time orientation*: When an individual or a family goes through changes, a time perspective is essential to identify past, present, and/or anticipated issues as each of these issues relates to the client's future environment. In therapy, the practitioner must help the client address past events, describe current issues, and plan future actions to deal with the crisis and prevent problems from recurring. This time perspective also aims at an integral examination of all facets of life events that may have a significant impact on the client's future outlook.

2. *Technique analysis*: Techniques must be connected to three therapeutic foci:

   a. They must be experiential in nature: Help the client reexperience the past, identify current feelings, and imagine what it is like to go through the proposed change.

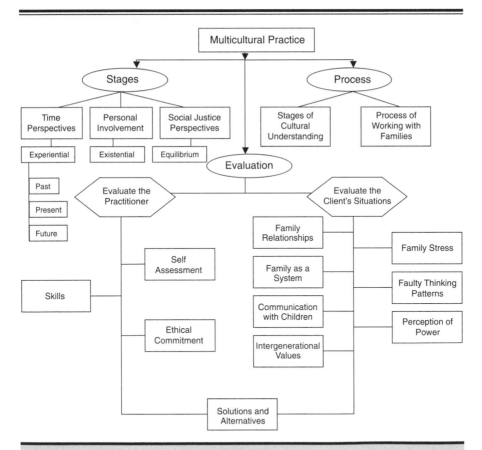

Figure 1.1

A Stage–Process Approach to Evaluation of Cultural Competence

b. They must have existential meaning: Identify the meaning of individual, family, and system existence because each individual represents a set of unique characteristics, and each family/system represents the call for individual existence.

c. They must achieve equilibrium in outcome: Relate the intervention process to the anticipated outcomes that promote social, political, and economic justice, helping clients appreciate the work that they have done.

3. *Action focus:* These theories aim at promoting a sense of balance within a given culture at any given time. Time may change, but the essentiality of justice, equality, and respect remain priorities within any system. The goal of intervention, whether it is clinical or political, is to help clients achieve the goals of promoting justice, examining equity and equality issues, and instilling hope, with the practitioner's continued support and respect.

Practice Theories as a Foundation

The practice focus of this book is on integrated learning from psychosocial theories to multicultural applications. The book covers 11 theories with multicultural applications:

1. Psychodynamic
2. Adlerian
3. Family Systems
4. Structural
5. Client-Centered
6. Gestalt
7. Strategic
8. Behavioral
9. Cognitive–Behavioral
10. Feminist/Empowerment
11. Solution-Focused

Psychodynamic theory, Adlerian theory, family systems theory, and structural theory help families resolve past conflict by highlighting the psychological experiences of the individuals. Psychodynamic theory emphasizes events from the past; Adlerian theory links past events with the present; family systems theory describes present issues in relation to the surrounding systems that were established in the past; and structural theory discusses the cultural and structural root of a system in terms of how this root impacts the functioning of its individual members.

Client-centered theory and gestalt theory are communicator theories that emphasize the development of relationships in current situations; both of these theories emphasize present functioning and the experiential nature of the helping process, which leaves clients with an impression about their own thoughts and feelings rather than with the practitioners' suggestions. These theories require self-determination from clients who feel hesitant, resistant, and hopeless to help them realize the importance of a *self-and-others* perspective in the development of healthy relationships.

Strategic theory, behavioral theory, and cognitive–behavioral theory are action-oriented and promote the control of one's thoughts and behaviors to take progressive steps into the future. These theories can assist clients from a variety of cultural learning environments in managing their actions and in altering their thinking patterns from an unhealthy blaming mode to healthier cognitive and behavioral functioning.

Last, to promote the concept of social justice, feminist theory, with its empowerment focus, and solution-focused theory address the importance of resource assessment and support intervention. Feminist and solution-focused theories tap into clients' strengths and assets to promote concrete outcomes and to deemphasize problem-oriented language during the intervention phase. These theories also incorporate empathetic and listening skills into practice applications in order to stress the importance of having an empathetic worker serving the client, regardless of the theory choice. Figure 1.2 illustrates the theory integration framework.

The Family Process as a Practice Framework

To demonstrate how each theory is applied to multicultural practice, this book provides case examples from a variety of theoretical approaches, based on a family process framework. In the standardized case, the family deals with one stage at a time, demonstrating practice principles and skills. This model is similar to the family developmental framework adopted in family practice (Duvall, 1988). A unique aspect in this book, however, is its use of case demonstrations to highlight a developmental process within the multicultural environment of multiple family problem-solving stages. This developmental view also provides a means for practitioners to understand how diverse families deal with different and difficult issues.

In studies of a variety of families, Duvall (1957, 1988) identified eight stages of family development. These stages, which many family researchers have found to parallel an individual's developmental process, determine the process of studying a family. The process starts from the meeting of two families, then moves to this couple forming a new family, their having children, children growing up, children getting married, the couple gaining grandchildren, their reaching retirement, and finally facing family members' death and dying. Table 1.1 outlines the developmental process as a practice framework.

Over the past five decades, family structure has changed dramatically (Aquilino, 2005; Hernandez, 1993). Consequently, we must consider additional views of development to fit the new diversity of family configurations. When events such as adoption and divorce occur, the transition to a new family structure can be considered a stage in family development. Traditional and nontraditional families

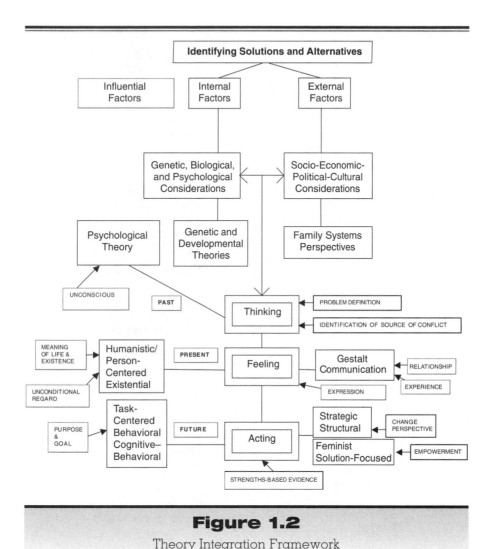

Figure 1.2
Theory Integration Framework

alike undergo developmental transitions, yet the configuration of these two types of families may differ depending on their experiences. For example, a family may consider adoption for many reasons, including infertility, the desire for another child, the need to support children left behind after a family member's death, and so forth. Other couples choose to remain childless. Different cultures may view this decision differently, especially because some cultures view the inability to bear children as a legitimate and socially acceptable reason for divorce. Thus, divorce is not a typical family developmental stage, but it can be regarded as a response to unexpected circumstances or to a life-cycle variation (Duvall, 1988).

Table 1.1

Developmental Process as a Practice Framework

Individual Developmental Stages	Traditional Views of the Family	Family Developmental Stages / Additional Views about the Contemporary Family
1. Infancy	Meeting of individuals from two families	Individuals with different lifestyles living in a multi-cultural environment
2. Toddlerhood	Formation of a new family	Family formation: definitions, values, and cultures
3. Childhood	The family with young children	The family with or without children
4. Adolescence	The family with adolescents	Decisions about additional household members: e.g., adoption, teen pregnancy, abortion, women having children after age 40, artificial insemination, or decision to remain childless
5. Adulthood	Marriage in the family	Relationships with additional household members: children moving out, parents moving in, divorce and the reconstituted family
6. Middle adulthood	Multigenerational families	Lifestyle adjustment: children moving back in
7. Later adulthood	Retirement	Re-retirement
8. Death and dying	Bereavement	Long-term care; simultaneously caring for aging parents as well as grandparents

To address the wide variations in modern families, this book describes 11 family stages:

1. Formation of the family
2. Development of cultural identity
3. Connecting two families
4. Families with children
5. Families in transition
6. Families with adolescents
7. Children leaving home

8. Families with adult children
9. Families in separation
10. Experiencing family diversity
11. Grandparenting

This family stage–process framework is based on research findings that support multicultural practice, as shown in Table 1.2. With practice examples integrated in

Table 1.2

Families in Multicultural Stages

Selected Family Development Stages	Characteristics	Research Findings
1. Formation of the family	—Definition of sex roles —Boundary around the couple within the family system —Relationship of the spouses to friends, activities, and community (Carter & McGoldrick, 1989)	—The role of the family is not limited to biological reproduction and intergenerational solidarity (Smith, 2004). —Families play a crucial role as production units, meaning that they also are a foundation for religious, work values, and social matters where traditions inherited from ancestors are executed (Ezra, 2003; Johnson, 2005).
2. Development of cultural identity	—Forming a cultural identity involves taking on world beliefs and engaging in behavioral practices that unite a community (Jensen, 2003).	—The extent to which one values autonomy and independence, or familial roles and obligations, and adheres to spiritual practices constitute important elements when forming one's own cultural identity (Jensen, 2003). —One of the variables that impact family functioning is its level of acculturation—the extent to which a family maintains traditional practices, values, beliefs, and preferences affect the family (Barbarin, 1993)
3. Connecting two families	—A change of two systems and an overlapping to develop a third system while realigning	How clients define "family," for example: —Americans in general:

(continued)

Table 1.2 *(continued)*

Selected Family Development Stages	Characteristics	Research Findings
	relationships with extended families and friends to include spouse (Carter & McGoldrick, 1989). —The ability of partners in all couple relationships to develop and sustain genuine relationships with the family-of-origin is critical for the well-being and satisfaction of the couple (Bowen 1978).	usually focus on nuclear family. —Italians: family refers to the entire extended network of aunts, uncles, cousins, and grandparents. —Black: family goes beyond blood ties and can refer to an informal network of kin and community. —Chinese: family may include all ancestors and descendents. (Carter & McGoldrick, 1989)
4. The family with children	—Becoming caregivers of a younger generation: —Struggle with disposition of childcare responsibilities and household chores. —Realignment of roles for extended family to include parenting and grand-parenting roles. (Carter & McGoldrick, 1989)	—Important for clinicians to evaluate family's childrearing practices in relation to their ethnic and social background (Carter & McGoldrick, 1989). —The lack of legal protection and knowledge of roles and language leave lesbian and gay families open to intrusion and invalidation (Slater, 1995).
5. The family in transition	—Family development theories caution the use of universality as an assumption when studying families in transition and the skew toward a single generational focus (Laszloffy, 2002). —All family members in transition face the issues of reorganization and renegotiation to define interpersonal boundaries (Wood & Talmon, 1983).	—Cultural and religious rituals "hold a special place in forming and sustaining family identity and contribute to feelings of safety on continuity." (Lanzet & Bernhardt, 2000, p. 239)
6. The family with adolescents	—Adolescents tend to do better in families in which they are encouraged to participate in decision making but in which parents have rational control and then ultimately decide what is	—Conclusions from previous studies indicate that many minority students first confront their ethnicity differences from the majority white culture during the period of adolescence (Portes &

(continued)

Table 1.2 *(continued)*

Selected Family Development Stages	Characteristics	Research Findings
	appropriate. (Henry, Peterson, & Wilson, 1997) —Parents who use effective strategies to transfer important values to their adolescent children have better parental control and parent–child outcomes. (Padilla-Walker & Thompson, 2005)	Zady, 2002). —Adolescence is the first time that individuals are able to foresee, contemplate, and worry (Chang, 1997). —Minority status and gender have an effect on worry for adolescents (Chang, 1997). —Lesbian and gay identity development is a complicated process (Martain, 1982), and the isolation and stigmatization that come from this may account for the high rate of suicidal behavior among these individuals. (Savin-Williams 1996)
7. Children leaving home	—Finding other life activities for the parent(s) — Renegotiating marital system as dyad —This stage includes the most exits and entries of family members. (Carter & McGoldrick, 1989)	—Must assess carefully what pathway a particular family considers "normal" for young adults in its cultural context. (Carter & McGoldrick, 1989, p. 77)
8. The family with adult children	— Shifting family roles, increased caregiving, grand-parenting, and maintaining independence in aging all need to considered when looking at this stage in the midlife (Ballard & Morris, 2003).	—In the dominant culture, the children leaving home initiates the midlife and later life stages. The household goes from a two-generational unit to a marital dyad or single-parent home where the parent–child relation is redefined and the focus of the parental unit is on individual and couple life pursuits (Carter & McGoldrick, 2005). —In healthy families, the marital subsystem is assumed to have more impact on parent–child subsystem than the parent–child subsystem has on the marriage (White, 1999)

(continued)

Table 1.2 *(continued)*

Selected Family Development Stages	Characteristics	Research Findings
9. The family in separation	Family adaptation to loss or separation usually involves shared grieving and reorganization of the family relationship system (Walsh & McGoldrick, 1991).	—Men and women, who invest in marriage differently, will have different emotional experiences as they go through the divorce/separation process (Carter, 1988). —Regardless of cultural or national differences, most people require 1½ to 3 years after the initial separation to stabilize their emotions (Cseh-Szombathy, Koch-Nielsen, Trost, & Weda, 1985).
10. Experiencing family diversity	—Ethnicity influences our patterns of thinking, feeling, and behavior externally and internally (Carter & McGoldrick, 1989).	—For gay and lesbian families, the traditional family life cycle model may not apply because (1) broader criteria are used to define a family (Weston, 1991); (2) childrearing may not be the central component of the family (Slater & Mencher, 1991); and (3) gay and lesbian individuals are labeled as a minority that their biological families are not a part of (Martain, 1982). —As families acculturate, members become increasingly involved with U.S. traditions, but internal family system variables remain intact even when English becomes the primary language (Portes & Zady, 2002).
11. Grandparenting	"Grandparenthood is a systematic transition that alters intergenerational relationships" (Spark, 1974).	After a certain time, spiritual faith, participating in religious services or activities, and support are key elements for the elderly to sustain resilience (Walsh, 1998).

theory applications, chapters 4 to 14 use this framework to structure the practice–evaluation integration with concrete examples.

This framework should be applied with cultural sensitivity, and practitioners must note three fundamental principles involved in working with diverse families:

1. Some families may not go through all these stages.
2. These stages do not represent an exhaustive list of family development.
3. The process is nonlinear in nature.

This practice–evaluation framework has the characteristics of fluidity and nonlinearity. *Fluidity* means that stages vary because of cultural diversity; and *nonlinearity* suggests that these stages may not move in a fixed order. Practitioners must analyze how to apply techniques through these stages based on the unique characteristics of the family system. Most important, these family process stages highlight the importance of connecting theory integration to practice and evaluation. We must approach any given family with its systems in mind. Every family exists in a multicultural environment that requires constant feedback if it is to improve and develop.

From a systems perspective of studying families, we must help families achieve system equilibrium. Integrated practice strategies, derived from many of these theories, should be applied. The combination of theoretical approaches will address the client's psychological, relational, cultural, and societal supports and will consider the changing demographics in the world that may affect the society in which the clients live. The society is more than a family's immediate surroundings. It also is the worldview that directs the family's growth, development, and change.

Globalization and Indigenization

Two major concepts that must be understood before we enter into a discussion about multicultural practice principles are globalization and indigenization. *Globalization* is the trend of observable social, economic, and political phenomena that are worldwide in scope and move beyond state and country boundaries (Ahmeadi, 2003). The connection between globalization and multicultural practice relates mainly to economic and political issues (Porter, 2007). In the fields of social work and counseling, however, globalization also refers to the development of a greater sense of community commitment that expands the scope of human services to promote social justice on a global scale.

Indigenization is an interactionist approach that examines the immediate environment of a group of people. The indigenization approach incorporates the values and cultures of individuals into the decision-making process to ensure that interventions reflect their needs (see Nimmagadda & Cowger, 1999).

From the globalization perspective, three major practice principles are required:

1. Cultural sensitivity
2. Observations of interrelated social problems across nations
3. Incorporation of the value of social justice in practice

From the indigenization perspective, these three principles hold true, and they place an additional emphasis on preventing the influence of the professional's own cultural background in treatment decisions. While globalization represents a macro-international perspective and indigenization values the micro-localization view in practice, these two concepts are complementary in establishing principles of multicultural practice.

With a close connection to the socioeconomic and political environment, multicultural practice takes on a postmodern social concept. Within the context of postmodernism, globalization can bring about knowledge of cultural traditions, boundaries between languages, and distinctiveness of ethnic groups. In addition to promoting social justice, multicultural practice can be connected to migration and the cultural adjustment of immigrants and refugees. To thoroughly understand the role that globalization plays in practice, practitioners should be knowledgeable about trends in international migration.

Migration Patterns in the World

Multicultural practice no longer focuses solely on "minorities," who are seen as lesser in number in a population. Today, migrant populations have increased substantially in many countries. Figure 1.3 identifies the many countries of origin of immigrant families. Practitioners must be educated about these original backgrounds because they represent a diversity of cultural, social, economic, and political orientations as well as family expectations and expectations toward cross-cultural, immigration, and refugee experiences. Although individuals from these groups may still be considered "minorities" because of their lesser socioeconomic and political power as perceived by others, they are increasing in number rapidly. Global migration affects every nation on the planet; countries may be places of origin, places of transit, and/or places of destination for migrants (British Broadcasting Corporation [BBC], 2007).

Migrants, including refugees, are defined as individuals who were born outside of the region in which they are currently residing. Nearly 145 million people lived outside of their native countries in the mid-1990s, and this number is now increasing to between 2 and 4 million each year (Population Reference Bureau [PRB], 2004). The countries with the highest *emigration* rates—movement of people out of the region—are China, India, and South Africa, along with some Eastern European countries. The countries highest in *immigration*—movement of people into the region—are the United States, countries in Western Europe, Australia, and the former Soviet Union (BBC, 2007). Globally, migrants comprise approximately 3% of the world population (United Nations, 2002), and in more developed regions, almost one in 10 persons is a migrant (International Migration, 2002).

According to the United Nations (2002), North America was home to 40.84 million migrants in 2002, representing 13% of its total population. International migration is at an all-time high in terms of absolute numbers (PRB, 2004) and accounts for the rise in different cultures, languages, and ethnic backgrounds in all

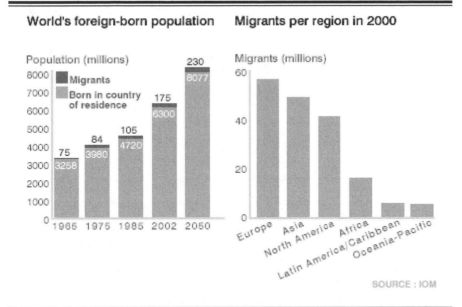

Source: From *Factlife: Global Migration,* by BBC News, 2007, Retrieved March 21, 2005 from http://news.bbc.co.uk/2/shared/sp1/hi/world/04/migration/html/migration_boom.stm

Figure 1.3
World's Migrant Populations

countries. The ethnic background of migrants coming to the United States has shifted in recent years. For more than 200 years, the majority of migrants entering into the United States were of European descent; during the first decade of this century, more than 90% of the nearly 9 million immigrants who entered the United States were from Europe. By the 1980s, however, the origin of migrants had shifted, with approximately 84% from Latin America and Asia and only 10% from Europe.

With a significant rise in the rate of legal immigration, especially from Asia and Latin America, we can expect continued growth in the future (PRB, 2004). Residing immigrants in a country, however, include documented and undocumented immigrants and refugees. For example, according to U.S. Citizenship and Immigration Services (2006), U.S. immigrants come from a total of 231 countries and territories: 56 European, 55 African, 41 Asian (including Middle Eastern), 25 Caribbean, 25 Oceanian, 14 South American, 7 Central American, and 2 North American countries (see Table 1.3). Although the representation from various countries may be consistent, the actual number of immigrants exceeds any official published number.

Table 1.3

Immigrants Admitted by Region and Country of Birth

Europe (N = 56)

Albania
Andorra
Armenia
Austria
Azerbaijan
Belarus
Belgium
Bosnia-Herzegovina
Bulgaria
Croatia
Cyprus
Czech Republic
Denmark
Estonia
Finland
France
Georgia
Germany
Gibraltar
Greece
Hungary
Iceland
Ireland
Italy
Kazakhstan
Kyrgyzstan
Kosovo
Latvia
Liechtenstein
Lithuania
Luxembourg
Macedonia
Malta
Moldova
Monaco
Montenegro
Netherlands
Norway
Poland
Portugal
Romania
Russia
San Marino
Serbia and Montenegro

Slovak Republic
Slovenia
Soviet Union (former)
Sweden
Switzerland
Tajikistan
Turkmenistan
Ukraine
United Kingdom
Uzbekistan
Yugoslavia

Africa (N = 55)

Algeria
Angola
Benin
Botswana
Burkina Faso
Burundi
Cameroon
Cape Verde
Central African
   Republic
Chad
Comoros
Congo, Republic of the
Democratic Republic of
   the Congo
Djibouti
Egypt
Equatorial Guinea
Eritrea
Ethiopia
Gabon
Gambia
Ghana
Guinea
Guinea-Bissau
Kenya
Lesotho
Liberia
Libya
Madagascar

Malawi
Mali
Mauritania
Mauritius
Morocco
Mozambique
Namibia
Niger
Nigeria
Reunion
Rwanda
Sao Tome and Principe
Senegal
Seychelles
Sierra Leone
Somalia
South Africa
St. Helena
Sudan
Swaziland
Tanzania
Togo
Tunisia
Uganda
Western Sahara
Zambia
Zimbabwe

Asia (N = 41)

Afghanistan
Bahrain
Bangladesh
Bhutan
Brunei
Burma
Cambodia
China
Cyprus
Hong Kong
India
Indonesia
Iran
Iraq

(continued)

Table 1.3 *(continued)*

Israel
Japan
Jordan
Korea
Kuwait
Laos
Lebanon
Macau
Malaysia
Maldives
Micronesia
Mongolia
Nepal
Oman
Pakistan
Philippines
Qatar
Saudi Arabia
Singapore
Sri Lanka
Syria
Taiwan
Thailand (Siam)
Turkey
United Arab Emirates
Vietnam
Yeman

Oceania (N = 25)

American Samoa
Australia
Christmas Island
Cocos Island
Cook Islands
Federate States of
   Micronesia
Fiji
French Polynesia
Guam
Kiribati
Marshall Islands

Nauru
New Caledonia
New Zealand
Niue
Northern Mariana
   Islands
Palau
Papua New Guinea
Pitcairn Island
Samoa
Solomon Islands
Tonga
Tuvalu
Vanuatu
Wallis and Futuna
   Islands

Caribbean (N = 25)

Anguilla
Antigua-Barbuda
Aruba
Bahamas
Barbados
Bermuda
British Virgin Islands
Cayman Islands
Cuba
Dominica
Dominican Republic
Grenada
Guadeloupe
Haiti
Jamaica
Martinique
Montserrat
Netherlands Antilles
Puerto Rico
St. Kitts-Nevis
St. Lucia
St. Vincent and the
   Grenadines

Trinidad and Tobago
Turks and Caicos
   Islands
U.S Virgin Islands

South America (N = 14)

Argentina
Bolivia
Brazil
Chile
Colombia
Ecuador
Falkland Islands
French Guiana
Guyana
Paraguay
Peru
Suriname
Uruguay
Venezuela

Central America (N = 7)

Belize
Costa Rica
El Salvador
Guatemala
Honduras
Nicaragua
Panama

North America (N = 1)

Canada
Mexico

Source: From *Persons Obtaining Legal Permanent Resident Status by Broad Class of Admission and Region and Country of Last Residence: Fiscal Year 2006,* by the U.S. Citizenship and Immigration Services, 2006, Retrieved August 30, 2007, from_http://www.dhs.gov/xlibrary/assets/statistics/yearbook/2006/table11d.xls

Camarota (2002) reports that 11.5% (33.1 million individuals) of the total population of the United States consists of immigrants. Kocarek, Talbot, Batka, and Anderson (2001) estimate that by the year 2050, 47.2% of the U.S. population will be non-white. In the United States, immigrants are represented disproportionately in lower income brackets, as one in four people in poverty is a migrant (Camarota, 2002). Actually, as immigrant populations grow in number, the poverty rate for immigrants and their U.S.-born children (under 18) is 20% higher than that of natives and their children—22% versus 18% (Greenberg & Rahmanou, 2007).

International migration, along with technological advances, has led to globalization in many diverse areas including economic, political, and social. The diminishing importance of geographical boundaries has led to a direct impact on people's living standards and ideals (Ahmeadi, 2003). Crow (1997) wrote, "It can no longer be assumed that people sharing a particular geographical space will also have the common social ties and culture by which a society has conventionally been defined" (p.10). The inevitable differences in cultures, traditions, and ethnicities will call for practitioners to be sensitive to immigrants and refugees who retain the values of their country of origin, and also to the first- and second-generation children and grandchildren of these immigrants and refugees who adopt values from their homeland and host country.

From a global perspective, cultural sensitivity is a key element in working with clients and their families. Special attention must be directed at how variations in cultural or ethnic heritage, gender, socioeconomic status, perceived level of power, and personal characteristics affect each individual's perception of problem definition and solution identification. A list of dos and don'ts is provided in Table 1.4 as a practice guide for developing a cultural understanding in practice. Alessandria (2002)

Table 1.4

Essentials in Multicultural Practice

Dos	Don'ts
• Recognize that multicultural counseling is inclusive of race, gender, sexual orientation, age, disability, culture, ethnicity, social class, rank, and location, as well as education.	• Don't blame clients based on their race or other differences.
• Learn from clients about the values of each particular tribe, religion, social group, etc.	• Don't assume that all persons from a given culture or social group have the same belief system.

(continued)

Table 1.4 *(continued)*

Dos	Don'ts
• Gain a perspective of sociopolitical issues and ways that these issues may impose on professionals and clients.	• Don't assume a particular meaning of a soft or firm handshake.
• Establish trust, particularly with those who do not openly trust others.	• Don't overemphasize or underemphasize your handshake.
• Show patience.	• Don't assume that the identified client is always the focus in therapy.
• Appreciate the use of silence.	
• Be aware of nonverbal communication, especially with cultures where eye contact, direct questioning, and hand shaking may become signs of disrespect.	• Don't assume that eye contact, handshakes, and body contact (pat on the back, etc.) is understood in the same context as in the United States.
• Show consistency.	• Don't assume that assertiveness is interpreted in the same manner in all cultures.
• Communicate with appropriate questions such as, "How does your family/culture see this?"	• Don't assume that mental health is defined uniformly in all cultures or societies.
• Explore the client's perception of the difference between individualistic versus collectivist values.	• Don't generalize the cultural values or traditions to every individual in that culture.
• Gain a sense of understanding for the strong level of respect for elders, particularly elderly women, in certain communities.	• Don't assume that that all cultures devalue old age or the female gender.
• Convey a sense of respect through a desire to understand and help.	• Don't leave the clients to wonder what the next steps of the helping process will be.
• Maintain awareness of institutional barriers that prevent ethnic minorities from using mental health services.	• Don't assume that ethnic-minority clients avoid seeking help because of their personal belief system.

Source: Adapted from *Counseling American Minorities,* by D. Atkinson, G. Morten, and D. Sue, 1989, Dubuque, IA: Wm. C. Brown, *Theories and Practice of Counseling and Psychotherapy* (7th ed.), by G. Corey, 2005, Belmont, CA: Brooks/Cole, and *Multicultural Counseling Techniques,* by Metropolitan Community College, 1999, Retrieved April 3, 2005, from http://ids dev.mccneb.edu/dcarter/counseli.htm

acknowledged that professionals should pay attention to all ethnicities, whites and non-whites, because they represent a variety of backgrounds and ethnic cultures. Therefore, in a manner similar to the way politics and economics have surpassed their national boundaries, social work and counseling practices must incorporate various techniques and processes to cater to these distinct cultures and ethnic groups.

Defining Culture and Ethnicity

The United Nations Educational, Scientific and Cultural Organization (UNESCO, 2005) defines culture as

> a set of distinctive spiritual, material, intellectual and emotional features of society or a social group that encompasses, in addition to art and literature, lifestyles, ways of living together, value systems, traditions and beliefs. (para 3)

Ethnicity is defined as a social group composed of people who

> [share] a sense of common origins, claim a common and distinctive history and destiny, possess one or more dimensions of collective cultural individuality, and feel a sense of unique collective solidarity. (Ministry of Economic Development, 2003)

Culture and ethnicity often refer to a common thread, such as unique cultural traits, a sense of community, ascribed membership, territoriality, and ethnocentric identity, through which individuals and families share values and customs (Marger, 2003). An individual's culture and identity are both deeply tied to family and are often reinforced by the community. To gain a full understanding of a family's history and sense of belonging, the practitioner must become familiar with its culture and ethnicity. By understanding the family's culture and ethnicity, the practitioner will build trust and respect with clients.

Over the course of human history, multiple meanings have been ascribed to terms such as ethnicity, race, diversity, and culture. These terms serve as the connection between the individual and the community and its social change. Their variations affect the individual and family at the micro, meso, and macro levels. In examining diversity from a holistic viewpoint, *human diversity* now encompasses the multifaceted principles of our clientele. Individual systems are composed of multidimensional layers—gender, cultural background, socioeconomic status, ethnic makeup, and other diverse differences.

The concept of human diversity has gained significant momentum in social work and counseling literature. Guadalupe and Lum (2005) write that

> human diversity has opened the floodgates to consider simultaneously such diverse characteristics as age, class,

skin color, culture, disability, ethnicity, family arrange-
ment/structure, gender, marital status, national origin, religion, sex, sexual orientation, and so on. (p. xxii)

Nezu (2005) prefers to use the term human diversity to address inclusively the needs
of our diverse clients and further suggests that practitioners should not overlook the
social component when adopting a biopsychosocial model in practice. Because
diversity has expanded to include *all* people, we must incorporate the concept of
human diversity into our practice when addressing cultural competence and multiculturalism. The ability to value differences among families and individuals will aid
the practitioner in becoming a stronger clinician and in appreciating family diversity
and its strengths as well.

In multicultural practice, respecting a person's ethnic identity is only the first
step. Whereas studies of multiculturalism emphasize the importance of cultural
diversity and the coexistence of two or more cultures in a relationship-building
process (Suinn, Khoo, & Ahuna, 1995), ethnic identity literature has emphasized
whether and how closely an individual feels invested in his or her own specific ethnic group (Johnson, Wall, Guanipa, Terry-Guyer, & Velasquez, 2002). A client's ethnic identity, then, forms in large part within personal identity development, which
plays a major role in the counseling process. In clinical practice, practitioners have
an ethical obligation to develop sensitivity to cultural distinctions and thereby be
able to create interventions consistent with their clients' values (Corey, 2005). Thus,
the concept of multicultural counseling has been defined as the joining of two or
more people from different cultural backgrounds in a helping relationship (Torres-
Rivera, Phan, Madduz, Wilber, & Garrett, 2001).

According to Ponterotto, Gretchen, Utsey, Reiger, and Austin (2002), from a
clinical perspective, multicultural counseling competence or *cultural competence*
consists of three components:

1. Awareness of one's own cultural socialization and accompanying biases
2. Knowledge of the worldviews and value patterns of culturally diverse populations
3. Specific intervention skills that are effective with these populations

Over the past two decades, many researchers and practitioners have focused on the
importance of multiculturalism in counseling, research, education, and organizations
(Kocarek, Talbot, Batka, & Anderson, 2001). The implementation of multicultural
training is necessary for practitioners to adequately address the needs of a diverse
clientele. According to Sue, Ivey, and Pederson (1996), most of the training in the
United States during the 1980s was monocultural, which inevitably resulted in ineffective work with ethnic minorities. Once the multicultural perspective came to light,
many researchers began to incorporate self-awareness and cultural sensitivity within
their field of practice.

Ponterotto and associates (2002) anticipate that by 2010, the commitment to
diversity will be identified as a core value in the field of counseling psychology.

Comparatively, in social work, cultural and ethnic diversity is already a core content area in the BSW and MSW curricula, as evidenced by the Social Work Code of Ethics, which states that "social workers are sensitive to cultural and ethnic diversity and strive to end discrimination, oppression, poverty, and other forms of social injustice" (National Association of Social Workers, 2007). Eventually, all social sciences are expected to emphasize human diversity in their respective curriculum and to address development and assessment in multicultural competency through their research.

Defining Evaluation as Practice

When providing human services, practitioners often face multifaceted questions:

How do we measure service outcomes?
How do we monitor programs or services?
How do we assess the needs in our community?
How do we assess service effectiveness?
How do we ensure that our agency has provided quality services?
How do we know when we should keep or discontinue a program, continue to treat a client, or refer the client to another service provider?
How do we assess the impact of a service?
What is the most efficient way to deliver services?

To move beyond a mere description of best-practice evaluation, this book provides appropriate measures within each chapter to integrate evaluation with multicultural practice.

Practice evaluation has several distinct components. In using these components, the practitioner is able to understand the dynamics of program evaluation and, more important, to select the most appropriate measures for specific types of evaluation.

In macro practice, these evaluation components include the following:

- Needs assessment: a method to identify the needs in an organization or a community
- Formative evaluation: an evaluation method to help an organization refine its mission, value, vision, goals, objectives, and outcomes
- Efficiency analysis: an evaluation method to assess the *best* way to accomplish the goals and objectives of an organization
- Process evaluation: an evaluation approach to monitor whether the target populations are being served and whether the programs are implemented according to their plan(s)
- Outcome evaluation: a method to evaluate whether the goals and objectives are being met
- Summative evaluation: an evaluation method to compare program X (intervention) with program Y (without the intervention)
- Impact assessment: a method to identify the net effect of a program after controlling for all confounding variables

In micro practice these evaluation components become the following:

- Needs assessment → Intake and case assessment
- Formative evaluation → Formulating goals and objectives
- Efficiency analysis → Selecting treatment
- Process evaluation → Monitoring progress
- Outcome evaluation → Evaluating treatment success
- Summative evaluation → Comparing treatment outcomes
- Impact assessment → Net effects of the treatment

Figure 1.4 identifies the components of practice evaluation. A practitioner cannot identify the problem until an intake and case assessment is conducted. Once the problem is identified, the practitioner will formulate appropriate goals and objectives with the client to resolve the problem. The practitioner will then identify and select the best treatment method to achieve the goals and objectives. When the treatment is selected, constraints and resources both must be taken into consideration. Therefore, the best treatment may not simply be the most *effective* treatment; instead, it should be the most feasible and effective treatment. *Feasibility* involves a careful examination of resources and constraints. When a treatment is implemented, the practitioner

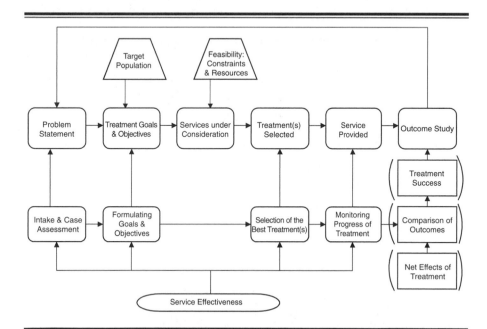

Figure 1.4

Practice Evaluation: A Conceptual Framework

will monitor whether progress is made towards the goals and objectives. Finally, the practitioner will assess whether the goals and objectives are achieved.

In assessing outcomes, the practitioner will monitor the accomplishment of the stated goals and objectives. Thus, the treatment is subjected to ongoing evaluation, especially when various modalities are being implemented. For example, if any selected treatment modality has not shown its total effects as anticipated, the practitioner may want to check the impact of other components within the treatment process, including environmental and emotional changes, to help clients achieve the maximum outcomes. In addition, the skilled practitioner should be mindful, in making comparisons among various treatment methods, to apply the most suitable techniques to the client's unique situation. Furthermore, even though the goals and objectives are achieved, the outcome cannot necessarily be credited to the treatment alone. The practitioner should constantly assess changes in the environment and the client's conditions. Consequently, a *net effect* assessment should be conducted to identify whether the selected treatment has contributed to the outcome.

Figure 1.5 presents an example of a single-system evaluation design to identify whether treatment success came from one of the two selected interventions when applied to a client system. The data show that, compared to Intervention #1, the outcome in Intervention #2 was more successful when the measured rating moved in the desirable direction, downward. Furthermore, when the two interventions were combined in the third intervention, the practitioner could see clearly that

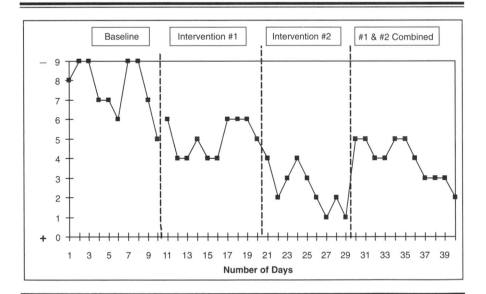

Figure 1.5

Evaluating Effectiveness of Two Interventions in One Client System the combination of the two interventions, although not as successful as using Intervention #2 only, pointed to the same pattern of reduction in the measured rating; that is, a better outcome was indicated in the latter days with both treatments.

If the goals and objectives have not been achieved, information or data collected from the evaluation process will be redirected to the problem identification stage, and the problem statement will be reexamined. The goals and objectives and the selected treatment approach will be revised and monitored continuously, and the evaluation cycle will continue. The practice evaluation should focus on the services provided by a practitioner or an organization—the activities that benefit clients and their families directly. In behavioral health, it is imperative to assess and evaluate the targeted behavior and other related issues to be able to identify the effectiveness of services. These evaluations provide a sense of achievement from the client's perspective, evidence of accurate application of efficacious techniques from the practitioner's perspective, and identification of whether the problem has been resolved from the family's standpoint.

Evidence-Based Practice

To demonstrate multicultural competency, practice evaluation must be conducted. Evidence-based practice is vital in the human services. It promotes the use of data to support continuation of the best practices and identifies ineffective or harmful practices so they may be changed or eliminated. In evidence-based practice, decisions are based on previously tested interventions that are likely to produce the desired outcomes (Roberts & Yeager, 2004). The integrated framework utilized in this book adopts this practice knowledge to enhance the understanding of selected theories pending further testing within a variety of client systems.

Through the study of practice techniques presented in the dialogue examples in each chapter, practitioners can polish their skills and adjust their practice techniques to accommodate clients' unique characteristics and presenting issues through culturally appropriate interventions for their respective clients. In Table 1.5, core skills in working with individuals and their families are listed for the reader for practice purposes before studying the applicability of the theories with the standardized case. In addition, the practical examples provided throughout this book will allow practitioners to evaluate the process and outcomes using specific measures, tools, and procedures.

This integrative practice–evaluation model is conceptualized under the premise that human service professionals must demonstrate a commitment to delivering evidence-based practice in order to

1. close the gap between practice and research,
2. provide data to document the multicultural applications of using various techniques, and
3. develop strategies that facilitate the growth and expansion of knowledge, skills, and value domains within each profession and across disciplines.

Table 1.5

Core Skills in Family Interventions

1. Rapport building: joining with the individual, group, family, or community	Communication Skills: • Active listening: use minimal encouragers • Brevity and building trust: "I hear you." "I don't understand this point." • Congruence: "I appreciate what you just said." (No "…but…") • Directness: "Do you mean…?"
2. Information gathering	Questioning techniques: • "Tell me what brought you here." • "Tell me about your relationship with your family." • "Tell me more." • "Give me an example of that." • "Thanks for the information, X. At this point, I would like to hear from Y about the situation."
3. Structuring	Time limits: "We'll have one hour today to talk about your situation." Role: "I see my role as helping you …." Process: "I will help you by …" Action: "By the end of this session today, I will ask you to try new ideas and…"
4. Reflecting content and clarifying	Draw out the content: "Joe, I noticed you avoid looking at others when you talk to them." Identify the content: "Most of you seem to have trouble with certain subjects, I've noticed…. Do you have other observations?" Reflect the content: "It seems to me that several of you are expressing concern about the same problem…. What's your view of my perception?"
5. Reflecting feelings	Listening for feelings: observing nonverbal cues: "I noticed that you've been kicking your feet. Tell me how you're feeling." Timing: "You've been looking around for the first ten minutes. Do you feel uncomfortable being here?" Reflecting: "It appears that you feel like no one has been listening to you. Is this right?"

(continued)

Table 1.5 *(continued)*

6. Self-disclosure	Feeling: "You seem angry to me....Can you respond to my feeling?" Experience: "I had this experience before and felt the same way you're feeling now." Focus: "I'm not your focus today. Let me hear from you first."
7. Confrontation	Feeling: "You laughed when Mary expressed her sad feelings. Tell me more about this." Validation: "If you didn't care, you wouldn't be this upset. I think you care more than you're willing to admit." Action: "I bet you'd lose your temper if you did that. What do you think?"
8. Redirecting	"Wait—before you tell me about Ami, let's finish what you were saying about your mother. You said she ...." "Thanks for your input. At this point, I'd like to hear Ami's thoughts about this."
9. Summarizing	"From what you've told me, three things are really important to you: first, ...; second, ...; third, ... Did I miss anything?"
10. Closure	Time: "It's time to end for the day. Let's talk more next time." Task: "We've accomplished a lot today, and the most impressive thing was that..." Homework: "Between now and our next meeting, would you do...?" Wishes: "We're about to finish now. Please let me know what you'd like to do next." Goal: "We'll talk about X next time."

CHAPTER TWO

The Case Approach: Purpose and Process

This book takes a unique approach to learning multicultural practice through a case study that presents a family going through various life-change stages. The case is hypothetical, and the family characteristics in the description are based on composite information gathered from actual families representing various ethnic backgrounds and sharing similar characteristics.

For learning purposes, the standardized case used throughout this book is a family composed of a heterosexual couple and their two children. This is not to imply that this family represents the *typical* family. Instead, by using the same case throughout, readers will learn to apply the skills and techniques from each approach one at a time, with the case as a constant, fixed entity. Thus, at the conclusion of this applied learning, the reader can appreciate the importance of integrating multiple approaches when working with families of distinct demographic characteristics including race and ethnicity, culture, gender, physical or mental ability, sexual orientation, family composition, or socioeconomic status.

In addition, practitioners often find themselves having to integrate several theoretical approaches when the presenting problem changes from a micro-oriented mental health issue to a macro-oriented community concern. Indeed, readers will come to see the disadvantages of using one single theoretical approach or of generalizing a set of characteristics onto every client system. Instead, readers will gain an appreciation for integrating multiple approaches in a variety of situations, especially when compared to the drawbacks of applying a narrow set of skills within the limited parameters of any given individual approach.

The Standardized Case

Before working with a family, practitioners should familiarize themselves with the core skills of family intervention. Each chapter highlights these skills using a generalizable case, or so-called standardized case, to provide readers with a baseline for examining various theoretical approaches. Practitioners must also understand how individuals and families communicate problems to helping professionals. The theory of constructivism contends that people do not comprehend external reality directly but, rather, construct models to make sense of their experiences (Glaserfeld, 1984). The narrative approach, based on this theory, helps us understand how individuals of any culture communicate their own concepts of their life's meaning and purpose through story-telling (Holland & Kilpatrick, 1993). The narrative approach is utilized throughout this book to illustrate how potential clients may tell the stories of their own problems and difficulties through their own cultural lens.

By working with the same standardized family through its various developmental stages, the reader will identify family issues and apply various intervention techniques with the family. In addition, the chapters analyze the strengths and limitations of each approach in their application to the family's cultural issues. Finally, the book explains the benefits of integrating various theories from a culturally competent perspective to enhance the selection and integration of various approaches in practice. Because there is no "typical" case in social work and counseling practice, this scenario will help students understand the limitations of using only one theory with their client system and learn to critically examine the skills that have been applied.

The standardized case scenario is presented with limited psychosocial information. It does not provide ethnic, cultural, or specific socioeconomic background of the family. This same case with modifications will then be used to identify practice and evaluation issues for different ethnic and family groups. Once the case has been demonstrated with theoretically supported techniques, it may be altered in some respects to address issues that arise when family characteristics vary. Variations may include, but are not limited to, race, ethnicity, gender, family composition, family of origin history, sexual preference, mental or physical disabilities, income, housing/neighborhood, education, religion, language, healing preferences, political orientation, and so on. To illustrate applications of techniques that are cross-culturally relevant, additional demographic details may be added and other information subtracted from the family situation at hand. This demonstrates how in reality a family's cultural diversity can be assessed further, even with the limited information provided.

Each chapter provides practice dialogues with these family members to demonstrate various approaches with the same family while remembering that clients within the same family, ethnicity, culture, community, or neighborhood differ. With the standardized case in mind, common American first names are used throughout the book to develop a baseline for the case approach discussion, not to ignore cultural variations. Ethnic names, however, should be considered for role-play demonstrations when ethnicity is a variable in the case study.

Practice With a Family

With limited information provided through the intake process, the practitioner will assess the family in terms of composition, age, educational level, career, income level, and other demographic information The standardized case in this book offers the following information for learning purposes:

Composition: a family of four (a married couple with two children)
Education of the couple: college-level
Income: middle-class
Careers: mechanical engineer and teacher/graduate student
Presenting problems: communication between the couple; parent–child relationships
Service requested: family counseling

A popular approach to sorting the family's intake information is a genogram, a diagram that examines family relationships (McGoldrick, Gerson, & Shellenberger, 1999). Figure 2.1 illustrates a genogram with Joe and Mary as the identified clients

Intake Information of a Selected Family for the Case Studies

Intake: This family is composed of Joe (42), Mary (38), and their two children, Ami (16) and Kevin (8). The couple has been married for 17 years. In the past two years, they have had communication difficulties with their children and, therefore, are seeking help to "glue" the family back together. Joe is a mechanical engineer, and Mary is a substitute school teacher who has recently begun attending a graduate social work program. They describe themselves as a middle-class family and note that both of their extended families do not expect women and mothers to work outside of the home.

Initial Assessment: Joe has expressed complaints about Mary's inconsistent parenting style. He disagrees with how Mary handles the family's finances and their children's unreasonable spending. Mary has presented symptoms of emotional distress with no recognized physical cause. She believes that both children are concerned about her constant arguments with Joe, and the children seem to be having trouble concentrating on their studies.

Ami and Kevin disagree with this interpretation and believe that the issue lies within their parents. Both children are willing to attend family counseling with their parents in an effort to clarify their parents' miscommunication. The family has not had a shared activity for many years, and the children's social activities have been limited.

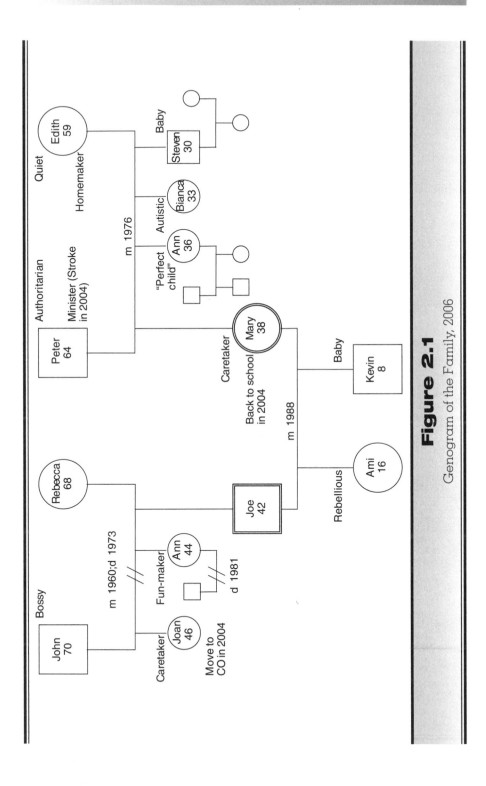

Figure 2.1

Genogram of the Family, 2006

and illustrates the composition of their families of origin. The couple was married in 1988. Mary describes her role as the "primary caregiver" in the household, their daughter as "rebellious," and their son as the "baby." Mary could not think of a term to describe her husband.

Using the genogram, relationship lines can be added to illustrate a strong, fused, or distant relationship between a pair of individuals within the family. Throughout the chapters, this genogram can be a tool to add and modify information about the family, but it typically does not allow enough space to specify cultural elements that have an impact on family functioning. A culturagram, therefore, is an additional aid to identify information relevant to assessment that can be useful for designing the intervention (Congress, 1994, 2004).

Figure 2.2 illustrates the culturagram for the family in this book. In Mary and Joe's case, Mary thinks it is time for her to seek employment. She believes strongly that she has the ability to handle a new job but at the same time worries about the children not having enough supervision. When information on this standardized case changes to demonstrate cultural diversity, the culturagram will be edited to reflect the changes.

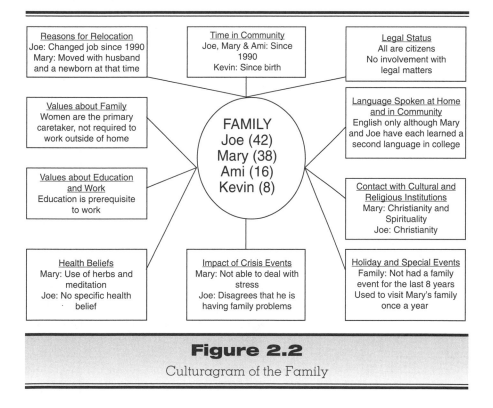

Figure 2.2
Culturagram of the Family

Beyond the Standardized:
Racial/Ethnic and Compositional Variations

Variations in families can stem from socioeconomic or political factors, health or mental health factors, human diversity factors, and technologically related factors. The family may be very poor, having a hard time making ends meet. Or it may be a refugee family trying to adjust to a new culture. A family may be facing death and dying issues involving a parent recently diagnosed with cancer. A family may be challenged by a member's recent suicide attempt. A minority family may be stressed by an incident of racism and discrimination, as exhibited by the recent bullying of a child at school. A family may be struggling with issues surrounding the future of a child with a disability and a current educational system that does not meet his or her special needs.

To avoid further complications in the theory learning process, we are using only a single case so variations can be analyzed in future discussions. Specific variations, some of which are used in the following chapters, are introduced below. This list is not meant to be comprehensive or all-inclusive.

Family composition:	a heterosexual couple with or without children; a cohabiting couple with or without children; a single parent with children; a gay or lesbian couple with or without children; a transgendered member in the family; a grandparent (or grandparents) living with grandchildren
Education:	no formal education; grade school; high school; college-level or degree; graduate level or degree; extremely different levels between the adults in the household
Income:	Unemployed; low income; average income; high income; described by the client as middle class; on welfare
Race/ethnicity:	African American; Asian American; Hispanic/Latino; Native American; immigrant; biracial individual(s); multiracial family; transnational and other specific ethnic groups

Before varying the demographic or compositional information of this standardized case, the reader should be familiar with human diversity information and the rationale behind applying and integrating multiple approaches in practice. Although the primary emphasis of this book is on psychological theories within ethnic minority families, we also include nontraditional families—adopted families, single-parent families, gay and lesbian families, and families with bisexual and transgender individuals. With an increasing number of nontraditional families seeking human services, professionals should be cognizant of the importance of utilizing multicultural knowledge, skills, and unbiased attitudes when working with these clients. Table 2.1 summarizes how these various cases are incorporated in each chapter for analysis, practice, and evaluation.

Race and Ethnicity

Recent history is replete with discussions concerning ethnic classifications and race categories for census and statistical purposes. Because race and ethnicity are the major variants for understanding practices with the standardized case, information from four racially and ethnically different composite cases will be used here. Again, keep in mind that each race and ethnicity represents a wide range of cultural expectations and family characteristics. African Americans can be individuals with origins from any of the black-race groups originiating in Africa. Asian Americans can have origins in Asia, Southeast Asia, or the Indian subcontinent, including but not limited to countries such as Cambodia, China, India, Japan, Korea, Malaysia, Pakistan, the Philippine Islands, Thailand, and Vietnam, as well as from Pacific Islands such as Hawaii, Guam, Samoa, Fiji, and of Polynesian, Micronesian, and Melanesian cultural backgrounds. Hispanic or Latino Americans identify their ethnic origin as

Table 2.1

Organization of the Chapters

Chapter	Theory Presented	Alternative Family Characteristics for the Case Approach	Focus of Developmental Stage
4	Psychodynamic	African American	Formation of the Family
5	Adlerian	Asian American	Cultural Identity Development
6	Family Systems	Latino American	Connecting Two Families
7	Structural	Native American	The Family With Children
8	Client-Centered	Adoption	The Family in Transition
9	Gestalt	Drug Problems	The Family With Adolescents
10	Strategic	Single Parent	Children Leaving Home
11	Behavioral	Adult Children in an Interracial Marriage	The Family With Adult Children
12	Cognitive–Behavioral	Divorce	The Family in Separation
13	Feminist/ Empowerment	A Lesbian Couple With Children	Experiencing Family Diversity
14	Solution-Focused	Poverty	Grandparenting

Mexican, Puerto Rican, Cuban, Central American, or South American. Native American Indians encompass more than 771 federally recognized tribes in the United States (Valentan, 2002).

Although Caucasian families are not the focus of this book, they, too, comprise a wide variety of ethnicities, including origins in Europe, the Middle East, and North Africa. In addition, practitioners should be sensitive to clients' personal definitions, as they may be native-born, new immigrants, or a family that has been living in the United States for many generations.

The U.S. Census Bureau (USCB, 2004a) provides statistics that describe the current demographics in the United States:

- From 1990 to 2000, the total population in the United States increased from 248.7 million to 281.4 million, with an increase in the ethnic minority population from 60.0 million to 86.9 million—a 44.83% increase.
- In 2000, the overall population was represented by approximately 81% Caucasians, but this figure is estimated to fall to 72% by the year 2050.
- The Latino population is expected to grow exponentially faster than any other subpopulation, with a current representation of 12.6% of the total population in 2000 and a projected representation of 24.5% in 2050.
- The Asian and Pacific Islander population is expected to grow from 4% in 2000 to 8% in 2050.
- African Americans currently constitute 12.7% in 2000 and are expected to comprise 14.6% by 2050.
- Based upon the 2000 Census data, the most rapidly growing ethnic groups in the United States are Hispanics and Asians. In 2000, the population of Hispanics was 35,305,818—a 57.2% increase from the 1990 Census. The population count of Asians was 11,898,828, up from 6,908,638 in 1990—a 72.2% increase.
- The immigrant population is composed of 28,910,800 immigrants (foreign-born population) in the United States. Within this population, 46.4% are Hispanic/Latino, 25.9% are Asian, 22.1% are white, and 5.5% are black.

Table 2.2 breaks down ethnic populations in the United States by number. The statistics are presented to create awareness of demographic trends and are not representative of all individuals from any specific background. Familiarity with these statistics, however, enables more effective interventions by discussing the trends with the client(s) to provide validation and support. With this in mind, we give capsule reviews of four ethnic groups.

African Americans

According to U.S. Census data, in March 2004 the 36 million African American people in the United States constituted 12.5% of the civilian noninstitutionalized

Table 2.2

Ethnic Populations in the United States

Hispanic	35,300,000	Vietnamese	1,200,000
African-American	34,700,000	Japanese	1,100,000
Russian	7,000,000	Hmong	300,000
Jewish	7,000,000	Cambodian	200,000
Islamic	7,000,000	Laotian	200,000
Chinese	2,900,000	Pakistani	200,000
Native American	2,500,000	Thai	150,000
Filipino	2,400,000	Indonesian	63,000
Haitian	2,000,000	Bangladeshi	59,000
Polish (Chicago area)	2,000,000	Other Asians &	
Asian Indian	1,900,000	Pacific Islanders	420,000
		Total	109,792,000

Note: All statistics listed reflect the reports of April 2003.
The total estimated ethnic population in the United States is 97 million.

Source: From *Ethnic Populations in the U.S.,* by the Christian and Missionary Alliance, 2003, Retrieved March 13, 2005 from http://web2.cmalliance.org/ncm/intercultural/population.jsp

population. In March 2004, the unemployment rate of African Americans was twice that of Caucasians (10.7% and 5.1%, respectively). African Americans accounted for about one-quarter (8.8 million) of the population in poverty in 2003 (USCB, 2004b). Culturally sensitive therapists must acknowledge the African American experience. Because of the long history of racism in America, African Americans traditionally have relied on internal rather than external resources to seek help and have a more collectivist, community-oriented perspective than Anglos. African Americans also are less likely to seek private psychotherapy, choosing community mental health clinics instead.

As with all families, African American families have a variety of structures, but the number of female-headed black households has increased since 1980. Perhaps because of this trend, African American fathers are often assumed to be absent, lazy, unreliable, and uninvolved in their children's lives, especially if the child is born out of wedlock. African American families have consistently demonstrated role flexibility throughout history. All members of the family help members of the extended family, and every family member develops a degree of competence in various family roles. In addition, African American families and communities have learned to utilize the extended family network and kinship system creatively to maximize support for individual and group needs, such as sharing households, food, money, childcare services, emotional nurturance, and support in the face of stress, poverty, unemployment, and the racism of the dominant white culture.

Because African American children may be more likely to be exposed to negative environmental influences (poverty, violence, racial discrimination), individuals who work with African American children should provide information on the use of resources, promote help-seeking behavior, and encourage social mobility. In addition, spirituality is important to many black individuals and families, and the church is often a significant resource to the black community. Thus, therapists should assess clients' spiritual beliefs to ensure the most effective treatment.

Asian Americans

The U.S. Census reported that in March 2002, 12.5 million Asians were living in the United States, representing 4.4% of the civilian noninstitutionalized population (Reeves & Bennett, 2003). After passage of the Immigration and Nationality Act of 1965, immigration contributed greatly to the growth of the Asian population (Chang, 2003, p. 79). The majority of Asian households are family households. Asian Americans are less likely to divorce and more likely to have a large family than Caucasians. Asian Americans are more likely than Caucasians to have earned at least a college degree, but at the same time they are more likely to have less than a ninth-grade education. Asian Americans are concentrated in managerial and professional specialty occupations. In 2003, 11.8% (1.4 million) of Asians lived below the poverty level (USCB, 2004c).

Asian Americans tend to place high emphasis on the group and on family values. Filial piety, the concept of respecting and caring for one's parents, also plays an important role in the traditional Asian family. Generally, Asian American families value respect, work, and achievement, and Asian cultures have a more collectivist perspective, including "values of interdependence, conformity, and harmony" (Zane, Morton, Chu, & Lin, 1999, p. 194).

In terms of communication, Asians tend to avoid direct confrontation. At times they have been described as a model minority because they are often socially well adjusted and consistently successful in scholastic and economic achievement (Chang, 2003). Some researchers, however, contend that the successful image of a few elite, individual Asian Americans has had drastically negative effects on the welfare of the Asian American group as a whole (Sandhu, Leung, & Tang, 2003). Although many Asian American cultures prize academic achievement and education, Asian American children often feel driven and controlled by parental pressures and guilt. This emphasis on academic pressure can lead to achievement anxiety and desperation when students lack academic ability (Chang, 2003).

Like other ethnic groups, Asians have been subjected to considerable discrimination in the United States, historically being the target of legislation seeking to limit their immigration (Chinese Exclusion Act), internment during World War II, and antimiscegenation laws. More than other ethnic groups, Asians are likely to be perceived as foreign by others, even if they are American-born, and they are more frequently asked the specifics of their ancestry.

Asian societies have traditionally maintained strict concepts of gender roles, but more modern Asian families are moving away from this inequity. Parents still tend to be more permissive with sons than with daughters. Asian Americans tend to perceive mental disorders as dishonorable and embarrassing and, therefore, may be reluctant to seek help.

Latino Americans

Though "Hispanic" is used to refer to Spanish-speaking immigrants from Latin America and their descendants, the term "Latino" is now preferred because it reaffirms their native, pre-Hispanic identity. Latino is a more democratic alternative to Hispanic because Hispanic is a term strongly supported by politically conservative groups that regard their Spanish European ancestry as superior to the "conquered" indigenous groups of the Americas. Latino is also more accurate geographically because it includes the native-born Indian ancestry people from Latin America.

In 2004, there were 40.4 million Latinos in the civilian, noninstitutionalized population of the United States, representing 14% of the total population (USCB, 2004d). In the Latino population, two-thirds (65.9%) were of Mexican origin and 40.3 % were foreign-born. Latinos of Mexican origin were more likely to live in the West (51.6%) and the South (36.0%) and had the highest proportion under age 18 (36.4%). Overall, Latinos comprise a young population with relatively high birth rates to teens and single mothers (Brendel & Sustaeta, 2003). Two issues greatly affecting many Latinos are education and poverty status (Brendel & Sustaeta, 2003). More than two in five Latinos aged 25 and older have not graduated from high school, and Mexican Americans are less likely than others of Latino origin to have at least graduated from high school (Ramirez & de la Cruz, 2003). Many of their educational problems relate to lack of proficiency with the English language (Brendel & Sustaeta, 2003). Overall, Latino workers, especially Mexican workers, earn less than Caucasian workers. In 2002, 22.5% of Latinos were living in poverty, which constituted 25.2% of the population living in poverty (USCB, 2004d).

Traditional Latinos place high emphasis on community, cooperation, modesty, and hierarchical relationships. The value of familism (*familismo*) refers to the concept of family or collective needs as superior to individual needs. In many Latino families, grandparents, uncles, aunts, or cousins live with or near the nuclear family, temporarily or permanently. The family is highly protective of its individual members, and in return it demands loyalty. Latino families are typically large, with the expectation that children will care for their parents in times of illness and in old age. Besides blood relatives, familism includes close relationships in which people are perceived as kin because they are closely associated with the family.

Gloria, Ruiz, and Castillo (1999) used the term *personalismo*, or personalism, to describe a cultural value that holds interpersonal interaction in high regard, often higher than task or material achievement. As a result, Latinos and Latinas may seek a more personal relationship with the therapist, perhaps inviting the therapist to events or giving gifts. Therapists should handle these situations delicately and with respect.

A third cultural value is general likeability (*simpatía*), often leading Latinos and Latinas to emphasize courtesy and manners, and to avoid direct conflict. Autonomy and individual achievement are not particularly emphasized, especially among females (Brendel & Sustaeta, 2003).

Much emphasis is placed on views of gender roles in Latino culture, including the concepts of *machismo, hembrismo,* and *marianismo* (Gloria et al., 1999). The husband often assumes the role of provider and protector of the family, and the wife assumes the expressive role of homemaker and caregiver. The concept of *machismo* conveys the notion of an honorable and responsible man rather than the negative stereotype of aggressive virility (Brendel & Sustaeta, 2003). Latinos in general have a strong spiritual orientation (Arredondo & Perez, 2003; Brendel & Sustaeta, 2003; López & Carrillo, 2001), with Catholicism as the prevalent religion. Therapists should be cautious when making assumptions about gender roles in Latino families, as these concepts are often used stereotypically. In addition, even in situations where traditional gender roles are present, therapists must appreciate the strengths and the value that lies in these concepts (Gloria et al., 1999).

Native Americans

Native Americans comprise approximately 2.3 million self-identified people, with a population that is steadily growing (Garrett, 2003). Only 52% of Native American youth complete high school, and only 4% graduate from college. Seventy-five percent of the Native American workforce earns less than $7,000 per year, and 45% live below the poverty level. In addition, one in six Native American adolescents has attempted suicide, a rate four times higher than that of all other groups. Alcohol mortality is six times the rate for all other ethnic groups. Tuberculosis is 7.4 times greater than for non-Indians002C and diabetes is 6.8 times greater than for non-Indians (Russell, 1998).

The long history of atrocities perpetuated against Native Americans has affected many aspects of their modern life. Extended kinship networks, however, have been maintained and have allowed many Native Americans to uphold their traditional communal perspective of family life. Native traditional values include the importance of community contribution, sharing, acceptance, cooperation, harmony and balance, noninterference, extended family, attention to nature, immediacy of time, awareness of the relationship, and a deep respect for elders (Garrett, 2003).

Native American culture is deeply rooted in religion and spirituality and in the concepts of balance and harmony. The cultural identity of many Native Americans is rooted in tribal membership, community, and heritage. Native Americans tend to view mental health professionals negatively, usually because these practitioners are not perceived as sharing or understanding their cultural values.

Adoptive Families

"Adoption is a nontraditional way of creating a family that establishes life-long bonds among children, adoptive parents, biological parents, and this presents unique challenges, stressors and joys" (O'Brien & Zamostny, 2003, p. 379). Available data collected by the federal government remains incomplete for several reasons:

- States report summary statistics voluntarily on all types of finalized adoptions using data primarily drawn from court records.
- The number of states and territories participating in the reporting system has varied from year to year.
- States use their own definitions when reporting data.
- Some data include only those children who are in or have passed through the public child welfare system, and most of them are adopted through public agencies, which handle less than half of all adoptions.
- Some data are obtained from several types of records and the record-keeping procedures vary significantly.
- If the data are collected through adoption agencies, the statistics on independent adoptions are usually not included.

Although many research studies target adoption issues, their small sample sizes are often not representative and do not allow national estimates. Other national survey data are problematic because the surveys focus primarily on the collection of a variety of information rather than the specific issues of adoption, and they rely upon self-reporting. In addition, some statistical analyses cannot be performed reliably because adoption is relatively rare and the number of adoptions included in these national surveys is small. Therefore, we cannot provide a confirmatory conclusion to state how many families have been impacted by adoption.

The most useful data concerning adoptive families are provided by the U.S. Census and collected by the U. S. Department of Commerce, Economics and Statistics Administration. These sample data are regarded as "the most comprehensive national data on adopted children available since 1975" (Kreider, 2003, p. 20) because the data were collected from approximately one in every six households. Although it cannot provide a comprehensive count of all adopted children in the United States, the Census 2000 special report, *Adopted Children and Stepchildren,* reports that there were 2.1 million adopted children in 2000, including 1.6 million under age 18 and 473,000 over age 18. Of the 45.5 million households in 2000 with children of any age, 1.7 million households had adopted children living in their residence.

In addition, in 2000 and 2001, approximately 127,000 children were adopted annually in the United States. Since 1987, the number of annual adoptions has remained relatively constant, ranging from 118,000 to 127,000 (U. S. Department of Health and Human Services, 2004).

Negative myths and stereotypes abound regarding adoptive families. Many people believe that adoption is inferior to having a biological child, that children who are adopted will exhibit numerous problems, that adoptive parents will have difficulty attaching to their children, and that birthparents are uncaring, promiscuous, and living in poverty (O'Brien & Zamostny, 2003; Zamostny, Wiley, O'Brien, Lee, & Baden, 2003). Moreover, therapists often discount the role of adoption when providing therapy to adoptive families. Many practicing psychologists indicated that they need additional education about adoption (O'Brien & Zamostny, 2003).

Families With Drug Problems

The National Survey on Drug Use and Health, formerly called the National Household Survey on Drug Abuse, is the primary source of information on the use of illicit drugs, alcohol, and tobacco by the civilian, noninstitutionalized population of the United States for ages 12 years and older. SAMSHA (2007) estimated that among youths aged 12 to 17 in 2003, 2.8 million were current illicit drug users, 2.7 million were current binge drinkers of alcohol, and 3.6 million reported the use of a tobacco product within the past month. Of adults aged 18 or older, 16.7 million were illicit drug users, 51.1 million were binge drinkers of alcohol, and 67.1 million used a tobacco product within the past month. Of all the illicit drugs reported, marijuana was the most commonly used, with 14.6 million adult users and approximately 2 million marijuana users among youth aged 12 to 17 in 2003 (SAMHSA, 2004).

The Child Welfare League of America (CWLA) surveyed its member agencies regarding the impact of alcohol and other drugs (AOD) on the delivery of child welfare services. The data were collected through a survey in ten states: Alabama, Kentucky, Massachusetts, North Carolina, New Hampshire, Rhode Island, South Carolina, Tennessee, Washington, and Wyoming. Of the 305,716 children served during the 1991 fiscal year in those states, 112,552 (36.8%) were affected by problems associated with AOD, such as living with a caregiver who had AOD problems. In five states (Alabama, Massachusetts, New Hampshire, Washington, and Wyoming) out of 164,639 children served, the child's own use of AOD was judged to be at least one of the presenting problems in 18,067 cases (11.0%) (Curtis & McCullough, 1993, para. 6). Of the 111,927 children served by 129 voluntary child welfare agencies throughout North America, 64,200 (57.4%) were reported to be affected by problems associated with AOD. In addition, of the 89,106 children served in 100 voluntary child welfare agencies, the child's own use of AOD was judged to be at least one of the presenting problems in 18,917 cases (21.2%). Fifteen out of the 36 public agencies (41.7%) reported they routinely screen referrals for problems associated with AOD, and in the voluntary agencies, the ratio was 125 out of 176 (71.0%) (Curtis & McCullough, 1993, para. 7).

In 1997, CWLA conducted a national survey of its state public child welfare agencies on AOD issues. Results from this survey show that parental chemical dependency was a contributing factor in the out-of-home placement of at least 53% of the 482,000 children and youth in the custody of the child welfare system. Approximately 67% of parents with children in the child welfare system required substance abuse treatment services, but child welfare agencies were only able to provide treatment for 31% of them. On average 51% of child welfare workers receive training on recognizing and dealing with substance abuse issues during their first year of service. Eleven percent of the child welfare/AOD experts surveyed believed that children and parents with AOD problems can be treated in a timely manner (less than one month) (CWLA, 2007). CWLA (2001) reported another recent estimate that 40% to 80% of the families involved in the child protective service (CPS) system have problems with alcohol and/or drugs.

It is often hypothesized that substance use is an issue primarily among black Americans. Based on current estimates, however, the vast majority of substance users are white Americans. Regarding alcohol use, another stereotype is that Native Americans as a whole are afflicted with alcohol problems. Substance abuse issues and stereotypes related to racism and discrimination deserve further research.

Teenage Pregnancy

Teenagers engage in risky behavior for many reasons—curiosity, excitement, emotional support and outlet, and self-identity and attachment. The most common risky behavior is sexual behavior. According to Smith and Elander (2006), six risk factors that lead to teen pregnancy are:

- early sexual activity,
- low life expectations,
- lack of knowledge and beliefs about contraceptives,
- relaxed attitude to abortion,
- mixed beliefs about love, and
- lack of use of local sexual health services.

Many school-based programs have been established throughout the United States to address sex and healthy life issues.

In a study of outcomes of a pregnant teen program in an alternative school setting, the researchers found that students had higher educational aspirations, better reproductive health outcomes, more contraceptive use, and better breast-feeding practice and intention after they attended the program than did non-enrollees of the program (Amin, Browne, & Ahmed, 2006).

The National Institutes on Health have funded research in this area, hoping to reduce the number of teen pregnancies and promote teen health. Their website, MedlinePlus, provides information for teens, which educates about pregnancy, demonstrates the proper use of contraceptives, and promotes understanding of sex-related issues and problems (2007). The aim is to identify problems at an early stage, help teens make healthy decisions, and prevent problems from escalating. It also publicizes research findings that promote better reproductive health among adolescents and that encourage fathers to participate in providing support to their pregnant partners.

Another driving force that prohibits, and even condemns, early marriage or teenage pregnancy is the increasing societal and family expectation that youth must obtain at least one higher education degree. In one study, a youth's perceptions of parental support and self-efficacy beliefs independently predicted his or her expectations to attend college (Ali & Saunders, 2006). In the family development process, parents' involvement in their children's lives is complex but influential. It is complex because of the interactive effect between the two generations' expectations and values. Research has confirmed that positive support by parents will eliminate obstacles to obtaining academic accomplishments.

Single-Parent Families

Parents without Partners International (2005) reported that single-parent households increased from 9% of all households in 1990 to 16% in 2000, and that the number of single parents who had child custody reached 13.5 million. Of these custodial parents, 85% were mothers and 15% were fathers. In these families, 13.8 million children under the age of 15 lived with single mothers, 2.7 million lived with single fathers, and 5.6 million lived with grandparents. In addition, 46% of single-mother households had more than one child. According to this same source, 89% of single fathers and 77% of single mothers were in the work force. It also reports a declining proportion of custodial parents and their children living below the poverty level from 33% in 1993 to 26.1% in 1999. These data are yet to be updated.

Estimates from a survey of social service agencies in the U.S. found that 33.4% of all clients in 1997 came from single-parent households and 59.7% of them had children under 17 (Second Harvest Network, 1997). In the past three decades, much of the research focused on the negative effects of father-absence on male children in single-mother homes (Hanson, 1986). More recently, in addition to describing father-absence as a factor in juvenile delinquency, research has continued to address inadequate sex role identification, drug abuse, poor school achievement, poor personal adjustment, poverty, and other forms of pathology (Becker & Liddle, 2001; Helburn & Bergmann, 2002; Spruijt, DeGoede, & Vandervalk, 2001). Research themes are related mostly to problems—10 times more than to strengths. Other deficits include single mothers' reliance on welfare, stereotypical assumptions about ethnic minorities being single parents, and lack of opportunities (see also Ford-Gilboe, 2000; Nelson, 2002).

Among the few studies looking at the strengths of single-parent families, Wuest and associates (2003) suggested that these families are often viewed as deficient and, therefore, they believed they were being intruded upon when their problems were being assessed. Research investigating the strengths of single-parent families stresses that not all single-parent households have problems, nor are all children affected adversely by divorce or family separation (Anderson, 2003; Barnes, 2005). Anderson (2003) analyzed the strengths of single-parent families from a *social health* perspective and noted that these families can be empowered to engage in social services when they need help because they can use their power to eliminate risky family structure and routines, exercise appropriate parental authority, and build on natural connections. Ford-Gilboe's (2000) study heightens the awareness that single-parent and two-parent families share similar strengths in protecting their children and exercising their contributions to the society.

Domestic Violence

Domestic violence is a term used interchangeably with *spouse abuse* or *partner abuse.* To be consistent with most of the literature, the issue of domestic violence described in this book is related to partner abuse, not other types of abuse within families.

An overwhelming majority (90%–95%) of domestic violence victims in heterosexual relationships are women (U.S. Department of Justice, 1994). In 2001, women accounted for 85% of the victims of intimate partner violence (588,490 total) and men accounted for approximately 15% of the victims (103,220 total) (USDOJ, 2003). According to the most conservative estimate, 1 million women each year are subjected to nonfatal violence by an intimate (USDOJ, 1995).

Over time, domestic violence has been statistically consistent across all racial and ethnic boundaries (USDOJ, 1995). Studies consistently demonstrate that at least 50% to 60% of women receiving welfare have experienced physical abuse by an intimate partner at some point during their adult lives, and some studies indicate rates as high as 82%. Moreover, these studies indicate that as many as 30% of women on welfare report abuse in their current intimate relationship (Lawrence, 2002; Lyon, 2000; Tolman & Raphael, 2000). The studies suggest that rates among the general population are approximately 22%.

In the past, domestic violence was a problem that was largely ignored or regarded as a private matter for families to resolve, a social problem of little consequence. Today, this problem is considered critical, occurring along many dimensions, taking many forms, and arising under a range of different conditions (Mears & Visher, 2005). Domestic violence was once seen as resulting from "normal stress and interpersonal conflict" within families (Worden, 2000, p. 222), but currently people are aware that domestic violence has many causes and is not typically associated with healthy individuals or families (Mears & Visher, 2005).

The illegal status of immigrant females compounds their vulnerability and isolation. If their abusers are citizens, they may threaten to prevent them from obtaining legal status through marriage if they report the abuse (Menjivar & Salcido, 2002). To remedy this dilemma, the federal Violence Against Women Act (VAWA) along with Battered Spouse Waivers create exceptions to the requirement that a woman's spouse must file her paperwork, so she may become a permanent lawful resident through family sponsorship without her batterer's cooperation (New York State Judicial Committee on Women in the Courts, 2004). Immigrant females who are abused may also be eligible for U-Visas, a special category of visas for the benefit of victims of serious crimes.

Interracial Couples

According to the 1990 U.S. Census, the population included approximately 1.5 million interracial couples—an increase from nearly 1 million in 1980 and from 321,000 in 1970 (Bentley, Mattingly, Hough, & Bennett, 2003). The U.S. Census (2000) reported that within 6% of married-couple households, the householder and the spouse were of different races and 3% of interracial married couples included one Latino partner (Simmons & O'Connell, 2003, p. 11). Overall, 7% of married couples had spouses of a different race or origin.

This report also stated that unmarried partners consistently had higher percentages of partners of different races or origins, ranging from 12% to 15% for household types of different gender composition. Another Census report cited by Fields and Casper (2001) documented 165,000 unmarried and about 1 million married interracial male–female couples. For male–female couples of Latino origin difference, there were 222,000 unmarried couples and about 1.7 million married couples (Fields & Casper, 2001). In 1990, all but 8% of interracial couples included one spouse (or unmarried partner) who was white. The data suggested that within interracial couples the non-white spouse was black in 14% of all interracial couples; American Indian or Alaska Native in 22%; Asian or Pacific Islander in 31%; and of other, mostly Hispanic origin, in 25% (Bentley, et al., 2003, p. 4).

Census data indicate that the number of children in interracial families grew from under half a million in 1970 to about 2 million in 1990. In 1990, for interracial families with one white partner, the non-white parent was black for approximately 20% of all children, Asian for 45%, and American Indian or Alaska Native for about 34% (Bentley et al., 2003, p. 4). As indicated by the National Center for Health Statistics, the number of multiracial babies born since the 1970s has increased more than 260%, compared to a 15% increase of single-race babies (Wardle, 2001). Since 1989, it is estimated that one million first generation biracial babies are born annually in the United States (Root, 1996).

Although the negative stigma has lessened, some members of all races view interracial marriage unfavorably. Interracial marriage is believed to destroy family traditions, cause problems for the couple and their children, and result in a loss of racial purity. Research by Lewandowski and Jackson (2001) suggested that individuals who marry outside of their race may have an exaggerated phobia of incest, low self-esteem, self-loathing and feelings of inferiority, deep-seated psychological sickness, excessive idealism, and a need to rebel against parental authority. To some extent, such research findings have influenced societal views about interracial marriages and have reflected a negative image about biracial or multiracial children (McClurg, 2004).

Families of Divorce

According to the National Center for Health Statistics (Sutton, 2007), the 2006 provisional estimate for the annual U.S. divorce rate was 0.36% per capita. (This rate is representative only of the states that record the number of divorces and does not include California, Georgia, Hawaii, Indiana, Louisiana, and Minnesota. Because every divorce involves two individuals, the percentage of divorces should double to obtain an accurate prevalence rate within the given population. The published divorce rate should be presented for the official count of married people rather than that of the population.

In the United States, the divorce count, excluding the non-counting states, is rising: 947,384 in 1998, 944,317 in 1999, and 957,200 in 2000. The National Center for Health Statistics reported that 43% of first marriages end in separation or divorce within the first 15 years of marriage (Bramlett & Mosher, 2001).

According to Census 2001 data, divorce rates (defined as "ever divorced" for those 15 or older) were 21% for men and 23.1% for women—a 1% increase since 1996. The highest divorce rates were found in the 50–59 age cohorts for both men and women—41% and 39%, respectively (Kreider, 2005). The median divorce age at first marriage was 39.2 for men and 36.7 for women. The divorce rates varied among ethnic groups, but Asian and Pacific Islander men and women were oldest at first marriage, compared to other groups. In 2001, census statisticians calculated that men who had ever divorced were more likely to be married currently than ever-divorced women. On the average, first marriages that end in divorce last about 8 years (Kreider, 2005). Table 2.3 gives divorce rates by ethnicity and gender.

From a global perspective, statistics show that the divorce rates tend to be lower in Asian countries than in European and North American countries. The countries with the five highest rates of divorce, per 1,000 inhabitants (Gulnar Nugman of the Heritage Foundation [GNHF], 2002) are

Maldives (10.97),
Guam (4.34),
Russia (4.3),
the United States (4.1), and
Ukraine (4).

Table 2.3

Divorce Rates by Ethnicity and Gender

Ethnicity	In Percentage	
	Men	Women
Non-Hispanic White	43.5	45.2
Black	38.4	39.4
Hispanic	33.1	35.5
Asian & Pacific Islander	37.7	39.1

Source: From *Number, Timing, and Duration of Marriages and Divorces: 2001,* by R. M. Kreider, 2005, Washington, DC: U.S. Census Bureau.

Divorce is often regarded as a social problem. From a historical point of view, divorce was assumed to reflect a breakdown of the moral order. In the contemporary context, children are generally portrayed as "victims of divorce." From the perspective of some family moralists, divorcing parents are considered inattentive, selfish, narcissistic, and abandoning their families for the purpose of self-gratification. Other couples, however, remain in unhealthy and unhappy marriages "for the sake of the children." In these cases, divorce actually may minimize the pain and disturbance to all involved, especially the children (Scott & Michele, 2003).

Gay and Lesbian Families

The current literature has offered some broad estimates regarding the number of gay and lesbian parents in the United States. Two sources published more than a decade ago gave the figure of 1 to 5 million lesbian mothers (Falk, 1989; Gottman, 1990) and nearly 1 to 3 million gay fathers (Gottman, 1990) in the United States. These wide-ranging figures are included only as an indication. Further, many gay and lesbian parents do not report their sexual orientation for fear of discrimination. Patterson (2000) suggested that many gay and lesbian families fear losing custody of their children if they were to disclose their sexual orientation.

Indications are that gay and lesbian parenting is on the rise in the United States, with an estimated 5,000 to 10,000 lesbians having given birth after coming out (Lambert, 2005). In addition, gay men and lesbians are not only adopting but also becoming foster parents. Considering these trends, professionals must recognize that the definition of family is changing and the traditional view of the family may not be valid for many of our clients.

Although the needs of ethnic minorities remain a central point within multicultural family practice, the increase in number of gay and lesbian, bisexual, and transgender (GLBT) families also has to be recognized as a distinct component of multicultural counseling. A difference between ethnic minority individuals and GLBT individuals is that GLBT individuals are brought up in families and communities that do not share their minority status (Lambert, 2005). Also, the topic of sexual orientation can be particularly difficult for some to address, but the therapist should bring it up to foster a healthy therapeutic relationship.

Again, developing self-awareness, sensitivity, and knowledge are foundational in working with nontraditional families. Often, gay and lesbian families are in need of advocacy, because the parents and children may experience social isolation, stress from lack of acceptance, and environmental challenges. As a result of such marginalization, support and advocacy on their behalf is necessary to promote social justice (Speziale & Gopalakrishna, 2004).

One of the main considerations in working with gay and lesbian families relates to the children who are growing up with two mothers or two fathers. Gay and lesbian families have unique concerns and complex dynamics in this homophobic and heterosexist society (Adams, Jaques, & May, 2004). A frequent presumption is that lesbians cannot be good mothers because they are considered less maternal than heterosexual women, and relationships with sexual partners leave gay fathers and lesbian mothers with little time for ongoing parent–child interactions (Lambert, 2005). In addition, lesbian mothers are assumed to be masculine and to therefore be inclined to interact inappropriately with their children (Lambert, 2005).

The main judicial concerns about the children of gay and lesbian parents are that children brought up by lesbian mothers or gay fathers may become gay or lesbian themselves. In addition, the children of gay and lesbian parents may face difficulties in personal development and peer relationships (Lambert, 2005). When gay and lesbian parents consider coming out in their communities and telling their children, concerns include child-custody disputes, family-of-origin reaction, fear of discrimination, peer ostracism, and how and when to tell (Ryan & Martin, 2000; Strong & Callahan, 2001).

Families in Poverty

According to the Office of Management and Budget's Statistical Policy Directive 14 (OMB, 1978), the Census Bureau uses a set of income thresholds that vary according to family size and composition to determine who is in poverty. If a family's total income is less than the poverty threshold for a family of that size, all individuals within that family are considered to be in poverty. The official poverty threshold does not vary geographically, and different levels of poverty are not distinguished, but the poverty threshold is updated annually for inflation, using the Consumer Price Index (CPI-U). The official definition of poverty includes income before taxes and does not include capital gains or in-kind benefits such as public housing, Medicaid, and food stamps (DeNavas-Walt, Proctor, & Mills, 2004, p. 39).

In a report by DeNavas-Walt, Proctor, and Mills (2004), the poverty rate for the United States population in 2003 was 12.5—9.9 percentage points below that in 1959, the first year for which poverty estimates are available. From the year 2000 to the present, both the number of individuals in poverty and the poverty rate have risen consecutively, from 31.6 million and 11.3% in 2000, to 35.9 million and 12.5% in 2003 (p. 9). Of the 76.2 million families in 2003, the family poverty rate was 10.0%. The report addressed the poverty rate for different types of families, and the poverty rate for female householders with no husband was found to be the highest, followed by male householders with no wife present, followed by married couple families. In the year 2003, the poverty rate of married-couple families was 5.4%, male householder with no wife present was 13.5%, and female householder with no husband present was 28.0%.

In addition to family composition, poverty rates were found to vary according to race and ethnicity. The poverty rate for white non-Hispanic individuals was the lowest, followed by the poverty rates of Asian and Pacific Islanders. The highest poverty rates were for blacks and those of Hispanic origin. According to 2003 statistics, the poverty rate was 6.1% for white non-Hispanics, 9.9% for Asian and Pacific Islanders, 21.5% for those of Hispanic origin, and 23.1% for blacks.

Although statistical measures are utilized to determine poverty thresholds within developed countries, poverty measures in developing countries are based on estimates of consumption by the World Bank indicator. Estimates of consumption are the values placed on the goods and services that people consume. In recent years, the per-capita consumption threshold referred to as "extreme poverty" is $1 per day, and the $2 threshold is used as the more general poverty indicator (Klass, 2002, para. 3). Klass (2002) cited regional trends for international poverty rates around the world. Poverty rates in the majority of Asian countries have declined dramatically over the past two decades, while poverty rates in the former Soviet Union countries have increased since 1989. In addition, poverty rates in the Middle East, Africa, and Latin America have remained relatively constant during this same period.

According to Cozzarelli, Wilkinson, and Tagler (2001), stereotypes about the poor were found to be significantly more negative than stereotypes about the middle class—that the poor are uneducated, unmotivated or lazy, and socially irresponsible (e.g., characterized by alcoholism and substance abuse). In addition, participants were most likely to blame the poor themselves for their state of poverty. Attitudes toward the poor, stereotypes about the poor, and attributions for the causes of poverty varied among individuals with different sociodemographic backgrounds. In addition, many of these stereotypes are related to core American values, such as the emphasis on work ethic and belief in a just society. Attitudes toward the poor and attributions for poverty are related to positions on public issues concerning welfare, availability of health insurance and health care for the working poor, and so on (Cozzarelli et al., 2001).

The Integrated Framework

In a multicultural environment, practitioners work cross-culturally with clients from a variety of cultural and ethnic backgrounds. Besides the diverse racial and ethnic heritages among clients, human diversity is evidenced in sexual orientation, religious/spiritual orientation, physical or mental ability, and other characteristics. Today, multicultural competency is a requirement within this multidimensional construct of reality (Coleman, 2005). From a micro viewpoint, Pederson (as cited in Torres-Rivera, Phan, Maddux, Wilber, & Garrett, 2001) describes this reality as "the coming together of two or more people from different cultural backgrounds in a helping relationship" (p. 28). From a macro perspective, the National Association of Social Work Code of Ethics emphasizes cultural and ethnic diversity and strives to end discrimination, oppression, poverty, and other forms of social injustice (NASW, 2005a).

Regardless of theoretical orientation, multicultural competency in practice is the ability to apply theories to practice with sensitivity (Ponterotto, Gretchen, Utsey, Reiger, & Austin, 2002; Torres-Rivera et al., 2001) by

- acknowledging one's own cultural socialization and accompanying biases,
- knowing the worldviews and value patterns of culturally diverse populations,

■ applying techniques with fluidity and flexibility that reflect adjustment to human diversity factors, and

■ integrating skills that provide culturally relevant interventions for diverse populations.

Multiculturally competent professionals assess how cultural differences between clients and practitioners may influence clients' perception toward the helping relationship and their ways of defining problems and applying solutions.

Stages of Studying Theory Integration With the Family

Carter and McGoldrick (2005) reiterated the importance of studying families through a family life cycle approach. The stages in the family life cycle approach can be applied to most families, with flexibility to accommodate today's forms. For the purpose of applying this theory to the case example in this book, the family life cycle approach is a guiding framework that allows for skills and techniques to be demonstrated under the assumption that the family is going through life stages. Because the learning process requires multicultural applications with this standardized case, these stages serve as pathways for discussion when the family formation represents another race or ethnicity, family composition, or family lifestyle:

Stage 1: Formation of the Family
Stage 2: Cultural Identity Development
Stage 3: Connecting Two Families
Stage 4: Family With Children
Stage 5: Family in Transition
Stage 6: Family With Adolescents
Stage 7: Children Leaving Home
Stage 8: Family With Adult Children
Stage 9: Family in Separation
Stage 10: Experiencing Family Diversity
Stage 11: Grandparenting

The multicultural family processing stages proposed in this book integrate the life cycle stage approach (Carter & McGoldrick, 2005) and the process-stage approach with a focus on cultural identity development (Lum, 2004). These stages are developmentally fluid and do not necessarily progress linearly. The purpose of the stage approach is to illustrate skills and identify multicultural issues from which each professional can learn. In each of the following chapters, one of these stages will be described briefly, followed by a series of related issues and dialogues between the clients and their family. These dialogues demonstrate the application of the selected approach or theory.

CHAPTER THREE

Practitioners as Practice Evaluators

This chapter introduces methods to help practitioners build a knowledge base for practice evaluation. It expands on how practitioners use culturally sensitive techniques to measure service or program outcomes in a variety of diverse settings. A single-system design method is described thoroughly and includes the six evaluation steps to use during practice implementation. An ASK evaluation model is presented, describing how to evaluate the three major practice elements: attitudes (A), skills (S), and knowledge (K). The chapter concludes with an integrative model relating each of the evaluation stages to the chapters in Part Two of this book.

Practice–Evaluation Integration

When working with a client system, the major practice components are:

1. define the problem,
2. identify resources and constraints,
3. conduct a psychosocial assessment,
4. undertake case planning and goal setting,
5. deliver the intervention or treatment, and
6. evaluate the outcome.

Figure 3.1 illustrates this process. During the intervention, from identifying the client's problem(s) and resources to case planning, the practitioner uses both direct questioning and indirect observations to obtain information (Blender & Sanathara, 2003). This assessment process has two aims: (1) measure the client's needs, and (2) predict the effectiveness of the service.

The first aim includes three initial goals: (1) to design and plan service input, (2) to establish a baseline regarding a client's needs and/or problems, and (3) to assess the family's readiness to use available services. The second aim examines the service effectiveness for the individual client. The practitioner continues to collect data regarding the identified needs and problems during and after the intervention process to be able to examine changes from the baseline and determine whether the selected service has achieved its stated goal. Thus, while the first assessment component focuses on the client system, the second component focuses on the service delivery system.

This data collection process, before, during, and after the intervention is the assessment base for practice evaluation (Briggs, Feyerherm, & Gingerich, 2004). An example is given in Figure 3.2. The utilization of intervention data in assessing

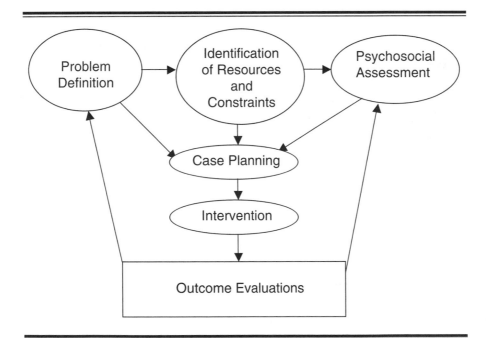

Figure 3.1

The Intervention Process

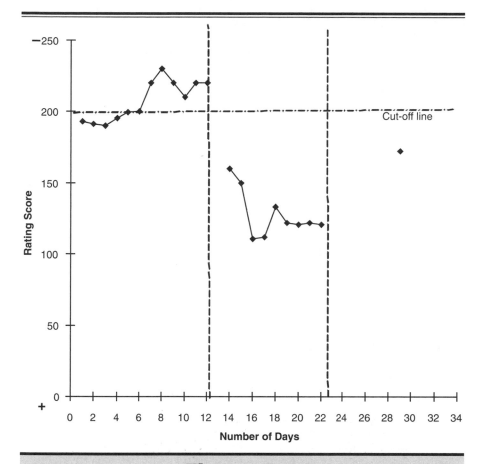

Figure 3.2
Baseline-Intervention Follow-up Measures: An Example

practice effectiveness and determining continuation or referral of services is called *practice–evaluation integration*. This integration involves two important considerations (Herie & Martin, 2002; Kuperminc, Blatt, Shahar, Henrich, & Leadbeater, 2004):

1. Cultural variations are a major component of assessment.
2. The power of cultural exchange between clients and practitioners is a treatment factor.

Practice Evaluation Stages

In clinical practice, two questions are central to practice evaluation:

1. How do clients know that their target behavior of concern has changed?
2. How do helping professionals know that their intervention has caused the change?

Clinical practice uses single-system research to measure each client system and compare changes before, during, and after intervention. In community-based services, practice evaluation questions are directed to the definition of service needs, characteristics of program goals and objectives, efficiency of service delivery, implementation process, and measure of the outcome. Community practice measures the service and outcome effects from a collective view, mostly cross-sectional in a given timeframe, using methods such as needs assessment, formative evaluations, implementation studies, and outcome studies. Because this book describes cases in a clinical setting, the community-based approach is described within single-system research as an integral evaluation component based on the person-in-the-environment principle of multicultural practice.

Steps in Single-System Research

The single-system research proposes six steps (see Bloom, Fischer, & Orme, 2003):

1. Define the service target or problem.
2. Define service goals and objectives.
3. Identify constraints and resources to select an appropriate treatment.
4. Measure monitoring actions.
5. Analyze data.
6. Report results and make recommendations

Define the Service Target or Problem (Intake and Case Assessment)

A major step in practice evaluation is to identify the central target(s) of the presenting problem. Some clients view the problem as an individually owned issue, and others relate an individual problem to its external cause and connection. In either situation, the practitioner must address the target behaviors and the specific situation in which these behaviors occur. During this step, professionals must obtain input from clients to accurately identify the service target, because definitions of the problem can vary from the practitioner to client. Helping professionals must also be aware that encouragement is an important ingredient to success at the stage.

To identify the service target, helping professionals must conduct an intake and case assessment to evaluate the client's needs. Needs assessment is a methodology that involves collecting empirical data to identify the needs in an environment. Needs are expressed in terms of the following formula:

$$\text{Needs} = \text{Resources Desired} - \text{Resources Available}$$

That is, needs are the gap between the resources that are desired and the resources that are available.

When conducting a needs assessment, Aramony (1982) suggested that the following major needs assessment questions be considered:

- Who is in need?
- What is in need?
- What is available?
- What is desired?
- Where are the services needed?
- How much are the services needed?
- Is the demand greater than the supply?
- Is the issue access and distribution rather than supply and demand?
- What is not needed (or less needed)?
- How much will it cost to provide the services needed?
- Who is going to pay for them?
- How long are the services needed?
- Does the client have access to the services?

To identify clients' needs, the practitioner must collect data via interviews with clients, their family members, friends, and other significant figures such as religious leaders, medical doctors, and other mental health professionals. Consent must be obtained from the clients at the first interview (see Appendix A for an example of Consent). Additional data that can be collected from clients include services requested, medical history, employment, income and expenses, family background, and culturally related data such as cultural adjustment issues, languages spoken, and cultural values and beliefs that the practitioner should know about.

Define (or Formulate) Service Goals and Objectives

In many cultures, problems are not to be shared outside of the family. Some clients seek help only because they believe the practitioner can help them locate supportive resources. Because clients consider concrete services important, they generally participate in the intervention process if a mental health treatment is reframed as a "service" and both short-term and long-term life goals are included. This perspective is congruent with the multicultural mission of helping clients enhance their quality of life. Cheung and Leung (2006) suggested the following evaluative areas in this step:

1. Define the rationale for setting up short-term goals.
2. Search for motivating factors to get the clients involved.

3. Identify specific steps in the self-contracting process.
4. Match the service target with the life goals of each individual in the family.

The emphasis of cultural values in practice–evaluation integration should be an integral component to this step. With this emphasis, the goal-setting step can be viewed as parallel to the community-based formative evaluation, in the same way that services are provided to the individual client or family and programs are provided to a group of clients or families. Before a service is implemented, the practitioner must formulate the service goals and objectives so its effectiveness can be evaluated and communicated with the community (or the client system) during the course of service implementation or at its completion.

Formative evaluation is a process of developing, assessing, and modifying goals, objectives, programs, services, activities, and service tasks. Early pioneers in this area, Herman, Morris, and Fitz-Gibbon (1987), identified the following questions for formative evaluation within a service or program:

- What are the program's goals and objectives?
- What are the program's most important characteristics—materials, staffing, activities, and administrative arrangements?
- How do program activities lead to attainment of the objectives?
- Are important characteristics of the program being implemented?
- Do program components contribute to achieving the objectives?
- Which activities or combination of activities best accomplish each objective?
- What adjustments in the program might lead to better attainment of the objectives?
- What adjustments in program management and support (staff development, incentives, etc.) are needed?
- Is the program or some aspects of it better suited to certain types of participants?
- What problems are there, and how can they be solved?
- What measures and designs could be recommended for use during summative evaluation of the program?

For clients from various cultural backgrounds and with situational differences, formative evaluations are useful when they are conducted in either a clinical or an agency setting, especially when the emphasis is on (a) how to help the practitioner and organization strengthen goals and objectives that are measurable and subject to later evaluation, (b) how to use existing and new resources to achieve the mission of multicultural practice, and (c) how to select appropriate measures to assess the success of a service or program. Therefore, a formative evaluator performs the multiple roles of helper, facilitator, consultant, and advisor.

In a clinical relationship, the practitioner who conducts a formative study is trying to assess the helping relationship. This includes evaluating three major components:

1. Level of trust with the clients

2. Assessment of potential problems in the treatment process
3. Guidance to help clients complete the entire process

The final product is to help clients develop a set of self-directed goals and objectives that will address the problems they face.

Identify Constraints and Resources and Select Treatment

Identifying formal and informal constraints and resources is critical to enhancing the success of an intervention. During this step clients identify any impediments in their immediate environment. In multicultural practice the practitioner must be sure to consider cultural and acculturation factors and evaluate how cultural differences between the client and the service provider might contribute to positive (or negative) outcomes. The practitioner can also help clients identify language difficulties, express thoughts and ideas, and understand how communication constraints affect the extent of cultural adjustment within a family.

Many times, the provider's assessment and the family's own assessment of needs diverge. This constraint can impede the development of a treatment plan. The client's input should be taken into consideration to identify the client's needs. Then, based on an objective assessment, the provider can better explain the directions of potential treatment.

Finally, lack of emotional support within the family is a constraint that leads to clients' seeking social services. Because the family is a vital resource for individuals regardless of cultural background, the practitioner must empower clients to assess and locate resources within their family network and provide intervention for clients who cannot obtain this support.

After identifying the constraints and resources, the practitioner can select the appropriate intervention. When formulating a treatment hypothesis, more than one service or intervention may be identified. The question becomes: "Which treatment or service should be selected for immediate implementation?" Obviously, this question does not concern only effectiveness but also efficiency. Efficiency is defined as the most cost-effective way to achieve the goals and objectives of a service, an intervention, or a program. Although efficiency can be assessed in many ways, the two most common methods are cost–benefit analysis and cost-effectiveness analysis.

Cost–Benefit Analysis

Cost–benefit analysis requires that both the cost and benefit (or effect) are expressed in monetary terms. The ratio between benefit and cost provides an indicator that reflects whether the intervention is cost-effective. If the ratio is larger than one, the benefit exceeds the cost. If the ratio is smaller than one, the cost exceeds the benefit.

To illustrate this in a simplified example: Suppose a single parent is dealing with a drinking problem. She finds that the cost of combined individual, group, and family therapy is $5,000, and that the cost of individual therapy for her alone is $2,000. Within the same timeframe, if the combined program would save the client $10,000 in family expenses toward the identified problem (for example, the client stops drinking and finds a better job), and if the individual program would save only $2,000 in family expenses (for example, a reduction in alcohol expenditures), the benefit–cost ratio for the combined program would be 2:1 (the benefit exceeds the cost by two times) and 1:1 for the individual program (the benefit does not exceed the cost). If everything else remains constant, the combined program is recommended because it would be more cost-effective for the client.

This example, of course, oversimplifies the problem, but it provides a straightforward illustration in monetary terms. It does not address the full benefits of each of the therapeutic programs and, as a result, cannot be used in isolation.

Cost-Effectiveness Analysis

Cost-effectiveness analysis refers to the ratio between cost and outcome. Outcome is expressed in units of expected results rather than in monetary terms. Similar to the cost–benefit analysis, the ratio between effectiveness and cost reflects whether the program is cost-effective.

Let's use the previous example to illustrate. Suppose this family would spend $5,000 for a combined therapeutic program (individual, group, and family) to eliminate 10 problems identified by the client. The individual program, costing $2,000 per person, would cost a total of $8,000 for four individuals in a family to eliminate the same 10 problems. The combined therapeutic program, thus, is more cost-effective.

Again, this example is oversimplified and cannot be used in isolation for decision making. In multicultural practice, benefits that contribute to the family's process of adjusting to a new environment or that help the individuals deal with social stigma, for example, cannot always be measured in dollars. The treatment selection must also involve the clients' input so they will be likely to benefit from the treatment effect as a result of their willing and hopeful participation.

Measure the Monitoring Actions (Monitor Progress)

As stated previously, concrete measures are imperative in the evaluative procedure. First, professionals must help their clients understand and practice self-analyses and self-observation. Clients who learn about their feelings and behaviors through personal reflection can gain further perspective from observing their interactions with others. Second, repeated observation throughout all intervention phases is essential. This measurement step aims to monitor progress and evaluate implementation of the intervention. The end result is that clients realize the importance of collecting relevant data consistently over time and visualize the impact of the intervention.

In this book these concrete evaluative tools are suggested in the form of standardized measures—that is, measures designed by researchers and tested to be valid to measure the target problem. Simple evaluative measures also can be used. These may include a self-rating scale; for example, a ratings scale to assess the impact of anxiety on a person's daily functioning. This scale can ask a simple question, such as: "On a scale from 1 to 5, with 1 being extremely relaxed and 5 being extremely anxious, rate your level of anxiety." The measure can be repeated at the beginning of each individual session, or implemented by the client every morning at the same time. Many clients from a culture that values concrete measures find a simple recording form helpful for the repeated measures of a stated and observable behavior (see Figure 3.3).

By recording the level in a continuous and repeated manner, a graphic presentation of the data can help the client monitor any changes. This scale also can be measured by someone other than the client, such as a relative, a friend, a teacher, or the practitioner. When working with a multicultural population on various issues, even a simple measure can add a variety of components.

For example, for a teenage client, the measure can use the same scale in six areas of interpersonal relationships. A practitioner can ask: "On a scale from 1 to 10, with 1 being the least important and 10 being the most important, indicate how important each of the following items is to your quality of life:

1. Communicating with my parents
2. Having fun with my peers
3. Knowing that I can succeed academically in school
4. Learning new skills from school
5. Dating someone I like

The practitioner may add other areas based on the initial assessment of the identified problem. These items can be determined through initial assessments with the client or with the client's family. With repeated measures, changes can be assessed and perceptions of the target problem can be validated.

Analyze Data: Are the Goals and Objectives Achieved?

After a treatment or service has been implemented, the client and the practitioner should discuss whether the intervention has achieved its overall goal. Throughout the evaluation process, data will have been collected to support an outcome evaluation. The overall evaluation question is: Has the service achieved its desirable goals and objectives?

Three types of outcome studies involve the following:

1. *Success of treatment* refers to whether the treatment goals and objectives have been achieved regardless of any confounding variables that may have contributed to the success. A one-shot case study, a one-group post-test-only design, or a time-series design will address the success of treatment.
2. *Comparison of treatment* outcomes emphasizes the assessment of whether the treatment should be continued or discontinued after comparing it with other treatment (or no treatment at all). A post-test design with the comparison group will address the treatment outcomes.

Target Problem or Issue:

Step 1: Choose a scale to measure the level of the target problem. An example is provided:

Low 1——2——3——4——5 High

Step 2: Describe in concrete terms or with behavioral indicators that can represent each level. Use the same measure throughout our process.

Low 1 =
     2 =
Mid 3 =
     4 =
High 5 =

Instructions:

Please use the scale developed by you and your practitioner to circle the level of your _____ **as it occurred today.** Record the time and date. Then write three words below to describe your feelings, and write down one or two events that happened today that are worth mentioning.

Record Time (may be prescheduled)	Level of Target Problem	Three Words to Describe Feeling at Time of Recording	Events That Happened Today	Other Comments
1.				
2.				
3.				
4.				
5.				
6.				
7.				

Figure 3.3

Self-Reported Scale to Measure Anxiety: An Example

3. *Net effects of treatment* asks whether the treatment alone contributes to the accomplishment of the goals and objectives. A pre-test post-test design with comparison group or a time series design with comparison group will address the net effects (see Table 3.1).

In addition to performing any outcome studies, the practitioner should utilize the literature and evidence-based sources to inform practice. Such sources include tested interventions on a specific problem such as alcohol and drug use (http://www.samhsa.gov/), research on national issues such as poverty and health problems (http://www.rand.org/), treatment tests that are based on a specific client population, such as health care information provided through the Cochrane Collaboration (http://www.cochrane.org/index.htm), and intervention testing through publications at the Campbell Collaboration (http://www.campbellcollaboration.org/). Journals that are published in paper and online are important sources to update service effectiveness (http://www.sw.uh.edu/communityoutreach/cwep_title_ IVE.php). Through tests and retests of the many theory-based interventions, practitioners can now utilize a combined and integrated set of modalities into their practice, especially when the publications have tested the use of interventions with a specific cultural or ethnic group or clients from various backgrounds.

Table 3.1
Types of Outcome Studies

Type of Evaluation	Major Evaluation Question	Clinical Example
Evaluation of treatment success	To what extent have the outcome objects been achieved?	The treatment has reduced the level of anxiety by 20% in 6 months compared to baseline.
Comparison of treatment outcomes	Should we continue or discontinue the treatment or service?	Gestalt therapy will help the family members who participate in treatment to have a significantly lower level of anxiety (compared to behavioral therapy).
Net effect of treatment	What is the net effect of the treatment after controlling for the extraneous factors or variables?	Clients who have received treatment will have a significantly lower level of anxiety than those who have not received this treatment.

Report Results and Make Recommendations

Data collection is a means to allow both client and practitioner to define their roles in the process of evaluation. They share perceptions and analyze the outcomes of the selected measures. Once the client clarifies his or her perceptions and listens to various views of the originally defined problem, the practitioner will be able to draw a conclusion based on observations of the client's situation. Recommendations, therefore, will come from mutual assessment of the target problem.

Practice Evaluation Designs

Responding to the evaluation questions requires selecting from a variety of practice evaluation designs. Some designs are more rigorous than others that require frequent observations, random assignments of subjects into treatment and nontreatment groups, the inclusion of comparison or nonequivalent groups that are treated with different interventions, and the inclusion of multiple timeframes. In multicultural practice evaluation, common evaluation designs are identified in Table 3.2 and briefly explained in their relevance to multicultural practice using the standardized case example (Mary and Joe's family) identified in Chapter 2. More sophisticated experimental and control group designs (such as the Solomon's four-group design) are available; however, their applicability to clinical evaluations is limited because only naturally occurring environments may help to structure such designs, not the use of artificial assignments that place clients into the various design groups. For this reason, they are not discussed in this book. Readers are encouraged to study these designs in details by reading research methodology books such as Cook and Campbell (1979).

One-Group Post-Test-Only Design

A one-group post-test-only design is one of the simplest and most practical methods by which to evaluate treatment. Observation is done immediately after the intervention is completed with one individual or a group. Using this design, practitioners may determine whether an effect has occurred subsequent to the intervention, but they cannot know whether the intervention itself produced the effect, because the design does not control for other variables that may have produced the outcome.

Most practitioners use this design for their evaluation of treatment success because it is feasible, economical, and practical. This design, however, does not identify net effects of treatment because it lacks a control environment. It is also not appropriate for comparison of treatment outcomes, because the evaluation data come from one reference point.

Table 3.2
Evaluation Designs

Type of Design	Graphical Description	Utility	Chapters
One-group post-test-only design (one-shot case study)	X O	Treatment success	4
One-group pre-test and post-test design	O_1 X O_2	Treatment success	5 & 6
Post-test design with comparison group	E X O_1 ———————— C O_2	Comparison of treatment outcomes	7 & 8
Pre-test post-test design with comparison group	E O_1 X O_2 ———————— C O_3 O_4	Net effects	9, 10
Time series design	$O_1 O_2 O_3 O_4$ X $O_5 O_6 O_7 O_8$	Treatment success	11 & 12
Time series design with comparison group	E $O_1 O_3 O_5 O_7$ X $O_9 O_{11} O_{13} O_{15}$ ———————— C $O_2 O_4 O_6 O_8$ $O_{10} O_{12} O_{14}$ O_{16}	Net effects	13 & 14

Meanings of abbreviations:
- X = treatment
- O = observation of a condition (subscripted numbers indicated the sequence of the observations)
- E = experimental group (individuals who receive treatment)
- C = comparison group (individuals who do not receive treatment)

CLINICAL EXAMPLE

Ami told the practitioner that she was having trouble understanding her mother's concerns about her leaving for college. Ami was angry at her mother's unrealistic expectations because in American culture most adolescents leave home after high school. The practitioner encouraged Ami to approach her mother and discuss the issue.

In the next session, Ami shared that she tried harder to understand her mother's cultural expectation that children should stay in the home until marriage. She had listened to her mother's reasoning and her fears. She expressed that her mother's concern was not unreasonable and she was able to comfort her mother. The practitioner concluded that the mother–daughter relationship had improved.

One-Group Pre-Test- and Post-Test Design

The one-group pre-test and post-test design requires a pre-test prior to treatment implementation and a post-test after the treatment is completed. Evaluation is planned to ensure that the target behavior or problem is identified and measured using the same instruments. In this design practitioners record changes in condition after implementing the treatment. This design is also known as the A-B design. *A* refers to the baseline, and *B* to the observation after treatment.

Although this design is stronger than the one-group post-test-only design, the practitioner still does not know whether the intervention itself or other factors actually caused the changes. This design, however, is relatively easy to use and has been adopted by many practitioners for outcome evaluations. This design is not appropriate for net effects or for the comparison of treatment evaluations because a control group or comparison group is not included in the evaluation process.

CLINICAL EXAMPLE

Mary's initial complaint was related to her unexplainable headaches. In the first session she identified a 9 on a 10-point scale of pain intensity and noted that she had "noticeably bothersome" headaches at least three times a day. Mary's husband said he believed that Mary's headaches were related to the stress she had been under since their daughter left for college. Mary agreed that this might be the cause and was able to relax and share with the daughter her concern about her separation anxiety.

A week later Mary told the practitioner that she had only one headache that week. Further, the intensity of the headache had been reduced to a 4.

Post-Test Design With Comparison Group

This post-test design requires a comparison group for the evaluation. A comparison group is composed of those who by choice do not receive treatment. If the targeted condition changes in the family or group receiving the treatment but not in the family or group not receiving the treatment, the treatment is likely to be responsible for the change. This design is not feasible when an appropriate comparison group with similar characteristics cannot be identified. The design is most applicable in comparing treatment effects in a population in which outcomes can be compared between those who receive treatment and those who do not. Nevertheless, this design is not appropriate for evaluating net effects of treatment because extraneous factors may not be easily detectable.

CLINICAL EXAMPLE

Mary's practitioner encouraged her and Joe to join a parent–teen communication program with their daughter, Ami. After this 3-week, six-session program, the parents shared with the practitioner that their relationship with Ami had improved. After comparing the result with another couple who did not take the advice to participate in the parenting program, the practitioner concluded that the parenting program was effective.

Pre-Test Post-Test Design With Comparison Group

The pre-test post-test design is similar to the post-test design with comparison group. Both designs include a comparison group that receives no treatment. A pre-test is conducted in both the experimental group and the comparison group prior to intervention. This design is more difficult to implement, though, as it includes a comparison group *and* pre-test and post-test for the study. The design is more appropriate for net effects assessment because it can control for many extraneous variables and may identify net effects of the treatment.

CLINICAL EXAMPLE

Two practitioners randomly divided a parent support group into two subgroups, with 10 couples attending a new evening parenting class designed for couples and teens (experimental group) and 10 couples taking a 3-week vacation (comparison group). As a pre-test measure, the practitioner measured all the parents' perceived relationships with their teenage children. When all the parents returned to the support group, the practitioners measured their perceived relationship again. The average score of the experimental group was higher than that of the comparison group. In addition, the pre-test and post-test comparison of each individual was found to be higher among those who joined the parenting class. As a result, the practitioner encouraged the comparison-group parents to join the class for the next three weeks.

Time Series Design

The time series design requires a pre-test and several post-tests that involve repeated data collection of the same measure. This design is appropriate for identifying the success of treatment. Because the design does not include a control group or comparison group, though, it is not appropriate for net effects evaluation or the comparison of treatments outcomes. It can be used as a clinical evaluation because clients can compare their own data at several treatment points.

CLINICAL EXAMPLE

Mary's self-image was measured at the beginning of a behaviorally oriented treatment program (baseline). After Mary had received a series of assertiveness training exercises over 5 weeks, the practitioner measured her self-image using the same scales. The data during this time were not significantly different from the original tests at baseline.

Then Mary was prepared to aid the practitioner to teach a group of teenagers a class on how to promote self-image. After 5 weeks in this teaching assignment, the practitioner measured Mary's self-image again. The data showed significant improvement in all three scales.

Time Series Design With Comparison Group

The time series design with a comparison group requires selection of an experimental group and a comparison group using several pre-tests and several post-tests. This is a rigorous evaluation design that has the capacity to control for confounding variables. This design is most appropriate for the net effects evaluation, as it includes pre-test and post-test as well as a comparison group.

CLINICAL EXAMPLE

Mary and nine other clients with similar problems were selected to receive treatment in an experimental group. The members of this group assisted the practitioner in teaching a self-image class, and another 10 clients with the same self-image problems were assigned to the comparison group. After each teaching or training week, self-image was measured for both groups. Overall, the improvement was more visible for Mary's group in each measured point than for the clients in the comparison group.

During the data collection process, the practitioner identifies what is important to the client and assesses how the outcome of the intervention is related to the clients' well-being and environment. These two pieces of information help the practitioner answer the questions related to the change of target behavior and the cause of the change. Individually focused measures are used, but the emphasis is on how the clients themselves and the clients' families and significant others perceive the benefits of treatment.

Although data collection increases clients' awareness of their problem-solving ability, the purpose of data analysis is to bring clients closer to their goals. The measure of this achievement must be concrete and straightforward. When data are analyzed with the clients, the practitioner may use graphic presentations of a selected rating scale to measure each of the client's feelings (e.g., from 1 to 5, with the client's own definitions of the low, mid, and high points), frequency observations (number of times), and duration (time, days) of target behaviors (such as positive self-talk, parent–child mini-conferences). Based on these observable data, the clients themselves draw a conclusion, with the practitioner's input. In a clinical setting, a description of the average change (in terms of number and percentage) of the target behavior or action helps the individual client or group of clients understand how much progress they are making after a specific intervention has been implemented.

Practice Evaluation in Multicultural Environments

Practice evaluation in a multicultural environment has demonstrated five major characteristics: (1) time orientation, (2) intervention process, (3) intervention focus, (4) intervention outcomes, and (5) cross-cultural exchange.

First, in terms of *time orientation,* the choice of an evaluation method must suit the before-during-after timeframe of data collection. The evaluative question to be posed is "Does the client show any improvement from one time period to the next?" The use of different timeframes to compare the client's change is essential because practice evaluation must include an intervention process, not just a treatment.

Second, the *intervention process* represents the application of various approaches to suit the needs of the individual client, taking into account the client's unique culture that may provide strengths or constraints to the success of treatment. This requires a thorough understanding of the client's view of the problem and its possible solutions.

Third, an assessment of the client's view is linked to the *intervention focus* defined in this process as related to the client's cultural background and expectations. This focus takes the client's perspective into consideration through an evaluative question: "Does this intervention bring about change that is culturally acceptable and reinforced?"

Fourth, the *intervention outcomes* will show measurable change based on the problem definition determined jointly by both the client and the practitioner. If the measuring procedures and methods are presented clearly to and agreed upon by the client, this will further enhance the client's participation in the intervention process and produce visual impact when time series data are collected and plotted.

Fifth, the *cross-cultural exchange* must take place in a multicultural environment. The practitioner's role is not only to implement services or intervention but also to help clients and practitioners learn how different cultures may view the same evaluative results in different ways. By providing evidence-based results with respect to cultural relevance, the client will be encouraged to share how the outcomes may lead to self-directed behaviors interacting with the multifaceted environment.

These five characteristics explain the importance of practice–evaluation integration. With this integration in mind, some examples are provided here. In the evaluation process, it is essential to define the service target in measurable terms (i.e., observable behaviors or actions). For example, if a Chinese client says, "I'm depressed," the practitioner would ask for the client's own problem definition. The client defines depression as "loss of sleep, feeling anxious and unhappy most of the time, crying with no apparent reason." The practitioner may use a standardized measure such as the Chinese Depression Inventory (see Yeung, Neault, & Sonawalla, 2002) to identify a baseline score. With the focus on family interventions, this book introduces evaluation measures based on the family stages analyzed in subsequent chapters.

The suggested evaluation measures will help identify service outcomes. In a multicultural environment, it is important to assess the input from and impact on the client system and its surrounding environment, as they are related to the stated problem. For practice–evaluation integration to be successful in multicultural settings, the practitioner must evaluate three major multicultural practice elements first identified by Leung, Cheung, and Stevenson (1994):

1. Examine of the practitioners' attitudes and personal beliefs prior to evaluation.
2. Incorporate of culture into practice when applying intervention strategies.
3. Build a knowledge base from evaluative data in multicultural situations.

Self-awareness is essential to avoid incorporating biases into the problem definition phase. Thus, selecting an appropriate evaluation measure is based on how the problem is defined by the client and reexamined with the client's input and the practitioner's objective assessment. (More information on self-awareness is presented later in this chapter.)

The ability to conduct multicultural assessments is extremely important in our increasingly diverse society. Current census projections estimate that by 2025, 40% of all Americans will be non-white (U.S. Census Bureau, 2004a). There is considerable evidence of current ethnic and racial disparities in social services, demonstrating the need to reach and effectively serve ethnic-minority clients (Stanhope, Solomon, Pernell-Arnold, Sands, & Bourjolly, 2005). Culturally competent practitioners are the best hope for fulfilling this need.

Therefore, helping professionals must learn, practice, and evaluate cultural competence in social services. Evaluating cultural competence plays an important role in measuring service effectiveness. In his pioneering stage-based model, Cross, Bazron, Dennis, and Isaacs (1989) explained that cultural competence occurs developmentally along a continuum: (1) cultural destructiveness, (2) cultural incapacity, (3) cultural blindness, (4) cultural pre-competence, (5) cultural competency, and (6) cultural proficiency. Cross et al. indicated that most human service agencies serving children and families fall between cultural incapacity and cultural blindness on this continuum. Practitioners must develop the capacity for self-assessment of cultural competency to be able to measure and improve practice standards.

Evaluation of client progress is regarded as culturally insensitive when the client's input is not consulted when selecting an evaluation measure, when a measure that is selected to target the client's problem has not been validated with the client's cultural expectations or at least with similar clientele, or when the practitioner does not measure success based on the client's definition. The value of problem definition can also be seen as culturally relevant if the client or family is being consulted. An evaluation of practice can be seen as culturally insensitive if it does not truly intend to help the client understand the situation or if it does not value slight improvements made with effort. It is also considered culturally irrelevant if the client does not fully understand the meaning of the measure.

As an outsider to a family's situation, the practitioner must remain neutral when interpreting the outcomes with standardized measures. After presenting concrete data, a practitioner may ask, "What do you see in this data?" or, "What do you think would cause the change in this behavior or problem?" to help break barriers to cross-cultural understanding. Inviting clients to participate in the evaluation process encourages them to appreciate their own cultural definition of success.

Best Practice Evaluation: The ASK Model

As described previously, one of the three elements in practice–evaluation integration is evaluation of the practitioner's self-awareness of multiculturalism. Self-awareness is the first step in multicultural practice, and practitioners who work with diverse populations have to be cognizant of their own values and beliefs regarding their own culture and the cultures of others. Social workers and counselors must recognize that the values and beliefs of diverse populations may differ from those of Western ideologies (Hodge, 2004; Maiter, 2004). This awareness can be attained through a variety of self-assessment tools, and then the results can be interpreted as strengths and limitations.

The continuous use of self-assessment tools to gauge cultural sensitivity will result in a heightened sense of awareness and an ability to better serve the needs of clients (McPhatter, 1997; Mederos & Woldeguiorguis, 2003; Nybell & Gray, 2004). To fulfill the goal of identifying practitioners' strengths and limitations through self-assessment and supervision, it is also essential to adopt a tool so supervisors can identify unmet training needs.

Self-assessment tools that measure one's cultural competency are not a new concept in the fields of social work, psychology, and other mental health professions. The recent development of self-assessment tools indicates that cultural competency self-assessment tools should be tested to be reliable and valid instruments—which means that only a limited supply is available for practice use. In addition, evaluative areas should include awareness, knowledge, skills, racial identity development, and multicultural terminology. In the Holcomb-McCoy study (2000), the results from a factor analysis of the Association for Multicultural Counseling and Development's (AMCD) Multicultural Competencies instrument indicate that these five evaluative areas correlate with the measure created by Sue, Arredondo, and McDavis (as cited in Geron, 2002; Holcomb-McCoy, 2000). Such correlation has demonstrated the fact that self-assessment tools should include these areas.

One of the major concerns with cultural competence self-assessment measures is that they identify only the practitioner's skills and do not take the client's perspective into consideration as much (Geron, 2002). With a strong emphasis on assessing the client's situation from a process–stage approach, the ASK instrument is suggested here for practical use. Based on a framework developed by Leung, Cheung, and Stevenson (1994), this questioning framework is built conceptually as a strengths-oriented model with consideration of three dimensions: (1) a seven-phase process, (2) an attitude-skill-knowledge (ASK) analysis, and (3) a worker–client interaction pattern.

Through a systematic analysis of this approach, a matrix with 21 evaluative areas (three competency areas across seven practice phases) is utilized to help caseworkers assess their competencies during inservice training. Questioning techniques can assist supervisors in providing ongoing feedback for their workers to enhance their understanding of cross-cultural factors in client–worker relationship and service tasks.

A short version of this instrument derives from analyzing data from caseworkers, supervisors, and graduate students. It focuses on three distinct areas: (1) awareness or attitude, (2) skills, and (3) knowledge. The awareness section contains questions pertaining to the individual's knowledge about beliefs and attitudes of a culture. The skills section concerns the creation and implementation of culturally appropriate interventions. The knowledge dimension concentrates on an individual's ability to understand distinct cultural views (Geron, 2002; Holcomb-McCoy, 2000).

Practical Use of ASK

With a Likert-type scale, the helping professional can use the ASK Instrument (see Figure 3.4) to evaluate his or her own competency in terms of working with culturally diverse populations. This scale does not indicate right or wrong answers but, instead, provides an opportunity for ongoing self-evaluation and cultural awareness measures. Practically, in working with a client system (an individual, a group, a family, or a community) the professional can assess how ready he or she is in three areas: (1) attitude and cultural awareness, (2) skill applications, and (3) the use of knowledge base. The self-rated score should fall between 1 and 5, in which 1 is "totally unprepared" and 5 is "competent."

With each client system as the focus, if the total score (total of the 14 items on the ASK Scale) falls below an average score, which is 42 (the norm based on Cheung & Leung, 2006), the practitioner must consult with a supervisor or professor to address any area that needs improvement or further learning.

The practitioner may also initiate opportunities with client systems to obtain information that is not available from the practitioner's previous experiences. Clients are the experts on their own situations, including cultural information that affects their definition of the problem. Practitioners should learn from their clients. Practitioners can also learn from case studies and case reviews. If the practitioner's self-assessment indicates a lack of multicultural awareness, hypothetical case situations highlighting areas of weakness can be presented and analyzed. Many of the cases presented in this book can be used as a means to understand the cultural and other types of variations among clients in a practitioner's

**Working with People of Diverse Cultures:
Attitude (A), Skill (S), and Knowledge (K)**

Use the following scale between 1 to 5 to assess your readiness in terms of Attitude, Skill, and Knowledge when working with a specific family/client:

    1 = Totally Unprepared
    2 = Somewhat Prepared
    3 = Neutral
    4 = Ready
    5 = Competent

Attitude Assessment

1. I am open to hear the clients' perceptions.   1   2   3   4   5
2. It is crucial that clients be allowed to clarify their
   perceptions of the problem.   1   2   3   4   5
3. I understand that attitude toward the use of authority
   may be so important that it may influence the family's
   willingness to participate in the assessment process.   1   2   3   4   5
4. I enjoy learning from my clients about their culture.   1   2   3   4   5
5. I use my previous experiences in working with clients from
   a specific culture as a guide in selecting services for new
   clients from that same culture.   1   2   3   4   5

Skill Assessment

6. I openly ask questions and share information concerning
   cultural differences with clients to help identify possible
   problems and barriers that my clients and I might encounter.   1   2   3   4   5
7. I ask clients to reflect back to me what they hear me saying
   about their problems.   1   2   3   4   5
8. When I encounter what appears to be resistance, I
   explore other possible meanings of this behavior in my
   client's culture.   1   2   3   4   5
9. I assess family strengths within the context of cultural
   norms when appropriate.   1   2   3   4   5
10. I acknowledge culturally specific practices with which I am
    not familiar.   1   2   3   4   5
11. I address the client's inappropriate behaviors that inhibit
    successful goal attainment without judging particular
    cultural values or beliefs.   1   2   3   4   5

Knowledge Assessment

12. I know several ways of greeting that may work well with
    the family.   1   2   3   4   5
13. I understand that information specific to the culture of the
    family may be useful in developing goals and objectives
    with the clients.   1   2   3   4   5
14. I realize the importance of including culturally relevant
    information in the outcome evaluation.   1   2   3   4   5

Figure 3.4

ASK Instrument for Use in Cultural Competency Assessment

caseload. The practitioner should not expect to repeat the same skills without considering differences in clients.

After you finish reading this chapter, you will respond to the 14 items on the ASK Scale (Figure 3.4) and record your total score in Figure 3.5. Then, after you have finished reading each of the chapters 4 to 15, repeat this procedure. If you evaluate yourself consistently, you will have 13 observations by the time you finish reading chapter 15. Plot the ASK Scale score in Figure 3.6 and identify what changes you have made. By following this format, you can evaluate your own cultural competency as you work through the cases applying the theories and skills explained in this book. Through an honest assessment of your own skills and areas of improvement with this scale, you will identify areas in need of improvement prior to further practice. Because this is a self-evaluation tool, you need not be cautious about admitting a lack of professional readiness. This is a developmental process to establish multicultural competencies through awareness of your limitations. Typically, individuals evaluate themselves more critically in a post-test than in a pre-test because of the contrast between their heightened awareness of the expansive knowledge base available and their limited abilities.

Week	Reading	ASK Score
1	Chapter 3	
2	Chapter 4	
3	Chapter 5	
4	Chapter 6	
5	Chapter 7	
6	Chapter 8	
7	Chapter 9	
8	Chapter 10	
9	Chapter 11	
10	Chapter 12	
11	Chapter 13	
12	Chapter 14	
13	Chapter 15	

Figure 3.5
ASK Self Assessment Scores

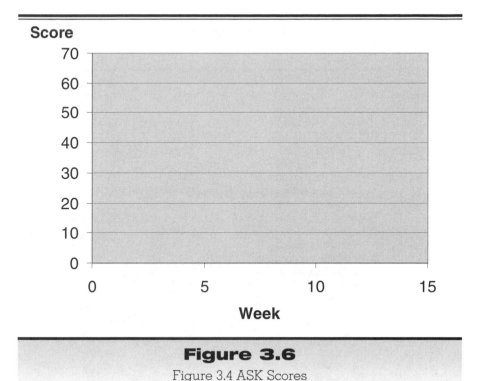

Score

Figure 3.6
Figure 3.4 ASK Scores

As a result, you are encouraged to provide qualitative responses in an effort to explain your scores for future reference. A cautionary statement: When supervisors ask their staff to utilize the ASK self-assessment tool, it is not to be used as a performance measure but, rather, as a means to help their staff move to a state of cultural sensitivity and develop a sense of cultural competency.

Multicultural Practice and Evaluation: An Integrative Model

After describing the conceptual framework in working with multicultural families (chapter 1), the case approach to evaluate theories to practice (chapter 2), and the various practice evaluation steps and methods (this chapter), we describe an integrative model to combine practice and evaluation in chapters 4 through 14. Table 3.3 is a summary linking chapters to evaluative steps and tools, to help practitioners identify the process of establishing multicultural competencies. As a process-oriented structure, chapter 5 evaluates family relationships using the Family Involvement

Table 3.3

Multicultural Practice and Evaluation: An Integrative Model

Approaches in Practice Evaluation	Multicultural Focus & Suggestions	Suggested Tool	Evidence-Based Example With a Selected Practice Evaluation Method
1. Conduct self-assessment	■ Practitioners evaluate their own perceptions of multicultural counseling development in areas of awareness, attitude, knowledge, skills, and communication. ■ Culturally skilled practitioners should evaluate their self-development on a regular basis.	Ch. 3: ASK Instrument Ch. 4: Multi-cultural Knowledge Awareness Scale (MKAS)	One-group post-test-only design
2. Evaluate family relationships	■ It is assumed that an increase in family involvement in children's early education experience will strengthen family relationships. ■ In different cultures, family involvement may vary depending on the characteristics of family members, time of involvement, and communication methods.	Ch. 5: Index of Family Relations (IFR)	One-group pre-test and post-test design
3. Evaluate the family as a system	■ Families are systems that are complex and ever-changing. ■ In multicultural practice, seven areas of family functioning are addressed, based on each member's perspective: task accomplishment, role performance, communication, affective expression, involvement, control, and values and norms.	Ch. 6: Family Assessment Measure (FAM)	One-group pre- and post-test design

(continued)

Table 3.3 *(continued)*

Approaches in Practice Evaluation	Multicultural Focus & Suggestions	Suggested Tool	Evidence-Based Example With a Selected Practice Evaluation Method
4. Assess problems within the family	■ Family functioning is measured based on the family's strengths. ■ The six dimensions of family functioning can be assessed in terms of the family's ability to do: problem solve, communicate with each other, assume roles, respond to each others' emotional needs, promote family togetherness, controll behavior that is counter-productive.	Ch. 7: Family Assessment Device (FAD)	Post-test design with comparison group
5. Assess changes and impacts	■ Life change (or stress) in one member affects all other family members. ■ Family members are connected through various life events and cultural experiences. ■ Cultural expectations are influenced by environ-mental factors.	Ch. 8: Family Inventory of Life Events and Changes (FILE)	Post-test design with comparison group
6. Communi-cate with children & adolescents	■ Communication is a tool that guides families to adaptability and away from stagnation. ■ It is assumed that balanced families have more positive com-munication. ■ Further assessment is needed to address the varied definitions of a balanced family and family openness across cultures.	Ch. 9: Parent–Adolescent Communication (PAC)	Pre-test post-test design with comparison group

(continued)

Table 3.3 *(continued)*

Approaches in Practice Evaluation	Multicultural Focus & Suggestions	Suggested Tool	Evidence-Based Example With a Selected Practice Evaluation Method
7. Measure intergenerational values	■ Adolescents' adjustment to a new phase of life is measured. ■ In immigrant and refugee families, various levels of understanding and satisfaction between the child and the immigrant parent may affect parent–child relationships.	Ch. 10: Intergenerational Congruence in Immigrant Families (ICIF): Child and Parent scales	Pre-test post-test design with comparison group
8. Measure family stress	■ A systems perspective explains how the events in a young adult's life can affect each family member. ■ Stress and adjustment are key concepts to understand family functioning, especially of a newly migrated family. ■ Immigrant and refugee families have many levels of cultural adjustment, depending on the duration and status of immigration. ■ Measuring immediate influences on stress is a must to facilitate cultural adjustment.	Ch. 11: Perceived Stress Scale (PSS)	Time-series design
9. Identify faulty thinking patterns	■ The intervention challenges rational/irrational thinking.	Ch. 12: General Attitude and Belief Scale (GABS)	Time-series design

(continued)

Scale. Chapter 6 examines the family as a system using the Family Assessment Measure. Chapter 7 assesses problems in the family using the Family Adaptability and Cohesion Evaluation Scales. Chapter 8 assesses changes and impacts using the Family Inventory of Life Events and Changes scale. Chapter 9 addresses parents'

Table 3.3 *(continued)*

Approaches in Practice Evaluation	Multicultural Focus & Suggestions	Suggested Tool	Evidence-Based Example With a Selected Practice Evaluation Method
10. Measure perception of power	■ Perception of power encompasses all cultures and social lifestyles. ■ Family empowerment is a process by which families access knowledge, skills, and resources that allow them to take control of their lives.	Ch. 13: Family Empowerment Scale (FES)	Time-series design with comparison group
11. Map out solutions and alternatives	■ Family coping strategies are justified through a combination of various meanings families have given to events as well as their use of resources to handle the stressful events. ■ Greater number of stressful events is related to lower adaptation.	Ch. 14: Family Crisis Oriented Personal Evaluation Scales (F-COPES)	Time series design with comparison group

communication with children and adolescents using the Parent-Adolescent Communication scale. Chapter 10 assesses intergenerational values using the Intergenerational Congruence in Immigrant Families: Child and Parent scales. Chapter 11 assesses family stress using the Young Adult Family Inventory of Life Events and Changes. Chapter 12 identifies faulty thinking patterns within a client system using the General Attitude and Belief Scale. Chapter 13 addresses the perception of power using the Family Empowerment Scale. Chapter 14 maps out solutions and alternatives, using the Family Crisis Oriented Personal Evaluation Scales to measure outcomes. Finally, Chapter 15 highlights the principles of multicultural practice and evaluations.

Practice evaluation is unique because evidence can be obtained from an individual, a group or family, or a community. With this respect for a basic understanding of practice–research integration, all of the theory chapters in this book will be demonstrated through a selected practice–evaluation method with the entry of data from an identified client system and its counterpart of an experimental or comparison group based on the standardized case described in chapter 2. A selected method may be used in two consecutive chapters, starting from chapter 3, to stress that its practical use can be applied across problems and across clients. These evaluation methods are easy to use and should be used consistently so aggregate data can be generated to support a scientific call of practice evidence.

PART
TWO

Practices With Cross-Cultural Analysis

In the multicultural integrated framework, practice means the application of theories to the healing or helping process, and evaluation is the systematic process of determining whether the application impacts the targeted issue or problem effectively and efficiently. The essential components in this integrated framework are theoretical techniques, practice process, intervention focus, and outcome measures, all of which are connected to the practice philosophy and evaluation of success.

When practitioners work within a cross-cultural environment, they must accept the client-centered philosophy that the client knows best. Although the practitioner may take on the role of an educator or change agent, he or she still must realize that teaching and effecting change begins only after he or she is knowledgeable about the audience. One of the basic principles of practice is to maintain a strong sense of self-awareness toward learning to be able to achieve the greatest benefit in practice. With the target of self-awareness in mind, techniques can be applied effectively and delivered efficiently.

Multicultural applications begin with a specific time orientation—past, present, or future. A multitude of approaches and techniques can be applied to help clients understand that all time perspectives are essential in the helping or healing process. From a multicultural perspective, the terms "helping" and "healing" are used interchangeably to indicate the benefits received for the well-being of an individual, a family, or a community. In a study by Tang, Sevigny, and Mao (2007), one fourth of the Chinese clients turned to folk healing as their primary health care service. To these clients, service effectiveness can be achieved only if the service fits in their cultural context.

During the healing process, engaging the clients is based upon the triad connections between the body, mind, and environment. The steps the practitioner should take to motivate clients to tell their stories and talk about their issues include thinking, feeling, acting (doing), and integrating the various applications and theoretical approaches. The intervention will be based on these four steps so the therapeutic view can be examined from the professional's experience, the clients' views, the types of actions taken, and the environmental factors involved.

A final component in this framework is the measurement of therapeutic development throughout the process and outcomes that result from intervention. Some theories may address insight or awareness, and others may evaluate change or diverse feedback.

PRACTICE FRAMEWORK			
Theory	**Time Orientation**	**Intervention Focus**	**Therapeutic Outcome**
Psychodynamic	Past	Thinking	Insight
Experiential Relationship	Present	Feeling	Awareness
Cognitive & Behavioral	Future	Doing	Change
System	All	Thinking–Feeling–Doing	Integration

Within the practice framework, the first therapeutic tool in multicultural practice is directed to the clients. After establishing rapport with the clients, the practitioner should ask the clients to tell their stories through direct talking or a variety of other means, such as drawing, story-telling, sentence completion, and so on. In family therapy, the narrative approach has proven effective in assessing multigenerational issues (Goldenberg & Goldenberg, 2004; Liem, 1997). Kerl (2002) asserts that narratives help clients address important aspects of their self identity as it relates to race, ethnicity, gender, and other human diversity variables. Goldenberg and Goldenberg (2004) advocate the use of self-narratives and cultural narratives when working with persons of diverse cultures. They place high value on the flexibility of narratives to accommodate clients' cultural values. Narrative therapists attempt to engage families in conversations that discover, acknowledge, and deconstruct those cultural beliefs and practices (from customs, laws, institutions, language, and so on) that help perpetuate the problem story.

For most theories that support multicultural counseling, therapists utilize narrative techniques in their approach. The various theories, however, tend to utilize narratives in slightly different ways:

- **Psychodynamic:** rooted in psychoanalytic theory, it assumes that unconscious motivation in early life can affect later development of personality, and it treats patients with an in-depth analysis of life experiences. It utilizes the narrative approach by encouraging clients to describe the past.
- **Adlerian:** uses techniques such as the family constellation, lifestyle assessment, and challenging faulty assumptions to help clients evaluate views of human nature. It utilizes the narrative approach by identifying life stories related to sibling and other family relationships.
- **Family System:** assumes that relationship problems are caused by the rigidity of structure, functions, and roles within a family, as well as lack of interconnectiveness among major components in the family. It utilizes the narrative approach by focusing on family events that describe relationship issues.
- **Structural:** purports that restructuring can take place once clients discover that problems are manifested from the rules and structure enforced in the family. It utilizes the narrative approach by empowering the clients to talk about family structural concerns.
- **Client-Centered and Communication:** focuses on acceptance, active listening, and reflective techniques that guide clients to find their potential, capabilities, and destinations. A nurturing environment is the key to open the door of communication, and communication is the key to open the door of relationships. It utilizes the narrative approach by addressing clients' interpretations.
- **Gestalt:** sees the body–mind connection within a here-and-now environment to stimulate clients to think about and look for personal growth. It utilizes the narrative approach by emphasizing clients' participation in dialogue about the perceived conflict.

- **Strategic:** assumes that symptoms should be the focus of attention and uses experiential strategies to find solutions. It utilizes the narrative approach to allow for paradoxical descriptions of the problem.
- **Behavioral:** focuses on how self-directed learning can lead to modifications of behavior. It utilizes the narrative approach by focusing on clients' progress and encouraging them to describe improvements and obstacles to such progress.
- **Cognitive–Behavioral:** challenges cognitive distortions as a means for clients to fully recognize the underlying causes of malfunctioning personal relationships. It utilizes the narrative approach by encouraging clients to express their thoughts.
- **Feminist:** identifies major socioeconomic forces affecting men and women and stresses the importance of utilizing internal strengths to evaluate the personal, social, and political conditions surrounding a given problem. It utilizes the narrative approach by encouraging clients to identify and explore societal issues through stories about their environment.
- **Solution-Focused:** searches for exceptions and solutions to help clients move forward. It utilizes the narrative approach by allowing clients to recall incidents that are exceptions to the rule and provides future-oriented questions to help clients identify possible solutions to achieving stated goals.

All of these theories can be applied in situations in which the client and his or her family are telling their stories. From an outcome perspective, these theories can be grouped into three categories of practice to achieve healing, experiencing feelings and relationships, and planning for the future.

1. Healing based on psychoanalytic therapy
   a. Purpose: to gain insight
   b. Technique: memory recall
   c. Therapist role: analysis
2. Experiencing based on humanistic therapy
   a. Purpose: to achieve self-awareness
   b. Technique: subjective experience
   c. Therapist role: listening
3. Developing the future based on cognitive and behavioral therapy
   a. Purpose: to change
   b. Technique: action-oriented assignments
   c. Therapist role: empowering

Within this practice framework, narratives are incorporated through various theories to assist practitioners with the integration of change concerning self-awareness about all human diversity variables. In applying narratives to multicultural counseling, Semmler and Williams (2000) identify key narrative techniques: deconstructing the dominant cultural narrative, externalizing the problem, reauthoring the story, and providing a context for the new story. The use of these techniques is well supported by gestalt, strategic, and solution-focused theories. In this textbook, the case approach demonstrates these techniques. Through description of a situation, event, or life story in a narrative, change is integrated into the client's life, enhancing his or her self-development. All theories and applications are based on the principle that self-awareness is the first step toward change and acceptance.

CHAPTER FOUR

Psychodynamic Theory

This chapter presents an introduction to psychodynamic theory with an emphasis on its strengths and use in multicultural practice. The stage is set for utilizing this theory and its techniques in practice through a case approach to the first family stage: formation of the family. The chapter presents four issues to demonstrate how various techniques are applied to this standardized case family:

1. The client's perception of an unstable relationship
2. Children as the therapeutic focus
3. The family's reactions to unresolved conflict
4. Families of origin issues

The case examples emphasize that neutrality, reassurance, and choice/resource analysis are more essential than strict interpretations in therapy. The examples also facilitate understanding of how to integrate this theory into multicultural practice.

In addition, through demographic data and other case-specific information, we summarize how experts can work effectively with African American families during the helping process. The evaluation process is addressed through a self-assessment, with the suggestion that all practitioners conduct a self-assessment and compare their results with the normative scores to gauge their proficiency in multicultural knowledge. Exercises for this chapter are directed to learning and healing, with an emphasis on cultural awareness, and they include the utilization of defense mechanisms in counseling and other practices.

The Psychodynamic Root

From a contemporary perspective, psychodynamic theory is a collection of theories that address the opposing forces within a system and potentially bring about motivation or conflict to the individuals within the system (Goldenberg & Goldenberg, 2004). These theories, though adopted from psychoanalytic theory, have a strong orientation toward relationship-building with the client and maintaining neutrality concerning practitioners' interpretations. Psychodynamic concepts and techniques are applicable to cross-cultural situations, particularly when practitioners closely examine the impact that gender and culture-related issues (such as the power issues

Psychodynamic Theory in Brief

Applicability to Multicultural Practice:
- Focus on past experiences related to the family culture; discrimination and racism issues.
- Identify key human diversity factors that can influence an individual's definition of well-being and self-image.

Major Figures:
- Sigmund Freud: personality development
- Erik Erikson: social development of personality
- Nathan Ackerman: integration of psychoanalytic and systems theories
- James Framo: object relations theory

Assumptions:
- Personalities are determined by unconscious motivation, forces including the id, ego, and superego, sexual and/or aggressive impulses, as well as childhood experiences.
- It is important to examine ego development from early childhood experiences.
- Family-of-origin issues are important sources for analyzing past experiences.

Therapeutic Process:
- Understand early history and past situations: Use recollections to identify past issues that may have an impact on current relationships.
- Use projective testing as part of an assessment: Assess the client's thinking patterns through the use of associated words, games, drawing, and other tools of a projection nature.

(continued)

involved in domestic violence situations) can have on the client's problem, without imposing a subjective assessment or biased interpretations.

The psychodynamic approach has been proven effective in cross-cultural practices when it is combined with a person-centered approach that considers safety and resources and when it is used with a treatment plan that considers cognitive–behavioral approaches in setting up goals and treatment objectives (Liggan & Kay, 2006; Spangler & Brandl, 2007). Given these combinations, the past can be dealt with if the treatment process evaluates the current situation with an action plan that can be implemented in the near future (Fraser & Solovey, 2007).

Kovel, as referenced by Corey (2005), noted that as the unconscious becomes conscious, choice will replace blind habits. Among the contemporary psychodynamic-oriented theories, family-of-origin and object relations theory seem to be the most culturally relevant to serving the needs of a diverse client system (Goldenberg &

- Analyze parental introjects: Identify the client's memory of parents' values and judgments.
- Address the use of self: Understand the importance of self-disclosure when it aims to uncover thoughts that the client has not previously considered.

Goals:
- Explore the unconscious: Examine the thoughts the client has not considered when certain tasks were done.
- Work through repressed conflicts: Identify conflicts that are not spoken but require individual attention before bringing to the family's attention.
- Gain treatment insight: Discover thoughts that have not been taken into consideration previously.

Multicultural Practice Techniques:
- Gather family history data: Identify all the relevant historical events and information that have impacted the client's well-being both positively and negatively.
- Dream analysis: Develop strategies to analyze the content of dreams that would provide meaning to the client's current situation.
- Analysis of resistance: Understand the power and meaning of resistance or conflict that may have contributed to the existing problem.
- Transference analysis: Identify the reflected images that are projected through the helping relationship between the client and the practitioner.
- Family-of-origin analyses: Analyze the family from which the client came, including its function, structure, problem, and relationship dynamics, to understand if any unresolved conflict would have spilled over into the client's current family or relationship.

Goldenberg, 2004). These theories emphasize the importance of practitioner neutrality in the interpretation process and the multidimensional aspect of history in the family (Framo, 1992).

Although some mental health practitioners continue to accept and utilize psychodynamic theories as their theoretical approach, others are highly critical of this approach. Some who reject the theory believe that it does not apply to multicultural practice because its emphasis on the sexual motives behind behavior may be viewed as inappropriate and offensive. Psychoanalytic theory is also criticized for its male-dominant nature and lack of attention to women's issues. Nevertheless, many practitioners adopt psychoanalytic techniques in a dynamic manner to help clients work through past issues and explore unknown forces, including psychological, sexual, family, cultural, economic, political, and other societal concerns. As Freud (1959) explained, "above all, our interest will be directed toward their family circumstances" (p. 26).

A major contribution of the psychodynamic aspect of practice theories is the assumption that an individual's past experiences provide insight into the impact of unresolved present-day issues within the individual and his or her family. These experiences contain cultural and ethnic elements that influence the individual's definition of well-being, self-image, socioeconomic status, ability to deal with power struggles, and connections with the family-of-origin.

If this past perspective is applied to a family seeking counseling, the practitioner may focus on the presenting symptom as a recurring matter that disrupts family functioning and role relationships. In this sense, the application of psychodynamic theory to multicultural practice is

> to accommodate to new experiences, to cultivate new levels of complementarity in family role relationships, to find avenues for the solution of conflict, to build a favorable self-image, to buttress critical forms of defense against anxiety, and to provide support for further creative development. (Ackerman, 1966, pp. 90–91)

From a cross-cultural perspective, all of these application functions enhance the client's healing and learning—the two main processes for achieving successful therapeutic outcomes.

On the Multicultural Stage: Formation of the Family

According to the functionalist theory, the creation of a family has a purposeful intent, aimed at fulfilling an individual's self-interest through reproduction and economic security; enhancing a couple's sense of togetherness, loving, and caring for each other; and promoting the society's culture and transmitting its values. For all of these functions and others, the formation of a family is a long-term commitment. From the structural perspective, families are relationship-based through their biological, emotional, and legal ties to one another. These connections establish boundaries for the family and allow both multigenerational and kinship ties to be maintained. From a psychoanalytic point of view, both the functionalist and structural theories identify a strong sense of membership and agreement. When individuals within the family do not communicate well, however, they begin to resent their membership and focus on their disagreements.

In cross-cultural counseling, it is evident that family functions are defined through a variety of perceived notions based on individual beliefs and expectations. As a result, family roles should not be based on the practitioners' view. Instead, the roles should be defined by each of the family members, to enable an understanding of each person's perception of the family from formation until therapy.

As Framo (1982) indicated, the multicultural strength of psychodynamic approaches is their emphasis on the use of

> the psychology of intimate relationships, the interlocking of multi-person motivational systems, the relationship between the intrapsychic and the transactional, and the hidden transgenerational and historical forces that exercise their powerful influences on current intimate relationships. (p. ix)

This approach stresses an understanding of how interpersonal interactions impact our relationships. The examples provided below are therapeutic dialogues illustrating techniques the practitioner uses. Definitions of the techniques follow the dialogues.

The Case Approach

In the following example, the psychoanalytic approach was utilized with the client, Mary. Since her last session, Mary has called the office frequently, complaining about the instability in her family. In this fourth session, the multicultural counselor (MC) helps Mary gain insight into some of her problems by analyzing how past experiences with her family-of-origin (especially regarding her attachment to past issues with her father) have affected how she views her relationship with her husband, Joe.

Issue #1: Unstable Relationship

MC: Mary, I noticed that you've been late for our sessions recently. You mentioned that you've been sick. Has something been troubling you lately?

Mary: (sigh) Actually, I was very uncomfortable in our last session, and I couldn't find a reason for it.

MC: Let's talk about that. How about doing something new? Close your eyes and go back to our last session. (pause) Tell me what you recall seeing and feeling from last time.

Using Past Feelings

Mary: I was doing all the talking, all the time. I know I must have looked like a fool, saying whatever came to my mind. But once I started, I couldn't stop. I found myself getting anxious about everything, worrying about what you might think about me as a person. I don't think Joe or my father would like this.

MC: What does not pleasing your father mean to you?

Mary: Well, I think I got sidetracked, sorry. I didn't mean to bring my father into our discussion.

MC: It's okay. Tell me anything that comes to mind for you right now.

Free Association

Mary: I guess I felt so powerless mainly because I sensed some control over me.

MC: Do you feel like you were controlled by me?

Mary: (nods)

MC: Did this "control" remind you of somebody?

Mary: I don't know. Maybe my father.

MC: Your father was the first important authority figure in your life. What is the strongest impression you have about him?

Transference

Mary: He's a controlling person.

MC: Do you see your father in Joe?

Mary: (nods)

MC: Through this projection process of seeing your father in me, you're expressing that you have a need to gain approval and acceptance from an authority figure. Now that you have your family and your father isn't living with you, do you think you still can't be separated from your father?

Seeking the Unconscious

Mary: I guess I can. But I find it difficult to believe that my own children now want to leave me. How can they do this to me after I've tried to model to them that they should always like to live with their parents?

MC: You seem to place your own expectations on your children.

Interpretation

Mary: That may be true. But I'm afraid if I don't, they won't be close to me any more.

MC: That's a feeling that has to be explored further.

Issue #2: Children as the Focus

Mary is concerned about her relationship with Joe as the children are growing older. She becomes depressed after finding out that Ami wants to attend an out-of-state college. Mary believes that Ami is leaving her because she wants to form her own family. Mary's relationship issues with her children continue to bother her. The therapist encourages Mary to open up and talk about her fear.

Mary:	I'm not sure about my relationship with my children any more. It won't be long before they both leave me.
MC:	(silence)
Mary:	I used to just accept it, but now I'm not sure about myself. I mean, my children are my life. I gave my best to them and I know they'll all desert me soon. I worked hard to provide my children with what they wanted. I need them but I don't know where they're going to be. (sigh) They don't seem to care about all I've done for them. (long pause)
MC:	(silence)
Mary:	No, I don't mean that. I don't know what I mean at this point. I'm confused. I even have this recurring dream about losing Ami in a dark place, and that drives me crazy!
MC:	Your statements about how you feel seem to tell me that you have a great deal of anxiety about separating from your children. I also sense that you fear losing your relationship that you've just reestablished with your husband. You seem to be having difficulties managing your own behaviors. Tell me if any of what I'm sensing is valid.
Mary:	I guess you're right.
MC:	Tell me more about your recurring dream about Ami.

Analysis of Anxiety Root

Mary:	Sure ... this dream has always been the same, and that puzzles me.
MC:	When did you start to have this dream? Do you dream it every night?
Mary:	It started about a month ago. Well, I don't remember if I've dreamt every night since then, but I think I might have had the dream six times already. (pause) It always starts out with someone chasing me. I'm running after Ami in the dream, but I never can catch up with her. Finally I catch her clothes, but she disappears. I always wake up seeing her again inside some dark place. Can you tell me what this means?
MC:	Well, the dream has an overtone that relates to your anxiety and separation. You seem to be afraid that Ami has matured fully and eventually you will lose her too. Is it true?
Mary:	Yes.
MC:	At what age did you leave your parents?

Dream Analysis

Mary:	When I was 18.
MC:	Tell me what happened.

Exploration

Mary:	My parents were very strict. They didn't allow me to date when I was in high school. I always had a fantasy that I would meet a nice guy and we'd have lots of kids and be very happy. You know … as it was, I married the only guy I had ever dated. I guess I shouldn't have left home that soon.
MC:	Did you say that at the time you left home, you shouldn't leave?
Mary:	No, I don't think so. It was my mother who would have liked me to stay at home longer. Now that I think about it, my mom should feel proud of me because I took just as good of care of my kids as she did with me.
MC:	Do you think you're important to your parents?

Projection

Mary:	Oh, I guess so. But they've never told me that, especially not my father. He was critical of almost everything I did, and I was always trying to get his approval. I used to take care of my brother and sisters, but he'd never say thank you or show his appreciation.
MC:	In what way does your relationship with your husband compare to the relationship with your father?

Transference: Uncovering the Unconscious

Mary:	Now you've really asked—I always try to gain acceptance from Joe. I think I followed my father's directions, and now I follow Joe's.
MC:	Do you want to talk more about this "acceptance?"

Issue #3: Unresolved Conflict

Recently, Mary has had anxiety attacks, and initially she did not want to tell her husband about her problems. During her last individual session, however, she realized that she could no longer hide her feelings and problems from her family. So she made the decision to have Joe come with her to the next session.

Mary:	This is my husband, Joe.
Joe:	Mary wanted me to come, so I'm here.
MC:	Nice to meet you, Joe. Thank you for coming. Mary wanted to talk about what we've been discussing in our sessions. Last week Mary and I were talking about her family and her relationship with her father. Mary, why don't you tell Joe about your relationship with your dad?
Mary:	(hesitant) Oh, I don't know. I love my father. He's a wonderful person, but he's a very hard person. It was hard to live up to his expectations.

(pause) I mean, I always wanted my father's approval but was never good enough.

MC: Tell me about your relationship with your husband, Joe.

Intrapsychic Conflict Analysis

Mary: I don't think my marriage is the way it should be, but Joe seems to think it's fine. We don't talk about anything, and I'm afraid to tell him what I really want because he'll be angry at me.

Joe: That is not true. We talk all the time. (showing stress) I don't get angry!

Mary: See—you're angry right now—just like my dad used to be.

MC: Let's relax. (pause) So, Joe, how do you see Mary's relationship with her father?

Reexperiencing Unresolved Family Conflict

Joe: He's a great guy. All of his kids turned out really well because he always kept them in line. Sure, he doesn't talk a lot, but when he does say something, everybody had better listen.

MC: So does that sound controlling to you, Mary?

Confrontation

Mary: I don't know what I want, but I don't like someone always telling me what to do! (tearful)

Joe: What are you talking about? I work hard, and you decided to go back to school, but now you want to go back to work. I never told you to do any of that!

MC: Mary, are you actually saying this to your father, not to Joe?

Projection

Mary: I don't know.

MC: I understand that this has been difficult for you. What if we practice it—what you would say to your father?

Joe: Well, I think she's going to need a lot of practice because she never says anything to her father.

Mary: I'm so tired of carrying around all this baggage. I just want to face my past and move on and work on my relationship with Joe and the kids.

MC: Let's imagine that your family is here right now, and we'll do a role-play. Assume that your father Peter, your mother Edith, your sisters Ann and Bianca, and your brother Steven are all here today. Close your eyes and imagine that scene. (pause) I'll ask you questions while you're thinking about possible answers from them. Let's start. (clear voice) Welcome everyone. Thank you for coming. What did Mary tell you about why you're here tonight?

(Everyone looks at Dad—He'll nod in approval for them to speak.)

Mom says, "Mary has problems, and we're here to help her."

Ann says, "Yeah, she's been acting a little strange lately, and we want to help get her straightened out."

Everyone continues looking at Dad. (pause)

Enactment

MC:	Mary, is there anything you want to change about this scene?
Mary:	Not really.
MC:	How about you, Joe…. Do you want to change anything?
Joe:	Nothing.
MC:	Mary, what would you like to tell them?
Mary:	Well, I want them to know that I came to see you because I've been having problems lately. I feel panicky, especially at night. I don't sleep well, and I worry all the time. My whole life has been structured and disciplined, and all I've ever done is to take care of my husband, my children, and my home. I think there should be more to life than this. I want to go to school because I want to have something for myself, but now I worry that it might mean I'm selfish. I want to have a career as a teacher or social worker, but I worry that I may not be successful. But I have to do something. My kids aren't listening to me. Ami is growing up and moving on. She thinks I'm too strict. Kevin thinks I'm not happy. Joe thinks I worry too much.
MC:	Mary, close your eyes. Now tell your father why you're seeing me.

Exploration

Mary:	Tell my father?
MC:	Yes. Imagine you're talking to your parents.
Mary:	I came to therapy because I felt sick all the time, and I couldn't find a reason for it. And Dad—I think I married Joe to get away from you, but Joe is just like you! You never supported me. You never approved of me, and you never thought I was worthy of anything. All my life I tried to do things to please you, and all I got in return was constant disapproval. (pause)
Mary:	And Mom, you never did anything to show me how you felt either. You always did exactly what Dad told you to do. We all only did what Dad told us to do. So we weren't allowed to have any choices until we left home. And then you were still in my head anyway—disapproving of whatever I did. (pause)

Mary: Dad, you're so controlling. Can't you see what you've done to all of us?

MC: Mary, keep your eyes closed. Take a deep breath and relax. Joe, how do you feel about what you've just heard?

Joe: I don't know. Mary is just not happy. I guess I always had high expectations for her, too.

MC: Mary, from what I heard—you feel that your dad wasn't able to communicate his true feelings, and that came across as disapproving and controlling. Has this affected you and Joe in your relationships as adults?

Resolving Past Issues

Mary: I don't know.

Joe: I can see that it has.

MC: Now, open your eyes and look at each other and tell me how the past has affected each of you and what you bring to this current relationship.

Issue #4: Family-of-Origin Issues

Mary explores her weight issue with the counselor, but she does not want to discuss this issue any further in her individual session because she believes it is a family issue rather than a personal issue. She is unhappy about the way Joe reacted to her weight problem and wants to address the issue in a couples counseling session.

MC: Mary, you stated during our last session that it was hard to tell your husband what you really want and feel because you're afraid. Why is that?

Using Past Feelings and Experience to Gain Insight

Mary: Did I say that? I don't know. I may be afraid he won't like it and leave me.

MC: Has there been an experience that led you to believe that he will leave you?

Mary: No… Well,… Joe… Joe thinks our marriage is okay. He sees nothing wrong with it. You know… he didn't want us to come in today because he thinks I'm being silly. I don't know how to say this, but all I know is that I don't want my marriage to be like my parents', and it seems to be headed that way. (about to cry) I feel like I'm doing so much to hold it together, and it all seems to be falling apart anyway. Sometimes I'm afraid to change the way I've been doing things for fear we'll break up. I'm sorry—I seem to babble every time I come in.

MC: Don't worry. That's why you're here. You can say whatever you feel…. Joe, what do you think about what Mary has said?

Joe: Look…. The only reason I came is because Mary has been making herself sick. I took her to the doctor the other day, and the doctor said there's no medical explanation for her problems. He said it was probably related to stress. I only came so you can tell her that.

MC: Joe, do you believe that Mary has been making herself sick on purpose? Why do you think she would do that?

Seeking the Unconscious

Joe: Mary has been gaining a lot of weight, and she's upset about it.

MC: Did Mary or the doctor say it was a weight issue?

Joe: No. Mary said it was our marriage. But I don't think there's anything wrong with our marriage.

MC: Joe, have you ever considered that the problems your wife is having can lead to the medical problems she's now facing? You mentioned that the doctor said he couldn't find any medical reasons for her problems. Can you possibly see a relationship between your wife's medical problems and her anxiety?

Joe: I don't really understand what the problem is. I know she's been a little down, but how is that my fault?

MC: Joe, it's not your fault, and this isn't meant to be a blaming session. The intent here is for each of you to understand what the other is feeling. Keep in mind that all families have problems. Don't you agree?

Universalization

Mary: Joe never seems to give me credit for knowing anything at all. He doesn't even trust me to know when something is wrong with my own body or mind. I have had a weight problem for a very long time, and I can't seem to do much about it. I know I've gained a lot more weight lately, but that's not why I'm here, Joe.

Joe: Look, I think she's really overreacting. What does she want me to say? I mean, I go out and work all day and she doesn't give me any credit for that. She thinks that when I get home, I should just spend time with her, but I don't have time for that. I wasn't raised that way. By me marrying her, that should tell her something. My father never told my mother all that mushy stuff.

MC: Joe, why did you marry Mary?

Joe: Because I care for her.

MC: Do you care for her or love her?

Joe: Yes.

MC: Would you look at Mary and tell her?

Joe: (looks at Mary) I care for her and love her.

MC: Joe, it's good that you praise your wife for a job well done and express how you feel.

Joe: It's hard for me to do it. I just wasn't raised like that. It's not that I don't appreciate what she's done for me or the family. I just don't understand why she needs me to tell her these things all of the time.

MC: I understand how you feel, Joe. Now, how about telling me a little about your childhood?

Investigating the Family of Origin

Psychoanalytic Techniques

Analysis of Anxiety Root: Finding the root cause of anxiety from analyzing the client's past experiences.

Confrontation: Identifying the client's resistance and/or action that can be modified.

Dream Analysis: Interpreting the meaning of the dream based on the tone, content, process, and components in the dream.

Enactment: Playing the role of each family member by re-creating a scene from the past.

Exploration: Probing to obtain further responses.

Free Association: Encouraging the client to talk about the first thought that comes to mind.

Interpretation: Providing meaning or symbolism to the thoughts or actions that are described.

Intrapsychic Conflict Analysis: Opening up the conversation to address issues that have been creating conflict within the mind.

Projection: Pointing out the client's use of self-deception that attributes one's own unacceptable desires to another person.

Reexperiencing: Creating an atmosphere to allow the client to go back to past experiences.

Resolving Past Issues: Linking the past issue to the present relationship issue.

Seeking the Unconscious: Finding out more about what is hidden in the mind.

Transference: Relating to a person or event by projecting past feelings onto someone who is present at the moment.

Universalization: Describing the client's feelings or experiences as being the same general reactions that most people also have in like situations.

Using Past Feelings: Reflecting on the client's feelings that are associated with the past or a past event in order to bring out unconscious thoughts.

Multicultural Practice Applications

The examples demonstrate the use of both classical and contemporary techniques based upon psychoanalytic theory. During the individual session, the counselor acts as an expert and utilizes interpretation and dream analysis as the preferred techniques. In the couples session, the role of the counselor changes from an expert to a supportive function while remaining analytical. In the couples session, the psychoanalytic therapist maintains a neutral position and provides minimal interpretations to support the client. The goals of both sessions are to strengthen the client's ego, focus on self-awareness, and recognize that current feelings might be influenced by the way a person handled his or her problems in the past. Free association is a central technique in the psychoanalytic approach. It encourages the client to express his or her views toward something that may have a deeper meaning than what appears on the surface.

One of the key characteristics of therapy is the support the practitioner provides. A psychoanalytic therapist may appear authoritative because of the extensive use of interpretations during the therapeutic process. Therefore, therapists should provide reassurance, empathy, and support in lieu of the interpretations in certain circumstances. The following example is an individual session that demonstrates these qualities.

Mary: I find it difficult to believe that my own children now want to leave me. How can they do this to me after I've tried to model to them that children should always like to live with their parents?

MC: Tell me what this type of role model behavior teaches your children.

Mary: They don't really recognize that I'm a role model for them. They really think that I'm overprotective and live a disciplined and structured life. But, you know, I'm afraid of the day when I won't be able to be with my family.

MC: You'll have your family no matter where they are.

Mary: Well, I guess you're right.

Another example that can help practitioners demonstrate the use of neutrality can be found in the dream analysis exercise. As seen below, multicultural counselors would use a "blank screen" approach when analyzing dreams.

Mary: It started about a month ago. Well, I don't remember if I've dreamt every night since then, but I think I might have had the same dream six times already. (pause) It always starts out with someone chasing me. I'm running after Ami, but I never can catch up with her. I finally catch her clothes, but she disappears. I always wake up seeing her again inside some dark place. Can you tell me what this means?

MC: You probably have put some thought into the meaning of this dream. Tell me what thoughts came to your mind when you were telling me about this dream.

Mary:	I think it just makes me feel nervous.
MC:	Nervous about what?
Mary:	About Ami leaving me.
MC:	At what age did you leave your parents?
Mary:	When I was 18.
MC:	Tell me what happened at that time.

Transference issues can take place in cross-cultural counseling because clients recognize the differences between the counselor and themselves and often project a sense of disbelief or mistrust. As expressed in the previous individual session, the use of transference can be modified to a more culturally sensitive therapeutic approach:

Mary:	I guess I felt so powerless mainly because I sense that you're in control of me.
MC:	How does your culture define "control" within the family?
Mary:	I don't know. I guess every family has a dominant figure.
MC:	Who is the first important authority figure in your life?
Mary:	Definitely my father.
MC:	Tell me about how you viewed your father as an authority figure when you were little.

Sometimes it is important to uncover the root cause of a problem before moving on to its solution. When applying this theory in supervision, a supervisor again would consider the three major elements in the psychodynamic approach: neutrality, reassurance, and choice/resource analysis. In the following case, the practitioner is Betty and her supervisor is MC.

MC:	Betty, what did you see in Mary's situation?
Betty:	I don't see her being strong enough to tell her father about her current relationship issues.
MC:	What makes her not strong enough?
Betty:	Her past.
MC:	What is your interpretation of her past?
Betty:	I don't know. I guess her way of dealing with relationship.
MC:	Absolutely. It's true that relationship can be affected by past experiences. What else did you do with Mary and her family?
Betty:	I helped Mary look into her choice and made sure that she had a support person in her family, someone she can always talk with.
MC:	The use of resources is a must. Focus on how she utilized her resources in the past and how she will find resources from now on. You've done a great job in analyzing her situation.

Psychoanalytic theory can be used in cross-cultural situations only if it provides therapeutic insight for both the practitioner and the client in a culturally sensitive manner. Critics of psychoanalytic theory say it is subjective, narrow, and pathological in focus and does not address evaluative outcomes (Cohan, Chavira, & Stein, 2006; Ellis, 2006). Despite its emphasis on interpretation, the term "analytic" is no longer considered a culturally relevant term for therapeutic use because it may imply subjectivity. Contemporary psychoanalytic theory is dynamic and emphasizes the importance of respect for human diversity. The name "psychodynamic" reflects its transformation into a welcoming psychoanalytic therapeutic base.

Healing in a dynamic sense illustrates the use of a psychodynamic approach in building client–practitioner relationships. Its application is strengthened by attention to the mind–body connections, the analysis of brain–mind functions, and the use of action-oriented dialogues (Corey, 2005; Lothane, 2006). As Lothane (2006) put it, the psychoanalytic nature of the psychodynamic approach "stands as an autonomous science of the mind" (p. 298). From a psychological viewpoint, traditional healing, spiritual healing, and natural healing all stem from the strong cultural roots of a person's belief system. The mind–body analysis begins within a person's culture, including all learned behaviors from the person's environment.

If healing is considered key to the therapeutic process, all psychoanalytic concepts can be culturally applicable. To illustrate this point, three psychoanalytic theorists with distinct theoretical orientations addressed culture in practice:

1. Sigmund Freud believed that an internal drive dictates how we learn our behaviors and that our cultural heritage controls the release of this drive.
2. Nathan Ackerman examined the constant interaction between the person and the environment to gain insight into what experiences have shaped the roles the individual plays.
3. James Framo believed that intrapsychic conflict stems from a person's family-of-origin in that the interactions among family members shape the person's behavior.

In a dynamic view, "parental introjects" must be analyzed, as they are "the most powerful obstacle to change" (Goldenberg & Goldenberg, 2004, p.145).

Combining all of these concepts, a culturally relevant question for therapeutic use emerges: "What is the body–mind–environment connection to this problem?" If our body provides the self-concept, and it may be influenced by how a person learned to believe through his or her cultural background and socioeconomic-political environment, the theoretical applications should be directed to body image as it relates to the environment. All three aspects of these orientations are essential to examine issues that have occurred in the environment.

Variations from the Standardized Case

In each chapter we present a variation of the "standardized case" to check the applicability of therapeutic techniques to various groups of people. Some of the demographic and assessment information includes ethnicity, socioeconomic class, education, employment, family structure, and types of family problems. To examine techniques from a cross-cultural perspective, experts in the field provide insight regarding how to work with this family with culturally sensitive and relevant skills. Students and practitioners alike can use this input as a reference to design culturally relevant skills or techniques, or to discuss whether the suggestions according to the given theory are culturally applicable to this particular family. Role plays and skits can be developed to guide further discussions concerning the particular intervention approach described in each chapter.

Variation from the Standardized Case: An African American Family

Female-headed African American homes have increased steadily during the last 40 years (U.S. Census Bureau, 2005a), and African American families are disproportionately affected by poverty (U.S. Census Bureau, 2005b) and gang violence in their communities (Miller, 2001), leading to additional difficulties with child rearing. The following case study is based on these demographic trends, but this information cannot, and should not, be generalized to all African American families. Because poverty affects large numbers of Anglos, Hispanics, Asians, and other ethnicities, it might be helpful to also discuss the case in reference to other ethnic groups. How would this family be approached differently if the members were of a different ethnicity, or if the children were being raised by a single father?

* * *

Joe and Mary are African Americans. Mary, a nurse at a large county hospital near her home, often works double shifts to make extra money. Along with working long hours, she is raising a family that includes her two children, Ami, 16, and Kevin, 8. Her husband, Joe, has a fleeting presence in the family. His work as a construction day laborer forces him to change job sites frequently, and he often spends the night outside of the home to reduce his commute to work.

The relationship between Joe and Mary is inconsistent and often contentious. Because of Joe's unpredictable schedule and Mary's constant overtime, Ami and Kevin have been raised mainly by their grandmother, Granny Mae, who lives next door. Mary devotes any free time she has to her community and church. The entire family is dedicated to church, and Mary is considered one of the church leaders.

Ami, in the 10th grade, has been a relatively good student until recently, when her grades suddenly began to drop. Ami has always excelled in sports and is currently on the track team—one of the fastest girls on the team, and the anchor on her relay team. A few days ago, Granny Mae received a phone call from Ami's coach, who said Ami was on the verge of being kicked off the team because of missed practices and her inability to follow team rules. Lately, Ami has come home with bruises on her arms, and Granny Mae suspects that her boyfriend is abusive.

Kevin, in the 3rd grade, has recently been skipping church, which is unusual because he used to take pride in his church activities. Kevin also used to attend Sunday school regularly. Now, however, the church pastor reports that Kevin has not been showing up. Kevin's behavior has been deteriorating, and now he becomes so angry with his mother at times that he yells and storms out of the house and is nowhere to be found for hours. Granny Mae has some suspicions about the crowd that Kevin associates with because these boys roam the neighborhood and wear all-red clothing.

Experts Say...

Dr. Cheryl Waites, North Carolina State University, suggested that the cross-cultural practitioner should consider several cultural, ethnic, and societal factors during the helping process with this family. First, practitioners should assess the value of extended family members to build on family strengths and identify the role of the grandmother before designing an intervention. The practitioner should also thoroughly evaluate the role of the father in the family and how this role affects the mother's authority. A sensitive therapist will have some understanding of the value of extended family members, parents, siblings, and peers within African American culture, address the cultural heritage of this family, and assess the family's connection with other support systems in the community.

In addition, the therapist should gather more specific information about the family to be able to properly plan an intervention. For example: How frequently is Joe home? How has Granny Mae been raising the children? What is Joe and Mary's relationship with Granny Mae?

In addition, a culturally sensitive practitioner can take the following actions during the steps of the helping process:

- *Contact:* Clarify the role of the practitioner in the helping process. Always be willing to acknowledge cultural differences and similarities.
- *Problem identification:* Seek the cultural meaning of the problem, that is, what it means within the family's cultural context.
- *Assessment:* Identify extended family members who are physically available and emotionally supportive to assist with the family's needs. Identify supportive cultural community resources (e.g., church groups, civic organizations, and community programs).
- *Case planning:* Assess the family's financial situation for purposes of treatment planning or resource allocation. Assess the family's willingness and motivation to accept help and work on the problems.
- *Intervention:* Develop rapport with the children and grandmother during home visits, provide individual therapy for the mother, provide conjoint therapy with the couple, and focus on relationship building. Consider other forms of therapeutic intervention (e.g., narrative approach, pastoral counseling).
- *Evaluation:* Identify strengths of the extended family support system; develop a tool for the couple to use for evaluation purposes in their relationship with each other and with their children with a strong focus on family building.

■ *Termination:* Find a song that is representative of this culture to express feelings, draw a picture of the family with each of the members' contributions, or use a poem from an ethnic writer to capture what has been learning during this therapeutic process.

When working with this family, the practitioner must address his or her own attitudes, values, skills, and knowledge. For this family, the practitioner should not form judgments about the family's financial situation; instead, he or she should praise the role and contributions of the extended family. The therapist should attempt to gain a more thorough understanding of the family's cultural context by attending cultural events, reading relevant literature, and using key respondents to gather information. The practitioner can provide information about child development and parenting skills but should also attempt to gain a deeper understanding about how racism and oppression impact African American families.

Specific intervention approaches with this family may include the following:

■ Use the *behavioral* theoretical approach to help the children understand that they can make changes individually to build family strengths.
■ Adopt the *structural* theoretical approach to identify power differentiation and its impact within the current family structure.
■ Use *family-of-origin* analyses to help the mother recognize the impact of her past experiences—such as job searching and personal finance management—on her current behaviors.
■ *Observe important family events* and help each member identify the importance of their ethnic heritage.
■ Use the *narrative approach* by developing an understanding of clients' life stories and ways of reauthoring them through collaborative efforts between the practitioner and the clients. This approach emphasizes the client's history, the broader context that is affecting his or her life, and the ethics or politics involved in therapy or treatment (Carr, 1998; White, 1993).
■ Help the family identify other culturally specific resources for support.

From a micro-practice perspective intended to enhance intervention efficacy, the practitioner will have to gather additional information from this family to be able to identify its unique strengths and barriers. First the practitioner should assess each person's level of physical and mental health functioning. Then the practitioner might construct a family tree or genogram (possibly with photos of each individual) and include information about extended family members in terms of education, occupation, socioeconomic status (SES), any history of child or spousal abuse, and any history of alcohol or drug abuse.

The practitioner can assess family support by having each member detail his or her support system, including how faith and the church community enhance the family's support and functioning. The practitioner must build trust with each member and provide support by identifying family strengths and the members' contributions.

The practitioner should work to develop goals for each person in the family and identify family activities in which all members can participate.

In addition to this micro-practice perspective, the practitioner seeks to strengthen the family's image by providing general information about community resources. Using these resources, the family could access additional help available locally to help address the poverty issues. From a psychodynamic point of view, examining family history can help the practitioner understand the cause of poverty within the family for two or more generations.

After analyzing the situation, the practitioner can help clients advocate for their right to obtain support from the government. Advocacy strategies include presenting clients' stories to identify gaps in social services. All work should involve an analysis of the past as a base to explain present situations.

Best Practice Evaluation

From this chapter forward, best practice evaluation, comprising 11 stages (see chapter 1), will be described with suggested measurement for use in practice. The first of 11 stages in the evaluation process includes a self-assessment tool, designed for the practitioner to assess his or her own biases and prejudicial attitudes prior to working with a diverse population. According to Phinney (1996), helping professionals are to focus on three components of cross-cultural understanding when discussing American ethnic groups:

1. Connotation and attitudes developed toward minority status
2. Past experiences associated with working with diverse populations
3. Strengths of ethnic identity

Beyond gaining an assessment of one's attitude, skills, and knowledge, a self-assessment process adds a fourth component: awareness and learning of cross-cultural differences.

Evaluation Stage 1: Assess the Practitioner's Own Self, Skills, and Commitment to Multicultural Sensitivity

Suggested Evaluation Tool: Multicultural Counseling Knowledge and Awareness Scale (MCKAS) (Ponterotto, Gretchen, Utsey, Reiger, & Austin, 2002)

Description: The MCKAS, a revision of the Multicultural Counseling Awareness Scale, consists of 20 items involving knowledge and 12 items centering on awareness. The MCKAS has been tested and demonstrates high reliability (alpha = .85 on each subscale of knowledge and awareness), construct validity (tested with confirmatory factor analysis with coefficient alpha = .91 and .80, respectively, on the two aggregate factors), and criterion validity ($r = .74$ with the Counseling Relationship Subscale in the Multicultural Counseling Inventory [Sodowsky, 1996]).

How to Use the Tool: MCKAS is copyrighted by Joseph G. Ponterotto, PhD, at the Division of Psychological and Educational Services, Fordham University at Lincoln Center, 113 West 60th Street, New York, New York 10023-7478 (212-636-6480); Jponterott@aol.com. The MCKAS contains a 7-point Likert-type scale, with which the user will rate his or her awareness or knowledge level concerning work with diverse populations. This is a self-evaluation tool, and the user must respond honestly to each statement and complete this tool every 6 months. After each completion of the self-assessment, the user must reverse the score on items 1, 4, 7, 10, 11, 18, 20, 24, 25 and 30 (so the score will change in this fashion: 1 = 7; 2 = 6; 3 = 5; 4 = 4; 5 = 3; 6 = 2; and 7 = 1). This reverse scoring procedure is necessary for scoring purposes only, and the new score does not alter the face value of the original rating.

After replacing the original scores with reverse scores, add all scores and divide the sum by 32. If any scores are missing, subtract the number of missing scores from 32 and divide the sum by that number.

Based on Ponterotto and colleagues' (2002) study of 196 college students, the mean for the Knowledge Subscale is 4.96 (standard deviation [sd] = .80) and the mean for the Awareness Subscale is 5.06 (SD = 1.14). Multicultural practitioners are expected to score above these college students' means. If the score is lower, examine the answer to each of the items and become aware of your own biases and lack of knowledge in the areas that received a low score. For example, if the original score on item #1 is 7 and this item has a reverse scoring procedure, the MKAS score for this item about eye contact becomes a low score of 1.

The practitioner should be aware that many cultures, such as Asian and Latino cultures, treat direct eye contacts (staring) as disrespectful to authority, teachers, or parents. Cultural awareness is a first step in building relationship with clients. Examining one's limited view of various cultures is the foundation of cultural awareness.

Multicultural Practice Exercises

1. Learning

   ### Transference:

   ■ "Think of a person in your family. Does this person remind you of a significant individual in your life today? What characteristics do these two individuals have in common?"

   ### Five Years of Life:

   ■ "Use five index cards to write or draw key influences during each year of your first five years of development. Ask relatives questions if you are unaware of some of these influences."

Multicultural Counseling Knowledge and Awareness Scale (MCKAS)

Using the following scale, rate the truth of each item as it applies to you.

1 = Not at all true   4 = Somewhat true   7 = Totally true

1   2   3   4   5   6   7

1. ____ I believe all clients should maintain direct eye contact during counseling. (A)

2. ____ I check up on my minority/cultural counseling skills by monitoring my functioning—via consultation, supervision, and continuing education. (K)

3. ____ I am aware some research indicates that minority clients receive "less preferred" forms of counseling treatment than majority clients. (K)

4. ____ I think that clients who do not discuss intimate aspects of their lives are being resistant and defensive. (A)

5. ____ I am aware of certain counseling skills, techniques, or approaches that are more likely to transcend culture and be effective with any clients. (K)

6. ____ I am familiar with the "culturally deficient" and "culturally deprived" depictions of minority mental health and understand how these labels serve to foster and perpetuate discrimination. (K)

7. ____ I feel all the recent attention directed toward multicultural issues in counseling is overdone and not really warranted. (A)

8. ____ I am aware of individual differences that exist among members within a particular ethnic group based on values, beliefs and level of acculturation. (K)

9. ____ I am aware some research indicates that minority clients are more likely to be diagnosed with mental illness than are majority clients. (K)

10. ____ I think that clients should perceive the nuclear family as the ideal social unit. (A)

11. ____ I think that being highly competitive and achievement oriented are traits that all clients should work towards. (A)

12. ____ I am aware of differential interpretations of nonverbal communication (e.g., personal space, eye contact, handshakes) within various racial/ethnic groups. (K)

13. ____ I understand the impact and operations of oppression and the racist concepts that have permeated the mental health professions. (K)

14. ____ I realize that counselor–client incongruities in problem conceptualization and counseling goals may reduce counselor credibility. (K)

15. ____ I am aware that some racial/ethnic minorities see the profession of psychology [or other helping professions such as social work] functioning to maintain and promote the status and power of the White Establishment. (K)

16. ____ I am knowledgeable of acculturation models for various ethnic minority groups. (K)

(continued)

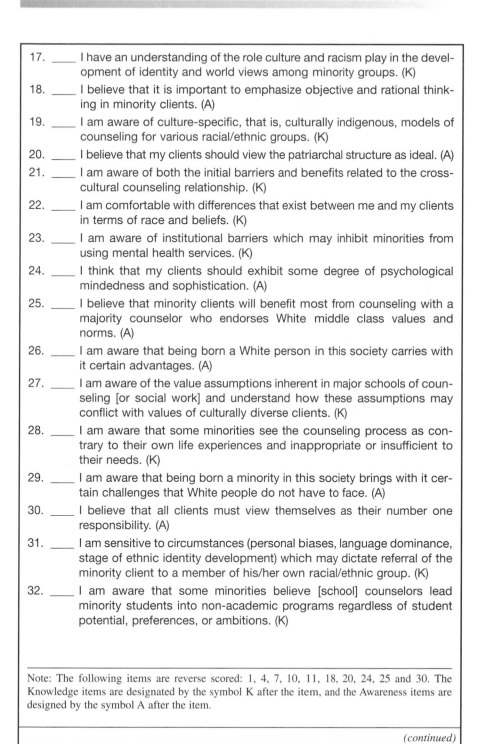

17. ____ I have an understanding of the role culture and racism play in the development of identity and world views among minority groups. (K)

18. ____ I believe that it is important to emphasize objective and rational thinking in minority clients. (A)

19. ____ I am aware of culture-specific, that is, culturally indigenous, models of counseling for various racial/ethnic groups. (K)

20. ____ I believe that my clients should view the patriarchal structure as ideal. (A)

21. ____ I am aware of both the initial barriers and benefits related to the cross-cultural counseling relationship. (K)

22. ____ I am comfortable with differences that exist between me and my clients in terms of race and beliefs. (K)

23. ____ I am aware of institutional barriers which may inhibit minorities from using mental health services. (K)

24. ____ I think that my clients should exhibit some degree of psychological mindedness and sophistication. (A)

25. ____ I believe that minority clients will benefit most from counseling with a majority counselor who endorses White middle class values and norms. (A)

26. ____ I am aware that being born a White person in this society carries with it certain advantages. (A)

27. ____ I am aware of the value assumptions inherent in major schools of counseling [or social work] and understand how these assumptions may conflict with values of culturally diverse clients. (K)

28. ____ I am aware that some minorities see the counseling process as contrary to their own life experiences and inappropriate or insufficient to their needs. (K)

29. ____ I am aware that being born a minority in this society brings with it certain challenges that White people do not have to face. (A)

30. ____ I believe that all clients must view themselves as their number one responsibility. (A)

31. ____ I am sensitive to circumstances (personal biases, language dominance, stage of ethnic identity development) which may dictate referral of the minority client to a member of his/her own racial/ethnic group. (K)

32. ____ I am aware that some minorities believe [school] counselors lead minority students into non-academic programs regardless of student potential, preferences, or ambitions. (K)

Note: The following items are reverse scored: 1, 4, 7, 10, 11, 18, 20, 24, 25 and 30. The Knowledge items are designated by the symbol K after the item, and the Awareness items are designed by the symbol A after the item.

(continued)

MCKAS Scoring Form

<u>Column K</u>
Truth Rating

<u>Column A</u>
Reverse Scoring

  1. (____) →   ____
  2. ____
  3. ____
  4. (____) →   ____
  5. ____
  6. ____
  7. (____) →   ____
  8. ____
  9. ____
10. (____) →   ____
11. (____) →   ____
12. ____
13. ____
14. ____
15. ____
16. ____
17. ____
18. (____) →   ____
19. ____
20. (____) →   ____
21. ____
22. ____
23. ____
24. (____) →   ____
25. (____) →   ____
26. ____
27. ____
28. ____
29. ____
30. (____) →   ____
31. ____
32. ____

(continued)

Scoring Methods:
(1) Add up the scores under Column K excluding those scores in parentheses:

_____
=> This is your Knowledge Score (K).

(2) Add up the scores under Column A (i.e., Reverse Scoring Items only): ____
=> This is your Awareness Score (A).

(3) Compute the Knowledge Subscale Score:
(K) ÷ number of items responded under Column K (out of a total of 22 items)
= ____ ÷ ____ = _____
=> This is your Knowledge Average Score (K").
=> If over 4.96, you are considered more culturally knowledgeable than an average student in counseling.

(4) Compute the Awareness Subscale Score:
(A) ÷ number of items responded under Column A (out of a total of 10 items)
= _____
=> This is your Assessment Average Score (A").
=> If over 5.06, you are considered more aware of multiculturalism than an average student in counseling.

(5) Compute the Overall Score: (K" + A") ÷ 2 = (___ + ___) ÷ 2 = ___
=> If over 5.00, you are considered more multicultural-competent than an average student in counseling.

Source: J.G. Ponterotto, D. Gretchen, S. Utsey, B. Reiger, & R. Austin (2002). A revision of the multicultural counseling awareness scale. *Journal of Multicultural Counseling and Development, 30*(3), 153–180. Reprinted with permission of Dr. Joseph G. Ponterotto. Please contact Dr. Ponterotto for permission to use the scale.

2. Healing

Psychological Need:

- "This is a safe place for expressing feelings and emotions. It is free of prejudice, discrimination, and racism."
- "When you think of a significant person of your ethnicity, what stands out the most about that person to help you relax or appreciate your culture?"

Counter-Transference Exercise:

- "Think of a person that you consider to be difficult in nature. This difficulty could refer to your relationship with this person or to the person's difficult personality. Then imagine that you were this person and take on this person's characteristics as fully as you can. How does this experience affect you? What aspect of your cultural background could help you deal with this difficulty?"

Additional Exercise:
The Defense Mechanisms (DM) Matching Game

Because psychodynamic theory emphasizes the importance of past experiences, some of the concepts of defense mechanisms can be used in role-play learning. Match each defense mechanism to its definition along with the two examples provided by Mary and Joe that best describe its use. In addition, write down your response to each of the dialogue examples and note which ones are culturally sensitive.

A. Compensation
B. Denial
C. Displacement
D. Introjection
E. Projection
F. Rationalization
G. Reaction Formation
H. Regression
I. Repression
J. Sublimation

   1. A defense through which painful thoughts and feelings are excluded from awareness.

     Mary: Sorry that I forgot to bring a picture of my father.
     Joe: I really couldn't remember what Mother said before she left us.

   2. A way of distorting what the individual thinks, feels, or perceives in a traumatic situation.

     Mary: No, my father was *not* an alcoholic.
     Joe: No, no—I don't think our marriage is in trouble.

   3. An expression that covertly demonstrates the opposite impulse.

     Mary: Yes, I think I like Peter, but I've tried to avoid him. As a matter of fact, I even told people that I don't like him.
     Joe: I like what you said … but …

   4. A self-deception that places one's own unacceptable desire onto another person.

     Mary: Ami is angry at Joe for not coming home for dinner.
     Joe: Mary doesn't have time to talk with me.

   5. A way to discharge impulses by shifting from a threatening object to a "safer target."

     Mary: When Ami was three, she always kicked her favorite bear when I sent her to bed.
     Joe: Nonverbal? Hmm … Mary throws her clothes on our bed when she's mad.

6. The use of good reasoning to explain a damaged ego.

    Mary: You think I'm controlling. But, you see, I have to make sure that
             Ami stays out of trouble. Otherwise she would have come home
             with a baby by now!

    Joe: See, I have to work to support this family. You can't blame me for
             being tired and giving you mean looks.

7. Redirecting aggressive or negative energy into creative and positive behaviors.

    Mary: Peter and I were in the play therapy class together last semester.
             During the entire semester, I was afraid to talk to him. You know
             what, though? I presented a project regarding fear and anxiety in
             play therapy session and got an "A" in this class.

    Joe: Mary, you said you were frustrated last weekend at your family
             reunion picnic. But you helped me plan such a wonderful activity
             for my family yesterday.

8. A way to demonstrate a behavior that has been outgrown.

    Mary: Yes, I noticed that too. I've been biting my fingernails while talk-
             ing to you.

    Joe: Yes, sometimes I scream like a little child.

9. Taking in and "swallowing" the values and standards of others.

    Mary: I agree with my mother that married women shouldn't have male
             friends.

    Joe: Of course, parents should have the right to control their children's
             behaviors.

10. Developing certain positive traits to make up for limitations.

    Mary: I did quite well in my play therapy class because of my artwork.
             Nobody in the class was aware that I don't have very good people
             skills.

    Joe: You know that I cannot spend much time with you, but I want to
             see what I can do to make you happy.

Answers to the Defense Mechanisms (DM) Matching Game:

1 = I; 2 = B; 3 = G; 4 = E; 5 = C; 6 = F; 7 = J; 8 = H; 9 = D; 10 = A

Topics for Discussion

1. List three elements in the psychodynamic approach that are appropriate for
   multicultural practices.
2. When gender is a concern, such as in domestic violence situations in which
   one gender is dominating the other, what practices should a psychodynamic
   counselor implement and avoid?

3. Although emphasis is placed on the importance of neutrality, psychodynamic theory does involve interpretation. What role do you think a supervisor should play in applying this theory in supervision?

4. Many theorists criticize the use of psychoanalytic theory when working with people of color. Suggest two reasons that support their criticisms and two reasons that dispute them.

5. How does a practitioner use psychodynamic theory as an advocacy tool to help clients who live in poverty?

CHAPTER FIVE

Adlerian Theory

This chapter outlines the theoretical concepts developed by Alfred Adler and provides a description of how the Adlerian approach can be applicable to multicultural practice. Adler highlights the importance of building family relationships to enhance well-being. By using stages of cultural identity development as the focal point to analyze a person's upbringing, individual perceptions about family relationships can be evaluated.

This chapter highlights sibling and family relationship issues from the standardized case of Joe and Mary's family to illustrate how Adlerian techniques can be used to resolve family problems such as personal connections, sibling relations, family relationships, and the parallel relationships with siblings and with parents. These techniques include *let's pretend, paradoxical action, happy button, constructive action,* and *family constellation analysis*. The case then is altered to illustrate the family struggle of an Asian American family.

Experts' input highlights the stage process from contact through how to assess the situation and plan a culturally sensitive intervention with the family members. The suggested practice tools are *lifestyle assessment* and *three wishes,* and the suggested practice evaluation tool is the Family Involvement Scale. Evaluation explores how to assess relationship building.

An Adlerian Purpose

The early practice of Alfred Adler was grounded in psychoanalytical theory. He later moved away from what he viewed as its limited view of human nature and expanded on the broad-based sociopsychological view of human behavior (Adler, 1982). According to Adler (1926), individual psychology is "a method of limitless encouragement" (para. 3). As he began to develop his own theories, Adler emphasized the analysis of social determinants that motivate an individual to act and behave in ways that reflect his or her family background and relationship pattern. He believed that

Adlerian Theory in Brief

Uniqueness in Multicultural Practice:

- It assumes each individual is unique, that personality development is shaped by the individual's own experiences.
- Application of techniques is based on the client's cultural and family background, rather than on what the practitioner knows best.

Major Figure(s):

- Alfred Adler (1870–1937): Individual Psychology

Assumptions:

- Human nature always has a positive side.
- Social influence is significant (much more so than biological).
- People can create a distinctive lifestyle at an early stage in life.
- Consciousness is the center of personality.

Therapeutic Process:

- The Family Constellation and Lifestyle Assessment is a tool assessing how early life can determine a person's current behavior.

Goals:

- To challenge clients' mistaken notions and faulty assumptions and encourage them to develop a positive view of life.
- To provide encouragement to help clients develop socially useful goals.

Multicultural Practice Techniques:

- A specific set of procedures is unnecessary.
- Techniques are selected to meet client needs, such as paradoxical action, encouragement, homework, and clients' interpretation of the family constellation.
- Encouragement is a major step in therapy.

all behaviors are purposeful and goal-oriented, and that they originate from a positive intent. This intent is expressed by individuals in their striving to achieve security while overcoming feelings of inferiority. When applying this theory to multicultural family counseling, practitioners must assess the cultural differences among the individuals in the family system, since each family member experiences his or her cultural background differently.

Adlerian theory is applicable to multicultural counseling because it inherently respects the experience of the individual: It assumes personal control of individual fate because of the basic human capacity to interpret and influence outside forces (Corey, 2005). Adler believed that working with an individual from a different culture means building the relationship of the individual to the outside world. Based on personal cultural references, most individuals have a subjective frame of reference that is phenomenologically oriented. With this orientation, we perceive our reality based on cooperative power, perceptions, beliefs, and influential conclusions from others.

Adler's theory of individual psychology is unique because of its use of the person-in-environment theme as a main therapeutic focus. Each person is treated as a holistic self whose thoughts, feelings, and actions are connected in a self-selected way. With this theme, Adlerian theory provides a way for the clients to see differences within one culture or across cultures. In interracial families, for example, the focus is to analyze the similarities and differences of each person's background in order to gain self-awareness. However, the use of family backgrounds as a starting point for analysis may be limited to those who have access to their families' information.

On the Multicultural Stage: Cultural Identity Development

Adler asserts that a holistic analysis of an individual's behaviors and actions is an avenue for understanding and interpreting personality. According to Adler, culture, orientation to life, social interest, birth order, and sibling relationships play a vital role in shaping an individual's personality. In describing family or lifestyle, the individual starts revealing his or her cultural or diverse identity. This approach to assessment can be particularly useful when the client is a new immigrant whose value system is rooted in their family and culture of their homeland.

Adler purported that self-perception is the beginning step in gaining insight in the therapeutic process. The therapist conducts a comprehensive assessment of the client's functioning based on information provided by the client on his or her family-of-origin. This process will assist the client in obtaining therapeutic insight about critical influences in the family as related to its culture, beliefs and values, and strengths and resources, as well as its limitations and constraints.

The Case Approach

In this example, the Adlerian approach is applied to help the client, Mary, connect her personal issues to family issues. It highlights the importance of analyzing the impact of Mary's past relationship with her siblings on her current relationship with others, particularly with her husband and children. Selected issues are: personal connections to family issues, sibling relationships, family relationships, and then connecting sibling relationships with parental relationships.

Issue #1: Personal Connections to Family Issues

Mary's worries are related to her physical illness with no medical explanations. The practitioner attempts to understand how her physical pain, such as headaches, is related to her feelings.

Mary: I've been feeling depressed lately.

MC: Is there something in your life right now that makes you feel that way?

Mary: I really don't know.

MC: I want you to do an exercise with me. Tell me about something that makes you happy.

Mary: I'm thinking about my children. They need me and enjoy my cooking. That makes me happy.

MC: Now tell me about an unpleasant incident.

Mary: I drove my children to the mall last weekend. On the way, they were fighting over something stupid…. I don't even remember what. I was so mad that I stopped the car in the middle of the road! I felt like they were making me mad on purpose.

MC: Tell me how the children's behavior was affected by your stopping.

Mary: They were quiet then, but they decided not to go to the mall. I guess they were embarrassed to be seen with me because I was so upset.

MC: Okay…. (Draws a happy face and cuts it out). Now I want you to push this button and pretend that it can make you feel happy again. Tell yourself that what happened in the car wasn't your fault. We all have feelings.

Happy Button

Mary: I guess I just didn't know what to do with them.

MC: Next time, push this button when you feel upset by their behaviors. Try it now. Before you press it, think about the happy feeling first.

Issue #2: Sibling Relationships

In this case, Mary is often anxious over matters that are related to others, especially her children. In this session the practitioner tries to uncover her early experience with siblings.

MC: Mary, at the end of our last session, I asked you to complete your lifestyle assessment. Did you bring it with you?

Mary: Yes... well, I did my best.

MC: Okay, Mary, on this self-assessment, it looks like you didn't get along very well with your brother during childhood.

Early Recollection

Mary: Yes, I didn't feel comfortable with him because he always picked on me.

MC: Many people have feelings of rivalry or competition with their siblings. Have you since found a way to overcome these feelings?

Mary: Not really. We don't really talk to each other.

MC: How about trying "Act As If?" In this coming week, you act as if you were good friends with your brother. Pretend that he has a lot to offer you or that you have a lot to offer him. Call him up, find out some more about him, and tell him how much you've missed him.

Let's Pretend

Mary: What does this have to do with my kids' problem?

MC: Through this exercise with your own brother, you may gain some insight about how your kids interact with each other.

(Later in the session)

MC: Mary, I've noticed that you have difficulty making direct eye contact with me. Tell me more about it.

Mary: I always feel that way when I look at another person. I guess our culture doesn't want us women look into someone else's eyes when we talk.

MC: Well, then, let's talk without you looking at me for the rest of the session.

Paradoxical Action

Mary: Huh?

MC: Try it.

Mary: Okay ... Well, I've been having some difficulties with my children. They fight all the time for no reason. (Looks at the counselor)

MC: Ahhh, wait.... Remember—don't look at me.

Mary: (Clearly uncomfortable) It's hard.

MC: What's hard?

Mary: I mean, when I look for support, I want to look at you.

MC: What do you experience since I've asked you not to look?

Mary: I guess I realize it's not my choice. Even though it might have been my cultural preference, I'd rather have choices.

MC: So you'd rather have choices. What choices do think your children have when they fight?

Issue #3: Family Relationships

Mary is dealing with a family decision issue. She identifies her feelings toward others which actually projects her feelings toward her own self.

Mary: Joe didn't want to come in today.

MC: How does this "no-show" affect you?

Mary: It makes me feel like he's not concerned about me.

MC: Mary, think about this again and consider an alternative feeling.

Mary: How?

MC: If your feeling can't be replaced, how about your action?

Constructive Action

Mary: How?

MC: Think about what you can do without him here.

Mary: I guess I can talk about him without him disagreeing with me.

MC: What kind of disagreement?

Mary: He disagrees with me that I should get a job.

MC: What do the kids say?

Mary: They don't have an opinion.

MC: What do you say?

Mary: It's my life. I just feel too tired of taking care of others and forgetting about myself.

Issue #4: Sibling and Parental Relationships

A Family Constellation Interview was conducted with Joe. He is the second in a family of three children, the middle child with two siblings (Christine +7 in age and Peter -2).

MC: Joe, what insight did you gain from our last session about your relationship with Mary?

Joe: I guess I know that this is just a feeling, but sometimes I feel that Mary is just like my mother.

MC: Can you recall an early childhood incident with your mother?

Early Recollections

Joe: Well, let's see…. I remember when I was about five, I was playing out-side and I was almost hit by a car. My mother yelled at me and called me stupid.

MC: What are some of your other early recollections?

Joe: One time I remember I was playing with Peter, and I accidentally scratched him on his arm. Peter told Mom that I did it on purpose. She believed him, not me, and shut me in the house for the whole day.

MC: What kind of feelings did you have during these incidents?

Feelings Association

Joe: I often felt like I couldn't do anything right. I was punished no matter what I did. I felt lonely and never really felt understood or cared for.

MC: I bet that was difficult for you. How did your parents get along?

Parental Figures and Relationships

Joe: They never got along very well. She berated him and ran all over him, and he wouldn't ever stand up to her. He escaped into his work. They were never affectionate or close with each other.

MC: What was your siblings' view of your parents?

Siblings' View of Parents

Joe: Peter and Christine thought well of both my mother and my father. Peter respected Mom more, though. He had some trouble with Dad. I didn't have much use for either of my parents, and I didn't want much to do with them.

MC: How about your father's relationship with you and your siblings?

Parents' Relationships to Children

Joe: Well, my father really liked Peter and Christine and did a lot with Peter. He ignored me.

MC: How about your mother?

Joe: My mother seemed to like the other kids and have time for them, but not for me.

MC: (Silence)

Joe: I mean … she didn't have time for me.

MC: And you didn't like that.

Interpretation

Joe: No, but … (pause)

MC: (Slowly and softly) No, but …

Encouragement

Joe: I guess I think that she didn't really like me.

MC: That's a feeling. Did she ever tell you that?

Feelings Association

Joe: No, but I knew.

MC: How did you know?

Joe: I just knew it. She didn't like us, and we didn't like her ... except Christine. Christine might be most like her. They're both responsible and highly capable.

Adlerian Techniques

Constructive Action: A comment about what positive action the client might engage in rather than continuing to engage in a negative action.

Early Recollections: A systematic way to generate information and help the client realize how past events or relationships with family members can be connected to current situations or affect current relationships.

Encouragement: Using simple words to encourage the client to share more information related to experiences, feelings and perceptions.

Family Constellation: A set of questions to collect data about sibling relationships, parental relationships with each of the children in the family, and other childhood memories about relationships.

Feelings Association: A suggestion that helps the clients relate their current feelings to a relationship with someone in their family or to an event that happened within their family.

Happy Button: A technique to help the client relax while stopping any negative or maladaptive thoughts.

Interpretation: A therapeutic view perception about a comment the client makes.

Let's Pretend: A role-play technique that encourages the client to think through the problem within the parameters of feelings and thoughts associated with the problematic situation or individual(s).

Paradoxical Action: A technique that requires the client to take an action to do something extraordinary or contrary to the typical cultural or familial expectation in order to stimulate the client's thoughts about irrational or faulty assumptions

MC: I see. So tell me—what have you learned from talking about your rela-
            tionship with your mother?

Joe: I learned that women are harsh and uncaring.

MC: What about Mary?

Joe: She's different. She's caring. But sometimes she makes me nervous.

MC: What has Mary done that makes you nervous?

Multicultural Practice Applications

Adlerian theory has many applications in multicultural contexts. For example, for
first-generation immigrant families and their more "Americanized" children, Adler's
precepts can be used to help children challenge their assumptions about their parents. Immigrant children tend to think that their parents resist learning from a new
culture (Cheung & Nguyen, 2001). Children should be encouraged to listen to their
parents' perspective before they judge their parents' behavior. Instead of looking for
who is at fault and who is "right," the multicultural counselor should examine the
interactions of the two lifestyles. The counselor can then assist the client in understanding how these lifestyles were developed and explore with the client how the differences might be interpreted to increase self-awareness.

   Although the techniques are shown in the case demonstrations for illustration
purposes, Adlerian theory does not endorse a single set of techniques. For multicultural practice, this is a strength as well as a limitation. The flexibility of the therapeutic orientation will appeal to individuals whose cultures emphasize the value of
the group, community cohesiveness, and cooperation because the practitioner does
not impose definitions of values on the clients unless they have a shared value (Renik
& Spillius, 2004).

   But the Adlerian approach may have limited applicability to cultures that view
psychoanalytic subjectivity in a negative light. For instance, Mexican American culture, which emphasizes the importance of group cohesiveness and history, may
regard subjectivity as a pathological label in the therapeutic process (Pena, 2003). In
addition, clients' abilities to speculate on another individual's subjective world are
often limited among individuals raised in cultures in which verbal expressions rarely
include statements of subjectivity—for example, women growing up in a Chinese
rural community (Liu, 2004). Therapeutic questions create a challenge for clients
who cannot verbalize their thinking patterns, such as those who have been clinically
depressed or those who have not achieved language proficiency.

   Because of the moniker "individual psychology," many practitioners mistak-
enly label Adlerian therapy as an individual technique. Actually, Adler stressed the
unique undivided personality that an individual has learned from the family and
socialization process. In addition, Adlerian theory has recently been incorporated
into couple and group counseling (Corey, 2005). This is an important development,
as involving clients' families in multicultural practice is often essential.

Combined with choice theory (Lewis, 2005) and gestalt theory (Bitter, 2004; chapter 9 in this book), Adlerian theory has been demonstrated to be an evidence-based approach to family counseling, focusing on the sociobehavioral aspects of individual interpretations while strengthening the individual's communication with the family. Its multicultural emphasis on social interest, belongingness, and family environment makes relationship analysis a reality as the client's cultural background provides a meaningful resource for the practitioner in modeling ways to improve relationships (Brack, Hill, Edwards, Grootboom, & Lassiter, 2003; Carlson & Carlson, 2000).

In assessing the clients' perceptions toward their parents and siblings, individual differences become the most obvious cause of difficult behaviors and difficult feelings. From a multicultural perspective, differences can be addressed as diverse ways of coping, and difficulties can be reframed as perceptual reactions that can possibly be misunderstood when coping with those differences. In the case illustrations, the practitioner must search for instances when perceptions become obstacles because they change how the client sees situations. When using the technique "Act as if," for example, the practitioner must realize how cultural barriers may block the client's willingness to try new things for change. Referring to the earlier dialogue with Mary about her relationship with her brother:

MC: How about trying "Act as if?" In this coming week, act as if you were good friends with your brother. Pretend that he has a lot to offer to you or that you have a lot to offer to him. Call him up, find out some more about him, and tell him how much you've missed him.

Mary: I can't do it. He would think that I'm nuts.

MC: Okay… can you think of any values or ideas in your culture that may affect how you would approach this exercise?

Mary: Well, men are strong in our culture. He wouldn't understand my good intentions in calling him.

MC: Do you mean you don't have to go through this exercise because you already know what barriers your kids have experienced?

Mary: I already know?

MC: Didn't you tell me that men are perceived as strong in your culture? Tell me more about Kevin and Ami in terms of their perception of gender roles in your family.

In another example, Mary is encouraged to talk about her own needs. The practitioner's task is to help Mary understand more about how her upbringing has affected her perceptions toward others.

Mary: It's my life. I feel so tired of taking care of others and forgetting about myself.

MC: I see…. Tell me how your culture defines women's roles.

Mary:	Women are basically caregivers. We do everything and sacrifice for our family. We give everything we can give.
MC:	Does Joe agree that you should adhere to his rules and not voice any of your concerns?
Mary:	Not really. But I'm afraid to ask for his opinions. Men are strong.
MC:	Let's pretend that I'm Joe. Tell "Joe" about your feelings and how he can be of more help to you.

In a family session, each individual clearly expresses feelings and perceptions about which other family members have been guessing.

MC:	Now tell each other about what you're worried about. Mary—you go first.
Mary:	I'm worried about how the kids make us angry with each other.
MC:	How about you, Joe?
Joe:	I don't have any worries. It's just Mary's worries that make me nervous sometimes.
MC:	Mary, tell Joe what you told me the other day.
Mary:	Joe, I feel that you're too strong in stating your opinion. I don't know how to ask for help.
Joe:	I didn't know you think I'm unhelpful. You know—I think you're really caring. You're a good wife, but you make me nervous. That's why I ignore you sometimes.
MC:	Do you remember what we did in our previous discussions about your upbringing? Let's see what past experiences in your own family can help you clarify or gain insight into your perceptions of your current relationship.

All of these examples illustrate a major aspect of Adlerian approach in family interventions: promoting self-awareness through the analysis of past relationships. This helps the clients to realize the complexity of human relationships so that they do not blame each other for the behaviors they see. Similarly, a beginning practitioner must realize his or her own family-of-origin issues as a way to gain self-awareness and provide objective feedback to clients instead of maintaining a set of pre-assumed values. The following dialogues demonstrate how a supervisor (MC) provides educational supervision to a social worker, Betty.

MC:	Betty, tell me what you've learned from Mary and Joe's meeting last week.
Betty:	I learned that family values have always been directing the way we see things.
MC:	Since family values can be very different from one family to the next, how can you use the family values from two different individuals to

counsel them when you are trying to understand your own differences from them?

Betty: I tried to avoid using my values to judge theirs. As a matter of fact, by seeing how the couple deals with their conflict, I begin to realize how my own family values have directed my communication style.

MC: That's very true. We must gain awareness through the process of helping. Objectivity will guide our practice.

Self awareness is a productive way to understand our strengths and limitations. It can be achieved by asking ourselves two main questions:

1. What can trigger my emotions?
2. How did I handle an unresolved conflict in my relationship with my family member?

In the helping process, the practitioner continuously learns to adjust his or her style of communication based on learning that past relationships are reflective of current behaviors.

Variations from the Standardized Case: An Asian American Family

In this chapter, an Asian background is added to the standardized case to highlight the impact of cultural differences on social adjustment and the building of family relationships. See chapter 2 for a brief description of this population as related to multicultural practice.

***

Joe and Mary, whose real names are Siuming and Meiling, have been married for 20 years. After arriving from China to the United States in the late 1980s, they Americanized their names. They have two children, Ami, 16, and Kevin 8, and Mary's mother, Mrs. Chen, also lives with them. The family has strong cultural ties to the local Asian community, and Ami and Kevin often participate in the cultural festivities at their temple.

Ami is a sophomore in the local high school, where she ranks third in her class. Although most people would expect her to be pleased with her academic success, she is not. She believes that her parents are dissatisfied because she isn't ranked at the very top of her class. Ami states that her mother often comments how happy it would make her if Ami were valedictorian. Also, Ami is also dating a student from the same school, but she hasn't told her parents about him because she fears that they will not approve.

Mary has had recurrent bouts of depression for several years. Ami thinks that this stems from the death of Mary's brother several years ago. Mary has tried herbal medicines and other traditional healing methods that elders in the family have suggested to help treat the depression, but nothing seems to work.

Recently Mary saw their family doctor several times because of physical pain in her left hand, but the doctor was not able to find a cause for the pain or provide a diagnosis. He recently expressed to Mary that be does not believe anything is physically wrong with her hand. Although Joe does think that something is bothering Mary, he does not know how to deal with it, so he tends to ignore the problem.

Kevin is an average student in the third grade. He shows a great interest in soccer and would eventually like to try out for the local community team along with his friends. His parents, however, want him to concentrate on his studies because he will be entering junior high in a few years. Kevin's parents believe that soccer will not help advance his future, and they want him to forget about the sport all together.

Mrs. Chen, who speaks very little English, often cooks for the family and attends community functions at the Buddhist temple. Friends from the temple often drive her to different activities. Other families within the Asian community also look to her for guidance.

Experts Say…

According to Dr. Peter Nguyen, former clinical director at Spaulding for Children and current social work faculty member at Virginia Commonwealth University, Asian families are generally not open to external help. Culturally, mental health and family issues are seen as taboo, and families risk the loss of "face" or status if they are exposed. Further, Asian families are sometimes reluctant to receive assistance from therapists who do not speak their native language. Asian families are often concerned that non-native therapists do not understand the nuances and values of their culture. The multicultural counselor can address these issues by being sensitive in all aspects of the helping process:

- *Contact:* Assess each family member's readiness level for seeking help. Know how to greet each member of the family with appropriate manners. Observe the basic body gestures in the greeting and communication process: Customs and traditions are important in Asian culture. Learning and respecting these rituals is essential in building support and trust. For example, it would be appropriate to remove shoes upon entering the client's home, to avoid direct and sustained eye contact during communication, and to accept the family's offer of tea.
- *Problem identification:* Identify each individual's definition of the problem, based on his or her own unique view. Learn the Asian family structure, which in most Asian families is patriarchal. Approach issues gently during the assessment process to avoid offending the family members, especially the father.
- *Assessment:* Identify strengths of the family support system. Assess the presence and importance of extended family members in the household based on cultural expectations and living conditions. Explore ancillary issues, as Asian families in general are reluctant to address the primary issues immediately. Exploration of ancillary issues can provide data for the

practitioner to assess the person-in-environment and perhaps provide links or clues to the primary issues.

■ *Case planning:* Assess the language skills and comfort level of each family member in therapy. Evaluate the comfort level of each family member toward biculturalism and bilingualism. It is extremely important for the practitioner to involve all family members in case planning.

■ *Intervention:* Develop rapport with the children. Provide therapy for the mother and father individually and jointly, focusing on relationship building with their children. Consider family role definitions (including gender roles) and feelings of responsibility and respect for elders.

■ *Evaluation:* Develop a tool for the couple to use to evaluate their relationship with each other and with their children, with a strong focus on reducing stress.

■ *Termination:* Identify available cultural resources for the family before closure. Identify extended family members (including immigrants from the same country) who are physically available and/or emotionally supportive to assist the family.

When working with this family, the culturally sensitive practitioner must also be aware of his or her own attitudes, values, skills, and knowledge. For this family, the practitioner should not make judgments about the parents' motivation to maintain their original culture or the children's readiness to be bicultural. In addition, the practitioner should validate the parents' high expectations of their children and work to identify various ways to communicate these expectations without using threats or pressure.

The practitioner can provide information about child development and parenting skills but should also learn the history of immigration from the family and its effect on their lives. Practitioners should be aware of certain cultural values and expectations of Asian families. For example, in this culture extended family members are important, children are not expected to leave home after high school, and families tend to care for elderly parents at home rather than in nursing homes.

Specific intervention approaches with this family may include the following:

■ Use the *behavioral* approach to help the two children understand that they can make changes individually to build family strengths.

■ Adopt the *structural* approach to identify gender differentiation and its impact within the current family structure.

■ Use the *psychoanalytical* approach to help the children understand the impact of their culture on parental behaviors, including expectations of total obedience and demands for actions that preserve dignity and honor.

■ *Observe important family events* and help each member identify the importance of his or her ethnic heritage.

In addition, the practitioner should assess the acculturation rate of the parents and the children. The difference in acculturation rate may be a source of conflict and communication problems between the parents and children. Further, practitioners should assess the marital relationship and parenting style of each parent. This assessment can provide data for the practitioner to apply to the marriage, as well as ways to unify the parenting style to provide consistency and stability for the children.

The children's own perspectives and their understanding of the parents' perspective should also be assessed. This information will help the practitioner formulate a plan of action that may include educational materials for the family and also help prepare mediation techniques that may be appropriate during the helping process.

Best Practice Evaluation

Evaluation Stage 2: Evaluate Family Relationships

Following the first stage from chapter 4, the second stage of the evaluation process includes an evaluation of the family relationships (see chapter 1). In this chapter, we will use a one-group pre-test and post-test design (AB design) to demonstrate how the family relationship problems can be assessed in Joe and Mary's family.

Suggested evaluation tool: Index of Family Relations (IFR) (Hudson, 1997)

Description: The IFR consists of 25 items. The purpose of the instrument is to assess family relationship problems. The scale contains three levels of assessment. A score of under 30 indicates that the family does not have any clinically significant problems. A score between 30 and 70 indicates that the family experiences clinically significant problems. A score higher than 70 points to severe problems in the family. The scale was developed based on a sample of 518 subjects, primarily Caucasian with some Japanese and Chinese Americans. The scale has excellent reliability with a mean alpha of .95. It also has a strong correlation with the parent–child and family relationship rating scale.

How to use the tool: The IFR is available for purchase via www.walmyr.com, or at P.O. Box 12217, Tallahassee, FL 32317-2217, USA (Phone: 850-383-0045). A sample of the scale can be reviewed via the following web site: www.walmyr.com/ifr sampl.pdf. The IFR contains a 7-point Likert-type scale, with which the user will rate the severity of the problems in the family. Because this is a self-evaluation tool, the user must respond honestly to each statement. After the client completes the scale, the practitioner must reverse the score on items 1, 2, 4, 5, 8, 14, 15, 17, 18, 20, 21 and 23 (so 1 = 7; 2 = 6; 3 = 5; 4 = 4; 5 = 3; 6 = 2; and 7 = 1). This reverse scoring procedure is necessary for scoring purposes only, and the new score does not alter the face value of the original rating.

After replacing the original scores with reverse scores, add all scores. Subtract the number of responded items (N) from the total score (Y). Multiply this number $(Y - N)$ by 100 and divide the number by the number of responded items (N) times six $[(Y - N) \times 100/(N \times 6)]$. The final score should range from 0 to 100. High scores indicate that the family relationship problems are more severe.

How to evaluate the outcomes: As discussed in chapter 3, six steps can be followed to evaluate family relationship problems using the single-system research. These steps are demonstrated with Mary's data as follows:

1. *Define the service target or problem (intake and case assessment):* The family has experienced intrafamilial stress.
2. *Define (or formulate) goals and objectives:* To reduce stress in the family.
3. *Identify constraints and resources and select a treatment:* Constraints include no communication among family members and lack of understanding from one to the other; resources include willingness to meet with the counselor and maintaining strong Asian values.
4. *Measure the monitoring actions (monitor progress):* The family members are asked to complete the IFR scale each week for 7 weeks (baseline A). Adlerian therapy is applied for 7 weeks (intervention period B) after the baseline. The practitioner records the score each week for 14 weeks.
5. *Analyze data:* Using Mary's scores in an individual session, the practitioner helps her compare the average IFR score in the baseline with the average IFR score in the intervention period. The data in Figure 5.1 indicate that Mary's average IFR score is lower in the intervention period (37.14) compared to the baseline period (90.00).
6. *Report results and make recommendations:* In addition to the average score per period, the practitioner evaluates that the IFR score in the 14th week (20) is significantly lower than the score in the first week (90). Combining Mary's results with each of the family members' results, the practitioner concludes that Adlerian therapy has been effective in helping the family address their

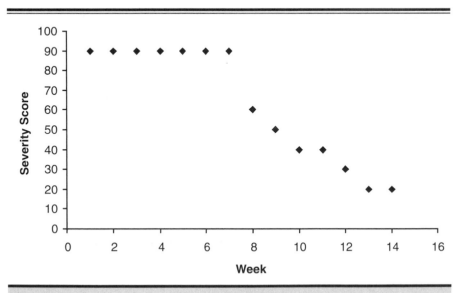

Figure 5.1

Index of Family Relations

family relationship problems. Specifically, Mary found that the lifestyle assessment helped her connect her family relations issues to some of the family-of-origin issues. It is suggested that Mary and Joe compare their data and address how their past family relationship issues affect their current relationship with one another.

Multicultural Practice Exercises

Lifestyle Assessment

Before utilizing the Lifestyle Assessment to assess clients, culturally sensitive practitioners must assess their own childhood experiences:

- List your siblings from oldest to the youngest. Write three to five words that best represent each person (including yourself), from the list below or of your own choosing. If you do not have siblings, choose three close friends.
- Among these siblings (or closest friends), who has the strongest trait on each of the following personality dimensions? Next to each trait, place the initials of all siblings (including yourself) from the most to the least next to each trait. For example, if you (Me) are the most assertive among your siblings, and your sister (Sis) is more assertive than your brother (Bth), the order will look like this:
  Assertive ___ Me Sis Bth ___

Personality Dimensions:

Assertive _____

Athletic _____

Bossy _____

Conforming _____

Critical of others _____

Critical of self _____

Demanding _____

Hardworking _____

Intelligent _____

Pleasing _____

Rebellious _____

Responsible _____

Sociable _____

Spoiled _____

Withdrawn _____

- Which sibling(s) is (are) the most different from you? How?
- What childhood fears did you have?
- What were your childhood ambitions?
- What were the most important values in your family?
- What memories of your childhood stand out the most for you?
- Write a summary about your parents in your early memories.

Three Wishes

- What is your current relationship with your parents? With your siblings?
- How do you see yourself in terms of your cultural identity *now*, compared to when you were about 10?
- What are *three* things you'd most like to change about yourself?
- What has been encouraging you to change or preventing you from changing those things?
- If you were 10 and were granted three wishes to change your family, what would you have asked to change? Would you change them now?

Topics for Discussion

1. Adlerian therapists typically begin the counseling process with the lifestyle assessment, which focuses on early recollections and family constellations. Which part of this assessment do you think can be applicable to a new immigrant family? Which part should be modified?
2. If cognition is the major focus of therapeutic analysis, how is Adlerian theory useful to clients with major depression, given their limited ability to provide answers to the therapeutic questions?
3. When thinking about working with clients from diverse cultural or socioeconomic backgrounds, which aspects of Adlerian theory would you recommend to a beginning therapist? Can you use Adlerian theory in clinical and educational supervision? Why or why not?
4. What are the limitations of applying Adlerian theory counseling with interracial couples?

CHAPTER SIX

Family Systems Theory

This chapter explores family systems theory based on the work of Murray Bowen. It highlights how the theory can be used to inform multicultural practice techniques and applications. It provides a comprehensive definition of the family, using both structure and function as major elements in the family system analysis. Dialogues with the standardized case center on family history and current relationships with extended family members. A major focus of the case study is differentiation of self. Three issues are presented with practice demonstrations with the standardized case:

1. Family history
2. Relationships with the extended family
3. The definition of a good family.

In providing a perspective of cultural variations, this chapter features a Latino immigrant family from Mexico. This ethnicity identifier is used to assist practitioners in providing culturally sensitive interventions and should not be interpreted as demonstrating "typical" characteristics of Latino families. The cultural values of Latinos should be assessed and incorporated in the intervention process (Corey, Corey, & Callanan, 2003; Pedersen, 2000; Sue & Sue, 2003). As mentioned in chapter 2, Latino populations strongly emphasize family and regard family values as superior to individual values (Gloria, Ruiz, & Castillo, 1999). This value of familism goes beyond the nuclear family to the extended family and significant non-relative relationships (Brendel & Sustaeta, 2003). Therapists should be aware of and utilize these unique values as strengths when the issues of interpersonal interactions, gender roles, and religious orientation are involved in therapy (Brendel & Sustaeta, 2003; Gloria et al., 1999). The Family Assessment Measure appears at the end of this chapter, and practical exercises provide ways to work across cultures.

Assessing Family Systems

Family systems theory evolved through Murray Bowen's work with patients who were diagnosed with schizophrenia and their families at the Menninger Clinic and the National Institute of Mental Health. In his research, Bowen demonstrated the synthesis of therapeutic concepts related to self–family differentiation (Bowen Center for the Study of the Family, 2004). Concepts including self-development, intergenerational issues, and family history are inseparable explanations of a family's structure and functioning.

To understand the premises of family systems theory, students must have an understanding of the definition of family. Such definitions, however, can vary widely and are based on a number of cultural, religious, social, and personal influences. In the authors' last 13 years of teaching, we have collected a variety of definitions of family from graduate students. A synthesis of these definitions is:

> A unit or group of two or more individuals (or beings) formally or informally connected through birth, law, and/or commonly recognized choices, circumstances, shared bonds, and personalities, who are connected by a structure of relationships and unique interests for achieving the functions of connection, guidance, and assignment of meaning, while also serving as a reflexive network that brings strengths, talents, and commonalities in providing emotional, spiritual, and/or social support.

This definition encompasses both the structure and the functions of a family and includes characteristics of traditional as well as nontraditional families. This definition also provides two insights for practice with multicultural families:

1. We work with a system of choices.
2. We exist within a system of relationships.

Practitioners who work with families must have an open mind in order to listen to and comprehend the client's definition of his or her family.

Family Systems Theory in Brief

Application to Multicultural Practices:

- The focus is on the family as a whole.
- Each person's role is identified in relation to the family.

Major Figure:

- Murray Bowen (1913–1990): Family Systems Theory

Assumptions:

- Each family member represents two life forces: self-identity and family dependency.
- Failing to differentiate from the family may cause problems.
- Individuals learn communication skills and decision-making skills from their family-of-origin.

Therapeutic Process:

- Analyze the family-of-origin (FOO) issues with the client's current perspective.
- Observe family interactions.
- Analyze societal, cultural, or familial forces supporting undifferentiation.

Goals:

- Distinguish between the subjective feeling process and the intellectual thinking process.
- Establish an "I position" to state the individual's own beliefs that are differentiated from the FOO's.
- Release the family triangle by refocusing the problem.
- Identify a family emotional system that is built within a triangle.

Multicultural Practice Techniques

- Develop a genogram or family tree.
- Separate the "I" from within from the "I" belonging to the FOO.
- Understand the family projection process.
- Analyze the multigenerational transmission process.
- Analyze sibling positions and triangles within a family.

On the Multicultural Stage: Connecting Two Families

When two persons come together to form a family, each of them brings at least one family-of-origin experience to this new connection. Language, culture, customs, values, and other things "learned" in the family of origin can all affect the attitudes toward and the view of the newly formed family. At first, the new structure of the family helps the individuals move away from their families of origin. However, when two individuals form a new relationship, they may continue their behavioral patterns as if they were still living with their families of origin. Typical examples include personal habits such as grooming, eating and cooking, ways of arranging household items, and communication styles, including the ability to handle emotions. Problems may arise when these individuals cannot adjust to each other's habits or cannot communicate about how the repeated behavioral pattern has become an obstacle to their new relationship.

The Case Approach

The following examples illustrate the use of family systems theory in understanding the impact of family history and of involvement with the extended family on a person's current functioning. Through personal projection processes, these examples identify three major aspects of a family system: its subsystems, its emotional ties, and the transmission of its values from one generation to the next. Selected issues include understanding the importance of family history, analyzing the relationship with the extended family, and defining a good family.

Issue #1: Family History

Joe agrees to come to this couples session because he wants to find out what Mary has done to help Ami. In previous sessions, Joe's view has been limited to his role as a father. In this session, he begins to realize how his attitudes about family have been influenced by his past experiences with his own family-of-origin.

MC: What's been going on this last week?

Mary: Well, we've really been having problems with Ami....

Joe: No, Mary. It's *you*, not we, who has been having problems with Ami.

Mary: Well, she's just not doing what she's supposed to do. She comes in at all hours of the night and doesn't help around the house. She calls boys all the time, and she's starting to wear those short skirts and too much makeup.... Joe just doesn't seem to care.

MC: Joe, what's your reaction to what Mary is saying?

Family Involvement

Joe: Ami has an eleven o'clock curfew, which she always meets. She dresses just like the other kids, and if Mary would ask her to help around the house, I'm sure she would. But the problem is that Mary never asks anyone for help. We never know what she's thinking.

MC:	Mary, do you agree with what Joe said about you never asking for help?
Mary:	Well, they should want to help me if they really love me, without even being asked. And if Ami cared anything about how I feel, she would come in earlier and dress more appropriately. She should know what that can lead to.
MC:	What does that lead to, Mary?
Mary:	Boys and girls in the middle of the night—do I have to spell it out for you?

Family Projection Process

MC:	Yes, please. I just want to understand more.
Joe:	(Rolls eyes and sighs)
MC:	Joe, I noticed you rolled your eyes. What are you reacting to?
Joe:	It's just that she's never been comfortable with this subject. I doubt if she'll talk about it.
MC:	Joe, tell me what you're referring to. What is it that Mary won't talk about?

Use of "I" Position

Joe:	Having relations.
Mary:	(Looking uncomfortable, shifting in her seat, chewing on her lip) Talking about this makes me very uncomfortable.
MC:	Mary, I think this is a safe place to talk about it.
Mary:	It's not something I'm used to talking about.

Family Projection

MC:	Joe, what do you think about this?
Joe:	Well, we've never talked about it before. Now that I'm thinking about it, maybe it's one of the major problems in our marriage.

De-Triangulation

Mary:	But Joe, I didn't think you'd want to talk about this. I didn't think you wanted anything to change. I thought you were perfectly fine with how things are.
MC:	Joe, are there things you would like to see change in your marriage?
Joe:	You know, we've been together for twenty years, and I've never felt that Mary has enjoyed it. She's never said no, but it's like she's not even there. It's like it's a duty to her.
MC:	What would you like to change?
Joe:	I would like to see that Mary enjoys our marital relationship.
MC:	Mary, how does it make you feel to hear what Joe just said?

Mary: I feel confused. Joe spends most of his time telling me how he doesn't want me to change. But now he wants change...

MC: Joe, what do you think?

Joe: Well, I don't really want her to change. I just want us both to enjoy each other. Recently she's been going to work, and that bothers me. I mean, Mary, you know what happened in my family....

MC: Tell me about what happened, Joe.

Joe: Well, when I was around eight, my mother got a job and started spending more time outside of the home. Before I knew it, she met a man and was gone.

MC: (To Joe) So she met someone.... Was there anything else you think made your mother want to leave?

Joe: I guess she had all these outside interests and activities. She just met a man who became more important to her than her family.

MC: That must have been really hard. How did your family cope with her leaving?

Joe: My father started drinking. I was the youngest and was too young to understand what was going on, so I relied on my older sister. She was the one who took care of me.

MC: This is interesting, Mary. You're the oldest in your family, and you grew up taking care of your brother and sisters. Joe, you're the youngest, and you grew up being taken care of by your older sister. Can either of you see any similarities in those backgrounds to your life now?

Sibling Position

Mary: Yes, I take care of Joe, and I've taken care of people all of my life.

Joe: Mary took over where my sister left off.

Issue #2: Relationship with the Extended Family

Many of the current issues and problems with this family stem from Mary's and Joe's families of origin. The extended family is connected in a way that can be rigidly perceived in terms of staying in each person's roles and responsibilities. The purpose of therapy is to untie this rigidity. In this family session, Mary, Joe, and the children discuss current family conflict. In most family situations, a triangle is created when an additional family member, such as a child or an in-law, is struggling between two individuals in a new relationship, and if the couple cannot adjust to each other's habits and styles. This triangle in the relationship may trigger problems at any time. One way to ensure that the couple can see this projection of their problem(s) onto a third person is to temporarily take that person out of the discussion, in other words, to de-triangulating the person from the triangle relationship.

| MC: | I would like each of you to tell us how you see your family. Kevin, you're the youngest. Would you please start? How do you see your family? |

Sibling Position

Kevin:	Me? I don't know.
MC:	Tell us how you feel about your family.
Kevin:	Well ... I feel happy about my family.
Ami:	I don't feel that.
Kevin:	That's you. You always make Mom unhappy.
MC:	Ami, tell me a little more about that.
Ami:	Everything was fine until Mom went back to school.
Kevin:	There's nothing wrong with Mom going to school.
Ami:	There's nothing wrong with Mom going back to school, but things sure have fallen apart around here.
MC:	Ami, explain what you mean by "falling apart."
Ami:	Mom was always strict, but now that she's going back to school, she's worse—always on my case about how I dress, my dating. I can't do anything right.
Mary:	Because you're out of control!
Joe:	No, she's not, Mary. You're being too hard to her!
MC:	Mary, how does "out of control" apply to Ami?

Detriangulation

Mary:	She comes in at all hours of the night. She calls boys all the time, and she wears those short skirts and too much makeup. Joe doesn't seem to care. She doesn't help me around the house at all.
Ami:	I never knew that you needed help around the house. You don't say anything.
Joe:	That's true, Mary. We can't read your mind.
Mary:	If they cared about me, they'd know what to do. I wouldn't have to ask. If Ami—and for that matter, any of them—had as much devotion to the family as I do, they would see that they could help bring in the groceries and put them away, fold their own clothes, and ... well, it's just so obvious that I could use their help.

Detriangulation

| MC: | Mary, from what you've told me about your family, I'm wondering—is that how it worked in your family? No one told you what to do? |
| Mary: | That's right. No one ever had to tell me. I looked after my sisters, did the laundry, cooked most of the meals, and cleaned the house so my mother could help my father with his church duties. |

MC: What motivated you to be so conscientious?

Mary: Conscientious? I never thought about it like that. I was just doing what needed to be done to help the family.

MC: How did the family express that need to you?

Mary: My father had very high standards about the condition of the house and how all of us presented ourselves to the outside world. It wasn't so much what he said it to me. It was just his disapproving look when I wanted to do something that he thought didn't reflect family unity. Dad's commandment was, "Work first." Nothing else was as important. If it was fun and didn't have anything to do with his work, we received swift judgment.

MC: How did you feel about that kind of discipline?

Mary: I didn't like it.

MC: Did you believe young people should have fun or shouldn't have fun?

Multigenerational Transmission Process

Mary: It's not that I think people shouldn't have fun, but the family should come first.

MC: So do you see a pattern here in the way you were raised and in the way you think about your own family?

Self-Differentiation

Ami: I don't know about her, but I sure do! She doesn't want anybody to have fun—just wash dishes and make beds like she did. But there's more to life than that. I'm not you, Mom. Just because Grandpa didn't want you to have any fun, it doesn't mean I can't. That old fart hates everybody!

Mary: Ami, don't talk about my father and your grandfather that way!

MC: Let's stay away from insults like that in here…. Mary, what do you think about Ami's perception that you don't want her to have any fun?

Family Projection Process

Mary: It's not that I don't want Ami to have fun. I just want her to have the same sense of family that I have. But I'm beginning to see that isn't working so well for me.

Joe: What do you mean it's not working for you? Maybe it's not working for *me*. Since Mary has taken so many interests outside the family, things aren't running as smoothly. We aren't as close as we used to be.

Mary: Joe, we weren't any closer before. I just didn't complain then.

Joe: Why did you have to go back to school? Weren't you happy?

Mary: Happy? I don't even know who I am as a person, let alone know if I'm happy!

MC: Some of the family thinks your return to school is okay, but others, including Joe, don't see it as positively. Joe seems to have some concerns about the changes you're making. Let's all look at the genogram (see chapter 2) and see if it shows us why Mary might have returned to school. If you look, you'll see some interesting patterns and dates that have some things in common. I've highlighted these. What are some of the things you all see?

Ami: Hey, I never noticed that Mom went back to school after Grandpa's stroke.

Kevin: That's also when Aunt Joanie moved to Colorado!

Ami: Yeah! There is a connection.

Emotional Cutoff

MC: Mary, what do you think about Ami's and Kevin's observations?

Multigenerational Transmission Process

Mary: I really admired my little sister for going back to school. But I knew my father wouldn't approve of my going to school because I had a family to take care of, and I've always thought of my family first. I knew my mother wanted to do something more with her life, but she never did. I don't want to end up depressed and lonely like my mother, but here I am, feeling depressed and lonely every day.

          When I first went back to school, I felt so empty. I just took one class, but I enjoyed meeting new people and having interesting, intellectual things to talk about beyond dirty laundry and "what's for dinner!" My school friends seemed interested in me, not just what I could do for them.

MC: Sounds like school was really a validating experience for you…. Joe, how do you feel about what Mary has just said?

Joe: I never knew Mary was so depressed and lonely. She looked happy to me. I thought she was doing what she wanted to do. I never knew about her thoughts about her father and sister, or her worrying about ending up like her mother. I want Mary to be happy, but I also want things to go back to the way they used to be.

MC: Joe, your mother left when you were eight or nine. Could this have anything to do with your feelings about the changes Mary is making?

Joe: I never really thought about it before. I've worked hard not to be like my father…not to have my wife leave me.

MC: What do you mean—not being like your father?

Joe: After my mother left, my father drank all the time and was never there for us.

Emotional Cutoff

Ami: Well, Dad, you don't drink… but sometimes it's like you aren't there for us.

MC: What do you mean by that, Ami?

Detriangulation

Ami: When Mom went back to school, Dad was around even less. He started playing tennis, and he wasn't ever home. Mom had to take us everywhere, and she went to all of our games by herself.

MC: Joe, how do you feel about what Ami just said?

Joe: I'm not sure how I feel.

Multigenerational Transmission Process

Ami: Instead of an alcoholic, you're a workaholic. It's pretty much the same thing, Dad.

MC: Joe, do you think it's the same thing?

Joe: No, it's not the same thing! I work hard to provide the family with everything they need. I thought I was doing what everybody wanted me to do. Then Mary went and changed everything.... I never understood why Mary wanted to go to school. I gave her everything.

         When she went back to school, I felt just like I did when I was a child and my mom started being away from home more and more. Everything seemed fine in my family, and then all of a sudden Mom was gone and nothing was ever the same again. There was nobody to take care of me except for my big sister.

Multigenerational Transmission Process

Ami: Oh? Is that why you married Mom? To have someone take care of you?

Joe: No, Ami, I married your mother because I love her. She took really good care of me—I mean us—before she went back to school. I guess I miss that.

Self-Determination

Mary: Joe, I need to have a life, too.

MC: So would you all say the problems in the family aren't so much about Mary having a life away from home but more about the fears some of you are having about the changes in the family?

Issue #3: Definition of a Good Family

This is the third session for Mary and Joe. They are joining another couple in therapy, Bianca and Bill, who have three children and are attending their sixth session. Mary's recent involvement with school has led her to a part-time job. The presenting problem is Mary's resentment that Joe isn't supportive of her new job.

MC: Mary, you told me in the last session that you're ready to meet another couple. Tell me what you expect to gain from this experience.

Mary: I don't know—I guess learning from them about our mistakes.

MC:	Joe, what would you like to gain from this experience?
Joe:	I'm not sure. I just want us to be happy.
MC:	Part of the reason I wanted us to meet all together is that you have something in common: Each couple has a member with a new job, and all of you have kids. Mary, why don't you start by telling us about your job?
Mary:	I really like it. I've been working there for three weeks.
MC:	How's the family adjusting to your work schedule?
Mary:	They still aren't used to me not being there when they get home. Ami, my sixteen-year-old, gives me a hard time for not having dinner ready. Joe complains that it's too much for him to handle.
MC:	Joe, what's too much for you?

Individual Assessment

Joe:	Nothing seems to be in order since she's been working. I'm worried that the family will fall apart. The children need Mary to be there for them.
MC:	Joe, your mother worked outside the home, correct?

Analyzing the Family-of-Origin

Joe:	Yes, she did, and it caused a lot of problems.
MC:	Bill, you and Bianca discussed the same issue when you first saw me. Did your mother work outside of the home?
Bill:	No, she didn't. But she died a very bitter woman. She told me that she regrets that she was never able to finish her education or get a job. I feel like we were selfish to expect her to stay home.
MC:	How did your father feel about her working?
Bill:	He wouldn't allow it. Even when the children were grown, he told her it wasn't respectable.
MC:	Bianca, did your mother work outside of the home?
Bianca:	Yes, she had to work. My father died when I was ten.
MC:	How was your family affected by her working?

Assessment of Family Reactions

Bianca:	We were fine. We just had to be responsible.
MC:	Mary, I recall that your mother has never worked outside the home. Is that correct?
Mary:	Yes, but I don't want to be like her. I want to live my life.
MC:	So in talking about our mothers, what do you all notice? Joe?
Joe:	Not every family is the same.
Mary:	I don't know if a woman should always be the caretaker.
MC:	Okay…. So Mary, what do you want from Joe, Ami, and Kevin?

Mary:	I've been thinking about it, and I believe I need more support from Joe before I can face the children's demands for my time.
MC:	Joe, how do you feel about this?
Joe:	I want to support her, but I hope she knows what she's doing.
MC:	Let me ask you, Bill—do you have any concerns about Mary working outside her home?

Group Feedback

Bill:	I want to ask Joe what his real fear is.
Joe:	(Silent)
Bianca:	Yes, I want to know the same thing. The children are in school. They're less dependent on Mary. I think you guys can make it work together.
MC:	Joe, what do you think?
Joe:	(Silent)
MC:	Mary, what are your thoughts about a mother working outside the home?

Analyzing the Family-of-Origin

Mary:	My parents taught me strong values. I stayed home to raise my children, but now that they're older and more independent, I think I deserve to find out who I am. And I should be able to work if I want to. I still want my family to be happy and my household to run well. I can work harder to get supper ready on time. I know that's hard on everyone.
MC:	Joe, you said your mother working outside the home was a problem. Could you tell us more about that?
Joe:	My mother worked long hours, and we had to fend for ourselves. My other siblings got into some trouble, but I was a good kid. I fear that my kids may get into trouble. I'm also afraid that Mary's parents think I can't take care of her. I don't make a lot of money, but I can support her. She doesn't have to work. After all these years, I think her parents are still upset that she married me.
MC:	So you're afraid of what Mary's parents are going to think. What are you afraid might happen if Mary continues to work outside the home?

Specifying Client's Problem or Need

Joe:	I do worry what they think. Her parents are very strict and they're still trying to run our lives. I guess I'm also worried how we can manage. Mary does a lot for us. It's just hard for me to get used to Mary not being home when I need her—but I guess I'm willing to try.
MC:	You're willing to try?
Joe:	Yes.
MC:	Mary, how do you feel hearing what Joe just said?

Mary: I feel good.

MC: Bill, let's move to you and Bianca. What it is that you want from Bianca?

Group Feedback

Bill: I really want her to take better care of herself.

MC: In what way?

Bill: She needs to pay more attention to the way she looks, and be better ... at just being a wife.

Family Systems Techniques

Analyzing the Family-of-Origin: Identifying past relationships between family members in the family where the person was born or raised.

Assessment of Family Reactions: Identifying how each family member (of the family-of-origin or the current family) responded to a situation similar to the one addressed by the client.

Detriangulation: A method to divert the attention from focusing on one person to find possible solutions for the presenting issues.

Emotional Cutoff: Exposing how a person may find a way to escape from handling a family issue.

Family Involvement: Providing opportunities to allow family members to respond to the perceived problem/issue.

Family Projection: A technique to help the client realize that the issue is related to some interpersonal issues within the family.

Group Feedback: Receiving feedback from other individuals about the strengths of the family, with the goal of building more healthy family relationships.

"I" Position: The use of an individual's first-person view to see how the situation is handled.

Multigenerational Transmission: A technique used to reveal how current situations and issues are often repeated patterns of past experiences from individuals' families-of-origin.

Self-Determination: A technique to encourage clients to make decisions based on objective assessment.

Self-Differentiation: A technique to help clients realize that a certain behavioral pattern may be directly related to strong family values and to encourage clients to make their decisions based, instead, on objective assessment.

Sibling Position: A method to determine how a person's birth order may affect how he or she perceives current problems within the family.

MC: Okay. What are your ideas about what a good wife should be?

Bill: She needs to always look her best. Bianca doesn't keep house the way she once did, but I think we're fine. I'm helping to make it our home.

MC: Joe, what are your ideas about what a good wife should be?

Joe: I understand what he's saying. Couples should work together for the marriage to work.

MC: Good. Bianca, what are your ideas about what a good husband looks like?

Bianca: He works to make sure the home is a happy place.

MC: Mary?

Mary: Yes, he should understand me. Then we'll have a good family.

Multicultural Practice Applications

In this case study, differentiation of the self is the focus. Many cultures place a higher value on family connections than on the self (Brooks, Haskins, & Kehe, 1999; Garrett, 2003; Gloria, Ruiz, & Castillo, 1999; Zane, Morton, Chu, & Lin, 1999). For example, Latino culture, as mentioned at the beginning of this chapter, assumes that family or collective needs take priority over individual needs. Multicultural practitioners must realize that the very concept of differentiation is a Western ideal and, therefore, must be applied to diverse clients from a culturally sensitive perspective.

In the above dialogue, Mary relates her own rigidity to her family-of-origin. The dialogue does not suggest that Mary extinguish the family values she learned from her family-of-origin but, rather, that she learn from the patterns of her family-of-origin and how they affect her relationships and interactions with her own family.

Mary: It's not that I think people shouldn't have fun, but the family should come first.

MC: Do you see a pattern here in the way you were raised and in the way you think about your family?

Mary: I sure do! Should I change it?

MC: Well, you can't change history. But your awareness already has led you to change how you see things.

Ami: Does it mean that Mom understands how important having fun is?

MC: Mary, why don't you respond to that? What do you think about what Ami just said?

When working with clients who have different cultural expectations, the practitioner takes special care to provide opportunities for each client to express his or her own perspective. Potential misunderstandings can be minimized by continually asking for clarification.

MC:	Mary, I think this is a safe place to talk about it.
Mary:	It's not something I'm used to talking about.
MC:	I understand this feeling…. Joe, what's your expectation about coming here?
Joe:	I have no idea. I just want to make sure that things will go back to normal.
MC:	What's "normal?"
Joe:	Mary not feeling nervous. The family all feeling happy.
Mary:	I'm not nervous. I'm just not comfortable.
MC:	Tell us about your discomfort.
Mary:	I'm not comfortable with talking about my family behind their back.
Joe:	Mary, I'm not comfortable with that either, especially when I talk about you without knowing how you feel about it.
Mary:	I appreciate your understanding. This is exactly why I'd like you to come.
MC:	We're here to talk about how families can affect the way we behave, as well as how they influence our feelings. It's normal to feel uncomfortable. No one can tell us what to do when we feel uncomfortable about having a problem. It's important that we express what the problem is, though.

If a practitioner's family-of-origin issues are still unresolved, he or she may not clearly separate the client's current issues from his or her own or solve these problems without blaming another family member's preserved values. The first step is for the practitioner to realize that self-differentiation can be achieved without abandoning family values. From this experience, the practitioner can discern whether the client came from a family with strong family values or problematic experiences, as the client's perception of a problem may be very different than that of a person who comes from a different family-of-origin. The following supervision example illustrates how a person's family-of-origin issues may affect the way a person deals with other relationships.

MC:	I understand that you have a hard time dealing with the Mary's issues. Would you like to talk more about it?
Betty:	Yes, it is related to my own family issues.
MC:	(silent)
Betty:	My mom had a very similar situation to Mary's. I guess all women went through this struggle.
MC:	All women?
Betty:	Not really! I mean a lot of women. I saw myself similar to Ami, finally coming out from the strict discipline that was created by my mom. Now I am independent from my family, but I thought of telling my folks about my feelings.

MC: It seems that you have already resolved your issue. How about drawing
             a genogram of Mary's family and identifying a couple of your differ-
             ences from her?

             (Betty finishes the genogram and examines it.)

Betty: We all share similarities, and that's why the feeling about family disci-
             pline came to me so strongly. I know that I was affected by that feeling,
             and talking with you helped me release that burden. It wasn't Mary; it
             was me who held on to that feeling for too long.

The practitioner was able to overcome her past issue, but the feeling remained
unchanged. This supervision session identifies helpful tips for practitioners who tri-
angulate themselves into the client's situation. The problem presented in this example is obviously not a severe one, but it illustrates that triangles can occur anywhere.
It is surely a culturally universal concept because triangulation involves not only an
"in-between" person, but it can also be an event or an unresolved feeling.

Variations From the Standardized Case: An Immigrant Family From Mexico

The standardized case is modified with a different ethnicity than in the previous
chapters. Now the family represents an immigrant family from Mexico. Particularly
in the United States, immigrants are contributors to the demography and economy
of the country, but they are often discriminated against because of language, cultural,
and customary differences.

                                    ***

Joe and Mary emigrated from Mexico to the United States 10 years ago and
have been married for 15 years. Their names on immigration papers are José and
María. They have two children Ami, 16, and Kevin, 8. Joe is an industrious worker
and spends a great deal of time away from home managing his family's restaurant
business. Mary owns a dry-cleaning service company, which she manages with her
niece. Both parents have a strong work ethic, and their employees respect them.
Because the businesses are running well, Mary and Joe often devote extra time to the
businesses by staying late or covering shifts for other employees.

Although Mary and Joe are currently happy in their life, there was a time soon
after they were married when Joe had an extramarital affair. Although it was 14 years
ago and has not happened since, Mary still has difficulty trusting Joe and is particularly sensitive to him working late.

Ami is currently three months pregnant and is contemplating dropping out of
school. Mary has told Ami that if she decides to drop out of school, she can help run
the dry-cleaning business. Ami feared that her parents would kick her out of the house
when they found out about the pregnancy, but both Mary and Joe have told Ami that
although they think she has been irresponsible, they will help to raise her child.

Kevin feels lost within the family. He is jealous of Ami because she is receiving more attention from Mary and Joe. He does not think Ami deserves special attention because she "got herself pregnant." Recently, Kevin, formerly a hardworking student, has been spending time with the "wrong crowd" and skipping school. On most Sundays the family attends their Catholic church together. Several church members who are also close to the family have told Ami that they will help with childcare if she decides to work after the baby is born.

Experts Say...

Dr. Maria Puig of Colorado State University observes that many family values may be viewed as part of the problem. In order to understand these values and their relation to Latino culture, the practitioner must work closely with the family in a learner's mode; he or she must learn about the family's culture, assess the family's view of the problems, and incorporate the learned information into the intervention phase.

When working with this family, the cross-cultural practitioner should consider several cultural, ethnic, and societal factors. First, the practitioner should assess the value of extended family members to build family strengths. The helping professional should also address the family's cultural heritage and the impact of religion on the help-seeking behaviors. Finally, the practitioner should be aware of how immigration has impacted the family's level of functioning.

In addition, a culturally sensitive practitioner can take the following actions during the steps of the helping process:

- *Contact:* Know how to greet the entire family by demonstrating appropriate manners toward each of the members. In addition to establishing a treatment alliance foundation, ask about how various family members define the primary family stress, what brought them in today, how each member perceives his or her contribution to it, how each is affected by it, how each copes or is attempting to lessen or resolve the family stressor.
- *Problem Identification:* Identify each individual's definition of the problem, based on his or her own worldview.
- *Assessment:* Identify extended family members who are physically available and emotionally supportive, to assist the family with their needs. Ask them to define something unique or healthy about their family, which gives a systemic picture of how family members experience events, including coping mechanisms with family strengths as resources to draw upon.
- *Case planning:* Assess the family's financial situation for the purposes of treatment planning and resource allocation. Focus at the dyadic level to reestablish parental boundaries around arguments and insulate children from the more overt manifestations of "raw verbal" marital conflict that is likely occurring outside the polite facade that often is present at initial assessment.
- *Intervention:* Develop rapport with the children; provide individual therapy for the mother; provide joint therapy with the couple; focus on relationship-building with all of the family members. Use the "common factors" approach

(Asay & Lambert, 1999; Lambert, 2005a) as contributing to real change in clients. The common factors approach recognizes that to promote change the practitioner must:

□ pay attention to and mobilize multiple outside factors (40%),
□ constructively utilize the clinician's interpersonal and relationship skills (30%),
□ attend to instilling hope or positive expectancy for change (15%), and
□ attend to what therapeutic model and techniques (15%) best fits the client problems based upon evidence based practice research.

■ *Evaluation:* Identify strengths of the extended family support system. Develop a tool for the couple to use to evaluate their relationship with each other and with their children, with a strong focus on family relationship-building.
■ *Termination:* Find a cultural means that is representative of this culture to help clients express feelings; draw a picture of the family with each of the members' contributions; use a poem from an ethnic writer to capture the learning during this therapeutic process.

To maintain a high level of practice sensitivity, multicultural practitioners must possess specific attitudes, values, skills, and knowledge. In relation to this particular family, a sensitive practitioner should not, for example, make any judgment about the family's financial situation, especially related to the lack of contribution from all members. The practitioner should praise the support from the extended family and also provide information about child development and parenting skills.

Among several possible intervention approaches or strategies for this family, the practitioner may be the following:

■ Use the *behavioral* approach to help the two children understand how they can make changes individually to build family strengths.
■ Adopt the *solution-focused* approach to resolve problems.
■ Use *family system* analyses to help the mother recognize the impact of the family experience on behavior change.
■ *Observe important family events* and help each member identify the importance of his or her ethnic heritage toward healing.

To enhance the efficacy of intervention, the practitioner would have to gather additional information from this family to identify their strengths and barriers. First, the practitioner should assess each person's level of physical and mental health functioning. Then the practitioner might construct a family tree or genogram (possibly with photos of each individual) and include information about extended family members in terms of education, occupation, socioeconomic status (SES), any history of child or spousal abuse, and any history of alcohol or drug abuse.

The practitioner should also analyze the impact that past parent–child and sibling relationships have had on current relationships. In addition, it would be helpful to identify the value placed on education for each gender to understand the two children's roles in pursuing a high-quality education. Furthermore, it would be valuable to discover each individual's perception of how religious support enhances family functioning. The practitioner might assess family support by having each person create a list of his or her support system (financially, emotionally, spiritually).

As with every family, the practitioner must build trust with each member, affirm clients' feelings, model appropriate behavior, and provide support to each member by identifying family strengths and the members' contributions. The practitioner should develop goals for each family member, identify family activities in which all family members can participate, and assess cultural values in terms of how they relate to the identified problem. Again, examining how Latino cultural values are assessed is important to determine how they can be incorporated into the intervention phase.

Best Practice Evaluation

Evaluation Stage 3: Evaluate the Family as a System

Following the second stage from chapter 5, the third stage of practice evaluation includes an evaluation of the family as a system (see chapter 1). In this chapter we use a one-group pre-test and post-test design (AB design) to demonstrate how family functioning is assessed through the standardized case family as an example.

Suggested evaluation tool: Family Assessment Measure (FAM) (Skinner, Steinhauer, & Sitarenios, 2000)

Description: This scale has four self-report components: a general scale (50 items), a dyadic relationships scale (42 items), a self-rating scale (42 items), and a brief family assessment measure (14 items). The purpose of the instrument is to assess family dynamics through a systemic approach with seven constructs: task accomplishment, role performance, communication, affective expression, involvement, control, and values and norms.

The scale was tested in both clinical and nonclinical samples, and the overall FAM had high internal consistency. The internal reliability coefficients for adults were: .93 in the general scale, .95 in dyadic relationship, and .89 in self-rating. For children these were: .94 in the general scale, .94 in dyadic relationships, and .86 in self-rating. According to Skinner, Steinhauer, and Sitarenios (1983), FAM has achieved high discriminant validity, as reported through the results from its two research samples—"problem" (clinical) and "non-problem" (non-clinical) families. The results from these samples indicated that the measure could effectively differentiate the problem families from non-problem families.

Regarding construct validity, Bloomquist and Harris (1984) reported a high correlation between the FAM general scale and the special family scales in the MMPI (Minnesota Multiphasic Personality Inventory). They found that the FAM subscales for task accomplishment, role performance, communication, affective expression, involvement, and value and norms were strongly associated with the

MMPI's "family problems" special subscale. Similarly, the MMPI "family discord" and "family attachment" special subscales were highly correlated with task accomplishment, affective expression, and values and norms.

How to use the tool: The FAM is available for purchase via the Multi-Health Systems Inc. web site at: https://www.mhs.com/ecom/(b0z5xi55a5ooux550aw2dn 45)/inventory.aspx, or at P.O. Box 950, North Tonawanda, NY 14120-0950 (Phone:1-800-268-6011 (Canada); 1-800-456-3003 (United States). The FAM is also available via Multi-Health Systems (MHS), 65 Overlea Blvd., Toronto, Ontario, Canada M4H 1P1. Phone: 416-424-1700; 1-800-268-6011 (Canada); 1-800-456-3033 (United States). MHS also published a detailed manual outlining how to use the FAM scale. Users may also visit the MHS website for additional information at www.mhs.com. The FAM scale was translated into multiple languages, including French, German, Spanish, Portuguese, Japanese and Hebrew.

How to evaluate the outcomes: As discussed in chapter 3, six steps can be used to evaluate family functioning using single system research. These steps, as applied to Joe and Mary's family with Mexican ethnicity, are as follows:

1. *Define the service target or problem (intake and case assessment):* Based on the family's own definition, each member has experienced difficulties in performing his or her family function properly.

2. *Define (or formulate) goals and objectives:* To increase the level of family functioning.

3. *Identify constraints and resources and select a treatment:* Constraints include fear and lack of trust among family members. Resources include willingness to talk among family members to resolve the issues and their strong Mexican values.

4. *Measure the monitoring actions (monitor progress):* Ask the family members to complete the FAM General Scale each week for 7 weeks (baseline A). The family systems therapy is used for 7 weeks (intervention period B) after the baseline. The practitioner records the scores for each family member each week for a total of 14 weeks.

5. *Analyze the data:* Using Mary's data as an example, the practitioner compares the average FAM general score in the baseline (70.00) with the average FAM general score in the intervention period (34.28). The data in Figure 6.1 indicate that Mary's average FAM general score is more positive in the intervention period compared to the baseline period. Because lower scores indicate better family functioning, Mary's score, which has decreased 35.72 points from her baseline average, has provided evidence of the effectiveness of treatment.

6. *Report results and make recommendations:* The practitioner helps each family member plot a graph and examine the changes in data before and during intervention. As an illustration, in addition to the average scores comparison, Mary's graph shows that her FAM general score in the 14th week (20) is significantly more positive than the score during the first week (70), indicated by a lower score, and a trend of decreasing scores shows continuous improvement

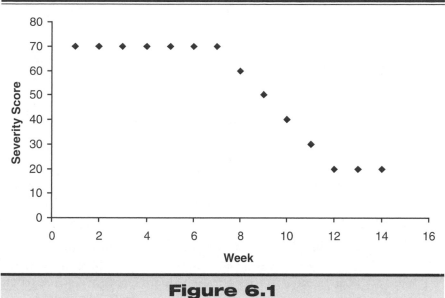

Figure 6.1
Family Assessment Measure

in family functioning. Mary's data can be compared to data from each family member to address the family's perception of issues. After 14 weeks of treating the entire family, the results suggest that the family systems therapy is effective in helping the family restore family functioning.

Multicultural Practice Exercises

Constructing a Genogram

Gather family history for at least three generations (children, parents, grandparents). Begin the genogram during a session, and ask the client and family to fill in any unknown information as a homework assignment. Genograms can be general or highly specific (see McGoldrick, Gerson, & Shellenberger, 1999).

The Therapy Triangle

Ask the client to draw an isosceles triangle. Put the name of the therapist on the top pinnacle and the names of the two individuals having communication problems below on the two equal sides. Ask the client to note how communication is directed.

Example:

MC: How does Joe make you sad?

Mary: I don't know. He hasn't been helping me lately.

MC: Who are you talking to now? Me or Joe?

Mary: You....

MC: Okay, now tell Joe. Look at him and tell him what you just told me.

Mary: Joe, you know…you haven't been helping me lately.

Joe: (Looking at MC) What's the problem? I've been really busy.

MC: Who are you talking to?

Joe: My wife.

MC: Okay then—look at Mary and repeat what you just said directly to her.

Questions from a Family of Three Generations

Have one chosen family member draw the family on a piece of paper, including his or her parents' generation and his or her grandparents' generation. Then instruct each member of the family to write down and then ask three questions about each generation. Questions can be directed to any individual in the family.

Letter Writing

If there is an unresolved conflict among two or more family members, encourage the individuals involved to each write a letter to the other person. The letter should focus on communicating about the issue, not just complaining. Encourage the use of "I" to express feelings, rather than "you" or "we." To prevent the letter writing from degenerating into venting and insults, help each of the letter writers to edit out the anger and overly emotional statements and reactions prior to delivering the letter.

Topics for Discussion

1. If family systems theory were to be applied to a sibling rivalry situation between an adopted child and a natural child, how would a practitioner know if the *differentiation-of-self* concept is applicable or not?
2. Would the techniques involving triangles be a helpful tool when children are involved in the assessment process? Why or why not? Are triangles a culturally universal concept for families?
3. What principles should supervisors or educators apply when using genograms in staffing or teaching?
4. Would the practitioner's family-of-origin issues affect how he or she sees the problems the client describes? In what ways? How can this be overcome?

Structural Theory

This chapter demonstrates the use of structural theory in working with individuals and their families. The family development stage described here focuses on families with children. The case approach with Joe's and Mary's family mapping illustrates issues related to children's independence, structural analysis of the family, family changes, and determination of priorities. The standardized case then is modified, and additional information is provided about a Native American family facing social isolation to further demonstrate the use of multicultural perspectives in the assessment and treatment process. In the best practice evaluation process, problem assessment should be conducted sensitively with input gathered from the clients. The recommended tool is the Family Assessment Device (FAD), which is utilized for assessing six dimensions of family functioning.

A Focus on Family Structure

The structural approach to family therapy was developed by Salvador Minuchin (1921–), who studied pediatrics in the early 1950s and began his psychoanalytic training in 1954 (Goldenberg & Goldenberg, 2004). After studying the interactions of children and adolescents in their families, Minuchin (1974) found that mental distress usually stemmed from issues related to the family structure, and that the closeness or distance among family members determined their interaction patterns. These patterns of communication, in turn, influence individual behaviors.

In addition to examining the structural formation of families, structural theory provides a framework by which to analyze family transaction patterns to better understand mental health symptoms or issues (Goldenberg & Goldenberg, 2004). This theory purports that the well-being of family members is influenced by the organizational structure, the sense of wholeness and togetherness, and the interdependent functioning of its members (Minuchin, 1974). This theory utilizes a structuralism perspective, in which the exchange of roles and responsibilities among family members helps to maintain the function or reinforce the behavior within a family (Turner, 1982).

Structural Theory in Brief

Application to Multicultural Practices:
- It applies to analyses that deal with authority, power, and control within a system.

Major Figure:
- Salvador Minuchin (1921–): Family Structure

Assumptions:
- Behavior within a family is a product of the family structure.
- The identified client's symptom is a manifestation of structural problems in the family.
- How a family organizes itself is important to the well-being and effective psycho-functioning of the members.

Therapeutic Process:
- Assesses the family rules and structure.

Goals:
- To restructure the family (to support or not support certain behaviors).
- To assist family members in learning alternative and/or more satisfying ways of relating with one another.

Multicultural Practice Techniques:
- Homeostasis analysis: Analyze the balance in each of the family members' roles and responsibilities within the family.
- "Alignments" exercise: Understand how one family member relies on another to be an ally to fight against a third family member.
- Detouring analysis (see example in case demonstration): Use visuals that focus on how changing the course of interactions between two or more family members could change the perception of relationships with each other.

Structural theory applies to multicultural families because the perceived level of functioning for many families is affected by how members define their roles and responsibilities in relation to others. Minuchin argues that rigidity in definition of roles and responsibilities within the family can create mental distress and communication problems, especially between parents and their children. In his work with immigrant families, Minuchin found that this rigidity can often be seen as a barrier to communication among family members, especially when parents hold on to more traditional values than their more acculturated children. Like family systems theory, structural theory focuses on analyzing family interaction patterns as a way for the family to understand each person's perception of the other members' needs or problems. Structural Theory uniquely connects family interactions to the roles perceived and played by each family member and uses the knowledge of these connections within the family culture to identify any maladaptive behavior.

Regardless of culture, families are the primary source in determining each members' individual concepts of functional demands, that is, perceptions of how to effectively perform a designated task, which govern the behavior of individuals in the society (Turner, 1982). Structural theory, with its focus on power differentials, can be applied to the analysis of many situations within a family's boundaries (Minuchin, 1974). The analysis emphasizes how two members' current roles affect how they interact with each other.

In multicultural practice, structural theory addresses "problems that are inherent in our present social order and, therefore, the focus of change should be mainly on social structures not individuals" (Payne, 2005, p. 237). In cases in which acculturation is an issue, clients will be directed to address structural composition in the family to attempt to understand how family communication is affected by the different perceptions of roles and responsibilities. Addressing the family's needs is the first step in getting acquainted with the family, even if the practitioner is not familiar with the family's customs or culture. The family may join together and connect more naturally when they are seeking to address a concern related to the family's structural roles than when confronting the functional (or dysfunctional) roles of any particular individual.

On the Multicultural Stage: Families with Children

Views regarding the role of children within families vary considerably by culture. Some cultures consider children to be a source of support for the family in the future, and others see having children as an obligation. For example, in Asian and Latino cultures, children are expected to care for the family physically, financially, socially, and psychologically when they are adults (Chang, 2003; Brendel & Sustaeta, 2003). In some countries, families' childrearing practices are restricted by national policy (for example, the "one child policy" in China), they may have limited access to family planning methods based on national policy or priorities (for example predominantly Muslim countries, rural India, Catholic countries), or they are encouraged to bear more children to counteract their population decline (for example, in some western European countries and recently in Hong Kong).

Regardless of this variation, the ultimate goal of structural theory–based therapy is that a family's structure determines the interaction patterns among its members and creates a certain rigidity in its definition of roles and responsibilities. In a family with children, the ultimate goal of therapy is to help the family reexamine each member's roles and expectations, develop appropriate boundaries between subsystems (such as parents, siblings, and parent–child relationships), and strengthen each person's understanding of the family's hierarchical order.

An analysis of the family's subsystems, boundaries, alignments, and coalitions helps each person understand the function or dysfunction of the family's current structure. According to this theory, family relationships may be drawn out by means of family mapping, to chart the family's current relationship connections (Figure 7.1). With an understanding of interpersonal communication and relationship patterns, clients will begin to see which efforts are necessary to alter rigid and unacceptable structures between or among members. By joining the family and adopting its communication style, such as repeating each of the members' word usage, the therapist will help each member observe how to define and transform the family structure to improve the overall functioning for all members. Structural theory assumes that the family's dysfunctional structure must be modified before the therapist can help to motivate anyone to make individual changes.

The Case Approach

The client, Mary, is working with the practitioner to identify how her emotions are affected by recent family changes. Utilizing structural analysis techniques, the practitioner shows Mary how to approach her issues with a sense of family stability by taking concrete actions. These issues demonstrate structural therapeutic skills: issues with children, structural analysis, family changes, and priority setting.

Issue #1: Issues with Children

This is the second individual session with Mary. She is not comfortable at the beginning of the session—avoiding eye contact, speaking rapidly, and fidgeting with her clothing.

MC: Mary, during our last session we were talking about your children. I remember you told me that Ami is leaving home soon for college, and it is hard for you to see her go. Can you talk more about that?

Accommodation and Joining

Mary: It's hard. It's even harder to imagine what I'm going to do after both Ami and Kevin have left.

Joe: (F) Father;
Mary: (M) Mother, also the Identified Patient (IP)

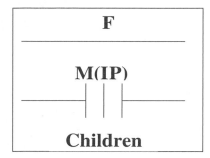

There is a rigid boundary between Joe and Mary. Mary is overinvolved with her children.

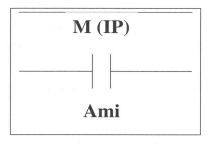

More specifically, Mary has a conflict with Ami, who is more vocal about her objection to her mother's overinvolvement.

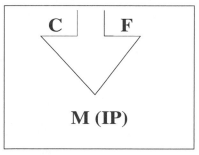

The children and the father all hold Mary responsible for their difficulties in transitioning to a new family life stage.

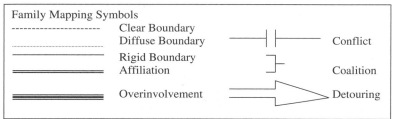

Figure 7.1
Family Mapping of Mary's Family

MC: You sound as though you're going to be alone very soon.

Tracking

Mary: Well, I know I won't be alone. I just don't know anymore…. (silent)

MC: What's bothering you right now?

Mary: I think I'm always the problem in this family. They don't seem to care … but I do have a lot of problems…

MC: Wait! Don't convince yourself that you're the problem.

Restructuring

Mary: It's hard not to see it that way.

MC: What do you mean?

Mary: I mean that my body is breaking down on me.

MC: You sound upset, but you still haven't told me what the problem is.

Mary: Everything is a problem. I can't sleep. I think about things too much, and I cry at almost everything and nothing. I just don't feel good about myself.

MC: That's why you think you're the problem?

Mary: Yes. Also, I can't concentrate, and I'm always doing everything for everyone else.

MC: What exactly are you doing for everyone?

Mary: I do everything around the house, in my school, with the kids. If I'm not around to do all these things, then….

MC: Then what would happen?

Tracking

Mary: Then everything will fall apart.

MC: Who told you that?

Mary: No one. No one had to. I just know.

MC: Mary, maybe you're right. There's no way around it. You have to do everything so nothing will fall apart. Tell everyone in the family and at work that you're going to do everything for everyone else. Call your friends and tell them you're going to do their laundry, iron their clothes, and feed their dogs and cats. If you still feel like you have time, cook for your neighbors, too. Is it enough?

Paradoxical Constructions

Mary: (Laughing a little) You think I'm crazy. I don't think I have time to do all of that.

MC: No, I just want you to think about your thought process and the way you hear what your family members say to you. Didn't you say you do everything for everyone else? Don't Joe and the kids think that Mom can do everything?

Mary:	I know I exaggerated that a little.
MC:	No, I think you're overfunctioning because you want to get closer to your family and your friends.

Reframing

Mary:	I think I'd better talk about this intention to be closer to my family with Joe and the kids. I don't want them to think that the reason I got a job was to get rid of them.

Issue #2: Structural Analysis

In a family session, because the clients have begun to recognize that the family structure may be causing some communication problems, the therapist decides to help them reexamine their role in these problems by conducting a structural analysis.

Mary:	They think I'm the problem. I'm always upset and nervous.
MC:	Is it *you* as a person who is the problem?... How?
Mary:	Yes, it's me. I just ... I want to do something for myself, but I feel nervous about getting it done.
MC:	So it's the behavior of not getting things done that's the problem then, not *you.*
Mary:	You're right. I shouldn't call myself a "problem."
MC:	Right. So who else in the family thinks the problem is about not getting things done?

Joining

Joe:	I think the problem is Mary worrying about getting a new job. She's just fine.
Ami:	I think Mom has too much to do.
Kevin:	Mom is fine.
MC:	It seems that your family has a structure of "doing."
Mary:	What do you mean?
MC:	Everyone is structured around what you're doing.

Structural Perspective

Mary:	Yes, I don't feel happy if I can't finish what I'm supposed to do.
MC:	Wow—I can never finish all my work. Then, I guess by that logic, I shouldn't ever be happy.

Paradoxical Restructuring

Joe:	It's just Mary.

MC:	Is it Mary's problem or the family's problem?
Joe:	I guess now it has become the family's problem.
MC:	Joe, Mary is really concerned about not completing her work at home. What can you do to address her concern?
Joe:	I tried to help, but Mary just didn't let me! She has her own way of working things out.
MC:	Mary, what do you think about what Joe just said?
Mary:	I don't know.
MC:	What is your role in this family?
Mary:	A wife and mother.
MC:	That's the traditional way of looking at your role. Are there any other creative ways of looking at it?

Restructuring

MC:	(Everyone is silent) Kevin, how do you see your family?
Kevin:	Me? I see a ball. It goes round and round.
MC:	What do you mean?
Kevin:	Like a ball you pass around. It starts from Mom and comes back to her at the end.
MC:	Wow—that's great, Kevin. So the ball is like all the family responsibilities? Ami, how do you see yourself interacting with this ball?

Metaphor

Ami:	I don't. I can't see myself.
Mary:	You just don't want to be there.
MC:	Ami, how do you feel about not being there or not seeing yourself being there?
Ami:	I guess I'm there but not really there.
MC:	That's a feeling. Mary, what role do you want Ami to play inside of this family structure?

Focusing on Structure

Mary:	To be one of us. To help out when I ask.
Ami:	You always ask me to do something, but you end up doing it yourself.
Mary:	That's because you don't do it.
Ami:	I would do it. I just…. Just give me some time to do stuff.
Mary:	I like to be clean.
MC:	Okay—so you're on different timetables then. And maybe you have different sets of standards for what a job well done looks like. Let's explore that….

Issue #3: Family Changes

This session started with a discussion about the issues that are important to each of the family members. Joe mentioned that he doesn't like the way Ami dresses and that she "bends the house rules" at times, and Mary pointed out that Ami has been ignoring her curfew.

The therapist took out a *detouring* wand (a yardstick with an arrow tied to one end) and asked Mary to hold it with the arrow pointing toward Joe. The purpose of using the detouring wand is for both of them to visualize how a joint effort may affect Ami's behavior. The remaining dialogue demonstrates how the family can examine each person's expectations of belonging and separation so boundaries between family members can be defined more clearly.

MC:	I have another wand. (Takes another yard stick and hands to Joe) Joe, take this wand and share what you think has to change for Ami to come home on time.
Joe:	(Taking the wand and pointing it at Ami) I would like her to come home for dinner and show more respect. And when she comes home, I would like her not to stay in her room all the time.
MC:	Joe, you just restated that you want Ami to come home. You haven't responded about how to help Ami change her behavior.
Joe:	I don't know how.
MC:	Ami, take the wand.
Ami:	(Quietly)…. I don't want to.
Mary:	You have to.
MC:	Ami, tell us what you would like to see happen.
Ami:	(Silent)
MC:	Okay…you can think about it for a minute. Mary, let's go to you. What do you want from Ami? Go ahead and take the wand.
Mary:	I really don't know. Ami has been fighting with Dad more than usual.
MC:	Mary, take the wand and put it in front of Ami with the arrow pointing at Joe.

Detouring

MC:	Now what do you see?
Mary:	I see Joe as a commander and Ami as resisting his commands … Ami is making him upset.
MC:	Ami, what do you see?
Ami:	I see them making me do stuff I don't want to.
MC:	Why would they do that?
Ami:	They say they want to protect me.

MC:	Hmmm…. How do you feel about that?
Ami:	I belong to this family, but I don't want to be controlled. I'm grown. I can make some of my own decisions.
MC:	Okay…. Now Joe, take both wands and point one toward Mary and the other one toward Ami. Ami, what do you see now?
Ami:	I see Dad's constant demands on us.
MC:	Okay, now Ami, you take the wands and point the arrows from you to your parents. What do you see?
Ami:	That I have been demanding to them too…. I don't really mean to be, but I know I am.
MC:	Okay, good. So let's talk about this. Joe … Mary—what are your thoughts about this exercise?
Joe:	I think we need two arrows on the wands—going back and forth. So it's not just demands from me to Ami or Ami to us, but more like we can talk about things. So we can respond to each other.
Mary:	I think so, too. More back and forth is needed. Not just one-way communication when we're talking to each other.
Ami:	Sometimes I would feel like talking if they'd allow me to speak.

Issue #4: Setting Priorities

In this session the family is planning to work toward a common goal and set priorities together. The dialogue demonstrates techniques used in the structural approach.

MC:	Today I'd like to talk about your experiences this week now that we've looked at some of the behavior patterns in your family. Joe, would you start us off?

Joining

Joe:	Sure. To me, things seemed to be a little bit better. But I guess it seems like Mary is still feeling bad and pretty stressed out.
MC:	Is that true, Mary?
Mary:	Not really. I mean, no more than usual. I've just been really busy with the house, laundry, garden, and everything else. I guess I've been tired. There's just not enough time to do all the things I should be doing.
MC:	Okay … well, let me ask you something. Who decides what you *should* be doing in your house? Who decides who is responsible for things?

Restructuring

Mary:	I don't know who *decides*. But I've always done all the household chores. My mother took care of our household. I left home and married Joe, and now my household is my responsibility. That's just the way it is.

MC: Okay—well, let's think about something. Pretend that the household isn't solely your responsibility, What if other family members have chores that are their responsibilities? Imagine what that would look like. Start by thinking about a typical Saturday at your home? What would each of you be doing?

Enactment

Joe: Well, I usually read the paper in the morning, and then in the afternoon I work on whatever I brought home from the office.

Ami: (Annoyed) Saturday is my mall day.

Kevin: I usually go to my friend Jerry's house to play video games.

Mary: (Laughing slightly) Well—I cook breakfast, do laundry, dust, mop the floor, water the plants, vacuum, clean the bathrooms, go grocery shopping—take care of all the little things I didn't get to during the week.

MC: Okay, good. Let's get up and move around a little, okay? We're going to act out our Saturday.

SCENE: (All family members pretend to do what they said they usually do. Everyone is calmly and slowly moving, some are sitting still, but Mary is rushing around—cooking, folding laundry, vacuuming, watering plants, dusting, sweeping—somewhat frantic.)

MC: Oh my goodness! Mary! No wonder you're tired. Do you see how much you're moving compared to the others?! Okay, now let's restructure that scene. This time everyone has to take one chore instead of their usual Saturday activity. Ami, can you vacuum? Joe, how about if you make breakfast? Kevin, you sweep.

Mary: (Smiling, looking confused)

MC: Mary, you can water the plants. Okay—begin!

(Scene continues for a few minutes until the therapist stops them.)

Restructuring

MC: Great job! Okay, let me ask you, Mary—how did that feel?

Mary: It felt kind of nice to have everyone pitching in.

MC: I bet. Okay, everyone, your assignment for next Saturday is to enact this for real. Then I want you to spend at least fifteen minutes talking about how it felt and how things could be better for each of you. Then the rest of the afternoon can be free for you all to do what you usually do.

Issuing Directives

Joe: (Raises hands in air, frustrated) I still don't understand why we have to change things. If Mary starts working, everything at home will be in shambles. Everything is fine as long as Mary keeps doing her wonderful job at being a mother and a wife. We don't have to change anything!

Structural Theory Techniques

Alignment: Explain how family members join or oppose each other in a given activity.

Detouring: Visualize how the alliances between two or more individuals in the family are built and changed by examining how the united pair hold other members responsible for a problem.

Enactment: Ask the family to visualize and function during the therapy session as in the home situation. This allows the therapist to understand the family's current structure. First, direct the family to think and act on how each subsystem (e.g. the couple, the children, mother and children, father and children) usually interact when they have to make a decision or deal with an issue or problem.

Family Mapping: Make a chart with family members' names, relationships, and connective lines to show organizational and transactional patterns within a given family.

Issuing Directives: Empower each member to work on homework assignments or exercises that will bring about change or improve interactions and relationships.

Joining with the Family: A three-step rapport building process to gain comfort when working with the client/family:

1. Tracking: Adopt the family's way of thinking about the situation.
2. Accommodating: Relate to the family's current rules and roles.
3. Mimesis: Become like a family member by adopting the family's style of communication.

Metaphor: Make use of clients' symbols or life forces to represent feelings, thoughts, and experiences during interpersonal interactions within a close system.

Paradoxical Constructions: Provide the family with a different (and even opposite) frame of experiencing the current situation to stimulate reactions toward change.

Reframing: Place an event or problem within a new context. Relabel what would occur to obtain a new perspective to resolve difficult feelings associated with the event or problem.

Structural Modification/Perspective: By means of an analysis of the family's structure, the therapist will examine the interactions of its members in order to achieve the following objectives:

1. Challenge the current family reality.
2. Create new subsystems and boundaries.

(continued)

3. Block dysfunctional transactional patterns.
4. Reinforce new and adaptive family structure.
5. Educate about family change.

Symptom Focusing: A reframing technique that examines the behavioral symptom of an identified client from an alternative perspective (i.e., things are different than they look):

1. Re-label the symptom.
2. Alter the affect or emotional expression of the symptom.
3. Expand the symptom.
4. Exaggerate the symptom.
5. Deemphasize the symptom.
6. Move the focus to a new symptom.

Ami: (Enthusiastically) Yeah! I agree with you, Dad. Why should Mom get a job and abandon us and dump all her responsibilities on our shoulders?

Mary: Ami, how could you say this!

MC: (Overexaggerating) Ami, wait a minute! I bet it would be *so* convenient for you when your mom was at work that you'd have a lot of freedom. With this freedom, your mom wouldn't pick up after you, make your lunches, wash your clothes, and make your beds. You'd have to iron your clothes by yourself, too! Joe, you would take these responsibilities if the kids demand it.

Paradoxical Construction

Joe: (Annoyed) It's not that we can't do these things, but Mary cares about us. I'm thinking about her feelings more than anything else. If she starts working, she may feel that she's abandoning us.

MC: Okay. Let's ask her…. Mary, do you think you'll feel that?

Mary: (Gathering courage; voice rises slightly; sits a little higher in chair) No. I don't think I'll be abandoning Joe and the kids. Working is just something I want to do at this point in my life. I want to do something where I can say, "I did this on my own" or, "I accomplished something." (Turns to Joe) Just because I'll be working doesn't mean that I don't love you and the kids.

Differentiation

MC: Okay, let's look at Mary's desire to work not as abandonment but, rather, as an independent goal that she wants to accomplish.

Symptom Focusing

Mary:	No matter what happens, I'll never leave you. You'll always be my number-one priority.
Joe:	I agree.
Ami:	I just want more freedom.

Multicultural Practice Applications

In families with more rigid concepts of gender roles or traditional concepts of familial roles, it is difficult to involve every member in the discussion of alignment and detouring. In the case of Mary and Joe, if Joe does not want to attend therapy or is reluctant to participate in any of the activities, theorists would respond in a variety of ways. Although some theorists think it is important to address his feelings, structural theorists suggest that the emphasis should be on analyzing his reluctance with a focus on family structure.

MC:	Joe, I'm glad to see you today.
Joe:	Well, I'm not sure why I agreed to be here. But here I am.
Mary:	I'm surprised he made the time to come in. He never has time for me.
MC:	Joe, it's important for Mary that you're here today.
Joe:	I'm here because she nagged me all week about it.
Mary:	Joe, come on. You know how hard it is for me to ask for anything for myself.
MC:	I'm sure this is hard for you, Joe. Let's explore how this might be a family structure issue.

Using enactment as a tool can be an effective technique to integrate the family structure into discussion. Many people, however, do not feel comfortable enacting a role in front of others, especially to explore sensitive issues like disciplining a child or disagreeing with a significant other. For example, in the exercise above with the detouring wand, Ami expressed that the exercise was too childish. In Joe's situation, he may even refuse to enact a family scene, thinking it is not his responsibility or not in his interest.

MC:	Joe, you stated earlier that Mary works hard. What do you mean?
Joe:	Well, I guess it started when Mary decided to go back to school. She still didn't ask for help. Ami is old enough to do some of the cooking, but Mary didn't ask her to help out with any of the household chores.
MC:	I think Mary likes to be the caretaker.

Reframing

Joe:	I guess she wants to be a responsible wife and mother.
Mary:	I just do my part.

MC:	Would you talk a little about what part you are playing, Mary?
Mary:	The housewife, mother, wife…
MC:	What is in these roles that you cannot ask for help?
Mary:	I have to do it so that I feel comfortable about being myself.
MC:	It sounds like it is all your decision.
Joe:	No, she just wouldn't listen.
Mary:	I don't know how to ask when you are not even showing any interest in these chores.
Joe:	I admit. I'm not interested. But it doesn't mean I cannot help. Think about the cancelled trip. It was caused by your not asking for help.
MC:	Joe, tell me about the cancelled trip.
Joe:	I canceled a leisure trip because of her.
Mary:	I was too sick that evening to handle anything, and I asked Joe not to go on that trip.
MC:	Let's reenact that evening for me.
Joe:	What?
MC:	Reenacting the situation might give you some insight as you're reexperiencing that event just like it is happening now.
Joe:	Okay!
MC:	Joe, I want you to start at the point when you walked in the door that evening, thinking about packing for the next day's trip.
Joe:	I smelled the food and said, "I'm home. Is dinner ready?"
Mary:	No, it's not ready. I'm too tired.
Joe:	What do you mean—you're too tired? Aren't you excited about tomorrow?
Mary:	I'm sick. I can't go.
Joe:	What?! Everything is ready, and you're telling me this now?
Mary:	I'm just too tired.
MC:	How did you feel when you heard Mary say that, Joe?
Joe:	I canceled the trip.
MC:	I know you did. But how did you feel just now when you heard Mary repeat what she said that evening?
Joe:	It's funny. Now I have a different feeling.
MC:	What is it?
Joe:	I felt angry that evening because I had to cancel the trip. Now I can actually feel sympathy for Mary because she was absolutely too tired to go.
Mary:	Thank you for understanding. I felt so guilty that I was actually sick for a few days.

Variations From the Standardized Case: A Native American Family

Assessing the cultural expectations of the clients and their family is important. The standardized case has been modified to represent a Native American family whose cultural expectations stem from the historical heritage of ancestors from both the maternal and the paternal sides of the family.

***

Joe and Mary have been married for 20 years, and they have two children, Ami and Kevin. Joe is of Navajo descent, and Mary is a Cheyenne. Joe's middle name is Hastiin, a Navajo name meaning "man," and Mary kept her maiden name, Knife, as her middle name because she believes her family are descendants of Chief Dull Knife, a prominent American Indian who signed the Treaty of Fort Laramie in 1868.

The family recently moved from a reservation into a suburb of a big city. At times Mary feels depressed and wonders why she has such a difficult time making friends outside of her own community. She senses that people turn away from her, and she does not understand why. On occasion Mary misses the life she had on the reservation because she felt more understood by others there. She realizes, though, that she and Joe moved to this current apartment so their children can attend a reputable school.

Recently Joe started drinking more frequently—an added concern for Mary. Ami currently is a sophomore in high school, where she receives average grades. Mary has been bothered that Ami has been staying out past curfew, frequently going out without telling her parents. Kevin is doing well in the third grade, but Mary has recognized that when Joe drinks, Kevin tends to pull away and become isolated. Mary tries to help the children understand some of the problems that can be associated with drinking and has been watching them more closely, demanding that they call home every hour when they are out with friends, and doing all the chores for them so they will have a stronger desire to be home.

Issue #1: Family Expectations

MC:	Joe, how have you been?
Joe:	I started running last week to get rid of my problems.
MC:	Running?
Joe:	Yes, I joined the marathon club. I think it will help me have more energy and get rid of my drinking habit.
MC:	Tell me about your drinking habit.
Joe:	Usually when I get up in the middle of the night, I think of my family on the reservation. When I couldn't sleep, I drank a little. When I got up in the morning, I couldn't help but drink another shot or two. When Mary started to attend college, I noticed that I drank a little more. She

told me that I couldn't drink in the apartment because it might affect Kevin. Last week after talking with you, I decided to join a health club, but I found this interesting guy who told me about the marathon club. Now I run every day.

MC: How does running affect your view about drinking?

Joe: It helps me concentrate on my body. When I'm running, I also think about Mary and the kids. I shouldn't oppose Mary's desire to get a job. I should quit drinking so I can be strong again to get a promotion. With more income, Mary won't feel obligated to help out on the financial part.

MC: Is Mary's job all about extra income?

Joe: Not really. Mary wants to use her knowledge, I guess.

MC: In your family-of-origin—your parents' household—did your mom work when you were in high school?

Joe: No. Mom took care of us.

MC: Does it mean that Mary's work will take her away from taking care of you?

Joe: No. I never feel this way. But for some reason I feel that I haven't provided enough for her, and that's why she wants to work.

MC: This is a strong feeling. Let's look at your family structure—mom staying home while dad works. Is this what you both want?

Joe: Well, that would be ideal, but, … I know, the world is different now. And that's why I wouldn't mind being a weak husband.

MC: What's your definition of being a weak husband?

Joe: Not able to provide everything for my family.

MC: To you, is drinking a way to hide your feelings about being a weak husband?

Joe: No, I don't think so.

MC: Joe, you're not a weak husband. In your family structure, there has always been a rigid definition of who you are. When something has changed, the image of being a nurturing husband has shifted. You tried to find a way to express it but couldn't. Do you think there's any truth to this observation?

Joe: I think you're right. I'm probably not weak, but I just didn't know how to express myself.

Issue #2: Joe's Alcohol Use

MC: Mary, you've told me before how upset you will be when your children leave home. Why don't we talk about this a little bit since your children are here today?

Mary:	Ami isn't home most days. I think she isn't comfortable with the apartment. I'm sure that when she goes off to college, she won't come back. Ami knows that I don't like the way she dresses, and she's been breaking all the family rules.
MC:	Ami, what do you think?
Ami:	Me? I have nothing to say.
MC:	Would you like to explain?
Ami:	I'm not going to bother her. She has too much on her plate already.
Mary:	What do you mean? I'm here to help you understand that your behavior isn't acceptable.
MC:	We're here to communicate. I sense some dissatisfaction. Now, Mary, tell us about Kevin.
Mary:	Kevin is sweet. He's very sensitive to his father's drinking because I told him that alcoholism is genetic—it's in his blood. Kevin has been extremely quiet lately. I guess he knows his dad is drinking again. I'm concerned.
MC:	Kevin, would you like to say something about your mom's comments?
Kevin:	I think Mom is right. I would never drink. I don't like to talk about Dad. Besides, I'm sad to see that Ami is constantly fighting with Mom, but I know my sister isn't a drinker.
MC:	It sounds like something is happening in your family. First let's focus on Joe's drinking.
Mary:	I told Joe not to drink in front of the kids. I bought him some books to read. He joined AA once, but then he decided he could quit drinking without help. He doesn't like the people at AA.
MC:	Did he tell you what kind of people he dislikes?
Mary:	He doesn't like to be looked down on. He told me that some of the people there thought he was trying to get on welfare. He thought people were discriminating against him.
MC:	Did he talk about how he could quit drinking without help?
Mary:	Not really! I tried to help him by not allowing him to bring any liquor home—even beer.
MC:	Who's responsible for controlling Joe's drinking in the family?
Mary:	I guess it was me—until I felt sad that I wasn't able to tell him anything.
MC:	When was that?
Mary:	It was … when Ami started to come home after curfew.
MC:	What is the connection between these two things—Joe's drinking and Ami's breaking her curfew?

Mary: It was me. Joe doesn't think curfew is important, but now I'm not able to tell them what's expected of them because I'm too sad myself.

MC: Ami, can you help your mom help your dad?

Ami: I didn't know that my curfew was all that important to Mom. Now I know. But, I don't know how to help.

MC: Mary, how would you like Ami to help?

Mary: I don't know. I just don't want to deal with so many things at once.

Ami: I'll come home early, okay?

Mary: That's my girl. I only want the best for you. (Looks at MC) I get anxious every time we talk about Joe's issue. In his family no one could argue with him, not even his own mother.

MC: How about his father?

Mary: His father hasn't talked to him for a long time now. They clashed every time when they used to talk, and now that we moved away from the reservation, his father doesn't talk to us anymore.

MC: Now your family is maintaining a family structure where Joe isn't making decisions for his own drinking or for Ami's behavior. You said you were afraid of the kids not coming home. Actually, you aren't comfortable being the person who tells everyone what to do. Joe has waited for you to be the one who makes the family decisions. Is there any truth to your roles of being a protector, decision-maker, connector, and problem-solver?

Mary: I know I'm tired. Now I know I'm the connector. I'll sit down to talk about my feelings with Ami. Now that she understands me a little better, I hope she'll help me feel comfortable by being home more often. Kevin needs his sister, too.

Kevin: Yep!

Experts Say...

Dr. Christine Lowery, University of Wisconsin at Milwaukee, identified a number of factors that may impact a Native American family, including socioeconomic, political, and cultural factors. At first glance, it appears that this family is socially and possibly culturally isolated. Dr. Lowery stated that a practitioner would need more information on this case before beginning the assessment and intervention process, especially related to their cultural practice, customs, family values, and socioeconomic background. Such information builds a base for the practitioner so that he or she can closely examine both internal and external factors that have built the current structure of the family.

Assessment: The family may have moved primarily because of Kevin. Ami makes average grades, and the family lived on the reservation for most of her school career. Assessing the reasons for the move, how the family came to the attention of the social worker, and the individual and family expectations is important. The social worker should also ask for details about individual and family activities and personal identities on the reservation and in the new environment. This information should yield some details about the family's social, spiritual, and cultural selves, including individual and family strengths and goals.

In addition, geography makes a difference for American Indians who may (or may not) be tied to the land, depending on whether they are part of the ceremonial community in their Indian or near-Indian environment. At home, the family would probably be a part of social networks (kin, friendships, employment, school, community). The social worker should ask how long the family lived on the reservation and their history there. Whom did they leave behind? How often do they return?

Experiences of racism also should be assessed. As many American Indians know, some communities are more racist than others, and this may be connected to geography. American Indians may have different racial or racism experiences in South Dakota than in New Mexico, where the Hispanic population is dominant. Coming from a social setting where one doesn't experience racism with one's own people (though there is intertribal prejudice) to a situation where racism is a daily experience could be quite stressful for the whole family.

Social class also should be considered. Did the family have a different social class standing in the reservation community? How has this changed? Critically, one partner may be more culturally comfortable in the suburban area than the other, and this should be explored.

The family's financial situation should be assessed. How is Joe's work? What are the demands? Does Mary have a job?

As far as Joe's drinking—is it with people from work or alone? His coping skills and current and previous drinking patterns should be assessed. Does Mary have a drinking history? She may be depressed, and this should be assessed. Assessment of Ami's and Kevin's developmental, emotional, and social needs must also be considered. What has the new school environment demanded of them? How have they had to change in response? Have they developed the coping skills needed for a school with people to whom they may not have close ties?

Intervention: Because Mary feels so isolated, a first step may be to foster American Indian connections in the new community. Often, families relocate where there is an existing network of kin, friends, or tribal members already established in the area. A cross-country move—which is likely in the professions (medicine, law, academic settings) where social and cultural networks may not be well known—could be an exception. Still, the Indian "moccasin telegraph," national conferences or paw-wows, email, and the Internet all allow for potential connections. In addition, many large cities have established Indian centers—gathering places for those who are longing for home, for those who have always been in urban areas, and for non-Indians who support Indian causes or just enjoy being with Indian people.

Other interventions should address relationship issues. After 14 years, Mary and Joe's parenting styles have been established, but they may be undergoing a change in power because of the environment or because the family is at a different developmental stage. The social worker should assess what unexpected changes Joe and Mary have seen in their children. Joe and Mary are from different tribes, one matriarchal and the other patriarchal. How do they interpret gender roles as they become older and in this new setting? How does this impact leadership, roles, and responsibilities in the family, including parenting? Changing communication styles and interactions are important to understand in this developing family. One way to examine their interactions is to ask about their views toward parental authority and address equality issues within the family.

Best Practice Evaluation

Evaluation Stage 4: Assess Problems Within the Family

Following the third stage of connecting two families from chapter 6, practice–evaluation integration in this chapter addresses the fourth stage of assessing problems within the family. We will use a post-test design with comparison group to demonstrate how to assess problems with a family.

Suggested Evaluation Tool: Family Assessment Device (FAD) (Epstein, Baldwin, & Bishop, 1983)

Description: The FAD contains 60 items to measure six dimensions of family functioning: problem solving, communication, roles, affective responsiveness, affective involvement, and behavior control. It also includes an overall general functioning measure. The scale has achieved internal reliability ranging from .72 to .92. It has also demonstrated some degree of concurrent validity, evidenced by a strong correlation with the Locke-Wallace Marital Satisfaction Scale. The FAD also predicts scores on the Philadelphia Geriatric Morale Scale.

How to use the tool: Readers may contact Dr. Epstein at the Family Research Program, Butler Hospital, 345 Blackstone Boulevard, Providence, RI 92906 for a copy of the scale or review the scale via the book by Fischer and Corcoran (1994), *Measures for clinical practice: A sourcebook* (2nd Ed., Volume 1) (pp. 239–242), New York: The Free Press. This 60-item measure uses a 4-point Likert-type scale with the following responses, 1 = strongly agree, 2 = agree, 3 = disagree and 4 = strongly disagree. Lower scores indicate more positive functioning in the family. Based on a study of 503 subjects, Epstein, Baldwin and Bishop (1983) report the means for the subscales of a clinical sample as follows: 2.20 for Problem Solving, 2.15 for Communication, 2.22 for Roles, 2.23 for Affective Responsiveness, 2.05 for Affective Involvement, 1.90 for Behavior Control, and 1.96 for General Functioning. The FAD is available from the Family Research Program, Butler Hospital, 345 Blackstone Blvd, Providence, RI, 92906.

How to evaluate the outcomes: As discussed in chapter 3, six evaluation steps are used to assess the family functioning using the single-system research design. These steps are demonstrated with Joe and Mary's family of Native American ethnicity.

1. *Define the service target or problem (intake and case assessment):* The family members have problems communicating with one another. Because their roles are unclear, family functioning has been disturbed.

2. *Define (or formulate) goals and objectives:* To increase the level of family functioning.

3. *Identify constraints and resources and select a treatment:* Constraints include the husband's alcohol use problem and social isolation. Resources include the wife's willingness to seek help and family members' strong Native American family values.

4. *Measure the monitoring actions (monitor progress):* Mary is referred to the practitioner for structural family therapy. From a research point of view, she represents the experimental group. From a clinical perspective, she is the one who will be helped to reframe family problems. Mary is asked to complete the FAD General Scale each week immediately after treatment has started for 7 weeks.

   The practitioner records the score each week. The scores are plotted in Figure 7.2. A parent from another family, Ann, who faces similar family issues, cannot participate in the treatment program due to her current job commitments. Ann has agreed to fill out the FAD General Scale in the same 7-week period while waiting for her work to slow down before coming to treatment. Ann is regarded as the comparison group because she is not receiving the treatment. Ann's scores are plotted in Figure 7.3.

5. *Analyze data:* The average FAD General Scale scores can be computed based on the seven observations in the experimental group and in the comparison group. Mary's average FAD General Scale score (1.28) is lower than Ann's (4.00), which indicates that Mary's family functioning is better than Ann's.

6. *Report results and make recommendations:* The results suggest that the structural family therapy has been effective in helping Mary to obtain a better perception of family functioning. For the nonparticipating clients, the practitioner can use average data from several clients in both the experimental group and the comparison group to plot two graphs to demonstrate (e.g., to Ann) that treatment will help achieve better family functioning. For confidentiality, no name will be attached to any examples shown to clients.

Multicultural Practice Exercises

1. Examining the Structure of the Family
   - Ask the family to write something down to represent the expected family structure.
   - Use sticky notes for each family member to write down the perceived role of one chosen family member.
   - Write down five characteristics (one on each sticky note) about this person and post it on the wall.

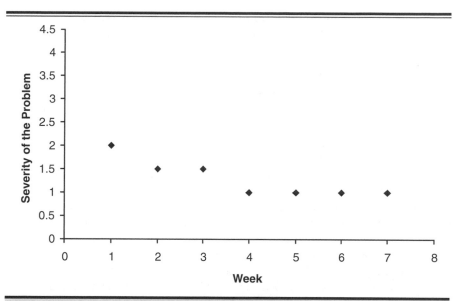

Figure 7.2
Family Assessment Device General Scale Score: Experimental Group

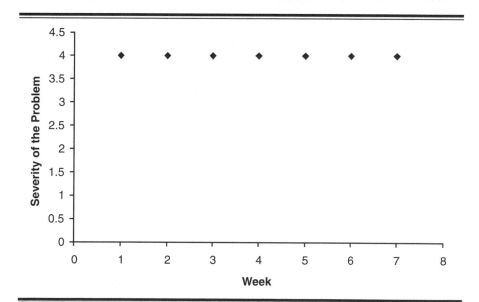

Figure 7.3
Family Assessment Device General Scale Score: Non-equivalent Group

- Have each person find his or her role and five characteristics.
- Discuss how all of these roles and characteristics fit the expected family structure.

2. Detriangulating the Child

   - Ask each family member to draw a triangle and then place the name of each family member next to an angle. If there are more than three participants, place more than one name next to an angle.
   - Use lines to indicate the relationship (close, distance, conflictual) between each pair of individuals.
   - Remove one child at a time from the triangle and see if the relationship lines change.
   - When a family has no children, ask each person to indicate how this triangle maintains its shape, such as drawing longer or shorter lines to represent contacts between the adults, conversation contents, feelings, etc.
   - Ask how the children get pulled in this triangle again. What might be the cause, event or conversation associated with this pull-in?
   - Explain the function of leaving the child out of the triangle when the adults are working through their own issues and feelings.

Topics for Discussion

1. Structural theory emphasizes the use of therapeutic efforts for each person in the family to understand the family structure. How does this approach differ from family systems theory in terms of setting the priority as the analysis of family interaction patterns?
2. In structural theory, the therapist joins the family in its communication style. How might a family react when the members do not see this as natural, especially in a cross-cultural relationship? How would the practitioner reply if it were to become a concern?
3. An assumption of structural theory is that the restructuring exercise could help family members learn alternative ways of dealing with one another to prevent future conflict. How would restructuring work with a family that has deep and protracted conflict when only one member seeks therapy?
4. Much of structural theory was developed for use in reestablishing parental authority or marital bonding. Would the mindset that one person's dominating position over the rest of the family be applicable to families that emphasize gender equality or parent–child equality?
5. Does this theory provide a conceptual base to challenge the socioeconomic, political, and environmental impacts on the family? How do we examine these factors before suggesting changes in the family structure?

CHAPTER EIGHT

Client-Centered Theory

This chapter describes the client-centered theory and its unique approaches when working with individuals, couples, and families. The first approach is rapport building, in which the practitioner gains the trust of the client. Building trust is necessary in establishing interpersonal relationships. Through the therapeutic process, clients become aware that they can safely express their feelings and share their problems openly with the practitioner, especially at the beginning of the therapeutic relationship.

The second humanistic approach is the enhancement of communication. The description of client-centered techniques is based on Carl Rogers's emphasis on positive regard and Virginia Satir's teaching on positive communication. When using the case approach to study this theory, students and practitioners can role-play how the family reacts to the identified client's symptoms of depression. Three issues are identified during the therapeutic process: difficulty expressing feelings, the impact of miscommunication on mental health, and communication issues between two or more individuals.

This chapter offers additional suggestions that center on responses to clients' resistance and hesitation. The chapter also demonstrates the use of the drawing of communication styles and family sculpture. It assesses the impact of change in evaluation of practice by means of Family Inventory of Life Events and Changes (FILE) and a post-test design with a comparison group.

The Client-Centered Atmosphere

In multicultural practice, the term "client-centered" is used frequently to highlight the importance of incorporating the client's perspective into treatment. This perspective encompasses a vast array of cultural expectations, religious values, societal influences, and family values. With an emphasis on human factors, client-centered practitioners integrate other aspects of practice (such as gestalt, communication theory, behavioral, and solution-focused approaches) to address the client's mind–body–behavior connections to the presenting problem.

The use of client-centered approaches takes into consideration the client's gender issues as well as his or her socioeconomic and cultural backgrounds because it aims to discover the client's position and how the client feels about this position in relation to the family environment. "Starting with where the client is" has become this theory's practice principle. The use of client-centered practice cannot stand alone in therapeutic interventions; it must move into the systems perspective after the clients' current feelings and views on relationships have been validated (Dagirmanjian, Eron, & Lund, 2007). Once the clients feel comfortable with disclosing their feelings and views, other therapeutic approaches can be integrated to help the clients examine their attitudes and look further into their abilities to resolve past issues or find future solutions (Irving & Dickson, 2006).

According to Abraham Maslow (1973), every individual has basic physiological and psychological needs that must be fulfilled before acquiring other higher level needs. Basic physiological needs include food, water, air, and sleep, among others. The next level specifies the need for safety, and this level is followed by levels involving psychological needs including self-esteem, a sense of love and belonging, and self-actualization. From a multicultural perspective, all of these needs are fundamental to our well-being and are essential for growth and development and should be fulfilled side-by-side or within a similar timeframe (Majercsik, 2005).

The culturally competent client-centered practitioner should assesses the client's needs from a hierarchical point of view but should also understand the multiplicity of needs that can be influenced by cultural and other factors (Yang, 2003). Based on this assessment, the practitioner can gain insight into the client's current state of functioning and the needs lacking for an improved quality of life.

Beyond the needs assessment, the culturally competent practitioner should demonstrate a sense of respect for the client and create a profound and personal relationship with the client that will help him or her reach the achievement need. Developing what Carl Rogers has termed "unconditional positive regard" and empathy with the client is foundational to all cross-cultural encounters, to be developed in the first two steps of therapy. Unconditional positive regard is a mirroring process that aims to provide a sense of trust and instill the belief that people are inherently good even when they are facing problems. Empathy is a basic technique in which the practitioner conveys genuine understanding of the client's needs, feelings, and concerns. With these two steps built into the working relationship, the practitioner will gain a sense of trust in the relationship, which will allow the client to feel comfortable about disclosing his or her concerns and problems.

While focusing on human nature, client-centered theory also includes a humanistic perspective proposed by Virginia Satir, which addresses communication and growth-enhancing techniques. Satir is recognized for her use of the humanistic approach in education and family therapy. Her main goal is to help people understand the importance of nurturing others and developing a supportive environment. The presenting problem is not the real focus but, rather, the client's inability to cope and manage the problems effectively. In Virginia Satir's model the family unit is

Client-Centered Theory in Brief

Uniqueness in Multicultural Practice:

Client-centered theory assumes that all individuals have the potential and power to understand their own problems. The practitioner's role is to act as a guide for clients in realizing their potential.

Major Figures:

Carl Rogers (1902–1987): Client-Centered Therapy
Virginia Satir (1916–1988): Communication Styles

Assumptions:

- We have the capacity to understand our problems.
- The client's self is the client's resource.
- Practitioners must show understanding, support, acceptance, respect, caring, and positive regard to gain clients' trust.

Therapeutic Process:

- The assessment process is subjective because the client is the one who knows the dynamics of his or her behavior.

Goals:

- To provide a climate of understanding and acceptance so clients can accept themselves.

Multicultural Practice Techniques:

- Active listening
- Reflection and clarification
- Probing for information
- Positive unconditional regard
- Empathy
- Self-esteem building
- Conjoint family drawing

treated as a whole through techniques such as family sculpture, self-esteem building, and family life chronology. She emphasizes the role of intimacy in family relationships and identifies the various patterns of communications that affect family relationships.

Each family's culture has its own unique forms of communication. Prior to analyzing the presenting problem, the practitioner must analyze the family's form of communication. Satir identified the following four communication styles that families use to hide their inadequate feelings:

1. Placator
2. Blamer
3. Super-reasonable
4. Irrelevant

The *placator* sets aside his or her own needs, tries to relieve the problems of others, and takes the blame for anything that goes wrong. The *blamer* does not take responsibility for his or her own actions but instead is consumed with his or her expectations and demands. The *super-reasonable* denies the feelings of self or others and gives the impression of being rigid and analytical to make the "right" impression. The *irrelevant* is the intended rescuer who tries to distract others and give others the impression that the problem does not exist. In addition to these four communication styles, Satir suggests using the *congruent communicator* as a healthy alternative to the four communication styles described above. The congruent communicator talks with people at their level in a consistent and nurturing manner. This analysis of communication style will help family members process their feelings and make new choices in terms of how to build their relationships.

Because humanistic theory focuses on the process, a trusting and accepting relationship develops between the practitioner and the client. This, in turn, provides a mirroring effect to the client, which allows the client to feel comfortable in trying new roles and making efforts to connect with his or her family. Every therapeutic session should aim to help the client understand how important it is to be a *congruent* communicator, one who takes the other person's perspective into consideration in order to build and maintain a healthy relationship.

On the Multicultural Stage: Family in Transition

Among "traditional" and "typical" families, Duvall (1957, 1988) identified eight sequential stages of family development:

1. Married couples with no children
2. Childbearing families
3. Families with preschool children
4. Families with school children
5. Families with teenagers

6. Families with launching young adults
7. Middle-aged parents
8. Aging family members

Over the past 50 years, however, family structure has changed dramatically (Hernandez, 1993), and we must consider additional stages of family development to fit a variety of family configurations.

When families face events such as adoption, foster-care placement, and divorce, *transition* can be considered a stage in family development. Traditional and nontraditional families alike transition developmentally, yet the configuration of the two types of families differs depending on the experiences they encounter. Unless infertility is a problem, most families do not utilize foster care or consider adoption. Although the divorce rate is close to 50% in most developed countries, including the United States (Americans for Divorce Reform, 2007a, 2007b), divorce is not a typical family developmental stage but, rather, a response to unexpected circumstances.

Duvall (1988) referred to divorce as "a life cycle variation." Families who experience circumstances such as adoption, foster care, and divorce can be considered families in transition. This chapter addresses issues related to families of adoption and foster care, and a later chapter will address divorced families.

The Case Approach

In the following examples, the practitioner attempts to use the client-centered approach to walk the client through her feelings at the present moment, to help the client define mental wellness, and to identify communication patterns within her family. Selected issues are related to expressing feelings, defining mental health in the family, and identifying communication patterns.

Issue #1: Feeling Expressions

This session explores Mary's defensive feelings to help her fully state and comprehend the ramifications of her interpretation of experience. This allows her to see herself more clearly and provides her with a moment of congruence. The therapist's unconditional positive regard, empathy, and congruence have allowed Mary to see her "self" and her struggles clearly.

MC: As I remember, Mary, last week when we stopped, you were saying how hard it was for you to tell other people what you want and how you feel about things.

Mary: Yes, it's hard for me to *feel*. Sometimes I'm not sure what exactly it is that I feel.

MC: Go on.

Active Listening; Using a Minimal Encourager

Mary:	I mean it's difficult for me to know what I'm feeling, let alone express it to someone else.
MC:	It seems that you have a hard time letting people know how you feel because you don't always notice how you feel.

Reflecting Contents

Mary:	Right. And actually, now that I think about it, I've had lots of practice in blocking off my feelings.
MC:	Lots of practice?

Active Listening; Clarifying by use of Questions

Mary:	Sort of … When I was a child, I was punished whenever I acted angry. If I cried, I was sent to my room and told to stop crying. I even remember being happy and playful only to be told to settle down.
MC:	You learned early that your feelings, good or bad, got you in trouble.

Reflecting Contents

Mary:	Yeah.
MC:	That must have felt constricting.

Accurate Empathy

Mary:	Yeah, I really felt suffocated.
MC:	So for most of your life, it's never been appropriate for you to express your feelings….

Reflecting Feelings

Mary:	And now all I feel is confusion.
MC:	Feeling confused doesn't make anyone mad at you.

Using Nonconfronting Technique to Reflect Feelings

Mary:	Yeah, but feeling confused makes me angry…. I mean, I'm really hurt.
MC:	Tell me more.
Mary:	(Pausing) Is it okay to feel angry? I'm so confused and scared. I'm afraid that if I say I'm angry, my husband and I will grow even further apart.
MC:	So you're afraid of your feelings and your husband's reaction to them?

Reflecting Feelings

Mary:	Yes, that's it. I don't know if I'd be able to control myself if I ever got started talking. I feel so angry, and I'm so afraid of his reaction … He might even leave me! Oh … I just don't know … I feel so *guilty* … It's such a mess.
MC:	You have a lot of conflicting thoughts going on inside your head right now.

Mary:	Yes, and I feel so tired and weighed down from not being able to under-stand myself. (pause) I guess I've felt guilty all my life, or at least for as long as I can recall. Seems like all I've ever done is what other people expected of me, or at least I tried to do what others wanted! First it was my parents, and then … oh, I don't know … I feel like screaming—or maybe even running away. Maybe it's better for me not to feel after all! Whenever I do feel, I'm more miserable than when I don't feel. I'm scared, and, oh, I don't know …
MC:	It seems that your contradictory feelings get in your way when you try to think about what you want from your family.
Mary:	Yeah, I just can't put into words what I want. I think I want something so strongly, but when I get up the nerve to talk to my husband or my chil-dren, I get tongue-tied. Nobody wants to listen to my fumbling around about what I want and how to say it.
MC:	You don't feel like your family would listen to you?
Mary:	Oh, … maybe a little, but they … Yeah. I don't think my family even cares enough to listen to what I want even if I could say what it was. They don't even seem to think about me except when I'm not there to keep them organized and do things for them.
MC:	It's easy enough for them, but hard work for you.
Mary:	I always give, and they just take.
MC:	You're just a kind person.

Positive Regard

Mary:	(Confused) But I can't tell them that!
MC:	You mean you're scared to tell them about your feelings?

Reflecting Feelings

Mary:	I mean … what would they think if I told them this is how I feel? They might think I don't love them.
MC:	It seems that their love and respect is totally dependent on your being, not on your feeling.
Mary:	I just feel uncomfortable about sharing my feelings, that's all!
MC:	How about trying to express your feeling to me now—as if I were Joe?

Issue #2: A Family's Mental Health

The definition of mental health varies from culture to culture. In some societies men-tal health is not considered a public concern because it assumes that people should work hard to rid themselves of any mental problems. As a result of this assumption, it is challenging for some people who have experienced mental health issues, such as work stress, family conflict, drug and alcohol abuse, or domestic violence, to address their issues.

In this case, the issue of an adolescent's rebellion illustrates how reluctant the family feels to address this issue as a mental health problem. Rather than using a "pure talk" approach to illustrate the use of client-centered techniques, the practitioner demonstrates the use of a creative visual–feeling approach (rope therapy) to overtly address the issue.

Ami: I don't understand why my mother doesn't trust me and won't let me go out and spend more time with my friends.

MC: She doesn't trust you?

Active Listening; Clarification

Ami: I don't think she trusts me, because every time I ask to go out, she starts asking me a million questions including whether or not I've done all my homework.

MC: (Smiling) A million of questions are a lot of questions, huh?

Ami: (Smiling) You know what I mean.

MC: So when this happens, how does it make you feel?

Ami: I get so frustrated. I usually rush off and slam my bedroom door so I don't have to hear her. It isn't worth it to even argue with her.

MC: Are there any family rules about going out?

Ami: Not really. Mom always seems to say no but never gives me any reason.

MC: Hmm … not having flexible family rules can feel frustrating.

Accurate Empathy

MC: Mary, how do you feel about this?

Mary: It's really important to me that Ami does well in school and goes to college.

MC: It's important to you?

Active Listening; Use of Minimal Encourager

Mary: Yes, it's important to me because I want Ami to be independent and be able to make a living for herself.

MC: Okay—Joe, what happens at home when Ami asks to go out?

Communication Patterns

Joe: Ami will usually ask me first, but I tell her to ask her mother. I can usually hear them arguing about it afterward.

MC: What do you do when Mary and Ami start arguing?

Joe: Well, I have an office at home, and I usually go in there and start working on one of my projects.

MC: Let me see if I have this right. Ami first asks Dad's permission to go out but is told to ask Mom. Then Ami will ask Mom, and they start to argue about it. Joe, when this happens, you go to your office, and Ami rushes to her room and slams the door. Does this sound right?

Reflecting Content

Everyone: Yes.

MC: Ami, tell me more about your requests to spend time with your friends.

Encouraging Communication

Ami: I'll be graduating soon and just want to spend some time with my friends. A lot of my friends will be going away to college, and I won't see them as much. You know, I'm an Honor Roll student and I don't know what else I need to do to satisfy my mother. And my father doesn't say anything at all, which makes me really angry.

MC: It makes you angry?

Active Listening

Ami: Yeah, he should say something at least! I don't know what else to do but get angry.

MC: Mary, how do you feel about Joe not being more involved?

Mary: Joe works really hard all day, and I think I should be able to handle this problem on my own. I don't want to bother him with this.

MC: How do you really feel?

Exploring

Mary: (Pausing) Well, it would be helpful if we could talk about this together.

MC: Let's stop here for a minute and try a technique that I call "ropes." This will help us get an idea of how your family is currently interacting, what that feels like for each of you, and how it affects the family. We're going to role-play what happens.

I'm going to give each of you a rope called the "self rope," which you will tie around your waist. Okay—here's self rope for each of you … Take a minute to tie it around your waist, please …

Now, I'm going to give you two other ropes. I call these "relationship ropes." Mary, here's a relationship rope that you can tie on your self rope, which represents your relationship with Joe. And here is the other rope, which will tie to Ami. Joe, you have two ropes, too—one to tie to Mary and the other to Ami. Ami, you have two ropes—one to your dad and one to your mom.

Rope Therapy

MC: Okay—let's get started.

Ami, let's start with your request to go out. Remember, we're role-playing all of this as it actually happens at home. You said you start by asking your dad, so let's start there.

Ami:	(Shaking the relationship rope toward Joe) Dad, can I go to Carol's house? We're going to watch a movie, and I'll be home by nine-thirty tonight.
MC:	Joe...
Joe:	(Pulling the rope) Ami, you need to ask your mother if that's okay.
MC:	Ami, you and your dad pull away from each other and feel the tension in the rope. (Both pull the rope tighter) Then ask your mom permission to go out.
Ami:	(Shaking the relationship rope toward Mary) Mom, I'd like to go to Carol's house. We're going to watch a movie. I'll be home about nine-thirty.
Mary:	Ami, have you done all of your homework? It's a school night, and I really think you should stay home.
Ami:	But, Mom, I've done all my homework, and I'll be home early.
MC:	Mary, you and Ami pull away and feel the tension in the rope. (Both pull the rope tighter against each other)
MC:	Joe, what happens now?
Joe:	I go to my office, and Mary and Ami argue about this. I can usually hear Ami slam her door.
MC:	Okay, so Joe, you try to turn away. Ami, you pull harder on your mom's rope, and Mary, you pull harder on Ami's rope. Joe, you're still turning away. You're turned away from your family.
	Now, really exaggerate the motions once more. Joe, you turn away, and Mary, you and Ami are pulling tightly on each others' ropes, very frustrating and very angry. Can you all feel the tension in the ropes?
Everyone:	Yes.
MC:	Okay, let's stop now, relax, and talk about how this feels. Go ahead and sit down. Joe, let's start with you.
Joe:	I feel like I'm pulling away from my family. I felt distant as I had my back turned toward them. Even though I'm trying to stay out of the situation, I can still feel the tension, especially when Ami gets angry with me. I don't like this feeling.
MC:	Is it fair to say that trying to stay uninvolved still affects Mary and Ami and tension still remains?

Reflecting Content

Joe:	Yeah, but I never realized this was happening until now. It feels awful to walk away from my family like that.
MC:	Mary, how do you feel?

Mary:	(Pausing a moment to reflect) The tension I was feeling reminds me of my relationship with my father. He was a very strict man and didn't allow me to make any of my own decisions.
MC:	How did you feel when you were Ami's age?
Mary:	I remember wanting to get out of the house so badly.... I just wanted to leave, and I even thought about running away.
MC:	What did you want your father to know?
Mary:	I always wanted my father to trust me. I knew I could make good decisions if he just had faith in me. Somehow, I guess I just wanted him to be proud of me.
MC:	Is this what Ami wants?
Mary:	(Mary becomes teary) Yes, I think this is exactly what Ami is asking for.
MC:	Joe, would you agree?
Joe:	Yes, Ami is a very responsible young lady, and she does very well in school. She has never given us reason to believe that we can't trust her. (Joe looks at Mary) Isn't this right, honey?
Mary:	Yes. You know, this whole time it hasn't been about Ami ... It's been about me.
MC:	Go on.

Minimal Encourager

Mary:	I just don't want Ami to have to depend on anyone to provide for her. I hope she'll be independent and have her own career. She doesn't need to get married right away. It's all the same things I always wanted for myself.
Ami:	Mom, I'm going to college after I graduate. You know I've already talked to my counselor at school and he's helping me get all the paperwork filled out. I'm so excited about starting college!!
Joe:	I'm really sorry for not helping you all discuss this. I've been parenting just like my parents. When my father came home from work, we ate dinner together, and then he would rest and relax. My mom was always the one to make decisions about all of us kids.
MC:	It's important that parents share in their parenting roles and responsibilities and that all family members are able to communicate with each other.

Active Listening; Reflecting Contents

MC:	Mary and Joe, what would you like Ami to know? Can you tell her now?
Joe:	(Looking at Mary for a moment) Ami, we love you very much, and we know that soon you'll be starting college. Gosh, it seems like just yesterday when we celebrated your very first birthday! Your mom and I

do trust you, and we know you're very smart and have a good head on your shoulders.

Mary: Yes, we do love you and trust you very much. Your dad and I are very proud of you, and we know now how important it is for us to communicate with each other. We want you to have a very happy life.

MC: How do you feel now that you've been able to sit and discuss your feelings, Ami?

Ami: It feels like the tension has gone away, and it's nice to hear my parents tell me how much they care about me. I love them, too, so very much.

Issue #3: Identifying Communication Patterns

This session explores the communication between Mary and Joe. Mary learns that she has been misinterpreting the lack of communication from Joe. She learns that Joe is committed to their relationship, and this realization will enhance Mary's self-esteem. Together they come to understand the need for improved communication of their thoughts, feelings, and dreams.

Joe: ·   Mary cries at every little thing now. The other day she told me she didn't even know *why* she was crying. She's been having a lot of trouble sleeping, too. Sometimes I wake up in the middle of the night, and she's sitting at the kitchen table with a glass of milk or is cleaning up the living room at three o'clock in the morning. The doctor has told her there's nothing physically wrong with her, but she needs to take it easy. Now Mary has told me she wants to get a full-time job, but I'm not sure if she can handle it.

MC: Joe, do you think working would benefit Mary?

Active Listening, Reflecting Contents

Joe: Maybe. But not just Mary…. It's for the whole family.

MC: What do you think, Mary?

Mary: I'm not sure.

Joe: The kids are all practically grown, and soon Ami will be in college. Kevin spends most of his time at football practice anyway.

MC: Joe, have you and Mary ever talked about her going to work?

Joe: Yeah, we talked about it awhile back. Since she has been so depressed, I've avoided the subject of work, because I thought it might be more stressful for her. I guess she thinks I caused all these problems.

MC: Mary, would you like to take this opportunity to respond and talk with Joe about how you feel about working?

Inviting Response

Mary: Okay. (Pausing) Well, Joe, since I've been coming to counseling, I'm figuring out that I'm not very good at expressing what I really want to do and how I really feel. In fact, I'm feeling very torn and am not sure what I really want to do. I've never said that you're the cause of all my problems, but it feels like nobody ever listens to what I have to say....

Joe: (Interrupting) I'm listening.

Mary: You all depend on me all of the time for everything, and it feels like I can't depend on anyone.

Joe: I don't know what to say. I thought our marriage was just fine. I've always supported this family.

MC: Let's hear Mary out. What she has to say is important.... Go on, Mary.

Use of Encouragement

Mary: I'm learning that I should take more time for myself—but I don't even know what I would enjoy doing. I'm scared that the family doesn't need me anymore. Ami and I barely speak a civil word to each other, and Joe is right—Kevin is almost never home. It seems like I'm just the cook and maid around our house. The kids seem to be slipping away, and it won't be that long before they're grown and married.

MC: It appears that your all-important role as a mother is changing.

Reflecting Feelings

Mary: Yeah, you're right. I'm afraid that in a few years Joe and I will be sitting alone with nothing to talk about. As it is right now, all we seem to talk about is the kids. When we were young, we used to talk about our dreams for hours on end, but we haven't done that in years.

Joe: Mary, don't you remember? You dreamed about having children and being a loving mother. For the most part, the kids have turned out great.

Mary: (Smiling, then sighing) I really miss when the kids were little.

MC: It feels good to reminisce about the past, Mary, but is there anything in your present life that makes you feel good?

Seeking Positive Exception

Mary: At times I feel pretty good about finishing school. I made good grades and got along well with other people in my class and with my professors. But I'm terrified to take the next step of becoming a teacher. What if I fail and get fired? What if the children don't like me?

MC: Mary, you just finished saying that you got good grades. You've told me before that your experience as a student teacher went very well. What is the likelihood that you will get fired from a teaching job?

Encouragement

Mary: I guess not very likely. (Quietly) I'm also afraid that if I fail, Joe will
            leave me.

Joe: What? Now come on, Mary. I never said I was going anywhere. (To MC)
            I had no idea she was thinking I would ever leave her!

MC: I'd like you both to have the opportunity to really listen to each other and
            be heard by each other. Let's make it easier for you to focus on each

Client-Centered Therapy Techniques

Accurate Empathy: Reflecting a genuine understanding of the client's feelings.

Active Listening: Acting as a neutral listener without providing any biased responses.

Clarification: Asking questions to clarify the meaning of an event, problem, or feeling.

Communication Patterns: The manner in which people talk with each other so the person does not feel threatened by the listener.

Encouraging Communication: Providing an opportunity for the client to disclose information related to interpersonal relationship issues.

Exploring/Inviting Response: Encouraging the client to discuss further by asking a simple question about what the client has just revealed.

Minimal Encouragers: Using simple responses such as "yes," "go on," "I understand," or simply nodding your head to indicate that you are listening.

Positive Regard: Treating the client as an individual, not a case.

Reflecting Content: A form of therapeutic interpretation with a follow-up question to check for its accuracy so the client does not feel that the therapist is imposing meaning onto the client's answer.

Reflecting Feelings: Interpreting how the client might have felt by observing nonverbal expressions or verbal clues.

Rope Therapy: The use of ropes around the waist of each individual with additional cords to link to others to show tautness or remoteness within the relationship or tension between two or more individuals in therapy.

Seeking Positive Exceptions: Identifying any responses to the complaints that are not perceived to be problematic.

Unconditional Positive Regard: Providing positive feedback without expecting any positive returns.

other. There's something we can try to make focusing easier. Can we try it?

Joe and Mary: Okay.

MC: I want you both to stand up and move your chairs so they face each other…. Okay, now Joe, move even closer so your knees are touching…. Good. Now let's allow Mary to finish her thoughts. Joe, please hold your response until Mary is finished.

Mary: Joe, there are times when I really feel unsure about our future together. It seems like we're drifting apart, and before we used to spend time just with each other. Now it feels like all I do is take care of the house and kids, and all you do is work. Even at home you lock yourself up in the den with that damn computer for hours! It seems like I only have a roommate now instead of a husband. I guess working comes naturally to you, but it feels like you prefer your work over spending time with me. The kids don't need me all that much any more either. I feel like I'm losing everything, and I don't know what to do. I'm really confused and feel like I don't have a plan or any direction in my life.

Joe: I guess you're right. I do spend too much time in front of the computer. It's just that I need to keep up with the younger folks at work. My boss seems to think they're better and more productive than I am. Mary, I'm sorry if I don't pay enough attention to you or to our marriage. All along I've been thinking that our marriage is a good, strong one. I'm very comfortable with our marriage and our family, but I had no idea that you felt differently. I really want to stay together and am willing to do what it takes.

Multicultural Practice Applications

In the multicultural environment, many clients find that expressing feelings is not an easy task. First, clients may feel culturally prohibited from expressing their feelings because it may mean revealing their "weak side." Second, it is difficult to ascertain the most acceptable form of feeling expression. Third, the language used to describe feelings can be culturally bound. Other barriers include family pressure and the collective value of not seeking psychotherapy (Dwairy, 2002). This session demonstrates these barriers notwithstanding the family's decision to come in for therapy.

MC: I want to start off today by letting both of you know that although I've been working with Mary for a while now, I'm not here to take sides. I will be a neutral participant during the session. I'd like to begin by asking each of you how you feel about being here today and what expectations you have for this session. Mary, let's begin with you.

Mary: Well, right now I'm feeling very nervous. (pause) And I guess what I want from this meeting is to be able to tell my family how I feel and what I want from them. I think if I am able to get this off of my chest it will be a real load off my shoulders.

Joe: I don't have a clue about why I'm here, much less why Mary is here. Everything was fine until Mary wanted to go back to school. What are we supposed to get out of this? ... If Mary is so unhappy ... I don't understand why ... I've done everything, I've given her everything.

MC: Joe, I hear your frustration, and you're being very supportive by coming here for Mary today. How about you, Ami?

Accurate Empathy

Ami: (Rolling her eyes) I don't know why I'm here either. I have my own life ... my own problems ... my own stresses. (big sigh) I just can't deal....

Kevin: Yeah, I don't understand what the problem is either.

MC: Well, I think it's important to understand that everyone can benefit from this session, not just your mom. It seems clear, based on my previous sessions with Mary and what I've just heard, that there is some miscommunication in the family. It appears that you are all having difficulty expressing your feelings and needs, and because of this, people are not being heard or understood.

Reflection of Feelings

Mary: Yes, that's exactly how I feel.

MC: Good ... good.... Then we're headed in the right direction. So what are some other thoughts and feelings?

Joe: If Mary is so unhappy, how come we don't know why?

Ami: Yeah, why are we here? What is Mom's problem anyway? We all have problems. I'm the one about to go away to college. (distracting)

Joe: (Annoyed) That's just like you, Ami, to be thinking of yourself when we're here for Mom.

Mary: I'm sorry I'm putting all of you through this. I just don't want any of you to be angry with me. Can't we give it a try? I think we need to make some changes.

MC: I understand it's hard to put your family in this position, and I hear you apologizing to them for that. I'm wondering how the rest of the family feels ... hearing Mom apologize.

Empathy

Joe: Mary is always apologizing. I don't think she even knows what she's apologizing for!

MC: Mary, do you hear yourself apologizing?

Mary: Well …

Ami: (Interrupting) How long does this session last anyway? I'm supposed to meet Johnny at the beach.

Joe: There you go again, Ami! Just let Mom answer the question. Don't you even care that you're not listening to her?

Mary: Well, I guess I do apologize often. I give and give to my family, and they just take and take. I'm so afraid of losing them if I make the changes I want. That's why I feel I should apologize.

MC: So, Mary, it sounds like you're afraid of what would happen if you express your true feelings, especially if your family doesn't like your changes.

Mary: Yes, I guess I do stop myself because I don't want to hurt my family.

MC: Mary, I'm very proud of you for expressing your feelings to your family in such an honest way. That took a lot of strength. When a client doesn't feel comfortable verbally expressing his or her feelings, drawing can be used as an alternative form of communication. I think now is a good time to try an exercise that I believe might help all of you understand the roles and communication styles you use within your family. The purpose of this exercise is to help you improve your communication.

          (Continue after distributing the handout in Figure 8.1)

MC: Let me explain the exercise. First, here's a summary that briefly describes some communication styles that are found in most families.

Figure 8.1
Communication Styles Based on Virginia Satir

For example, you see "the placator" at the top of the sheet, which means a person who always asks for pardon and feels weak in power and position. "The blamer" is someone who dominates, finds fault with others, and complains. "The congruent" is someone who takes another person's perspective into consideration and believes in interpersonal harmony. "The super-reasonable" is a deep thinker who suggests ways to do things based on factual information or statistical support, regardless of subjective human factors. "The irrelevant" distracts people's attention and diverts energy into something that is not of significance to the real issue. Any questions about these roles? (silence) I'm also giving you a blank sheet of paper to draw on. I would like each of you to draw how you see your family members in each of these roles, and then we'll discuss your pictures. Take a few minutes to think about it, draw your picture, and then we'll discuss your pictures.

Conjoint Family Drawing

Kevin: You mean I'm supposed to draw my family and put the names of each one of these things next to them?

MC: Yes, that's right. Draw your family according to how you see each one of them as they fit into these roles. Although this may be difficult, remember that this is a safe place to explore and express your feelings.

(Several minutes later)

MC: Okay. It looks like everyone is finished. Let's discuss your pictures.... Joe, would you go first?

Joe: (Showing drawing) Well, this is how I see it. Here's me, and I see myself as both super-reasonable and a little bit of a blamer. Mary is definitely a placator. Ami—she's the irrelevant one because she's rebellious and into her own problems. And Kevin—he's the congruent communicator because he's always expressing his need for Mary to take care of everything for him.

MC: Blamer and super-reasonable?

Active Listening

Joe: Yeah ... um ... because I don't like to get into all that emotional stuff like Mary wants me to. And I'm a blamer because I see myself as the dominant member of this family. Somebody has to take control!

Mary: (Showing drawing) See, I put Joe down the same way, too. He's emotionally detached from us, and he blames me for everything.

Kevin: (Showing drawing) Yeah! I have Dad down as the blamer, too. He doesn't just blame you—he blames all of us!

MC: What else do you have Kevin?

Kevin:	(Showing drawing) I have myself down as a congruent communicator because I let everyone know exactly what I need. I put Ami as irrelevant and we all know why.
MC:	Ami, what do you think about being labeled as an irrelevant?
Ami:	I don't like it.
MC:	Tell us more about this dislike.
Ami:	I am who I am. They are who they are.
MC:	I understand. Do you mean this is how you feel and that is how they feel about you? I am glad you all expressed your opinions. Is there anything you want to add?
Ami:	(Holding up picture of a beach) This is where I should be right now!
MC:	Ami, that's a good picture. Tell us how this picture reflects your communication style with your family.

Unconditional Positive Regard

Ami:	I'm an outsider. I don't know what I should say or do.
Mary:	I don't know how to talk to you either. You always make me feel unimportant.
Ami:	I thought I did that to calm you down.
MC:	Mary, how do you feel when Ami said that?
Mary:	I guess Ami is right. I need to relax.
MC:	Good. You see her point. Mary, let's take a look at your drawing again.
Mary:	(Showing drawing) Well, I put myself as the placator, and I can't believe that everyone else sees me the same way. I find it amazing that everyone's view of each other is actually the same.

Ami's Drawing

MC: I get the sense that we're beginning to understand which roles each of you play in the family and how it affects your communication with each other. Mary, I'm interested in the way you arranged your family. Will you tell me a little bit more about that?

Mary: (Showing drawing) I put them all on top of me because that's the way I feel. I mean, everyone's expecting so much from me all the time, and I feel like I can't do the things for me ... the things I want to do.

MC: Um hum....

Active Listening; Minimal Encourager

Mary: I need to make some changes, and I need my family to understand and help me make these changes. But I'm afraid that I can't become the person I want to be, and I'm afraid of losing my family in the process. I feel so guilty for not doing enough for my family.... I mean, after all, I've always been a housewife.

Joe: Mary ... gee ... you sound so confused!

Mary: Well, Joe, I am! But I'm glad you noticed (smiling).

More often than not, couples having marital problems do not seek help from professionals. They may discuss their ongoing problems with close friends, neighbors, or relatives or even think they may find peace by ending their relationship. In some cultures, however, ending a relationship is not a simple process or an individual decision. It may require ceremonial or spiritual support, the family's blessing, or other practices. In the situation of Joe and Mary, Mary presents their marital problem as a communication problem while Joe denies having any marital difficulties.

Mary: Joe isn't the same man I married so many years ago.

MC: How did he change?

Mary: He's not caring or affectionate toward me any more. He doesn't even look at me the same way or spend time with me.

MC: How did you react to his "non-caring" behavior?

Mary: I felt very upset.

MC: Did you do anything about your feeling?

Mary: Well, I told Anita, one of my close friends.

Another aspect of multicultural application within this approach is the use of alternative methods of expressing feelings. When individuals find it difficult to talk about their problems, it may be easier to express feelings through drawings or through other creative means. Virginia Satir suggests that family sculpture helps each individual visualize the interpersonal relationship among family members. Using the case approach again, the practitioner can demonstrate how this visualization occurs in Joe and Mary's family session.

MC: I'd like to ask Ami to place the family the way she sees it. Mary, please stand to the side and observe as she builds the family sculpture. I'll stand in your place.

Ami: I don't know how I would do it. Let someone else go first.

MC: Would you explain your reason for not doing it?

Ami: Mom never listens to me anyway. Why should I pretend I know how to do this thing?

MC: You feel that your mom doesn't acknowledge your words. That can make it difficult to want to share with her. Would you like to ask your mother to really try to listen and pay attention to you now?

Ami: Umm ... I guess so.

MC: Try it. Tell her directly how you feel.

Ami: Okay, I'll give it a try.... Mom, if I'm going to do this, I need you to try to hear what I'm saying. Will you promise to try?

Mary: I had no idea you thought I wasn't listening to you. I promise I'll listen and try to understand your point of view.

Ami: Okay, I want Dad over here. Mom stands there by Dad, and Kevin is behind Dad. Now all of you sit with your legs crossed and with your backs to each other. I'll sit over here. Now, Mom will be rushing from one of us to another with a smile on her face trying to get each of us to look at her.

(Ami places her dad, brother, and herself in a semi-circle. They are all sitting on the floor, legs crossed, with their backs to one another. Ami is a little farther out of the circle than the others. They are not close to each other in proximity, each having his or her own space. Mary is directed to go from person to person, in constant motion, as the others sit alone.)

MC: Ami, tell me about your mother in this sculpture.

Ami: Mom wants us...

MC: Tell your mom directly. She promised to listen.

Ami: Oh, okay. Mom.... You seem to want all of us to be happy with you, so you spend all your time rushing around trying to please us. You have that phony smile on your face, but you never tell anyone what you really think.

(MC plays the role of "Mom." Ami touches "Mom's" face, and MC exaggerates her "smile.")

Ami: We're each trying to have our own life, and you won't stay out of it enough for us to have any fun. We are your whole life, so you try to make yourself our entire life too.

MC: Mary, now you see the family sculpture. Do you want to respond to what your daughter just said?

Mary: Well, I do want you to be a part of my life, Ami. I have known and cared for you more than anyone since before you were born. I just want you to be happy, so that's why I try so hard to do things for you. But you seem to push me away the more I try to help.

Ami: But Mom—what are you talking about? I'm seventeen years old! I'm not a baby any more. I have a life, and it's not your job to make me happy.

Mary: So I guess you want me to step back a little and give you some space.

Ami: It would be nice.

MC: Mary, talk to Ami about how you feel about this family sculpture.

Mary: Well, in some ways it's a little hurtful, but at the same time it's accurate. I've realized recently how much I live and breathe for this family. I want everyone to be happy with me, but it's wearing me out. I can tell that everyone is turned away from one another in our family right now. It seems like I'm the only one trying to keep this family together!

MC: Joe, how do you feel, sitting on the floor with your back to everyone?

Joe: It's a little strange just sitting here not looking at anyone or doing anything. In some of our past sessions, I've learned a little bit about how Mary feels about everything. But now I almost feel like I've left her to do more than her fair share of the work with our family and stuff. This makes it look like I'm just like the kids.

MC: Just like the kids?

Joe: Well, Mary is trying so hard to please everyone, me included, while the rest of us sit in our own little world. It just seems like we should work together more.

Variations From the Standardized Case: An Adoptive Family

The structure and formation of a family can change after children become part of the family. In general, parents who adopt children have had little experience and often seek assistance in understanding parenting methods. In this variation, Mary and Joe had their biological child before adopting another child and thought they wouldn't face any parenting issues.

***

Joe and Mary have been married for 20 years. They have a 16-year-old daughter, Ami, who is their biological child, and an 8-year-old adopted son, Kevin. Joe and

Mary have been quite successful financially. Joe is a top neurosurgeon in his field and often provides consultation visits out of town. Recently Mary has caught Kevin staying in his room for hours at a time, and when he comes out, his eyes are blood-shot. His behavior has become quite impulsive, and he is often argumentative. At the same time, his grades have started to slip.

Kevin recently was diagnosed with bipolar disorder and has been on medica-tion since then, but lately his parents suspect that he is not taking his medication. Mary has been afraid to talk to Joe about Kevin's recent behavior because she does not want to add any more stress to his already taxing medical practice. In the evenings Mary enjoys having a glass or two of wine but lately has been drinking a glass of wine during the day as well.

As Mary makes an even more concerted effort to discipline her son, he seems to pull farther and farther away. During individual sessions, Joe has expressed complaints about their inconsistent parenting styles, his disagreement with how Mary is handling the family's finances, and her unreasonable spending on the chil-dren. At the same time, Mary has presented symptoms of emotional distress with no recognized physical cause. Ami and Kevin have had trouble concentrating on their studies. The family has not shared an activity for years, and the children's social activities have been limited.

Experts Say...

When reviewing intake information with limited information, practitioners first must determine what information is missing, what information is usable, and what infor-mation requires more development, clarification, or validation before considering it as useful data. Second, it is critically important to suspend any firm judgments or working hypotheses about client systems prior to conducting formal assessment. With this in mind, the following are examples of actions that might be undertaken during the steps of the helping process:

- *Contact:* Clarify the roles of the family and their presenting issues. Based on the information presented in this case scenario, Mary seems to be the primary caregiver. What is the extent of her emotional distress? What are her feelings about her ineffectiveness in her parenting role? Does she recognize the changes in her consumption of alcohol or poor communication with her spouse? Joe appears to be responsible primarily for ensuring that the family's financial needs are met. What is his role in the family? Is he physically or emotionally present or absent? Is he satisfied with the martial relationship?
- *Problem identification:* Verify, develop, clarify, expand upon and/or validate individual and family information before it can inform appropriate treatment planning. For example, before planning the treatment, the practitioner must ascertain whether Kevin is using substances and whether he is taking his medication. After determining the nature of the problem, conduct a thorough biopsychosocial assessment

- *Assessment:* Recognize that Kevin's behavior may, in part, have a biological basis. To develop any hypotheses about Kevin's behavior would be premature until it is known whether he is taking the appropriate dosage of his prescribed medication. Nevertheless, some evidence suggests that bipolar disorder has a genetic basis and occurs more frequently in children whose families have a positive history.

  Joe and Mary may want to review available adoption records or initiate contact with other members of the adopted child's birth family (if appropriate) to determine whether bipolar disorder or other genetically linked disorders of this type have been identified among other members of his birth family. In addition, the extent of Ami's difficulties in her studies has to be assessed. Does Ami feel isolated from her family or peer group?

- *Case planning:* It is essential to consider the status of all individual family members and the family's relationship with the environment. Is the family isolated from friends and extended family? Are there any support systems or environmental obstacles that might support or hinder change?

- *Intervention:* Mary and Joe are not functioning in a manner that supports the needs of the family or individual members. Parental roles and styles of communication need to be addressed. If the parental roles are ineffective, can the parents adapt or change their roles? Is it culturally appropriate to do so? Several other key elements of family functioning may be problematic or ineffective, such as family communication and family boundaries.

- *Evaluation:* From a person-centered and family-focused perspective, gather information about individual and family strengths—that is, what individual and family attributes are present that may be used to support the client in system change.

- *Termination:* Address termination issues with all family members before closing the case. Adopted children can be especially sensitive to termination issues. Be sure to ask children about their feelings about terminating the therapeutic relationship and provide them with contact information for future use.

During the assessment process, the practitioner must gain an understanding that the challenges this family faces may or may not be related to their status as an adoptive family. Adoptive families must address unique challenges or circumstances. Parents must have a well-developed plan for telling their adopted children about their adoptive status. Biological children, if present, must also receive this information. Professionals in the field of adoption have long recognized the need for children to be aware of their adoptive status and related issues as soon as reasonably possible.

For intervention to be effective, this information must be presented in a developmentally appropriate manner. Parents can expect their children to want to revisit the issue of their adoption again and again as they move through different stages of development and have new life experiences. Children adopted from non-relatives have different, and sometimes unknown, genetic factors and medical histories that may become significant at later points in their lives. More and more, open adoptions are becoming a standard for adoption practice. Thus, children are more likely to have birth family contact of one kind or another. Whether adopted children do or do not have birth family contact, however, it is important to remember that their biological and psychological identities are tied in some part to their birth families.

Some adopted children have been removed from their birth parent's home as a result of neglect and/or abuse. The consequences of this neglect and/or abuse will likely be imported into the adoptive family system. This may manifest itself as significant psychological and behavioral problems related to the broader construct of attachment.

Best Practice Evaluation:

Evaluation Stage 5: Assess Changes and Impacts

The fifth stage of practice–evaluation integration focuses on how to assess changes and impacts. In this chapter we use a post-test design with a comparison group to demonstrate how to assess the stress of family members by reviewing their life events and changes.

Suggested Evaluation Tool: Family Inventory of Life Events and Changes (FILE) (McCubbin & Patterson, 1991)

Description: The FILE is an instrument that helps individuals identify life events and changes that may induce stress in a family. FILE has nine different subscales: Intra-Family Strains, Marital Strains, Pregnancy and Childbearing Strains, Finance and Business Strains, Work–Family Transitions and Strains, Illness and Family Care Strains, Losses, Transitions In and Out, and Family Legal Violations. The internal consistency of the total score was .81, but a range of .30 to .73 reliability coefficients was found for the subscales. The test–retest reliability of the total score was .80. The test–retest reliability of the subscales ranged from .72 to .77. The authors also reported a strong correlation between the Family Environment Scales (Anderson, 1984) and the FILE.

How to use the tool: Readers may review the scale in Fischer and Corcoran (1994), *Measures for clinical practice: A sourcebook* (2nd Ed., Volume 1) (pp. 289–296), New York: The Free Press. The FILE contains 71 items. Responses on the items are based on a yes/no format. A score of 1 is assigned to the "yes" response, and a score of 0 is assigned to the "no" response. The total score on the scale may be in the ranges of low, moderate, or high stress. The stage of the family function will determine the score. High scores indicate greater stress in the family. The scale can be completed by one parent or both simultaneously. The scale is available from Dr. Hamilton McCubbin, Center on the Family, College of Tropical Agriculture and Human Resources, University of Hawaii at Manoa, 2515 Campus Road, Miller Hall 103, Honolulu, HI, 96822 (Phone: 808-956-2254).

How to evaluate the outcomes: As discussed in chapter 3, six steps can be used to assess the changes and impacts on family functioning using the single-system research. Applying this evaluation method to the case example of an adoptive family in which Mary is the adoptive mother with many worries, these six steps are demonstrated as follows:

1. *Define the service target or problem (intake and case assessment):* Mary has experienced tremendous stress because of life events and structural changes within the family.
2. *Define (or formulate) goals and objectives:* To reduce Mary's stress while handling life events and changes in the family.
3. *Identify constraints and resources and select a treatment:* Constraints include behavioral health problem of the adoptive child and different parenting styles between the two parents. Resources include support from family members and the family's ability to maintain some mutual understanding among family members.
4. *Measure the monitoring actions (monitor progress):* Mary is referred to the practitioner, and client-centered therapy is applied to help Mary realize the importance of maintaining a positive attitude. Mary is assigned to the experimental group and is asked to complete the FILE Scale each week immediately after the treatment, for 7 weeks. The practitioner records the score each week. The scores for the 7 weeks are plotted in Figure 8.2. A client from another family, Joann, who faces a similar problem but refuses to participate

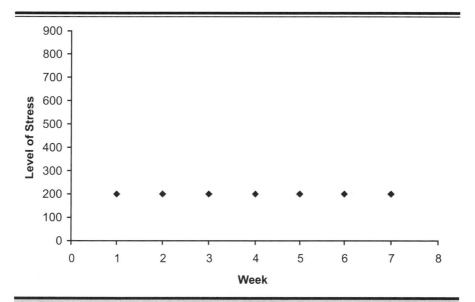

Figure 8.2

Family Inventory of Life Events and Changes: Experimental Group in treatment because of perceived difficulties in engaging the family in the subsequent treatment process, is assigned to the comparison group. While Joann was deciding whether to receive treatment, the practitioner asked her to complete the FILE scale over the same 7-week period. The scores for Joann are plotted in Figure 8.3.

5. *Analyze data:* The average FILE Scale score can be computed based on the seven observations in the experimental group (Mary's score = 200) and comparison group (Joann's score = 850). Using the average score as an example in each group (one individual per group in this example), the average FILE Scale score for Mary is lower than that of Joann, which indicates a lower level of stress.

6. *Report results and make recommendations:* If data are collected from more than the two clients in this example, the average FILE score in each group is to be used. In this case example, Mary's data have demonstrated treatment effectiveness. Mary's score is significantly lower than Joann's, which indicates that the client-centered therapy is effective in helping Mary reduce stress while handling life events and changes. The same data collection procedures can be applied to Joe to conduct a complete assessment of the couple.

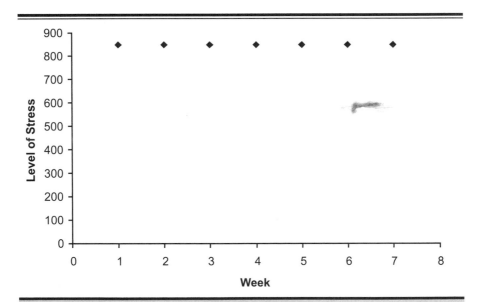

Figure 8.3

Family Inventory of Life Events and Changes: Non-equivalent Group

Multicultural Practice Exercises

1. Read the Self-Esteem Building Declaration from Virginia Satir (1972) and process the meaning of the terms self-worth or self-esteem.

   > I am me.
   >
   > In all the world, there is no one else exactly like me. There are persons who have some parts like me, but no one adds up exactly like me. Therefore, everything that comes out of me is authentically mine because I alone chose it.
   >
   > I own everything about me—my body, including everything it does; my mind, including all its thoughts and ideas; my eyes, including the images of all they behold; my feelings, whatever they may be—anger, joy, frustration, love, disappointment, excitement; my mouth, and all the words that come out of it, polite, sweet or rough, correct or incorrect; my voice, loud or soft; and all my actions, whether they be to others or to myself.
   >
   > I own my fantasies, my dreams, my hopes, my fears.
   >
   > I own all my triumphs and successes, all my failures and mistakes.
   >
   > Because I own all of me, I can become intimately acquainted with me. By so doing I can love me and be friendly with me in all my parts. I can then make it possible for all of me to work in my best interests.
   >
   > … I am me and I am okay.

2. Rope Therapy

   Demonstrate the rope therapy techniques with your own family, and check with your family members, asking how they feel about the tension and relaxation. Then discuss how a problematic relationship issue can be transformed into negative energy.

Topics for Discussion

1. What techniques are used in client-centered theory use to address the clients' ethnic, gender, or socioeconomic issues?
2. What might be some of the barriers to achieve practice effectiveness if the client-centered approach were to be the only treatment?
3. Demonstrate a client-centered technique that would encourage a resistant client to share his or her thoughts or feelings.

CHAPTER NINE

Gestalt Theory

Gestalt theory was developed by Frederick "Fritz" Perls and his wife, Laura Perls, in the 1940s. Breaking away from the psychoanalytic tradition in 1946 (Corey, 2005), Perls borrowed ideas from psychoanalysis, existentialism, and phenomenology (Wagner-Moore, 2004) to develop gestalt therapy. It is an interactive approach that focuses on body–mind connections to understand individual feelings. Gestalt represents the concept of the unified whole, which can help an individual see his or her full potential as a human being.

This chapter addresses the innovative nature of the gestalt approach in family therapy and includes case demonstrations with an identified client (Mary) in the standardized case and issues with her marriage, her dreams, and her failure to take responsibility. This chapter also discusses issues of families with adolescent children, and the standardized case is modified to present a family having boundary issues while trying to talk with their teen daughter about her possible drug involvement. The evaluation step centers on communication between parents and adolescent children. The tools include a parent form and an adolescent form measuring the quality of parent–adolescent communication.

Perls's View of Gestalt

Because gestalt theory emphasizes the wholeness of an individual, as well as the multiplicity of contact and process, it is highly applicable to clients from various cultures (Lobb & Lichtenberg, 2005; Wheeler, 2005). The theory addresses the constant influences on all facets of a person: body, mind, family, and environmental contacts, prompting practitioners and clients alike to consider the effect of cultural influences on behavior (Perls, 1969a, 1969b; Perls, Hefferline, & Goodman, 1951). Acknowledging the presence of all of these influential parts allows clients to recognize that feelings and thoughts are connected with the body and, therefore, can serve to either heal or harm the body. This theory does not stress outcome of the therapy; instead, it identifies the importance of being part of the human interaction process (Garcia, Baker, DeMayo, & Brown, 2005). It assumes that personal existence is a mechanism within a given boundary and that one person's existence affects others.

Incorporating the basic principles of existential philosophy, each individual is treated as a unique person who "is a possibility or potentially free to choose from among all possibilities from moment to moment" (Wulf, 1996, para. 30). Self-awareness and responsibility are key to determining how a person can move from therapeutic support to self-support, by taking responsibility to identify his or her own problems, abandoning bad habits, changing attitudes, collaborating with others, and modifying unhealthy lifestyles.

In addition to the traditional narrative approach to therapy, gestalt therapy utilizes a wide array of experiential exercises in which body language work links body, mind, and environment to therapeutic understanding of the here-and-now. Gestalt therapy also emphasizes the use of character analysis as a way of acknowledging the physical dimensions of the individual, including body movement, breathing, posture, musculature, and speech (Association for the Advancement of Gestalt Therapy [AAGT], 2007). The therapeutic process encourages clients to feel their current feelings, not just talk about them, so they will be able to connect feelings with the problem, and then describe the problem accurately and completely.

When applying gestalt theories and techniques, practitioners must consider some of the limitations of this approach. Gestalt therapy sometimes is considered to be an overly provocative technique for traditional families (Corey, 2005). Gestalt therapists can become highly personal and interactive with their clients by confronting, challenging, and demanding them to put into practice what they have learned in therapy (Nevis, 1983). Practitioners who have integrated the gestalt approach, however, consider the client's cultural framework and practice in a flexible way to ensure that the techniques are well received.

Another limitation of the approach is that gestalt therapy can assume that individuals have personal control over environmental influences. A premise of the approach is that human beings have the potential to choose from a variety of options based on situations and settings (Fernbacher & Plummer 2005). For families in poverty or facing discrimination, however, this assumption may have to be adjusted so practitioners can examine how the surrounding environment can constrain the potential options. Often the movement of individuals from dependence to self-sufficiency must be facilitated by environmental collaborations, rather than relying solely on individual efforts. Thus, people are encouraged to recognize environmental constraints but to avail themselves of resources and services they have not utilized that may be available to them.

When applying gestalt techniques to families of color or members of nontraditional families, practitioners must consider that

> (a) a person is a total system; (b) a change in one part of the individual affects the whole person; (c) humans seek closure, the completion of unfinished situations. (Coven, 1977, p.144)

Gestalt Theory in Brief

Importance to Multicultural Practice:

- It focuses on the whole person; a whole-family concept.
- It emphasizes concreteness.
- It attempts to identify the "how" rather than "why."
- It does not use pathological terms in assessment because the process is ongoing.

Major Figures:

- Frederick S. "Fritz" Perls (1893–1970): Originator of Gestalt Therapy
- Laura Posner Perls (1905-1990): Co-founder of the New York Institute for Gestalt Therapy
- Walter Kempler: Gestalt Family Therapy

Assumptions:

- People must find their own way in life and accept personal responsibility if they hope to achieve maturity.
- Awareness is important: conflict is reexperienced rather than merely discussed.

Therapeutic Process:

- Emphasis is on the client's direct experience of the here-and-now.
- Diagnosis is not stressed.

Goals:

- Challenge clients to move from environmental support to self-support.
- Gain awareness of moment-to-moment experiencing.

Multicultural Practice Techniques:

- Discussion about avoiding responsibility
- Dialogue with polarities
- Empty-chair
- Exaggeration
- Focusing on body messages
- Staying with certain feelings
- Reexperiencing past unfinished situations in the here-and-now
- Clients' own interpretation

From the perspective of working with families with multiple cultural expectations and demands, the emphasis should be on gestalt as a "totality" concept (Wheeler, 2005). This concept explains the connection from a whole person to another as the therapeutic focus. Vulnerabilities become an experience that brings out the cooperative effort, linking one system to another for the fulfillment of business completion.

Modifications to these techniques must take into account all aspects of the individual's or family's life situations—such as cultural, religious, political, social, economic, psychological, and emotional—that have had or will have an impact on the individual's or the family system's functioning. Enhancement of the client's personal awareness must focus on the chain effect that any one change may have on these various life aspects. Incorporation of client-centered, behaviorally oriented, and solution-focused approaches into gestalt is essential as a way to enhance clients' understanding of the importance of relationship building and goal setting, as well as outcome measures.

On the Multicultural Stage: Families with Adolescents

Having adolescent children often presents busy and stressful situations for families. As adolescents reach puberty, they tend to become more emotionally volatile because hormonal changes and the stresses accompanying these changes are compounded by more complex school and family demands, peer pressure and courtship issues, and intensive preparation for college and career development. Working with adolescents is a strenuous task for professionals because it requires a thorough understanding of "growing pains," peer pressure, and parent–child relationships. Solid communication skills are imperative to understand teens and their subculture connections.

From a gestalt point of view, this is a fulfillment stage that helps families realize the significance of unfinished business in individual growth and development. Unfinished business refers to unresolved issues from past experiences that elicit unexpressed feelings such as resentment, rage, hatred, pain, anxiety, grief, guilt, and abandonment. These kinds of unexpressed feelings may interfere with effective intrapersonal and interpersonal communication and will likely continue until the individual recognizes and processes the feelings (Corey, 2005).

Parents' unfinished business from their own adolescence may become a burden on their adolescent children as the parent may demand that the child obtain a higher level of accomplishment than their own. Gestalt therapy urges that parents recognize their own unfinished business so they can better understand their intentions when raising a family, as well as decide whether the changes they want are in themselves or in their children (AAGT, 2005).

The Case Approach

The practitioner uses Gestalt techniques to identify basic communication issues between the client and her family members. The therapeutic purpose is to bring the client to her present awareness level to help her secure a sense of power over her issues. These selected issues are related to unclear personal boundaries, as well as drug and alcohol abuse.

Issue #1: Privacy and Boundary Setting

In this family session with Mary and Joe, Mary has been having trouble communicating with her family members. She wants to get Joe's full support to deal with Ami's teen issues.

MC: Mary, I want you to sit face to face with Joe…. Now I want you to finish this sentence: "I'm not looking at you because I'm trying to avoid _____." And I want you to fill in the blank.

Statement Completion

Mary: I'm not looking at you because I'm trying to avoid an argument.

MC: Okay—good. What do you see happening if you and Joe start arguing?

Re-Experiencing Past Unfinished Business in the Here-and-Now

Mary: (Crying) Joe is going to blame me and think it's all my fault.

MC: Mary, what are you feeling right now?

Mary: Afraid of being alone. (continues crying) I feel like I can't breathe.

MC: Okay, Mary, let's take some deep breaths. Close your eyes. I know it's painful, but I would like you to stay in touch with your feelings.

Staying With the Feeling

Mary: (Crying more softly) I feel a little better now.

MC: Joe, when the two of you argue, what is it usually about?

Joe: It's almost always about Ami.

MC: Give me an example.

Joe: About her make-up, her schoolwork, her boyfriend….

Mary: Don't you worry about her, Joe?

MC: Okay—hold on a second…. Joe, what are you aware of right now when you heard Mary say this?

Joe: I'm aware of Mary's fear when Ami's not with her.

MC: So you feel that it's more of an overprotection issue here.

Joe: Sort of.

MC: Mary, I want you to put yourself in the position of a teenager right now. Can you describe the relationship you'd like to see between you as a teenager and your parents?

Mary: Close and warm.

MC: Okay—to the point that both of you can't breathe?

Mary: Well, no. Maybe a little freedom.

Joe: Sure.

MC: Do you both feel alone when Ami's not at home?

Mary: I feel scared.

Joe: (Touching Mary's shoulder, conveying "Don't feel scared. I'm here.")

MC: Joe, can you repeat that gesture?

Joe: (Pats Mary's shoulder)

MC: Pat with both hands, Joe.

Body Exaggeration

Joe: (Uses both hands and looks at Mary)

MC: Mary, how do you feel now?

Mary: Joe wants me to relax. I guess I'm a little too nervous about Ami.

Joe: (Nodding)

MC: Joe, is there anything you want to say to Mary?

Joe: (Quietly) I don't know what to say. I just notice that I haven't given her enough support. Ami is fine if Mary calms down. Mary can calm down if I'm there.

Mary: Ami's not a bad child.

MC: Repeat this and add, "… and I'm not a bad mother."

Mary: Ami's not a bad child, and I'm not a bad mother.

MC: Joe, say it about yourself, too.

Joe: Ami's not a bad child, and I'm not a bad father.

Issue #2: Drug and Alcohol Abuse

In this session, Joe and Mary express concerns about Ami's possible drug and alcohol abuse. Although they believe that Ami is not currently taking drugs, their worry has made Ami feel uncomfortable, and she refuses to talk with them. The Empty Chair technique is an effective way of getting the client to externalize the introjections or the incorporating aspects of others, usually parents, into the client's ego system. Gestalt therapy holds that taking the values and traits of others is inevitable and desirable (Corey, 2005). The danger, however, is in the uncritical and wholesale acceptance of another's values as one's own, which makes becoming an autonomous person difficult.

MC:	Let's talk a little about American teenagers. What do you think they do in their spare time?
Mary:	Drugs, sex, go to college someday….
MC:	How about you, Joe?
Joe:	Drinking, not sleeping, hanging out….
MC:	Okay, good … Let's talk about drugs and alcohol as an example and do an exercise here.

(Places one chair between Mary and Joe)

MC:	This exercise is called "Empty Chair." We're going to pretend that Ami is here in this chair, and we're going to talk a little about drugs and alcohol. If you don't feel comfortable continuing, just let me know, and we'll stop. Okay? All right. Mary, Ami is here to talk about her perception of drugs and alcohol. What do you think she might say?
Mary:	She'd say, "Mom, don't worry about me. I know what I'm doing. I can control myself."
MC:	What would you tell Ami?
Mary:	I would tell her….
MC:	(Interrupting) Remember—we're pretending that Ami is here in the chair. Look at Ami and tell her.

Empty Chair

Mary:	Ami, I trust you, and I know you're fine. But I would feel uncomfortable if I didn't warn you about the dangers.
MC:	Joe, what do you want Ami to hear from you?
Joe:	(Sounding demanding) I don't like kids to stay out late. They're doing things that we don't know about!
MC:	Joe, how do you tell Ami this? Look at her. Pretend she's still sitting on this chair.
Joe:	(Softer) Ami, I'm your dad. Of course I'm concerned about what you're doing. I just want you to know that you shouldn't be taking drugs or drinking.
MC:	Mary, what did you see when Joe was talking to Ami?
Mary:	I saw a different Joe. He's not yelling.
MC:	Joe, how do you feel now?
Joe:	I know Mary is nervous about Ami. I didn't know she's nervous about what I would tell Ami.
Mary:	Yes, I'm nervous all the time. When Ami comes home late, I'm afraid that you both would fight. When you two talked about drinking the other night, it was like you were accusing her. Ami was very upset.

Gestalt Techniques

Body Exaggeration: Helping clients understand through body work the emotional connections with the body.

Empty Chair: Stimulating frank discussions by pretending that a key person in this discussion is sitting on a chair next to the client (or family).

Reexperiencing Past Unfinished Business in the Here-and-Now: Encouraging clients to address unfinished business as if it is happening at the moment so they can grasp the present feeling as related to the past event or situation.

Statement Completion: Starting a few words of a statement (such as, "I feel ...") and encouraging the client to complete the statement so feelings and perceptions can be further identified.

Staying with the Feeling: Encouraging clients to sense and experience a feeling they try to avoid by asking them to stay with this feeling silently for a few seconds and then encouraging them to recall events or situations they associate with this feeling.

MC: Now Ami is here. What would you say to her, Mary … and then Joe?

Mary: Ami, just do what your father says, and don't argue.

Joe: I don't mean to be so demanding.

MC: What does Ami usually do or say when Joe lectures her?

Joe: She doesn't listen, and she slams her bedroom door. I become angry … and I guess Mary gets nervous.

MC: To your knowledge, does Ami take drugs or drink alcohol?

Mary: No, not that I know of. I *hope* she doesn't.

Joe: I get it. She's not doing it, and she thought I was accusing her.

Mary: Then when I went to comfort her, I asked if she's doing drugs or drinking.

MC: Now let's stop the exercise. Remember—this is only an experiential exercise. Ami is indeed not here. Let's process what we have just said.

Multicultural Practice Applications

Because gestalt is a technique-oriented approach, it is important to identify ways to use these techniques effectively. Bryant (2001) provides case evidence to support gestalt techniques used in a brief therapeutic setting. With a brief modality format, the practitioner can apply a few techniques to refocus clients on feelings and relationship issues. The following demonstrations with Mary and Joe's family illustrate some of the most relevant techniques for diverse families, with an emphasis on "total connections," or what Wheeler (2005) calls "multidimensional contacts." All of these techniques are very task-oriented, each aiming to find a concrete outcome.

Multicultural Practice Exercises

Exaggeration Exercise

This exaggeration exercise enables clients to become more aware of the subtle signals and cues they are sending through verbal or body language. The client is asked to exaggerate a movement, gesture, phrase, or statement repeatedly, which usually intensifies the feeling attached to the behavior and makes the inner meaning clearer. In this vignette, Ami explores the inner meaning of her body language.

Ami: (Crossing her legs and kicking her right foot)

MC: Ami, I'd like you to continue to kick your foot and exaggerate this movement.

Ami: (Exaggerating the kicking)

MC: Kick more—higher.

Ami: (Kicking higher)

MC: (In an encouraging voice) Kick higher!

Ami: (Kicking higher and starting to laugh)

MC: Ami, what do you feel when you kick your foot higher and higher?

Ami: Agitation … anxiety. I don't know…. It's funny. I guess I hadn't realized I was feeling that way.

Rehearsal (using the Empty Chair Technique)

Much of our thinking is rehearsal. In our minds we rehearse performances we think we are expected to play. We often experience anxiety because we fear we will not play our role well enough. To address this anxiety, gestalt therapists can ask the client to rehearse aloud the pros and cons of a given situation. Members of a therapy group can practice their rehearsals with one another. Clients become increasingly aware of how they try to meet others' expectations of them and the extent to which they want others to approve of and accept them. They also discover the extent to which they will go to gain acceptance.

MC: How have you been, Ami?

Ami: Well, something happened at school the other day that made me very uncomfortable.

MC: Let's talk about what happened.

Ami: During a track meet last Friday, I ran into a childhood friend that I hadn't seen for a while. He seemed to have a crush on me and asked me to go to have coffee with him after class. He said it so casually that I said "yes." Toward the end of the conversation, I started to panic and thought, "What am I going to say and do with this guy?" What would my classmates think about this? I've never been out with him. Peter is just a childhood friend. He used to laugh at my teeth. I used to be friends with him, but I don't know if I like him now.

MC: Then what happened?

Ami: I got scared and so nervous that I finally told him I forgot I had to be with my mom after the track meet. Then he said "No problem. We can go next week." I don't know what I'm going to say to him.

MC: Why don't we try rehearsing what you can do and say? Pretend that he's sitting in this chair and has just asked you to go to have coffee with him. Can you do that?

Ami: Yes, I think so.

MC: Peter is sitting on this chair. I want you to talk directly to him. I want you to bring last week to the here-and-now—when he asked you for coffee. Tell him what you'd like to say.

Ami: I guess I'm not sure if I would have the time or interest to have coffee with him.

MC: Pretend that you're talking to him.

Ami: Peter, I don't have the time to have coffee with you.

MC: What if Peter says he could change the place or time?

MC: Tell him how you feel now.

Ami: I'm not sure about this. Are we just going to have coffee? Why do you want to go with me?

MC: What do you think Peter wants?

Ami: I don't know.

MC: Maybe he just wants to talk about your childhood.

Ami: Just talk? That should be easy. But what do I have to talk about with him? I'm not very interesting…. I guess I could talk about my parents. But what if I panic? What if he just walks away?

MC: Is that what you're afraid of?

Ami: I don't know. I hadn't really thought about that, but maybe I am.

MC: Why don't we rehearse what you would say to Peter when you see him during your next track meet?

Ami: What should I say?

MC:	How about starting with, "Hello, Peter."
Ami:	Hello, Peter.
MC:	I'm Peter now: *Hi, Ami. How's school?*
Ami:	It's fine—but hectic.
MC:	*I'm fine, too. Can we go to Star Coffee after the meet?*
Ami:	Sorry— I can't. I don't have time.
MC:	*Do you mean you don't want to go out with me?*
Ami:	No. I just don't have anything to say. I hope you don't mind.
MC:	*All right. I understand.* Ami, do you think you can tell him you don't have anything to say to him?
Ami:	I think so.

I Have a Secret

This is an exercise to explore fears, guilt feelings, and catastrophic expectations—"If I change, something horrible will happen." In this technique you ask the client to think of some personal secret. Tell him or her not to actually share the secret with others but to imagine herself or himself revealing the secret. Ask the client to look at these things: What fears do you have about people knowing your secret? How do you imagine that others might respond to you?

In this demonstration, Ami comes to the therapy session with a letter she composed for Eddy, her secret heartthrob.

Ami:	I wrote that letter you suggested I write.
MC:	Will you share it with me?
Ami:	It's embarrassing.
MC:	You don't have to. You can read it to me when you're ready, or you can keep it to yourself.
Ami:	Ooooooh … I'll read it. Okay, here goes …
	Dear Eddy,
	I don't know where to begin. It seems so stupid for me to write to you, because I barely know you. But I need to talk to you because I have no other friend I can talk to. I mean guy friends. There are all these things about me I wish you knew, though. I'm not sure why. Part of it could be because I want you to invite me to the prom. The other part might be related to my family. If you don't want to go with me, that would be fine. I mean it. Just don't talk to me when you see me next if you don't want to. I am fine. Ami
MC:	Thanks for sharing that, Ami. Tell me—what were you thinking when you were reading that to me?

Ami: I was thinking I couldn't have much fun because my family wouldn't let me.

MC: You seem to have very little confidence in yourself. If you were to write a letter to your mom about Eddy, what would you write?

Ami: I would tell her about wanting to go to the prom. Eddy is the only person I'd like to go with.

MC: Does your mom know?

Ami: Not really. I don't want her to know.

MC: You don't want her to know about the prom at all?

Ami: Well—she knows about the prom, but I wouldn't want her to know that I want to go with Eddy. It's embarrassing.

MC: It is typical to feel embarrassed. How about if you can talk about your prom dress first? Let's rehearse it.

Dialogue Exercise

The purpose of the dialogue exercise is to bring about integrated functioning and the acceptance of facets of the client's personality that he or she has disowned and denied. This technique enables the therapist and client to concentrate on the "war" between the "topdog"—the righteous, authoritarian, moralistic personality—and the "underdog"—the defensive, apologetic, helpless personality (Corey, 2005).

When working with multicultural families, this dialogue technique helps clients get in touch with a feeling or a side of themselves that they may be denying. Instead of using the terms "topdog" and "underdog," it is suggested to use terms the clients are familiar with, such as "my strong side" and "my weak side" to indicate two internal conflicting thoughts, and "I like" and "I don't like" to polarize the feelings about two decisions. "Active" and "passive" also can be used to avoid any negative implications of an internal struggle. This will help clients promote a higher level of integration between the polarities and conflicts that exist in every family. The aim is not to rid the client of certain traits but, instead, to help clients learn to accept their polarities.

MC: Ami, spend the next 5 minutes writing down all your thoughts about being a teenage athlete. In the left column list five of your strengths, and in the righthand column list at least five of your weaknesses or limitations that correspond to each of your strengths.
(Ami starts and finishes writing)

MC: Please read one item from the "strong" side of yourself. When you read it, say "strong" first.

Ami: Strong: I like sports.

MC: Good. Okay, this chair next to you is going to represent your weak side. Now sit in this chair and read one "weak" point of yours. Please start with the word "weak."

Ami: Weak: I don't like myself sometimes.

MC: Okay. Now continue with this exercise, alternating one strong and one weak point. Switch your chair after each statement, and don't stop.

Ami: Strong: It feels great to feel special and to feel loved by my teammates. I'm proud of being myself.

            Weak: (switching chairs) Sometimes being a teenager is tough. I don't know if I'm happy.

            Strong: (switching back) I'm a winner. I win my races most of the time.

            Weak: I feel sad because my parents can never come to my games.

            Strong: I'm always a leader with my friends. I always think about my friends.

            Weak: I feel alone sometimes, especially when I'm home.

MC: Okay, Ami, give yourself a strength that can help you overcome this "alone" feeling.

Ami: I'm a likeable person. I can talk with my friends.

Dream Work

Though Perls' training began in the psychoanalytic tradition, the gestalt approach does not interpret or analyze dreams (Corey, 2005). Instead, the intent of Gestalt dream work is to bring the dream back to life and relive it as though it were happening now. The dream is acted out in the present, and the dreamer becomes a part of his or her dream.

Gestalt therapy asserts that every person, scene, and object in the dream represents a projected aspect of the dreamer (Mageo, 2001). All of the different parts of a dream are expressions of the client's own contradictory and inconsistent sides. Thus, by engaging in a dialogue between these opposing sides, the client gradually becomes more aware of the range of his or her own feelings. The gestalt approach purports that the dream is the most spontaneous human expression (Coven, 2004). Dreams represent an unfinished situation and contain a message about the client and his or her current struggles.

In this vignette, Ami and her therapist are discussing a recent dream of Ami's.

Ami: I'm driving my car to an appointment with my academic counselor at school. I'm running late. There's a car stalled on the freeway. My gas tank is on "empty," but I think I can make it. It's summer, and I can see the steam coming off the pavement of the freeway. I'm sweating, and my body is shaking.

            My car is making a strange noise. I told my dad to check the car on Saturday, but he probably didn't do it, and now it is going to break down.

            I finally arrive at the academic counselor's office. I'm a mess. My clothes are wrinkled, and my hair and clothes are soaked with sweat. The counselor says he can't see me because I'm too late. Before I wake up, I tell him it is not my fault ... the traffic ... my car.... He says, "Next time plan ahead."

MC: Ami, I'd like you to become the car.... Speak for the car.... What is the car thinking, feeling, saying...?

Ami: You should have made sure that Joe had checked me. Now I'm going to stall. I need to be cared for and not neglected.

MC: Good. Now try to speak for the traffic....

Ami: It's crowded out here. I wish these people would plan better and stop blaming their delays on me.

MC: Okay.... now be the weather....

Ami: I'm just letting off a little steam. It's summer, and I get warm and need a release.

MC: Ami, now be the academic counselor....

Ami: Listen—it's your fault! You should have planned ahead for the traffic. I have a schedule to maintain!

MC: Ami, now be yourself.

Ami: It's not my fault. Everybody needs me to help them on their projects. They didn't follow through on what they were supposed to do. I tried to do my best. Why do these things happen to me?

MC: Ami, what is the main feeling you get from your many parts in the dream?

Ami: I don't have a clue. That's why I come to see you.

MC: Let's try another angle: What is the dream telling you?

Ami: It may be that ... I have a little trouble with taking responsibility?

MC: Which part of the dream tells you that?

I Take Responsibility For...

The purpose of this exercise is to help clients accept personal responsibility for their own feelings. The client makes a statement aloud, then adds, "...and I take responsibility for it." This exercise is an extension of the continuum of awareness and is designed to help clients recognize their feelings instead of projecting their feelings onto others in an unhealthy way.

Explain to the client that this technique is meaningful even though it may sound mechanical. Then have the client proceed.

Kevin: I'm tired. I always have my problem with my mom, and I can't seem to do much about it.

MC: Kevin, let's try to take responsibility for it. Try saying that you're responsible for your problem with your mom.

Kevin:	What do you mean? It's the parents' responsibility. You can't blame it on me. You have to listen to what your parents told you to do anyway.
MC:	We all have to take responsibility. Start with saying "I" instead of anyone else, and you'll hear what you say.
Kevin:	What do you mean?
MC:	Earlier you said *you* have to listen to what *your* parents told *you* to do anyway.
Kevin:	Oh, I did? Well, I meant *me*.
MC:	Okay, try saying it now.
Kevin:	I have to listen to what my parents told me to do anyway.
MC:	Do you do what "most people do," or do you do what you *want* to do?
Kevin:	I guess it's what I want to do. I guess my parents may be right sometimes.
MC:	As part of our exercise here, I want you take responsibility for that. Start by saying, "I take responsibility for...."
Kevin:	Oh, boy. (taking a deep breath) I take responsibility for my problem with my mom.
MC:	How does it feel to take responsibility for it?
Kevin:	I feel weak—and a little scared. If it's my responsibility, it's my problem to fix.
MC:	Do you feel any power?
Kevin:	Ummmm, I suppose I do. How can I use it? My mom just doesn't like it.
MC:	You both have to work together on this.

Staying with the Feeling

Clients frequently refer to an unpleasant feeling or mood. Then they want to avoid discussing this feeling to escape the fearful stimuli. Using gestalt techniques, the therapist asks the client to remain with his or her fears and pain and encourages him or her to experience the feelings. This takes courage and also expresses willingness to endure the pain necessary for unblocking and making way for deeper levels of growth.

MC:	Joe, I noticed that you sighed when you made the statement regarding your marriage. What made you sigh?
Joe:	(Shrugging his shoulders and sighing) I'm not sure. I guess I was thinking of how long we've been together, and I really don't understand what I'm doing here.
MC:	Joe, in gestalt therapy we do a lot of experiments. Mary is familiar with some of them. Would you like to try one?

Joe:	Sure. Why not?
MC:	Joe, sigh again.
Joe:	(Sighs)
MC:	Now sigh and say, "I really don't understand what I'm doing here."
Joe:	(Sighing) I really don't understand what I'm doing here.
MC:	What feeling do you have right now?
Joe:	Confused.
MC:	Joe, I want you to repeat this: "I really don't understand what I'm doing here, and I feel confused."
Joe:	I feel confused.
MC:	Repeat the entire statement.
Joe:	I really don't understand what I'm doing here, and I feel confused.
MC:	Would you repeat "I feel confused" three times as loud as you can?
Joe:	(loud and angry) *I feel confused!! I feel confused!! I feel confused!!*
MC:	Joe, what do you hear?
Joe:	Wow—I hear harshness, anger. (pausing) When I talk to Mary, I use this tone of voice a lot because I'm afraid she isn't listening to me. I can see why she feels upset.

Reversal Technique

The reversal technique involves taking a person's trait and acting out the opposite characteristic. This can be useful when a client has tried to deny or disown a side of his or her personality. Ami has been overly responsible for other people and afraid to make mistakes. This demonstration will show Ami drawing out her irresponsible side.

Ami:	I'm afraid to make mistakes and look like a fool.
MC:	Ami, I want you do an exercise where you take risks. During this exercise, I want you to be irresponsible and not be afraid to make a mistake. Maybe you can even let yourself be foolish.
Ami:	Oh, you want me to be irresponsible? Foolish I understand—though I hate it—but I'm not even sure I know what irresponsibility is.
MC:	Pretend that you do. I want you to act out irresponsibility, and through that, perhaps it will become clearer to you.
Ami:	I can't believe you want me to be irresponsible....
MC:	I do. What have you been wanting to do but haven't done?
Ami:	I don't know.
MC:	You couldn't say so because you felt it was *not* you?

Ami:	I guess … I haven't been able to tell Mom I love her (sarcastically, laughing).
MC:	What would it be like for you to tell your mom that?
Ami:	Different. Gosh, I don't know. It's hard to tell Mom anything.
MC:	What do you mean by that?
Ami:	Who knows? I guess she's always unhappy about me.
MC:	What does that make you think of?
Ami:	It's really weird, but it makes me think of my dad.
MC:	Tell me more.
Ami:	Dad doesn't like the way I talk with Mom. I guess Mom and I have a bad relationship. Dad doesn't want it to get worse.
MC:	How does your dad's intent affect you now?
Ami:	Now that I think about it, Dad may be right. I just have to shift a little bit.
MC:	If your dad is here now, what do you want to say to him about your future behavior with your mom?
Ami:	Dad, from now on I'm going to be a good daughter. I'm always good, but Mom just doesn't see it.
MC:	Good. How do you feel about what you just said?
Ami:	For the first time in a long while, I realize I can say something *with* my parents.

Making the Rounds:

This exercise involves asking an individual in a group or a family to approach each group member and either speak or engage in an action. The purpose is to confront, to risk, to disclose the self, to experiment with new behavior, and to grow and change.

MC:	Ami, you said no one seems to understand you. Please go to your family and ask each of them this question: "What would be your greatest comfort if you understood me?"
Ami:	Dad, what would be your greatest comfort if you understood me?
Joe:	I could feel happy.
Ami:	Mom, what would be your greatest comfort if you understood me?
Mary:	I wouldn't have to guess whether you would come home for dinner or not.
Ami:	Kevin, what would be your greatest comfort if you understood me?
Kevin:	I would be your friend.
MC:	Ami, what do you want them to understand about you?

Playing the Projection

In this technique the practitioner asks clients who have expressed criticism or concern for another person to restate the criticism or concern using reflective "I" statements. This will make the client hear the criticism more carefully and understand his or her own attempt to use projection as a defense mechanism to resolve inner conflict.

Mary:	I can't trust Ami.
MC:	Say it again, but this time say, "I can't trust myself."
Mary:	I can't trust myself.
MC:	Say it this way: "I can't trust myself when I criticize Ami."
Mary:	What?
MC:	Say it and see how you feel: "I can't trust myself when I criticize Ami."
Mary:	I can't trust myself when I criticize Ami.
MC:	Close your eyes this time, and repeat what you just said.
Mary:	I can't trust myself when I criticize Ami.
MC:	Listen to your heart. What can't you trust about yourself when it comes to Ami?
Mary:	I guess I can't trust that I can be a good mother if I allow her to stay out late.
MC:	Can you trust Ami if you trust yourself?

Variations From the Standardized Case: A Family Dealing with Drug Problems

Some families seek professional help because they not only suspect but actually discover drug or alcohol problems in their children. In drug and alcohol abuse treatment, the Gestalt process focuses on the patient's feelings of aloneness and addresses the patient's challenges in the current environment in order to replace dependency with self-support (Clemmens & Matzko, 2005). Moving from environmental support to self-support, the Gestalt style of processing, which emphasizes awareness in drug use, is an effective means to encourage patients to challenge detoured cognitive thinking in conjunction with their maladaptive behaviors, thus moving toward a better relationship with others (Sharps, Price-Sharps, & Day, 2005). To see clearly how gestalt therapy works with this type of family, the standardized case has added information to include recent drug use by Ami, the teenage daughter in this family.

***

Ami always has been an "A/B" student and plays the clarinet in her high school band, but her grades have recently dropped to "Ds," and she has missed several band practices.

One day, as Mary is changing the sheets on Ami's bed, she finds a plastic bag containing a pipe and marijuana. As Mary examines the items, Kevin walks into the bedroom, and tells his mom Ami didn't let him touch it. Shocked, Mary asks Kevin what happened, and Kevin explains that he saw Ami and her best friend smoke the pipe.

Mary tells Joe about the incident, and they both confront Ami that evening. Ami admits to smoking marijuana but tells her parents that "everybody at school does it." Ami also tells her parents that smoking marijuana helps her relax, and comments that it is not a "bad" drug like cocaine or ecstasy. Mary and Joe are concerned that Ami will start using stronger drugs.

Role Play

The following case demonstration identifies how to utilize gestalt techniques to help this family. Mary and Joe have brought Ami in to see the therapist despite her objections.

Mary:	Can you tell us how to stop Ami from using drugs?
MC:	Let's slow down for a moment. What feeling comes to your mind when you ask this question?
Mary:	Fear … uncertainty. I feel desperate.
MC:	How about you, Joe?
Joe:	I don't know how drugs got into our family. It's terrible. I feel trapped.
MC:	Ami, how do you feel when your parents say this?
Ami:	I don't know. I feel bad. I told them I wouldn't do it again, but they wouldn't accept my apology.
MC:	Ami, stay with this feeling for a few seconds. (pause) Now think about what you would do if you were the parent right now. What would you say to your daughter if you found out she had used drugs?
Ami:	I don't know. I don't want to have kids.
MC:	Well, let's just imagine for a moment that you did have kids and your teenage daughter was sitting on this couch here. Tell her how you feel.
Ami:	I feel upset because you made a mistake.
MC:	Say it stronger and louder, Ami.
Ami:	I feel upset because you made a mistake!
MC:	Stronger and louder.
Ami:	*I feel upset because you made a mistake!*
MC:	How do you feel now?
Ami:	I feel like my parents are scolding me. I don't want to upset them. I thought it was okay to try it once or twice.
MC:	Joe, how do you feel?

Joe: I feel horrible. Angry ... sad. I want her to be healthy.

Mary: Yes, Ami, I want you to grow up to be a healthy woman. That's all.

Ami: I know. If I was a parent, I would feel upset, too.

MC: Ami, earlier you said that you felt badly and that your parents didn't accept your apology. Why don't we try it again?

Ami: Mom and Dad, please forgive me. I'm so sorry. (starting to cry; parents move to hug her)

Experts Say...

Adolescence is a stage of transition between childhood and adulthood. Adolescents often share common struggles at this stage—with school, home, friendships, body image, physiological changes, romances, peer pressure, substance abuse, teen pregnancy, and other health and mental health issues.

According to Dale Alexander, a drug treatment expert teaching at the University of Houston, with the current economic and cultural expectations of academic and career success, many modern parents have delayed childbearing until their 30s, and thus are reaching the end of middle age as their children reach adolescence. This can increase the difficulty because some parents retire before their children enter college. Nearly all children and parents realize that relationships start with communication between two persons. At this developmental juncture, however, communication is more than just conversations between two persons. It is about changes, about perceptual biases between two generations and between two worlds of technological, cultural, and value differences.

Additional issues that minority adolescents face include discrimination, self-image, social and economic equity, and the struggle between maintaining one's ethnic identity and excelling in school in competition with peers (Spencer, Swanson, & Cunningham, 1991). This case does not identify the ethnic identity of the family, and drug problems can hurt any family regardless of demographics. A culturally sensitive practitioner, however, can take the following actions during the helping process:

- *Contact:* Clarify the practitioner's role in the helping process. Maintain willingness to acknowledge cultural and personal differences and similarities.
- *Problem identification:* Seek the cultural meaning of the issue of substance use—what it means within the family's cultural context.
- *Assessment:* Conduct a more formal screening and assessment of Ami's possible marijuana use, using new marijuana-specific screens by Alexander (2003) and Alexander and Leung (2004).

  In some cases, formal assessment of Cannabis Use Disorders is indicated, using evidence-based criteria refinements for DSM IV-TR Substance Use Abuse or Dependence Disorders. Also, parental involvement and assessment of their past or present cannabis use is necessary to gauge parental permissive attitudes about marijuana use, as well as psychoeducational updating on how marijuana use during their own adolescence may affect the current situation. Also, clinicians should stay up-to-date on new research on cannabis that is balanced and accurate (NIDA, 2007; SAMHSA, 2007; Smucker Barnwell, Earleywine, & Gordis, 2005).

- *Case planning:* Obtain information as to the severity of a cannabis use disorder that may require clinical intervention versus adolescent experimentation. Weigh and monitor outpatient treatment versus intensive outpatient versus inpatient treatment options, along with periodic random urine screening to biochemically determine or deter future cannabis use.
- *Intervention:* Determine clinical intervention based on the evidence of extra developmental risks of 'heavy' cannabis use on adolescents, the presence of school performance deficits suggesting "amotivational syndrome," and use of cannabis as a mood modifier for anxiety or depression—which may be at levels requiring formal assessment.
- *Evaluation:* Prior to any treatment or intervention program, identify strengths of the extended family support system. Before initiating treatment, establish an evaluation plan so client satisfaction and treatment effectiveness can be assessed post-treatment. Provide the adolescent with educational information about the effect of substance use on brain development and its contributing factors to mental illness (such as schizophrenia) and discuss this information.
- *Termination:* Recognize that ethnic minority clients may require extra time for recovery because of the stigma associated with the family's inability to cope with the problem. Practitioners may want to assess clients' readiness to receive additional psychotherapeutic support before hospital discharge.

Best Practice Evaluation

Stage Six: Assess Problems Within the Family

The sixth stage of the practice–evaluation integration deals with how parents communicate with their children and adolescents. In this chapter we use a pre-test post-test comparison group design to demonstrate practice evaluation with a focus on family communication.

Suggested evaluation tool: Parent-Adolescent Communication Scale (PACS) (Barnes & Olson, 1982)

Description: The PACS has two forms. One is designed for the parent and the other is designed for the adolescent. Both the parent and the adolescent PACS consists of 20 items using a five-point Likert-type scale in which 1 = strongly disagree, 2 = moderately disagree, 3 = neither agree nor disagree, 4 = moderately agree, and 5 = strongly agree. The instrument is composed of two subscales. One measures the degree of openness in family communication, and the other measures the extent of problems in family communication. Each subscale contains 10 items.

Olson and associates (1983) report the internal consistency coefficients of the Openness subscale and Problems subscale to be .87 and .78, respectively. A confirmatory factor analysis indicates that the factor loadings for the Openness subscale range from .48 to .71. The factor loadings for the Problems subscale are within the range of .26 to .60.

How to use the tool: Users may locate the scale via the following reference: Barnes, H.L., & Olson, D.H. (1982). Parent-adolescent communication scale. In D.H. Olson et al., *Family inventories: Inventories used a national survey of families across the family life cycle* (pp.33-48). St. Paul: Family Social Science, University of Minnesota.The scores for the items on the Problems subscale are reversed in value. A sum of the 10 items on the Problems subscale indicates that the level of perceived problems in communication ranged from 10 to 50. A high score indicates a lack of perceived problems in the family. The total score for the Openness subscale is also the sum of the 10 items on the subscale. Higher scores indicate higher levels of openness in family communication.

How to evaluate the outcomes: Applying the six evaluative steps discussed in chapter 3, the parent–adolescent communication is measured with a single-system research design with the standardized case when the family is dealing with drug problems.

1. *Define the service target or problem (intake and case assessment):* The clients have demonstrated a lack of communication within the family.
2. *Define (or formulate) goals and objectives:* To increase communication between the parents and adolescent.
3. *Identify constraints and resources and select a treatment:* Constraints include substance abuse and lack of communication between the parents and the child. Resources include willingness to seek help and the parents' acknowledgement of the problem.
4. *Measure the monitoring actions (monitor progress):* A total of 10 subjects are assigned to the experimental group to receive gestalt therapy. The family members are asked to complete the PACS Openness subscale each week for 7 weeks (baseline A). Gestalt therapy is used for 7 weeks (intervention period B) after the baseline. The practitioner records the score each week for 14 weeks. The scores from the 10 subjects are averaged and plotted in Figure 9.1.

   Another 10 subjects with similar characteristics who face the same problem but do not participate in the treatment for various reasons are assigned to the comparison group without receiving the therapy during the 14 weeks. The comparison-group clients are asked to complete the PACS Openness subscale each week for 14 weeks. The scores for the 10 subjects are averaged and plotted in Figure 9.2.
5. *Analyze data:* Compare average PACS Openness subscale score in the baseline with the average PAC Openness subscale score in the intervention period. The data in Figure 9.1 indicate that the average PACS Openness subscale score is greater in the intervention period compared to the baseline period, with

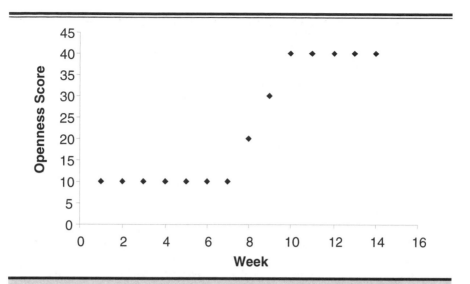

Figure 9.1

Parent–Adolescent Communication Openness Subscale:
Experimental Group

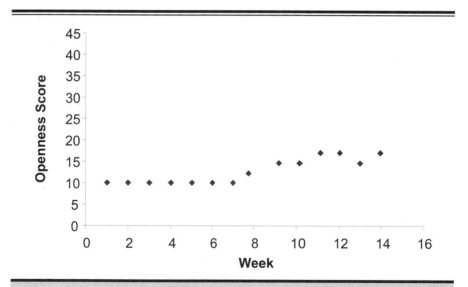

Figure 9.2

Parent-Adolescent Communication Openness Subscale:
Comparison Group

higher scores indicating that the family is more open to parent–adolescent communication. When comparing to the comparison group data (as shown in Figure 9.2 with no obvious changes), the practitioner can conclude that clients who received gestalt therapy in the experimental group are more open to engage themselves in communication.

6. *Report results and make recommendations:* The average PACS Openness subscale score is significantly greater in the experimental group than in the comparison group. The results suggest that the gestalt therapy is effective in helping the families address their communication problems. Additional cultural expectations are to be examined to further analyze the concept of openness.

Topics for Discussion

1. For which clients would this approach be most appropriate and least appropriate?
2. How would you modify the application of gestalt techniques to make them helpful for people from different cultural backgrounds or families with different characteristics?
3. To what other approaches is gestalt similar? In what ways?
4. How would gestalt approaches be helpful when combined with other approaches?

CHAPTER TEN

Strategic Theory

Strategic theory is derived from the work of the Palo Alto research group led by G. Bateson (see Dowd & Milne, 1986; Steinglass, 1987) and expanded through practical applications under Jay Haley's family-oriented approach of examining symptom formation and analyzing power control intent (Goldenberg & Goldenberg, 2004; Haley, 1980). This theory postulates that a problem involving a single family member can attract the attention of the entire family. In some instances, individuals use an illness or symptoms of an illness as a strategy to attract the attention of others. Although a person may not consciously plan to utilize the strategy, the attention it garners acts as reinforcement and drives the continuation of the illness or symptoms. With this psychological perspective, strategic theory can be used to identify specific plans or actions that aim to end behaviors or illnesses that have no organic, genetic, or physical cause.

These strategies are designed to be congruent with the client's cultural values, and this chapter describes in detail how strategic theory is applicable to multicultural practices. This chapter addresses three issues regarding children's growth and development and the resulting feelings of loneliness that parents may experience when their children leave home. As the case develops and the strategic techniques are applied, the standardized family of Joe, Mary, Ami, and Kevin demonstrates issues of parenthood and intergenerational conflict including mother–daughter relationships. Then, in an altered case scenario, the family is presented as a single-parent family, with Mary (the mother) as the sole caregiver and single parent without the support or presence of her husband Joe, who deserted the family.

Because strategic theory is a technique-driven approach, this chapter highlights demonstrations of various techniques. To measure the effectiveness of the treatments, it is suggested that clients use personal tracking to assess their progress. In addition, an evaluation tool of intergenerational values is recommended with steps to measure change.

Strategic Theory in Brief

Application to Multicultural Practices:

- Flexible techniques stimulate clients' thoughts about different situations.
- Systemic analysis helps clients reexamine their repeated patterns of behavior.

Major Figures:

- Cloe Madanes: Basic Intentions
- Jay Haley (1923–): Symptom Strategies
- Milton Erickson (1902–1980): Metaphonic and Hypnotic Therapy
- Mara Selvini-Palazzoli (1916–1999): Paradoxes and Counter-paradoxes; Rules of the Game

Assumptions:

- People have four basic desires: (1) to dominate and control; (2) to be loved; (3) to love and protect others; and (4) to repent and forgive (Madanes).
- A symptom is a strategy for controlling a relationship (Haley).
- It is important to find a difference that makes a difference (Milan's School).

Therapeutic Process:

- Assess here-and-now family communication patterns.
- Prescribe substitute behaviors and reframe negative thoughts.

Goals:

- To systematically search for differences
- To resolve the presenting problem
- To help people move on
- To avoid the focus on changing personality or family structure

Multicultural Practice Techniques:

- Re-labeling the meaning of symptoms
- Circular questioning
- Positive connotation
- Hypothesizing
- Rituals

Strategy as the Intervention Focus

Since 1959, the Mental Research Institute (MRI) has been active in developing therapeutic techniques and innovative ways of examining human behaviors (Goldenberg & Goldenberg, 2004). Strategic theory assists individuals in moving from previous behavioral patterns to new paradigms of change, and it contributes significantly to multicultural family therapy by helping families realize the impact of these repeated behaviors on their functioning. The original designs of strategic therapeutic techniques are highly directive and manipulative. When these techniques are applied to multicultural counseling, it is important to first establish trust and rapport between client and practitioner so clients will understand that the techniques being used are always purposeful. Recent developments in strategic therapy focus on the dynamic use of techniques with careful and culturally sensitive explanations of the purpose of each technique used (Gardner, Burr, & Wiedower, 2006).

Gender factors also play an important role in technique application. Walsh (1993) suggested, from the results of case consultation and practice evaluation, that clients' emotions must be assessed after applying certain techniques that exaggerate the gender roles within a family. Without cultural sensitivity in handling the use of the strategic techniques, clients may feel awkward or offended if they follow the directives provided by the practitioner to exaggerate gender role responsibilities. In a study conducted by Price (1994), a female adolescent with a developmental lag received benefit from strategic therapy because the client was able to connect the philosophical base of the therapy to her perception of what the problem was. In situations when the client does not reach an intellectual functioning level to comprehend the purpose of the strategies or techniques, it is advised that strategic therapy should be used with caution.

On the Multicultural Stage: Children Leaving Home

A family with children will eventually go through the so-called empty-nest stage when children leave home for college, for employment, or to form their own families. Since the 20th century, the empty-nest phenomenon has been described as a social concept, the stage in the adult life cycle when children are no longer living at home (Raup & Myers, 1989). In addition, it has been described as the stage when a couple spends time together after their last child has left home and before one of the spouses dies (Barber, 1989). Some researchers believe that the term "empty nest" carries derogatory ageist and sexist connotations by referring to women as "birds" or "old hens" (Oliver, 1982; Raup & Myers, 1989). Borland (1982) introduced the term *postparental period*—a more neutral but less common term.

A maladaptive response to the postparental experience has been called the *empty nest syndrome.* The role loss may lead to an identity crisis for some parents, especially mothers who have spent many years as caregivers (Raup & Myers, 1989). Others experience sadness, grief, dysphoria, and depression (Kahana & Kahana, 1982). Not all families, however, experience their children transitioning and moving out of the household—especially multigenerational ethnic families (Raup & Myers, 1989).

Because of the trend of adult children returning home after college, it may be argued that, for some, the postparental period may be shortened. This "boomerang generation" of adult children coming back home currently comprises approximately 18 million 18- to 34-year-olds who reside with their parents (U.S. Census Bureau, 2004a). Adult children return home for a number of reasons, many of which are characterized as negative. According to Mitchell (1998), the negative impacts associated with adult children returning home can be lessened if the adult child has taken on an adult role and is not as dependent. Additional benefits, such as intergenerational sharing and closeness, may also counter this negative impact (Mitchell, 1998).

The Case Approach

Using Mary and Joe's case as an example, the following dialogues apply strategic techniques to help the family realize the importance of understanding and solving certain family issues in actualizing family cohesiveness. Selected issues are related to the client's first child leaving home, her parenthood issues, intergenerational conflict, and mother–daughter relationships.

Issue #1: First Child Leaving Home

In the last individual session with Mary, the practitioner assessed her worries about being a perfect mother. In this session Mary is discussing her feelings about her parenting style. She is concerned about Ami's recent behavior and wants to know how to help Ami prepare for college.

Mary: Ami will be leaving soon for college. I don't know how to prepare her for it. She's been playing around too much lately.

MC: What do you mean by "preparing her?"

Mary: I want to help her understand how to be independent.

MC: In that statement, you seem to contradict yourself. You mentioned before that you would like Ami to be around longer.

Symptom Checking

Mary: I thought so, too. But the more I think about it, I realize that if I don't care about her wishes, she might think I'm not a good mother.

MC: Would you like to make a decision for yourself now?

Mary: What is it?

MC:	If you could make one change to be a better mother, what would that be?
Mary:	There isn't anything I'd like to change now.
MC:	It seems to me that, if you have nothing to change, you have been wrongly judged.
Mary:	Ami always thinks that I'm not a good mom.
MC:	It seems to me that you don't like being wrongly judged. As your assignment this week, jot down each occasion when you believe you were wrongly judged. Write down how many times it happens every day for a week.

Paradoxical Intervention

Mary:	That seems a little weird.
MC:	Whenever we face new things or act in new ways, we all feel anxious. Maybe it's easier not to think about the problem if you think it doesn't bother you.
Mary:	But I know I'm not happy, and I'm almost making myself sick worrying about what I should do.
MC:	If you allow the expectations of other people to guide your life, do you think you will be happier?
MC:	If you allow the expectations of other people to guide your life, do you think you will be happier?
Mary:	No.
MC:	If you are not happy, will Joe be happier?
Mary:	No. But I can't help it.
MC:	You can't help it or you want to keep it this way?
Mary:	No, I don't want to keep it this way.
MC:	Does "not keeping it this way" mean that you will try to do something different?

Circular Questioning

| Mary: | I guess so. I can record how and when I have been put down. I can even write down my feelings. However, I'm scared of how other people will react if I do something weird. (laughs) |
| MC: | That scary and weird feeling is what gets you to think that you are not able to help Ami. |

Issue #2: Parenthood Issues

In the last session, Mary was asked to do a homework assignment of "seeking put-downs." First she would find ways to be put down in her family. Then she would write down her feelings when she was put down by her family members and record the exact statements that made her feel she was being put down. In this session, Mary appears to be anxious. She is worried about how her parenting style is affecting her relationship with Ami and Joe.

MC: Hello, Mary. I sense that you're a bit more anxious today than you were last week.

Mary: This last week was much more difficult for me. I got an offer for a full-time teaching position at the private school where I've always wanted to teach. Then Ami stayed out late Saturday night, and Joe and I waited up. We called all of her friends and the boy's house where they were hanging out. She didn't get in until four a.m.! Joe hasn't spoken to her since.

MC: What else happened this week?

Mary: Oh—I almost forgot! I saw Kevin's teachers last week, and his grades have been dropping. He has several Cs now, and even a D and an F! He's not a young kid any more. What can I say to him?

MC: How do you feel right now?

Mary: I'm feeling pulled in all directions. I don't think I can continue like this. My kids have left nothing for me. (sobbing)

MC: Mary, it sounds like you've had a very trying week. What kind of support did you have? Were you able to talk with anyone?

Mary: No. (looks sad) Joe's silence after Saturday night has been directed not only at Ami but at me as well, it seems. Support—well I've always been the one to care for everything from the children's health issues to their education. If Joe would have done something, I would have… (looks off into space).

MC: You've done a lot to take care of your family. What a great job you've done this past week when they needed you!

Positive Connotation

Mary: I suppose I have … yes. I know I could have done better, but….

MC: But it would have been easier if you had some support or some sort of validation of your role?

Mary: Joe and I don't talk much…. (stares off)

MC: Mary, have you tried to talk with Joe about this?

Mary: I'm so afraid! It's been silent for so long between Joe and me.

MC: What can you do? What do you think you can do to engage Joe in discussing this?

Mary: I know I'm holding back about taking that step…. Everything is so chaotic right now that I don't think I could handle more! My head is spinning, and I'm having trouble breathing!

MC: Okay, Mary, let's take a deep breath. Try to relax. Breathe in ... and out.... Feel better now? Earlier you said you can't handle more. More of what?

Confronting

Mary: Joe's already been more silent since Ami stayed out. If I push, I don't know what he might do.

MC: It sounds like you're feeling trapped. Which way do you want to go? How long are you willing to feel this discomfort?

Mary: I've already pushed my limit. The assignment you gave me didn't work. It just seems to be getting harder! (looking angry)

MC: Your assignment about seeking putdowns ... yes, tell me what happened with that.

Ordeal Therapy

Mary: It seemed to be successful up until Ami's incident. Well, I felt just terrible! After several times of betting for putdowns, Joe finally gave me a funny look. Maybe that's why he's been so quiet around me, as well as Ami?

MC: Have you asked Joe why he's so quiet around you?

Mary: No. No. No. He gets like this at times, and I try not to put too much pressure on him. I've always handled everything.

MC: So, you are ... silent yourself?

Circular Questioning

Mary: (With an "aha" look) Why, yes! I've been silent, too—to keep the peace at home!

MC: And how has your chosen method of "keeping the peace" affected you?

Mary: My silence.... I feel so alone. (looking sad) I have these people around me I love so much, and I still feel so alone! (crying more)

MC: Mary, I hear you saying that your family's silence—you've also called it peace—has caused you a great deal of sadness, loneliness, pain.... Do you think this silence, or peace, is also affecting the way Joe feels?

Positive Connotation

Mary: I'm doing what Joe wants.

MC: Let's talk about some things you could do. And you choose one to try this week with Joe.

Mary: Where do I start?

MC: I think communication is where we need to start. I also want to talk about having a session with both of you next time. Do you think we can arrange for that to happen?

Mary: Yes, I think I can. Let me talk to Joe, and I'll call you about a good time to come next week.

MC: Okay, I'll wait to hear from you later this week…. Now, for homework, you could track your anxiety level and document it on a tracking form. (Hands Mary a tracking form—see the example anxiety scale presented in chapter 3). Rate your anxiety every day around the same time on a scale of 1 to 5, with 1 being "no anxiety" and 5 being "unbearable or extreme." You can write down anything that makes you feel anxious or not anxious for each day.

Tracking

Mary: How do I do it?

MC: Use one of these identical forms each day during the next week before our next session. Also, write down any event that may be worth mentioning, even though it may not seem to have anything to do with anxiety. For instance, how would you rate your anxiety level from 1 to 5 when Ami didn't come home until 4 in the morning?

Mary: That's a 5.

MC: What would be rated a 1 or 2?

Mary: Going shopping—yes, I'd probably rate that a 1. If Ami comes home early, it would be a 2.

MC: Try this for a week, and bring all your forms back.

Issue #3: Intergenerational Conflict

In an individual session with Ami, the goal is to examine the source of her value system to better understand what value she places on life and how her issue of "I'm afraid of telling my mother about my failure" is affecting her relationship with Mary.

MC: You look like you're feeling calm today.

Ami: Well, things went smoother with Mom this past week.

MC: Give me an example.

Ami: This morning we had breakfast together, which is really unusual. She was actually pleasant to be with. We talked a little bit about school, then about my boyfriend. I still worry that she can be too rigid at times, but she seemed to listen to me. I found myself thinking that she's learned something with you so she's is willing to talk about her feelings with me.

MC: Remember last time you told us that you would tell your mom about your problem?

Ami: Well … Mom still showed her worries. She said, "I just don't feel like a good mother." Since she's always worrying, I can't tell her about my problem.

MC: Can't or won't?

Confronting

Ami: What do you mean?

MC: We always have a choice, right? We make choices, take risks, or choose not to choose, don't we?

Ami: Not me. I've always been who I'm supposed to be. (laughs)

MC: Then what would you expect your mom to know when you're facing a problem?

Positive Connotation

Ami: I don't know. Mom will know one way or the other. I guess I'll tell her.

MC: And that's your choice, is it not?

Ami: (hesitating) I don't know if I have a choice.

           (After the practitioner works with Ami individually and identifies her wants, secrets, and perceptions toward the family problem, Mary and Joe join in as the therapist focuses on Ami's leaving home.)

MC: Ami, why don't you start off and tell your parents about the way you see your problems.

Ami: I think I stay busy all the time so I don't have to notice my problems.

MC: Don't you want to let out your secrets? Do you remember what you told me about what you think your parents think about your boyfriend?

Ami: I don't have secrets. It's a trust issue, and they don't seem to trust me.

Mary: (Interrupting) Ami, I don't want my daughter to spend the night with some unknown boy.

Ami: (Looking at MC) See—that's exactly what I told you.

Joe: I agree with your mom. You need to come home early.

MC: Let's focus on the behavior, not the person.

Symptom Focusing

Mary: When she comes home late after her curfew, I get nervous.

MC: Ami, what did you hear?

Ami: *Stop it!* I'm sick and tired of being treated like a little girl. I look like a fool leaving the dance at 11:30 when things are just getting started! Just because you two never had any fun doesn't mean I have to be made fun of by my friends!

Mary: Ami—behave!

MC: Joe and Mary, think about this question for a minute. When was the last time you both spent some fun time together?

Positive Connotation

Joe: It's different now.

Mary:	I don't have time to have fun. But that doesn't mean that Ami can stay out late all the time.
MC:	Ami, what did you hear?
Ami:	I know they've tried to do too much so that they couldn't even have fun.
MC:	Mary, I know we are dealing with two issues. Do you see how these two issues may connect? Now, let's look at the issues one at a time. Our focus right now is about your worries. (turning to Ami) Ami, please tell your parents how you feel about this.
Ami:	Well, I think they should know they can trust me.
MC:	Tell them directly.

Redefining the Symptom

Ami:	Mom and Dad, you can trust me.
Joe:	I trust you, Ami. I just don't want you to get hurt.
Mary:	Your father is right.
MC:	Tell Ami something positive about your trust.

Positive Connotation

Mary:	I trust you, Ami. I just want you to know that we're always here to protect you.
Joe:	We know you're not a little girl any more.

Issue #4: Mother–Daughter Relationships

Ami comes to her individual session first. Her intent is to help her mom understand her better and nag her less. Ami has experienced anxiety recently in connection with preparating for college. After sharing some of her personal issues with the practitioner individually, Ami agrees that she will be the one to calm her mom. Mary then joins the session.

MC:	Ami, would you tell your mother the concerns you have about college?
Ami:	Mom knows already. She knows that I'll probably go to an out-of-state college.
MC:	Is this something that both of you have talked about?
Mary:	Not really. I sure hope she would tell me what she wants to do.
Ami:	Mom, you're always keeping track of everything I do anyway. I don't have to tell you.
Mary:	Yes, you do. I pay for your school, and you must listen.
MC:	Mary, I'd like you to say, "Ami, tell me about your plans for college."
Mary:	(Impatiently) Ami, tell me about your plans for college.
Ami:	I've applied to a lot of colleges, but I think my top choice is New State College.

Mary:	I'm afraid I won't be able to see you if you go that far away.
Ami:	Mom, come on. This is America. You don't have to worry about it. No place is too far for me.
MC:	How about saying, "No place is too far to connect with my family?"
Ami:	No place is too far for anything.
MC:	Since our purpose is to examine your relationship with your mom and your family, how about if you try, "No place is too far to say hello to my mom?"

Insisting an Idea as a Strategy

Ami:	Okay! No place is too far for me to say hi to my mom.
MC:	How do you feel?
Ami:	I feel that you tried to force me to say something I didn't like. But once the words were out, I feel that I've told my mom something that I always wanted to tell her.

Strategic Theory Techniques

Circular Questioning: Asking a series of questions so the client will provide answers until the first question recurs or until the problem has an answer.

Confronting: Forcing the client to think about the issue or problem.

Directive: Leading or directing clients to say something that is positive to each other or helpful to the healing process.

Ordeal Therapy: Replacing the symptom with a new task that is more difficult so the client would rather give up the symptom than perform the task.

Paradoxical Intervention: Assigning the client to do something opposite from the client's liking to reach a higher awareness or better understanding of the problem.

Positive Connotation: Reframing the situation into something positive or transforming the situation into a learning experience.

Redefining the Symptom: Reframing the symptom to emphasize its original intent.

Symptom Focusing: Directly addressing the person's behavior rather than the person.

Tracking: Measuring the level of a specific feeling associated with the identified problem and finding ways to solve the problem by examining various situations that could increase or decrease the level of this feeling.

MC: Mary, how do you feel?

Mary: I really want her to be closer, even though no place is too far.

MC: Mary, it sounds like supporting Ami's decision contradicted your family values.

Paradoxical Intervention

Mary: Yes, my family comes first. I think it's hard to reach her even when she's nearby.

MC: Do you mean being near doesn't mean being close to her?

Mary: That's exactly right!

MC: Would being far away be worse, the same, or better when it comes to building a relationship?

Mary: Of course it would be worse to be too far apart!

Ami: Not really. I'll call or e-mail you, mom.

MC: Ami, it's even better for you because you'd think of your mom more often since she's far away and she wouldn't nag you! (joking; all laugh)

Exaggerating the Situation

Ami: Mom is such a worrier!

MC: Mary, I don't mean you actually nag Ami. I say that because I want you to know that being far away may actually mean becoming closer emotionally. Now, Ami, would you mind telling your mom directly, "Mom, don't worry, I'll be thinking of you all the time."

Ami: (Looking at MC) I'll be....

MC: (Interrupting) Please look at your mom when you're telling her this.

Directive

Ami: Sure. (looking at Mary) Mom, don't worry. I'll be calling you. I'll be thinking of you even though you might not know it.

MC: That's good!

Mary: I feel good!

Multicultural Practice Applications

One of the major contributions of strategic theory to multicultural practice is its flexibility and innovation to stimulate clients' thoughts in the therapeutic process. In cross-cultural situations, the practitioner must restate the presenting problem as interactional and situational rather than as dysfunctional or pathological to gain the client's trust. In the case of Joe and Mary, their symptoms are related to their ineffective communication. As they repeat these interactions, their symptoms intensify.

MC: Thank you for joining us today, Joe. What did Mary tell you about the purpose of this session?

Joe: It's all in her mind. I don't see the purpose of this, but I'm here.

Mary: I need you to be here.

MC: It's important you're here, Joe.

Trust Building

MC: Now we're going to do an exercise to analyze your interactions. Stay with me even if we exaggerate the event or feeling. Okay?

          (Mary and Joe nod)

MC: Mary, when you told me about the thoughts you've had recently about looking for a new job, I told you that it's unfair to keep Joe in the dark. Do you remember?

Joe: (In disbelief) Change jobs again?!

MC: Stay with us. There's a purpose to this interaction.

Joe: What is it?

MC: It focuses on how both of you see things from different angles. Please don't hide your true feelings or reactions. We need to see them. But if you feel uncomfortable talking about them, write down your thoughts or feelings on this piece of paper instead.

Not Manipulative

Joe: Okay.

MC: Now, Mary, tell Joe how you felt when I told you not to keep Joe in the dark.

Mary: I thought you were trying to give away my secret. But then I realized how pointless it would be if I didn't tell him.

MC: Joe, now share your feelings.

Variations From the Standardized Case: A Single-Parent Family

The case below has been changed in terms of its composition: Mary and Joe have been divorced for five years. Joe left the family in Mary's hands and has not paid child support. For further practice, this case can be changed to reflect commuting marriages and the lack of a spouse's support in a two-parent household.

***

Mary (38) has been a single parent for the last five years. She has two children—Ami, age 16, and Kevin, age 8. Ever since she and her husband Joe (42) divorced five years ago, Mary has had financial difficulties and tries to stay afloat financially.

Fortunately, Mary has support from her parents, who live nearby. Mary works as a secretary for a top executive of a large bank. Although she likes her full-time job and enjoys the time she spends with her children, she has very little time for herself or a social life. Often, Mary feels out of touch with her friends and is quite lonely.

As a single parent, Mary feels torn by her family and financial obligations, and she often suffers from feelings of guilt about not spending enough time with her kids. Recently Kevin expressed interest in joining the football team, but Mary knows that this will put a financial strain on her budget. At the same time, she does not want to deny her son the enjoyment of participating in sports. Mary has also noticed that Ami is struggling with her decision about what she should do after high school. During individual sessions, Mary has presented symptoms of emotional distress with no recognized physical cause. Ami and Kevin have had trouble concentrating on their studies. The family has not had a shared activity for years, and the children's social activities have been limited.

Experts Say...

According to Dr. Kay Stevenson, Director of Rocky Mountain Survivors Center, although this case does not specify the ethnicity or immigration status of the family, its scenario presents a realistic situation. The mother's emotional conflicts about having sufficient time for work, family, and self are common for single parents. Even though the client enjoys her work, at times she feels exhausted and overwhelmed because of her multiple responsibilities.

In support groups to help these families like this, culturally sensitive practitioners take the following major factors into consideration: choice, trust, and self-care. In this case, experts offer a process perspective about choice and trust when working with single-parent families so the stages from initial contact to termination can be incorporated into the process:

Choice

1. Ask the client to select the room and decide on where to place the chairs.
2. Incorporate rituals, stories, or activities selected by the client into the session's content.
3. Schedule the frequency and number of sessions based on the client's sense of time.
4. Pace each meeting around the client's needs, even if this means more meetings.
5. Avoid setting up choices with unequal or unknown consequences.
6. Avoid goals that are contingent on personal disclosure.

Trust

1. Earn the client's trust, but do not expect it.
2. Reaffirm the client's resources and strengths.

3. Self-disclose carefully and appropriately to humanize sessions and to narrow the distance between client and practitioner.
4. Direct additional interest to the client's family, community, and country.
5. Ask the client to teach the practitioner about his or her family and culture, because the family is the expert about the client and the situation.
6. Reinforce listening to the client after each disclosure of the problem situation.
7. Reaffirm to the client that others share his or her experiences and reactions are normal.
8. Be cautious about extending an immediate display of empathy so the client does not fear the level of intimacy too soon.

Self-Care

To increase clients' participation in experiencing here-and-now learning through a narrative approach regarding self-care take the following steps:

1. Allow sufficient time for the client to divulge the story, and include time for breaks, time-outs, and refocusing.
2. Expect circular, nonlinear stories.
3. Expect inconsistencies in the story-telling, as details may have been lost in the latest story.
4. Drive the gathering of details from the client by the client's need for clarity and not the listener's curiosity.
5. Distinguish between stories for integrating experience from stories for celebrating experience.

Methods of integrating these three culturally sensitive factors into practice are shown in the following dialogues:

MC: From what I'm hearing, your mom tends to yell at you but she's not doing it on purpose. Does it matter to you how your mom feels?

Ami: I guess so. But Mom has to understand that I'm no longer a kid.

MC: Close your eyes. Recall a time when you and your mom were having fun. What did you see or do?

Story-Telling to Bring a Feeling

Ami: I was swimming in our neighborhood pool. Mom came to join me in her old-fashioned swimsuit, but she looked so much younger. (smiling) We swam all afternoon, and then we talked at the poolside.

MC: What did you talk about?

Ami: School stuff and boy things.

MC: Now your mom worries about your school stuff and your boy things. Those things are no longer fun for her to talk about, right?

Ami: Right! Mom worries about almost everything now—even the fun things she used to enjoy.

MC: Who does your mom share her worries with?

Ami: No one. She doesn't talk. She just shows it.

MC: How does she show it?

Ami: She yells at us.

MC: Who does she yell at?

Ami: Me and Kevin.

MC: Why must she yell?

Circular Questions

Ami: We probably didn't listen to her?

MC: If no one is listening, why would she want to talk?

Ami: I guess she wouldn't. Now I understand why she needs a support group.

MC: When you go home tonight, please be a listener and tell her you're listening. Do this every night after dinner or before going to bed. Your mom needs your support.

Rituals

Ami: I'll try.

Best Practice Evaluation

Evaluation Stage 7: Measure Intergenerational Values

The seventh stage of the practice–evaluation integration, as outlined in chapter 1, is about measuring intergenerational values. In this chapter we use a pre-test post-test comparison group design to measure understanding and satisfaction levels between parents and their adolescent children in an immigrant family.

Suggested evaluation tool: Intergenerational Congruence in Immigrant Families Child (ICIF–CS) (Ying, Lee, & Tsai, 2004) and Parent Scales (ICIF–PS) (Ying & Tracy, 2004).

Description: The ICIF–CS contains eight relationship items measured with a 5-point Likert-type scale: 1 = strongly disagree, 2 = somewhat disagree, 3 = neither agree nor disagree, 4 = somewhat agree, and 5 = strongly agree. The ICIF–CS has two subscales: one for the father and one for the mother. In single-parent households, the client can fill out one of the subscales as the mother or father. The purpose of this instrument is to assess the levels of understanding of and satisfaction with the parent–child relationship, from the perspective of the adolescent child.

The parent version of this instrument, ICIF–PS, contains eight relationship items measured with the same 5-point Likert-type scale: 1 = strongly disagree and 5 = strongly agree. Reliability and validity were established for all the scales. The internal reliability coefficients of the first seven items of the ICIF–CS (father version) and ICIF–CS (mother version) are .85 and .84, respectively, indicating a high level of internal consistency. The test–retest reliability is assessed with r = .90 for the father items and .88 for the mother items. The internal reliability for the first seven items in the ICIF–PS is .90, indicating that the overall internal consistency is high.

For the ICIF–CS, convergent validity results indicate that the first seven items in both the father and the mother subscales are significantly correlated with overall relationship satisfaction with father and mother, with the r coefficients ranging from .35 to .66 (p<.01). Convergent validity has also been established for the ICIF–PS scale by examining the correlation of the individual PS items and the PS-total with overall parental satisfaction. The correlation coefficients range from .42 to .62.

How to use the tool: Readers can review the scale via the article by Ying and Tracy (2004), Psychometric properties of the Intergenerational Congruence in Immigrant Families—Parent Scale in Chinese Americans, *Social Work Research, 28*(1), 56–62. Users may need to change the wordings from Chinese to other ethnic group on item #7. An overall ICIF–CS score can be obtained by summing the first seven items of the scale. Scores can range from 7 to 37, with high scores indicating high levels of understanding and satisfaction with the parent–child relationship. The overall ICIF–PS score can be obtained by summing the first seven items of the scale. High scores indicate high levels of understanding and satisfaction with the adolescent child.

How to evaluate the outcomes: As discussed in chapter 3, six steps are followed to evaluate parent–adolescent intergenerational relationship using a pre-test post-test design with a comparison group. To understand Mary's situation as a single mother, these steps are as follows:

1. *Define the service target or problem (intake and case assessment):* Lack of understanding of the parent–child relationship.
2. *Define (or formulate) goals and objectives:* To increase the level of understanding of the parent–child relationship.
3. *Identify constraints and resources and select a treatment:* Constraints include the parent's emotional distress and lack of activities between parent and child; resources include employment and willingness to seek help from the counselor.
4. *Measure the monitoring actions (monitor progress):* Ten mothers are assigned to the experimental group to receive strategic therapy. The parents are asked to complete the ICIF–PS each week for 7 weeks (baseline A). Strategic therapy is used for the subsequent 7 weeks (intervention period B) after the baseline. The practitioner records the score each week for 14 weeks. The scores from the 10 subjects are averaged and plotted in Figure 10.1.

   Another 10 mothers with similar characteristics who face the same problem, but are waiting to get in the groups because of time constraints, are assigned to the comparison group without receiving the therapy in the 14 weeks. The comparison group is asked to complete the PACS Openness subscale each week for 14 weeks. The scores for the 10 subjects are averaged and plotted in Figure 10.2.

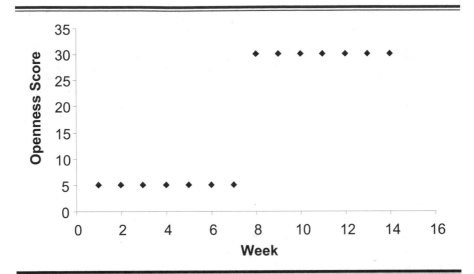

Figure 10.1

Intergenerational Congruence in Immigrant Families:
Parent Scale: Experimental Group

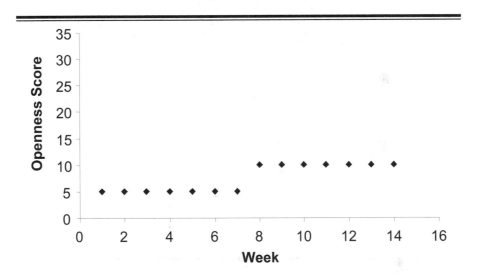

Figure 10.2

Intergenerational Congruence in Immigrant Families:
Parent Scale: Control Group

5. *Analyze data:* Compare average ICIF–PS score in the baseline with the average ICIF–PS score in the intervention period. The data in Figure 10.1 indicate that the average ICIF–PS score is greater in the intervention period than the baseline period. In this measure, higher scores indicate better understanding of the parent–child relationship. When comparing the data to the comparison group (see Figure 10.2), the practitioner is able to identify effectiveness of the planned intervention and pay attention to lower scores if they occur during the intervention period.

6. *Report results and make recommendations:* The average ICIF–PS score is significantly greater in the experimental group than in the comparison group. The results suggest that strategic therapy is effective in helping the parents understand the parent–child relationship so they will be more willing to talk about issues or perceived problems with their adolescent children.

Multicultural Practice Exercises

Paradoxical Intervention

Joe:	I don't understand why Mary is always fussing over something so minor.
MC:	If you don't understand, ask Mary now.
Joe:	Isn't she listening to me right now?
MC:	Yes, but try this instead and see how it sounds. Repeat after me: "Mary."
Joe:	Mary …
MC:	Why are you fussing over something so major?
Joe:	I said "minor."
MC:	Say "major" to see how it feels.
Joe:	Why are you fussing over something so major?
MC:	Mary, what did you hear?
Joe:	It doesn't make sense.
MC:	That's exactly what I want you to feel about your statement.
Joe:	You mean it doesn't make sense.
MC:	Who defines what is minor and what is major?
Joe:	Well …
MC:	Say it now about your earlier statement that Mary is fussing over something so minor.
Joe:	Mary, do you feel that it is important for me to say it now?
Mary:	Thank you for giving me a chance to determine what is major and important.
Joe:	Wow—that's it! I never thought about it from your perspective.

Pretend Technique

Kevin:	I don't see the point in me being here.
MC:	Do you mean it's not important for you to be here?
Kevin:	(silent)
MC:	Let's do a pretend game. Mary, pretend you're Kevin and say what he just said with his tone and expression. (Mary does this) Kevin, what did you see?
Kevin:	Mom just tried to be me—but she's not me.
MC:	Show your mom what you look like when you're not happy.
Kevin:	I'm not going to do it.
MC:	Mary, how about pretending to be Kevin and express his unhappiness?
Mary:	(Showing a sad face)
Kevin:	Mom, do you really think I look like that?!
MC:	If not, show your mom what you think it looks like.
Kevin:	(Showing a sad face)
MC:	Tell your mom how you feel when you're sad and what you would like her to know.

Ordeal Therapy

MC:	Joe, you mentioned earlier that you have never said anything negative about Mary's mother in front of Mary. How about trying this exercise tonight by calling your mother-in-law?
Joe:	Sure.
MC:	But I want you to say something extremely positive about your mother-in-law five times.
Joe:	I wouldn't do that, though.
MC:	If you're not willing to do that, you have to buy a fifty-dollar gift and take it to her house immediately.
Joe:	What's the point? I don't get it.
MC:	I just want to use this exercise to demonstrate that, if you are not willing to do something you don't want to do in order to fix the problem, you may as well give up the initial problem.
Joe:	I never want to start the problem.
MC:	Mary, what did you hear?
Mary:	It sounds like Joe doesn't want to connect with my mom. He has always said that my mom is controlling, but I think he's actually the one who is so controlling.

MC:	Joe, what did you hear?
Joe:	I am *not* controlling. I just don't want to have anything to do with her mom.
Mary:	That's it. My family isn't important in his eyes.
Joe:	I don't mean that.
MC:	You both have different perspectives about your relationship with your families.
Joe:	I don't want to give up the relationship, but I don't feel comfortable with her mom.
Mary:	What can I do to make you feel comfortable?
MC:	(To Mary) How about just saying, "It's okay. Let's put that problem behind us."
Mary:	I just love my mom.
Joe:	I understand. Please forgive me for starting the problem. It's really not a problem after all.

Circular Questioning

MC:	Who do you think is most upset about Ami's problem?
Kevin:	Mom.
MC:	How does your mom try to help Ami?
Kevin:	She talks to her for hours and sets a curfew.
MC:	Who agrees most with your mom's way of trying to help Ami?
Kevin:	Dad, I guess.
MC:	Who disagrees?
Kevin:	Ami. She thinks she should be allowed to do what she wants.
MC:	Who agrees with Ami?
Kevin:	I would, but I don't understand her.
MC:	What don't you understand?
Kevin:	Just about teenagers.
MC:	In your family, who have been teenagers before?
Kevin:	Mom and Dad, I suppose.
MC:	What kind of problems did your mom and dad go through as teenagers?
Kevin:	Don't know. The usual stuff, I suppose.
MC:	Can you guess who was most upset by their *teenage problem*?

Anxiety Scale Activity

Ask each of the group or family members to think of difficult situations within their family in the past and write a simple statement representing a feeling. The practitioner will collect the statements and modify the content to protect everyone's confidentiality.

In the next session or after a short break, the practitioner will read each statement and ask the participants to write down the anxiety level (from 1 = low to 10 = high) associated with this statement. For example, Scenario #1: "A girl stayed out late. The parents woke up at 2 a.m. and called all the girl's friends. The girl got in at 3 a.m. and saw her parents sitting in the living room." What is your anxiety level assuming you are the parents? What is your anxiety level if you are the girl? These responses can be used for group or family discussions.

Topics for Discussion

1. Because strategy therapy was originally developed from a male perspective, how does a family avoid power struggles between the two genders, especially when using a paradoxical intervention?
2. How does strategy therapy deal with resistance? What should you do if the client's family members do not want to participate in any of the strategic exercises?
3. If the client is not a high-functioning individual, how could he or she be made to understand the intent of a paradoxical intervention to avoid putting him or her at risk of completing the assigned task?

CHAPTER ELEVEN

Behavioral Theory

The topic of this chapter is behavioral theory as it has evolved from individual counseling to family therapy and from general counseling to task-centered, outcome-oriented multicultural practices. It stresses the concreteness of treatment plan and the development of cultural sensitivity with clients. With the standardized case, the practice dialogues address three issues:

1. Dealing with societal expectations
2. Balancing work and leisure and the postparental (empty-nest) syndrome
3. Children's returning home and the full-nest syndrome

In addition to applying behavioral therapy to Joe and Mary's family, this chapter presents a varied case scenario in which Mary has become a victim of domestic violence. In addition, to demonstrate the impact of multicultural issues on children, the standardized case then fast-forwards into the future, when Ami, the daughter in the family, is preparing to marry a man of a different race and ethnicity.

Because many cultures identify concrete behavioral change as the goal of therapy, behavioral concepts can be rather useful with multicultural clients because of the concreteness of the tasks assigned. This chapter illustrates specific behaviorist and social learning techniques. Evaluation consists of measuring family stress and changes in young adults' lives. Data from measuring Mary's Perceived Stress Scale are documented before and after behavioral intervention to demonstrate how to evaluate practice with a time-series design.

From Social Learning to Behavioral Action

Behavioral theory was applied to individual counseling about two decades before its application to family interventions in the early 1970s (see Bandura & Walters, 1967; Turner, 1996). The theory, which examines how behavior is influenced by events that precede or follow an action, emerged through the work of John Watson, Edward Thorndike, and Ivan Pavlov. Social learning theory later expanded on the traditional behaviorist view to account for the internal processes that occur in the learning process (Liberman, 1970; Spiegler & Guevremont, 2003). According to Wetter & Wetter (2006), people learn to use manipulation to control others, regardless of the type of problems encountered. Through the use of behavioral therapy techniques, practitioners can use concrete tasks to show clients the consequences of being manipulative.

Behavioral theory is a popular means to design therapeutic plans, especially when working with children and their families because of its efforts to provide concrete evidence to support the interventions (Niec, Hemme, & Yopp, 2005). When applying behavioral theory in treating families, practitioners consider family members to be a significant part of the client's natural environment. Consequently, observations within this environment can provide insight into a client's personal problems and the ways in which problems are related to family behaviors and interactions.

While every client may not have a full learning capacity, the practitioner can guide them to observe consequences which relate to the target behavior. The client can use this learning experience to identify barriers to his/her cultural adjustment. Barriers to achieving such consequence-oriented observations include the client's lack of motivation, refusal to participate, and defensiveness to admit mistakes. As a result, maladaptive behavior should not be framed as mistakes; rather, it is an adjustment difficulty. Especially in the case of a new immigrant, maladaptive behavior may be used as a defense mechanism to hide his/her feelings toward an inability to adjust to the new environment or to raise the person's self esteem through something that the person *can* perform (Nesdale & Lambert, 2007). Practitioners should use this opportunity, with regard to client defense mechanisms, to encourage the client to disclose any use of adjustment methods, which will lead to assessing the source of certain behavioral problems, as perceived by others.

Although behavioral therapy can be combined with cognitive therapy, it has a distinct theoretical origin that begins with the ABC theory: An antecedent event (A) causes the occurrence of a behavior (B), which is followed by intended or unintended consequences (C) that may affect the individual's future behavior (Corey, 2005). This antecedent–behavior–consequence theory explains how to facilitate an understanding of this learning process to help an individual modify his or her maladaptive behavior.

For individuals whose cultures focus more on concreteness, behavioral therapy is an effective choice. In a study of Japanese Americans, for example, Yamazaki (2004) found that cultural adaptation is considered successful after these immigrants have acquired concrete methods of learning. In another study, by Gil (2005), play therapy as a behavioral method of helping children verbalize concerns is effective with clients from all cultures because of its concrete nature. As applied to multicultural practice, many classic behavioral concepts that are used with individuals can be translated into actions to promote changes with families:

■ *Basic ID Model of Assessment* (Lazarus, 1986): Behaviors are assessed with a focus on seven interactive modals:

B = behavior
A = affect
S = sensation
I = images
C = cognitions
I = interpersonal relationships
D = drugs, biological functions, nutrition, and exercise.

These assessment areas identify how a specific behavior interacts with other biopsychosocial factors (such as the emotional and sensational effects arising from the behavior and the thinking process in association with personal and environmental factors), and thus creates a source for identifying problems as an assessment base.

■ *Classical conditioning* (Pavlov): Behaviors can be learned and unlearned (see Reilly & Schachtman, 2005, which discusses the recent emphasis on the function of learning rather than the conditioning process).
■ *Contingency contracting:* Behaviors are targeted for change during a process of enhancing the reciprocal exchange of desirable reinforcement (see Stedman, 1977).
■ *Contingencies of reinforcement* (Liberman, 1970; Skinner, 1969): Behavioral changes are assessed after an effort to restructure the reciprocal exchange process.
■ *Operant conditioning* (Skinner): Behaviors can be strengthened or weakened by connecting with selective rewards or punishments.
■ *Reinforcement* (Pavlov; Skinner): Behaviors can be changed by means of immediate consequences (see Davey, 1987).
■ *Shaping* (Skinner): Desired behaviors are achieved after successive use of reinforcement.

On the Multicultural Stage: Family With Adult Children

When children grow up and begin their adult lives, parents often struggle to find their new place in the family. The description of the empty nest phenomenon began in the 20th century and was defined as the stage in the adult life cycle when children are no longer living at home (Raup & Myers, 1989). It has also been described as the time a couple spends together after their last child has left home and before one of

Behavioral Theory in Brief

Importance to Multicultural Practice:

- Behavioral theory addresses concrete behaviors to be changed.
- Clients participate in defining goals.

Major Figures:

- Ivan P. Pavlov and B.F. Skinner: Conditioning and Social Learning
- Arnold Lazarus: Basic ID Model of Assessment
- Robert Liberman and B.F. Skinner: Contingencies of Reinforcement

Assumptions:

- Individuals are shaped by learning and sociocultural conditioning.
- Systematic goals guide us into action.
- Practicing and evaluating new behaviors are important ways to change problematic behaviors.

Therapeutic Process:

- Begin with a comprehensive assessment of present functioning, with reasons explaining how past learning is related to current behavior.

Goals:

- To eliminate maladaptive behavior and learn constructive behavior
- To develop self-directed and self-managed behavior

Multicultural Practice Techniques:

- Systematic desensitization
- Relaxation techniques
- Assertion training
- Self-management
- Reinforcement and modeling
- Behavioral rehearsal

the spouses dies (Barber, 1989). As we noted in the previous the chapter, some researchers consider the term "empty nest" derogatory because it perpetuates ageist and sexist attitudes by referring to women as "birds" or "old hens" (Oliver, 1982; Raup & Myers, 1989).

Borland (1982) introduced the term *postparental period*, which is a more neutral but less common term. A maladaptive response to the postparental experience has been referred to as the *empty nest syndrome* (Raup & Myers, 1989). This role loss may lead to an identity crisis for some parents, especially mothers who have spent many years as caregivers (Raup & Myers, 1989). Others experience sadness, grief, dysphoria, and depression (Kahana & Kahana, 1982). In some families, especially certain multigenerational ethnic families, youth do not move out of the household (Raup & Myers, 1989).

An emerging trend is for adult children to return home, so for some families the postparental period is shortened. The "boomerang generation" of adult children coming back home currently comprises approximately 18 million 18- to 34-year-olds who reside with their parents—a 85% increase from 1980 to 1989 (Casey, 2004; In Touch, 2005). Adult children return home for a variety of reasons, which may be characterized as negative, as in "divorce, unemployment, financial troubles, mental illness and chemical dependency" (In Touch, para. 1). The adult child can mitigate the negative impact of returning home by taking on an adult role and greater independence (Mitchell, 1998).

The Case Approach

Benefits such as intergenerational sharing and closeness may also counter the negative impact. The following issues demonstrate how societal expectations may impact a client's functioning and how the children's leaving and returning home have a significant symbolic meanings to parents. These issues include societal expectations and work and leisure.

Issue #1: Societal Expectations

The therapist uses the self-directed behavioral approach to help Mary develop her own goals and forms of reinforcement and to identify ways to monitor and evaluate her behaviors. At the beginning of this session, the therapist encourages Mary to imagine that Ami has finished college, has begun her career, and has formed her own family, and that Kevin has gone off to college. During this time Mary has become aware that the definition of her problem is influenced by society and that her behavior affects her view of her family.

Mary: I don't know what I expect of myself. You know … I've been doing everything for my children.

MC: Do you mean you can't find something new to do?

Focusing on Learned Behavioral Patterns

Mary: Well, I guess I can. But I really think my priority should be a weight-loss program. I need some help.

MC: Is your weight loss important to your children, too?

Mary: Yes, I think so. I think if I started something like that, they would see me as an important individual who can do things on her own, for herself.

MC: Great! Well, to help you do this, why don't we set up some goals and objectives for your immediate plan?

Mary: But I need you to push me to stick with my plan.

MC: Let's start by forming the plan, then we can talk about motivation, okay? Let's see ... you said you want a weight-loss program that will help you to strengthen your image. What would you say would be a satisfying change for you in terms of your weight?

Mary: Oh, I want to be as slim as Oprah.

MC: What size did you wear before you had your first child?

Realistic Goal

Mary: I would sound silly. Look at me ... I'll never look eighteen again.

MC: Think about it for a minute. What part of that look might you want to approach now?

Mary: This is silly! I can't get back to that size. I wore a size 12. That was the smallest I could get before my wedding day. I looked pretty good, but I remember thinking that I could have looked even better if I could have gotten down to a 10. It's kind of funny—now I'd be thrilled to be a size 12. I just want to look a little less ... dowdy.

MC: I understand. What would constitute looking "less dowdy" to you?

Mary: I saw a woman about my age in the supermarket yesterday, and she was wearing one of those workout outfits that people wear to aerobics or whatever. I think I'd like to be able to wear one of those without feeling uncomfortable.

MC: Okay. So you'd be thrilled to be a size 12 again, but you really want to feel like you can wear a workout outfit to the supermarket.

Mary: Oh, no. I wouldn't wear those things to the store—even if I were a size 12!

MC: Okay, then. What exactly do you want to accomplish in your weight-loss program?

Mary: I'm not sure ... but I guess my goal is really to wear a size 12 again. I'll aim for that anyway.

MC: That sounds reasonable. So your goal is to wear a size 12 again.

Mary: Yes, wearing a size 12 again sounds reasonable. I certainly could wear less dowdy clothes than I do now.

Target Behaviors

MC: Good. Now, in aiming for this goal, what behaviors do you need to change? Can you think of anything in your present behavior that you want to increase or decrease?

Mary: Well, everything I've read or heard says I need to eat less and exercise more. But I need someone to help me. I mean ... I've known that I have had to do this for years.

MC: Let's think about exercising more and eating less. How could you keep track of whether you're eating less and exercising more?

Mary: I could keep a list of what I eat and how much I exercise.

Measurement Tool

MC: That's a good suggestion. If you keep a list now for a week before you start your program, you'll begin to get a sense of what has changed along the road.

Mary: You mean I should start my diary before I actually do anything different?

Baseline for Observing Behavioral Changes

MC: Sure. It would be helpful to compare what you've done in the past to what you'll do with this new idea. Without a sense of what you're doing now, it might be hard to tell what specific changes might be good to make. And if your diary were to include what you eat, when you eat, and how you were feeling while you ate—as well as how much exercise you do—we might begin to see more of the kinds of issues that are involved in your eating and exercising behaviors.

Mary: Oh, I see.

Contracting

MC: Will you keep a diary this week, write down all those things daily, and bring it back next Monday? (Beginning to write a list) Don't forget to write down your feelings.

Mary: Okay … let's see. I'll write down what I eat, when I eat, and how I feel when I eat, and whether I do any exercise during the day, as well as how much I weigh that day at 9 p.m.

MC: Yes, and you might add *where* you eat to your list. That may be helpful to know—for example, whether you eat at the table, in front of the TV, in the car, in a restaurant, and anyone you eat with…. Remember—just eat and exercise as you normally do, and don't change anything yet.

Mary: Right. Got it.

(Next Session:)

Mary: Here's my diary. It was hard writing down what I ate without changing my behavior. I mean, when I saw how much I was eating, I think I cut down automatically. Also, I took a walk one day just so I would have something to write down in the exercise category.

MC: Yes. Sometimes writing things down is actually an intervention by itself. Did you write down anything about where you ate and how you felt while you were eating?

Mary: Yes, but I didn't like that part either. I notice that I eat more when I eat lunch in the car while I'm running errands or in front of the TV at night while I'm trying to wind down.

MC: That's a good observation. How did you feel during those times?

Reinforcement

Mary: At lunch I feel rushed and a little angry, like I'm doing all of this stuff and it's not even for me. I'm doing things mostly for my family, and I don't even have time to sit down and eat and relax. When I'm in front of the TV at night, I feel like that's the only time I have for myself all day, and that I deserve a treat for having gotten to the end of the day.

Issue #2: Work and Leisure

Mary and Joe are experiencing postparental (empty-nest) symptoms. Mary has noticed that Joe is working longer hours, and she is feeling increasingly lonely at home. Mary is now teaching full-time at a local high school. She does not want to go home too early because Joe is not home at dinnertime anymore.

Mary: I'm exhausted.

Joe: I don't understand why she's been so depressed lately.

MC: You just made a face, Mary.

Behavioral Manifestation

Mary: Well, I don't see myself having a good time. I'm really depressed.

MC: Remember that we discussed how you are in control of your feelings and behaviors? What do you think is the purpose of being depressed?

Goal-Oriented Language

Mary: I have no idea. It's just a feeling. At least it keeps me from getting angry.

MC: What would happen if you were to get angry?

Mary: It wouldn't be pretty. Actually, I'm afraid of what would happen. To imagine it scares me!

MC: Okay, let's explore that.... Joe, imagine a scene when Mary is getting angry. Describe it for us.

Joe: Mary never gets angry. She's depressed most of the time.

MC: Okay. Mary, let's examine this. Does anything good ever happen when you're depressed? Do you think that Joe is more attentive to you when you're depressed? Are you afraid that getting angry might push Joe away?

Mary: I never thought of it that way.

MC: So do you really want to change your present behavior?

Focusing on Change

Mary: I don't think I can, I think it's out of my control.

MC:	Let's see what you can change as a couple…. Joe, I want you to list some things you and Mary can do together for fun.

(Joe starts to write)

Concrete Planning

MC:	Okay? Now, Mary, imagine that you have to spend a lot of time and energy being depressed. Now transfer this time and energy to the list Joe just prepared for you. How many items would you use to replace depression?
Mary:	You're right. Being depressed is a waste of time and energy.

Issue #3: Children's Returning Home

Many families experience a "full-nest syndrome" after their adult children move back home to live with them. Mary is anxious about her continuous commitment

---

Behavioral Theory Techniques

Baseline: Defining one of more behavioral indicators before treatment begins to determine whether improvement can be made during and after treatment.

Behavioral Manifestations: Using concrete measures to identify whether the target behavior has changed in the desirable direction.

Concrete Planning: Developing a plan of action that includes a time schedule, measurable goals and objectives, steps of action, persons involved, and completion dates.

Contracting: The use of an agreement form to list goals and objectives so that the clients will have something concrete with which to follow through.

Focusing on Change: Directing the outcome to desirable change, defined specifically with the client.

Focusing on Learned Behavioral Goal: Helping clients understand that they can learn to make changes toward the desirable goal.

Goal-Oriented Language: Talking with clients about a concrete plan so they will think about how to work toward the stated goal.

Measurement Tool: Using an instrument to measure and check progress.

Reinforcement: Using prizes (e.g., verbal praises or rewards) to encourage the client to continue the plan of action.

Target Behaviors: Using a set of behavioral indicators to identify whether changes are moving in the desirable direction.

to being a caregiver in this household with the possibility of her daughter returning home.

Mary:	I always feel anxious.
MC:	When did you first notice it?
Mary:	Around this past Christmas.
MC:	Who has spent Christmas with you the past three years?
Mary:	When the kids were still at home, they had their own parties. Joe and I spent Christmas Eve together. Last year we were all together. Ami and Kevin came home for Christmas.
Joe:	Yes. Ami wants to move back home in the summer. She'll deliver her baby soon.
MC:	Mary, what would you see after Ami returns home?
Mary:	She may be busy. And so am I. But I'm happy that Ami needs my help.
Joe:	Mary wants to help, but she may not have the time.
MC:	Joe, what do you mean?
Joe:	Ask Mary.
Mary:	It's been quiet since the kids left. Now I've gotten used to my own schedule.
MC:	Would your schedule affect Ami's return home?
Mary:	Yes, sort of. No wonder I feel so anxious.
MC:	Experts suggest three basic house rules when kids move back home. First, care for yourself. Second, assign responsibilities. And third, set up weekly meetings. Have you had any of these concrete rules?

Multicultural Practice Applications

Maintaining a healthy weight and lifestyle is both an individual and a family issue. Women in Western cultures are especially pressured to ascribe to the thin ideal. This client should be asked about her definition of body image and how this definition is influenced by societal expectations.

MC:	What's Joe's reaction to your weight-loss program?
Mary:	Joe doesn't think I'm overweight. He said I just need to watch what I eat.
MC:	Joe, what do you think about Mary's appearance and her weight?
Joe:	She looks good. But we aren't that young anymore.... We've both gained some weight, but that's what happens in middle age. Mary's definitely not obese!
MC:	Mary, what are your thoughts?

Mary: I think I can make myself feel and look better with what I'm doing about my weight. I want to feel like I am doing something good for me and my health. I like to think I'm being a good model for Ami.

MC: Okay, Joe—can you see her point? Can you do anything to help Mary achieve her goals?

Joe: I do see her point. If losing weight is important to her, I'll do whatever I can to help.

MC: Mary, in what ways would you like Joe to help?

Mary: I'd like him to walk with me in the evenings. I want to spend time with him then, and if I go out alone, I feel a little guilty. If he would walk with me—I just go a mile—we could exercise and spend time together.

Women in particular feel as if their role in the household has diminished after children leave home. In many instances, however, responsibilities to maintain the household continue and can make some women feel trapped, especially when they are ready to move on to a new stage of life. Betz (2006) describes this as "work/family role convergence" in which many women bear the full responsibilities both in work and in their family. This feeling can be culturally reinforced if the family is male-dominant. To address some of these issues in the therapeutic session, clients may be asked to write down what they think their male counterparts may say in response to the following statement: "I feel trapped (or another feeling identified by the client) when…."

MC: Mary, write down how you feel now.

Mary: (Writes) I feel exhausted.

MC: Continue writing: "I feel exhausted when…."

Mary: I feel exhausted when Joe doesn't seem to understand me. He even yelled at me. (sobbing)

MC: How did he yell at you?

Mary: He said, "Don't cry! You're not a baby!" He was shaking his fist at me.

MC: How did you feel at that time?

Mary: I was scared. He seemed so angry.

MC: How do you feel now?

Mary: I'm okay now. I know he didn't mean it.

MC: Has he ever acted like this before?

Mary: Yes, when Ami was little. He didn't like to hear her crying.

MC: I'll talk about the past incident later. You said you were sad, but okay now, Mary. Imagine you are going to tell Joe about these mixed feelings. (pause) Now write down, or say, how you might say it to Joe and how Joe might respond to your feeling.

Mary:	I might say, "I was sad because you were angry at me." Joe might say, "Mary, I'm sorry. Cheer up."
MC:	Then?
Mary:	I would tell him, "I know you don't mean it, but your anger scared me." Joe might say, "I never meant you any harm."
MC:	It sounds like you're calm now. Let's go back to your issue of exhaustion. Imagine that someone is cheering you up. You feel happier. But you want to tell Joe why you've been feeling exhausted lately. What would you say? You can either say it or write it down.
Mary:	(Writes and then reads it) I prepare breakfast every morning. I rush to work and work, work, work. I pick up Ami's son at daycare before going to the grocery store. I cook. I clean. I take care of the lawn, the garden, everything. Then on weekends I clean, I do errands, and I do everything else—laundry, more cleaning....
MC:	Wow, what a list! Did you leave out anything else?
Mary:	(Writes more)
MC:	Does Joe realize how much you do?
Mary:	Probably not. This list surprises even me!

Variations From the Standardized Case: A Family Experiencing Domestic Violence

Many people, women, in particular, experience domestic or partner abuse. Although Mary and Joe, who represent an immigrant family, continue to be the main characters in the case, the practitioner should be aware that domestic violence can occur in any family.

***

Joe has been working at a manufacturing plant for nearly 20 years. His regular shift is from midnight to 8 a.m., but he often works double-shifts (midnight–8 a.m. and 8 a.m–4 p.m). One day, after a double-shift, Joe arrives home exhausted, wanting only to eat something and to get some sleep before the night's shift. When he gets home, Ami and Kevin are arguing over what to watch on television. Joe yells at them, telling them to "shut up" and go to their rooms.

Then Joe goes into the kitchen and finds some food burning on the stove. As he turns the stove off, his wife comes into the kitchen. Joe begins yelling, demanding to know why she's not watching the stove. Mary yells back, telling Joe that she's not feeling well.

Suddenly Joe slaps her, shouting that she should never raise her voice to him. Immediately he apologizes, puts his arms around her, and tells her that he'll never do this again. Mary has experienced Joe's physical violence and abusive language many times and is now unsure whether she can trust him not to show his temper again.

Role Play

MC:	Joe, would you tell me about what happened lately with your family?
Joe:	I have no idea. I'm too tired.
MC:	What made you feel tired?

Concreteness

Joe:	My family, my work, and everything else.
MC:	Mary, can you tell me your perception on this?
Mary:	I don't want to talk about it.
MC:	Please try. Joe needs to hear this, too.
Mary:	I think Joe is tired, and he dumps his emotions onto us.
MC:	How did Joe "dump" his emotions? Give me an example of this.

Specificity

Mary:	One night he came home, saw food overcooking on the stove, and slapped me. He forgot that I work very hard, too.
Joe:	That's not true. I was angry.

Experts Say...

- *Assessment:* First, assessment will address the history of family violence and patterns. Other important tasks during this stage include safety plans, including a possible need for shelter and therapeutic separation; assessing Joe for clinical depression with agitated type manifestations; and assessing Mary for clinical depression, major or dysthymic type.
- *Interventions:* Because the family is seeking help, it is essential to get Joe involved in the intervention process to help him develop skills in anger management and healthier styles of conflict resolution. The practitioner should pay attention to the damage done to Mary's self-esteem and trust and identify emotional damage to children who may have witnessed the violent events.

From a behavioral perspective, intervention with domestic violence should be related to the behavior manifested through interpersonal interactions. It is important to address cultural and ethnic values that reinforce female subordination and male dominance as an excuse for battering or using other forms of abuse by the husband. Because not enough information is available about the abuse, it is essential to assess whether the incident of shouting and slapping is occurring repeatedly in this household with the children as well.

In addition, the intake record should show how Mary was referred to this agency or counselor as a beginning assessment. Mary's reluctance to report may be related to her perception of gender differences, her cultural values regarding family cohesiveness, relationships between the father and the children, and her employment status or employability. Just as cultural and ethnic values are important determinants, economic security is crucial in Mary's decision to report or seek intervention.

Variations From the Standardized Case: Families Preparing for an Interracial Marriage

Another case example features Ami as an adult, preparing to marry John. This example does not identify the cultural and ethnic backgrounds of Ami and John's families so the focus can be on the general issues in an interracial relationship. The assumption is that these two families would have difficulty coming forward to address their cultural differences. In this case, Ami frequently discusses the interracial issue with her fiancé because she has been experiencing a direct impact from the families' disagreements. She is not coping effectively with her own ethnic identity in relation to her fiancé or with the potential conflict between the two families.

***

Ami (21) and John (22) have been engaged for 6 months and are trying to set a date for the wedding. Ami has been feeling frustrated recently because John's family cannot seem to commit to a date. Ami is also upset with her own family because even though they are polite, she knows that her family does not approve of John. Ami believes that her parents think that John, who is from a different racial and ethnic background, is not good enough for her. At the same time, she believes that John's family thinks she will not fit in with them.

To finalize the wedding plans, Ami knows that the families will have to sort out the venue, ceremony, food and alcohol, and number of guests. She is not sure that the families will be able to agree. Her family never has alcohol at any event, and it seems that John's family cannot have an event without alcohol. Ami has felt lonely when trying to plan the "greatest event of my life" because both families seem to feel that she and John are making a mistake. Ami has started to feel some resentment toward her parents for not seeming to be happy for her. At the same time, she feels guilty that she is "being selfish," because her mother, Mary, has accused her of this on several occasions. Ami has tried to talk to John about her feelings, but he continually says that she should not worry about what anyone else thinks and should just plan the wedding she wants.

Role Play

Mary: I feel sad that Ami is planning her wedding without my input.

MC: Did you talk with her about your feelings?

Mary:	No. I don't think they will listen to me, even if I share my feelings.
MC:	What makes you feel this way?
Mary:	John, Ami's fiance, came from a different ethnic background that seems to be totally different from ours.
MC:	Tell me what you would have liked to happen.
Mary:	For one thing, we would not want to serve alcohol at the reception, but John's family definitely wants alcohol.
MC:	What does "serving alcohol" mean in your family?
Mary:	We do not approve of it. It is against our family values.
MC:	What other conflicts can you anticipate?
Mary:	The choice of a place, John's family, John himself too.
MC:	Let's look at each of the conflicts and see if you can resolve these issues alone.
Mary:	Not a chance.
MC:	Then why are you upset about them, if you know nothing can change the way they are?
Mary:	Since I can't change them, it may be better for them to plan the wedding without us.
MC:	Yes, your input is important, but it can also create conflict. A wedding should be a happy occasion. Let's relax and have fun.
Mary:	How?
MC:	Let's do an imagery rehearsal about the planning. Close your eyes and imagine Ami was consulting you about the reception. You told her, "Ami, this is your wedding. Do whatever fits." You then relax and tell yourself, "I'm fine." Now open your eyes. What did you see yourself doing?
Mary:	I can't believe it. I feel much more relaxed after I imagined telling Ami to do whatever fits.

Experts Say...

Interracial marriage preparation may involve an inter-spiritual, cross-religious and cross-denominational issue that could be mobilized to lend additional outside spiritual resources, in the form of a priest or pastor, to help mediate with the clinician between the two different families. According to Nada Miocevic (2006), a private practitioner in Melbourne, Australia, very little research has provided skills for counseling interracial couples to build relationships. A developmental perspective is helpful as the new couple goes through one of the first tasks or first years of marriage that involve the transfer of primary emotional loyalties to one's spouse and the lessening of emotional loyalties to one's family-of-origin. A developmental perspective is also helpful to address one of the first tasks of newlyweds in the first years of marriage: the transfer of primary emotional loyalties to one's spouse and the lessening of emotional loyalties to one's family-of-origin.

This couple is being tested early, but that could be capitalized upon and reframed as a healthy challenge for the couple. How can "different" family, ethnic, and cultural traditions and rituals be respected during the ritual of marriage? How could the couple proactively take responsibility themselves to design a framework for the two different families to plug into, rather than expecting the two families to resolve all these differences in advance?

Assessment: Many issues surround interracial marriages. This case presents two major issues of

1. differences in values and behaviors stemming from cultural backgrounds and expectations, and
2. issues surrounding the meeting of these two sets of cultural expectations in a marriage.

When Ami and John have children, these children might face additional cultural barriers because of their biracial or multiethnic identity. Although the current situation does not mention anything about expectations of childrearing, the practitioner must assess past, present, and future concerns that may have significant impacts on this marriage.

Intervention: The couple should be prepared for a marriage ceremony in which language and ceremonial expectations may impose barriers. This couple has to cope with perceptions toward each other's families and accept that others also are assessing their differences. When John's reaction toward Ami's concerns does not sound supportive, the practitioner should encourage John to show support by verbalizing his understanding and caring, acknowledging that they will work through these barriers together, even though people might react negatively to their union. This approach, demonstrated with a behavioral orientation, may sound manipulative at times; however, it aims to take a directive approach to establishing concreteness through the therapeutic examination. With this concreteness, clients will be able to perceive a different perspective, instead of being manipulated to move forward.

Best Practice Evaluation

Evaluation Stage 8: Measure Family Stress

Following the seventh stage from chapter 10, the eighth stage of the evaluation process addresses family stress. In this chapter we use a time-series design to demonstrate how family stress can be assessed with a family having domestic violence problems.

Suggested evaluation tool: Perceived Stress Scale (PSS) (Cohen, Kamarck, & Mermelstein, 1983).

Description: The PSS consists of 10 items and provides a global measure of an individual's life event stress. The instrument has excellent test–retest reliability for assessing day-to-day changes with a coefficient of .85. Nevertheless, the instrument does not have good test–retest reliability for changes over a longer period, with a coefficient of .38. Therefore, it is used appropriately only for assessing daily or short-term changes. In addition, the instrument has an internal consistency of .78. Correlations have been achieved with the Health Youth Services Utilization Scale, the Life Satisfaction Scale, and the Psychosomatic Index.

How to use the tool: Permission for use of the scale is not necessary when use is for academic research or educational purposes. You may visit the following website to review the scale: http://www.macses.ucsf.edu/Research/Psychosocial/note book/PSS10.html. If you need written permission, contact Ellen Conser at conser@andrew.cmu.edu or at Department of Psychology, Carnegie Mellon University, 5000 Forbes Avenue, Pittsburgh, PA 15213, USA. The PSS uses a 5-point Likert-type scale (0 = never, 1 = almost never, 2 = sometimes, 3 = fairly often, and 4 = very often) to rate the severity of the stress in a family. Because this is a self-evaluation tool, the user should be encouraged to respond honestly to each statement to achieve a reliable and valid measure of daily stress. After the client completes the scale, the practitioner must reverse the score on items 4, 5, 7, and 8 for scoring purposes. After the reverse-scoring procedure, the composite score is the sum of all item scores.

How to evaluate the outcomes: As discussed in chapter 3, six steps are used to evaluate target behavior using the time-series single-system design. Applying the measure of family stress to the family experiencing domestic violence, these steps are as follows:

1. *Define the service target or problem (intake and case assessment):* The family has experienced a significant amount of stress. Mary (the wife) has been the most stressed.

2. *Define (or formulate) goals and objectives:* To reduce family stress as perceived by Mary after the husband's violent behavior has been controlled with behavioral interventions for 7 weeks.

3. *Identify constraints and resources and select a treatment:* Constraints include domestic violence and lack of trust between the parents. Resources include the husband's willingness to address issues and parental support provided for the children.

4. *Measure the monitoring actions (monitor progress):* Both Mary and Joe are asked to complete the PSS scale each week for 7 weeks (baseline A). After the baseline, the behavioral therapy is used with Mary and Joe individually for 7 weeks (intervention period B). The practitioner records the score each week for 14 weeks. For demonstration purposes, Mary's data are shown in Figure 11.1 to demonstrate the trend analysis before and during intervention.

5. *Analyze data:* One option is to obtain an average score from the baseline and another average score from the intervention period. The data from the 14

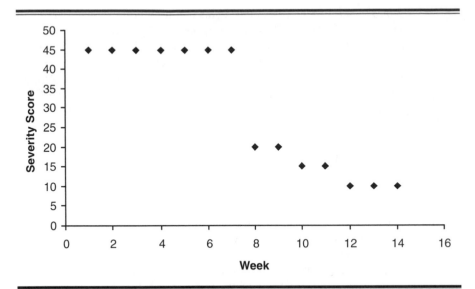

Figure 11.1
Perceived Stress Scale

weeks' observations show an obvious decrease immediately after the intervention has started, and the practitioner and the client visually examine the trend. The data in Figure 11.1 indicate that the PSS scores are much lower in the intervention period compared to the scores of the baseline period.

6 . *Report results and make recommendations:* The trend shows that PSS scores in the intervention period are significantly lower than the scores in the baseline. The results suggest that the behavioral therapy is effective in helping Mary to reduce her perceived family stress.

Multicultural Practice Exercises

Concrete Goals and Behavioral Changes

This is a concrete contracting process is used to allow clients to provide input as related to the current state of the problem and their future-oriented goal-setting.

Example 1: I will learn to express my feelings.

- Goal: I will talk with Joe at least 5 minutes a day about my feelings.
- Behavioral Change: I will not feel depressed for at least half of the day.

Example 2: I will improve communication with my family.

- Goal: I will make it a priority to be with my family.
- Behavioral Change: I will eat dinner with my family at least five nights a week.

Daily Affirmations for the Week

This is a common practice to encourage clients to engage themselves in self-directed exercises and to affirm their position in making changes.

Use sticky notes to post these or other affirmations on the bathroom mirror. Read each statement at a certain time of day:

Sunday: I make it a priority to be with my family.
Monday: I am a responsible person.
Tuesday: I will observe my way of communicating with others.
Wednesday: I like myself.
Thursday: I will relax today.
Friday: I will exercise at least 30 minutes today.
Saturday: I will talk with one of my family members today.

Relaxation

Relaxation is a culturally acceptable tool for any client. Practitioners can create an individually focused script to help a client find the best relaxation method. The following is a simple example. Additional statements can be used to encourage the clients' participation.

Close your eyes and think of a place you'd like to visit. Relax and tell me what you see.

Imagine that you are sitting in a peaceful place. What do you see? Who is with you? Relax and tell me how you feel.

Choose a person you trust. Tell this person in your heart that you would like to be relaxed.

Keep in touch with your place and environment. Now relax and let all of your tension go away. Come back to this place and be prepared to talk and share your feelings and thoughts.

Behavioral Rehearsal

Clients in different cultures have different rehearsal methods to share their feelings or ideas with their families. With the behavioral approach, the rehearsal will focus on the behavior to be demonstrated.

MC: Read this please. (hand the client a pretyped scenario)

Mary: I feel (<u>blank</u>) today because I've completed an assignment and understand how important it is to communicate with my family.

MC: Add your emotion as if you are about to read this to Joe.

Practice Guideline: Systematic Desensitization

Systematic desensitization is a method to progressively desensitize a person's anxiety through a series of relaxation exercises. This exercise requires careful planning with caution, as it can be anxiety-provoking. In a group setting you can adopt these suggested guidelines for setting up a systematic desensitization program.

1. Use a guided relaxation exercise with the group for the first three meetings as a rehearsal procedure. Do not include any anxiety-provoking elements in the exercise, but include a safe place in nature and suggest that the participant is very relaxed.
2. In the fourth meeting, ask each person to privately make a list of five specific behaviors or situations that can evoke anxiety.
3. Have each person list (or cut out pictures from a magazine) the five situations that evoke anxiety and arrange them in order from the most anxiety-arousing to the least.
4. Begin by using the first part of the same relaxation exercise as was used in the first three sessions. Then ask the members to imagine themselves in the least anxiety-arousing situation on their hierarchy. Then guide them to leave that situation by entering a peaceful and pleasant scene, and go back to the relaxation exercise.
5. In the same meeting (or the next meeting), ask the members to imagine themselves in the next most anxiety-arousing situation and apply the same relaxation procedure. After each relaxation, process their feelings.

Topics for Discussion:

1. The goal of using behavioral techniques in family interventions is to help the identified client change problematic behavior through learning experiences. What can be done if the identified client is not capable of learning? What cultural barriers have to be considered?
2. From a multicultural perspective, maladaptive behavior can be a defense mechanism that a person in the new cultural environment uses to communicate with his or her family about the problem. What would help the practitioner identify whether this maladaptive behavior is in fact a source of assessment, not a problem itself?
3. Critics say that behavioral approaches are manipulative. In what ways do behaviorally oriented techniques create this perception? What is the function of manipulation in clinical treatment? What could be done to eliminate this perception with clients?

CHAPTER TWELVE

Cognitive–Behavioral Theory

Although there are many forms of cognitive–behavioral therapy (CBT), rational–emotive behavioral therapy (REBT) is one of the more frequently used forms. REBT was previously referred to as rational–emotive therapy (RET) until Albert Ellis determined that *behavior* is an inevitable component in therapy (Ellis, 1996). REBT is a form of therapy that provides clients with a view that humans are born with potential for achieving rational actions by avoiding and modifying irrational and self-destructive thoughts. With the discovery of this potential, people will be able to avoid making repeated mistakes of self-blame, blaming others, intolerance, procrastination, and insensitivity to feelings (Corey, 2005).

The primary emphasis of this chapter is the analysis of perceptions that drive and influence behaviors. The chapter begins with an explanation of the concept of distortions in the reframing process. It then describes Ellis's cognitive–behavior theory and applies it to the standardized case situation targeting family changes precipitated by the mother's desire to work outside the home. The case then is varied to a divorce situation. Expert input and the evaluation of practice to identify faulty thinking patterns follow.

Our Mindset as a Therapeutic Component

Cognitive–behavioral theory is based on the assumption that individuals have the ability to overcome mood-related problems by learning to reframe their thoughts and cognitions (David, Montgomery, Macavei, & Borbjerg, 2005). This new way of thinking is culturally relevant because it looks at how perception and interpretation affect a person's feelings and experiences. By viewing the problem situation from a positive stance, irrational thoughts about being helpless can be reframed and understood as *distortions* that may affect the person's emotional state. To achieve the goal of positive change, the individual has to beware of thinking errors that reinforce negative behaviors.

Through active participation in the rethinking process, the multicultural practitioner is able to learn the cultural factors that influence a person's thinking. Although this process requires a change in mode of thinking to understand the relationship between emotion and irrationality, the skilled practitioner can help clients modify their deeply embedded cultural values by pinpointing the source of these irrational beliefs.

The cognitive–behavioral approach is a culturally relevant treatment method in that it assumes that people who grow up in different cultures not only think about different things, but they also think in different ways (Hofmann, 2006). Culture shapes and determines perceptions and reasoning routes. Although an individual's thoughts seem to be abstract and not measurable, they can be manifested in behaviors. As a result, culturally skilled practitioners must learn the client's cultural background and beliefs in order to effectively help them challenge unhealthy thoughts or thinking patterns that shape their various forms of behaviors. Since behaviors are learned, they can be unlearned, just as irrational thinking can be transformed into rational actions.

Ellis's (2002) ABC theory of personality illustrates this process. First, the activating event or *adversity* (A) does not immediately bring the emotional/ behavioral consequence but, rather, the *belief* (B) the person has developed before or during the occurrence has led to dysfunctional negative feelings as a *consequence* (C). A cultural belief that children absolutely must obey their parents (B) makes a young child feel awful and worthless (C) when he or she does not follow the parent's instruction (A). The (D) part of this theory is the dispute intervention. The cognitive way of helping this child is *not* to dispute the cultural belief, because the belief itself may be culturally relevant. The *dispute* (D), however, could be related to the child's mode of thinking that his or her parents would not accept the resulting action regardless of the child's reasoning and rationale for noncompliance.

The major intervention is that of disputing the irrationality, which in this case means challenging the client's fear of parental rejection that prevents him or her from taking action to offer an explanation. In this intervention, dysfunctional negative feelings (worthlessness and shame) can be translated or reframed into functional negative feelings (sadness or discomfort) or functional positive thoughts ("I can still explain it even though my parents may not accept my reason").

In couples therapy, the cognitive–behavioral model offers a means to increase a couple's satisfaction within their relationship and to decrease their negative communication patterns and styles. One method to achieve this goal is a *contingency*

Cognitive–Behavioral Theory in Brief

Importance to Multicultural Practice:

- Primarily focuses on a concrete plan of change that is measurable.
- Measures cognitive distortions from unrealistic expectations.

Major Figures:

- Albert Ellis (1913-): Rational–Emotive Behavioral Therapy
- Aaron Beck (1921-): Cognitive Therapy
- Donald Meichenbaum: Cognitive Behavior Modification

Assumptions:

- Our problems are created by our thoughts and our perceptions of life situations, rather than by the situations or past events themselves.
- Self-defeating beliefs are damaging.

Therapeutic Process:

- Assessment is based on patterns of thinking.

Goals:

- To eliminate the self-defeating outlook on life
- To acquire a tolerant and rational view of life

Multicultural Practice Techniques:

- Describe present beliefs
- Assign cognitive homework
- Change the use of language to reflect irrational thinking

---

contract, which can include items such as a "caring day request," in which each person lists things that he or she would like the other person to do. Listing the positive things in a concrete manner helps individuals gain awareness about a partner's needs. The emphasis on the positive allows a person to realize that negativity creates problems that hinder mutuality in relationships.

Cognitive–behavioral therapy emphasizes clients' roles in the therapeutic process. One of the goals of cognitive–behavioral therapy is to help clients identify stressors or problems they want to concentrate on in order to identify irrational thoughts and negative feelings that arise from these stressful or problematic situations. Clients are expected to come to the realization that they themselves have ownership of their problems or disturbances, but that they also have the ability to learn and change their circumstances based upon their experiences.

The learning process takes place if clients are aware that their irrational beliefs play a role by negatively influencing their perception of a person or an event, thereby creating a conflict. From this perception-checking process, clients also learn to accept rational alternatives and apply a new way of thinking that will lead to a positive feeling toward self and others.

On the Multicultural Stage: Family in Separation

In this stage, families may go through a physical or emotional separation. A physical separation may involve family members' living in separate residences as a result of parental separation or divorce, a husband and wife having jobs that cut into their time with each other, or a family member's engaging in a lot of traveling. An emotional separation may be manifested by the absence of mutual support or direct communication. Emotional separation may or may not involve physical separation, though physical separation eventually may lead to emotional separation because of the lack of proximity among family members. In any case, a no-talk symptom often stems from a pattern that begins with verbal arguments, which lead to assumptions about what the other person is thinking, and which may eventually lead to no communication at all.

The Case Approach

Issue #1: A Job Change

Mary has started a job. Both she and her husband have had problems adjusting to the time she has been away from home. The couple started seeing the family counselor to discuss their views.

Mary: (Looking at MC) As you know, Joe isn't happy about the changes I've been making in my life. In fact, I think he's trying to resist all my efforts.

MC: Mary, you've told me before that Joe is the one who needs to hear what you're saying. Turn and look at Joe…. Now tell him what you are thinking.

Mary: (Looking at Joe) Okay…. Joe, I feel like you're not happy about my changes—the way I look and my new job.

Joe: That's not quite true, Mary. You're overreacting. It just seems like your job is keeping you too busy.

MC: When you say "too busy," what do you mean, Joe?

Dispute Thinking

Joe: (Looking at MC) Well, Mary doesn't have any time for herself.

Mary: But this is my kind of job.

MC   Mary, are you saying that you're excited about getting this job?

Mary: Yup!

MC: Joe, do you dislike the idea of Mary's getting a job?

Joe:	No, not really.
MC:	Then what's on your mind concerning Mary's job?

Analyzing Thinking Pattern

Mary:	(Looking at MC) He thinks I don't earn enough.
Joe:	No…. That's not the problem. It's that I don't like her co-workers.
MC:	What qualities in these people do you dislike, Joe?
Joe:	They seem to occupy all of Mary's time, even her breaktimes.
Mary:	What's wrong with that? Don't I deserve a break?
MC:	What exactly are the behaviors you don't like, Joe?
Joe:	They remind me of my mother's co-workers.
MC:	What do you mean by that?

Analyzing Thinking as Related to Behavior

Joe:	They remind me of my mother when she was working. We kids knew that our mother left us because she was having an affair with a guy at work.
Mary:	My goodness! Do you think I'm that type of person? No wonder I've felt that something's been bothering you lately.
MC:	Mary, I understand your frustration…. Joe, what would you like to say to Mary?
Joe:	I don't mean that you would have an affair like my mother. I just couldn't help but be reminded of that. The reason I don't like your job is not because of you but because of the memories of the people my mother worked with.
Mary:	I've been with you for nineteen years. Please trust me.
MC:	What can you say to help Joe understand that his thinking isn't real?

Cognitive Restructuring

Mary:	Joe, I've been anxious about my job because I want to connect with my co-workers and have them accept me. Please accept me, too.
Joe:	I don't know what to say.
MC:	Just say, "Mary, I don't mean to think this way." And then share what feelings you have about Mary, not her job.

Issue #2: Divorce Issues

In lieu of the above illustration, Mary suspects that Joe doesn't like the idea of her starting a job because he doesn't want her to be working with a group of men. Actually, the couple's lack of communication concerning this matter is caused by Joe's fear related to his parents' divorce. In this session, Mary sees the counselor by herself.

MC: Mary, you said that you're worried about your marriage. Tell me what problem immediately comes to your mind.

Problem Solving Steps

Mary: Joe didn't ever want me to pursue a real job, but I've wanted to for quite a while.

MC: What do you think is on Joe's mind about your getting a job?

Mary: Joe thinks I'm around too many men every day. Besides, he didn't want to change things much at home.

MC: Do you and Joe think that change is a bad thing?

Dispute Irrationality

Mary: Not really! But Joe's mother left them when he was 9 or 10 years old. She got a job and met a guy there.

MC: Would your job make you leave your family?

Mary: No, it won't. This is all just in Joe's mind.

MC: Did you tell him that?

Mary: I thought he would understand without my saying so.

MC: If you haven't talked about it, how do you know that's the reason he dislikes your new job?

Dispute

Mary: I'm afraid he might think about divorce if I mention this connection.

MC: So if you share your feelings with him, he'll think about divorce?

Dispute

Mary: Well, I don't think it would happen right away. But, you know, he could become sensitive about the subject.

MC: Becoming sensitive is much different from wanting a divorce.

Mary: Of course, you're right! The world is a much different place now. I'm married to Joe because I love him. His mother wasn't happy with her husband from the very beginning. They got married because their parents wanted them to.

MC: What could you do now to make Joe feel like he felt at the beginning of your marriage?

Focus on Behavior

Mary: Well, I guess it came naturally before because I did most of the cooking and everything around the house. We were happy with our arrangement until I decided to look for a job.

MC: Do you mean you don't cook and clean for him now?

Mary: No, I still cook for him and the kids, but that's about it. I have less time now, and I'm tired when I get home.

MC: You mean (A) Joe is sensitive about your job, (B) he believes you won't have time to care for him, and (C) as a consequence, he will divorce you?

ABC Analysis

Mary: No, no—I don't mean that. I mean that (A) Joe is sensitive about my getting a job, (B) I believe I won't have time to care for him as much as I used to, and (C) the consequence will be that we won't see each other as much as before.

MC: So you're talking about not seeing each other as much, not about divorce.

Mary: Yup!

MC: Now focus on your own feelings. What can you do now to change your feelings to happiness?

New Feeling

Mary: I don't know how to change.

MC: Let's try this. Think about the happiest moment in your life. (pause) Got it?

Mary: Yes.

MC: Think about that happy feeling and remember how it feels. When you talk to Joe next time, keep this feeling in mind, and maintain a positive mood. Then ask him whether he wants you to keep your job. If he says no, ask him what he's concerned about in particular. This will validate what you're afraid of hearing, and it very well may be nothing to worry about.

Positivity

Mary: You're right. I feel happier already!

Issue #3: Family Involvement

Joe and Mary came in for a conjoint session. A main concern seems to be Mary's apparent depression, and the new job seems to be aggravating it. In this session, the practitioner discovers that both Mary and Joe had irrational thoughts about each other. Also, in this session the subject of the children enters the dialogue.

MC: Joe, Let's talk about the things that worry you most about Mary.

Joe: It's the times when she cries without a reason.

MC: Try to imagine the very worst thing that Mary could say or do when she's crying.

Joe: She could start yelling at me and hitting me.

MC: Joe, do you think Mary would do that?

Reality Check

Joe: No.

MC: Now, if she did that, what would be the reason?

Joe: I guess she might just want to release her anxiety.

MC: Is releasing anxiety something opposite to your belief system?

Dispute Irrationality

Joe: Not really.

MC: Now, Joe, tell me what is the best thing that could happen when Mary cries.

Joe: She would be able to talk to me and tell me what's going on. After that, she would probably feel better.

MC: Mary, would you like to react to Joe's comments?

Mary: First, I want Joe to know that I really love him. My getting a job has been hard on Joe, and the adjustment has been difficult for me, too.

MC: Mary, you said you're getting depressed lately. Why do you think that is so?

Mary: I'm afraid I won't be able to do a good job at home when I'm so busy at work.

MC: Does Joe tell you that you're doing a bad job at home? Or your children?

Dispute

Joe: (Interrupting) Nobody has said that.

Cognitive–Behavioral Techniques

ABC Analysis: Analyzing an irrational thought in terms of its activating event (A), emotional consequence (C), and the causal belief (B).

Cognitive Restructuring: Attempting to modify the client's thoughts, perceptions, and/or attributions about an event.

Dispute Irrationality: Identifying irrational thinking connected to an event that causes emotional discomfort.

Focus on Behavior: Redirecting the client to attend to specific behaviors that can be changed.

New Feeling: Pointing out alternative forms of thinking that can bring about a new and positive feeling.

Positivity: Focusing on the positive aspect of the event.

Problem-Solving Steps: Asking systematic questions to identify ways to solve the problem.

Reality Check: Encouraging the client to examine what is happening.

Mary:	Maybe not now, but they might say so at some point.
MC:	Did you just imagine that they would tell you something like this? Can you change this imaginary thought?
Mary:	Well, I feel like I don't have enough time to do everything.
MC:	So this is your feeling. How do you change this feeling into a positive one?

Positivity

Mary:	I believe I've been a good mother.
MC:	Since you don't think you have enough time to take care of everything anymore, what would you like your family members to do?
Mary:	I'll have to ask Joe, Ami, and Kevin to help with the chores, I guess.
Joe:	I know that Mary always puts us ahead of herself. I'm willing to help out as long as Mary will tell me what has to be done.
MC:	Good, Joe! Now imagine the best thing her job can bring you.
Joe:	Less financial strain on me now that we have more money coming in.
MC:	Can you imagine anything else?
Joe:	Well, Mary will understand how I feel after a full day of work, and we'll have a lot more to talk about.
MC:	Mary, when you hear Joe say this, what positive feelings does it bring about?
Mary:	It reminds me that Joe is wonderful!

Multicultural Practice Applications

From the beliefs and values instilled during their upbringing or culture, individuals develop an automatic thought process. The culturally sensitive practitioner does not attempt to modify a client's thinking without being aware of the impact of culture on the process. In Mary's case, she assumes that, above all, she must be a good wife and mother. In her culture, these roles are not to be changed, particularly because Mary herself deems them of primary importance. Instead of encouraging Mary to modify her thinking in regard to her taking a job, the counselor presents Mary with three possible options: (1) choose a good feeling associated with her competing roles, (2) ask the family to help her fulfill these roles, and (3) communicate directly with Joe about her expectations for change and learn his perspective.

Choose a good feeling:

Mary:	I don't think it's possible for me to continue being a good wife and mother if I work outside the home.

MC: What are your feelings when you think about your inability to maintain these roles?

Mary: Mainly sadness, I guess.

MC: Then why not keep these roles?

Mary: I can't do everything for the family if I want to do something for myself.

MC: Not being able to do *everything* for your family doesn't translate into being a bad wife or mother. Can you still feel happy even if you do less for the family?

Mary: How?

MC: Just feel happy, period.

Ask for assistance:

Mary: I can't feel happy if I can't manage to fulfill my roles.

MC: Then ask your family to help.

Mary: They won't help.

MC: Then you should communicate your unhappiness to them about not having their help. You're still happy about being a mother and wife, right?

Communicate directly:

Mary: Joe isn't happy about the changes I've been making in my life.

MC: Have you shared this thought with him?

Mary: Not really! He'd think it's my problem, not his.

MC: But you're assuming this. And even if he thinks this is your problem, you can tell him how you feel. How would you go about telling him your expectations for your life change?

Mary: I would say, "Joe, I'm planning to work outside the home from now on. What do you think?"

MC: What's on your mind now?

Mary: That Joe won't talk to me.

MC: What would you like him to say?

Mary: "Mary, I'm so proud of you for getting a job." But the problem is that I know he wouldn't say anything like that.

MC: Be positive. Tell him directly, "Joe, I would like to hear from you that you are going to be supportive and happy when I get a job."

Some families may not have a choice about both parents working outside the home. Say that this family is a two-income household, and Mary continues to feel unhappy about not fulfilling her family roles while she works. The cognitive–behavioral counselor explores how she can modify her feelings about what responsibility entails.

Mary: I have to have this job. Joe can't deny that we desperately need the money. But the problem is he still expects me to do all the chores, cook, and do the laundry. Basically he expects me to be the housekeeper!

MC: What's so bad about asking him to help out?

Mary: I feel so ashamed if I have to ask him or the kids to do my household chores.

MC: Where do you think this shame comes from?

Mary: I just don't feel comfortable asking for any help.

MC: But that doesn't mean they won't feel comfortable offering help. Try asking them for help, and then show them how to help.

Focusing on the cognitive influences of human actions rests on the assumption that we have a biological and cultural tendency to think irrationally, and thus we place ourselves in troublesome emotional situations needlessly. From a multicultural perspective, this assumption may imply that one must change the cognitive, emotive, and behavioral process in one of these three possible ways:

1. I can choose to react differently from the typical or culturally defined way if I evaluate the expected consequence in advance.
2. I can choose to follow my culture but accept the consequences and refuse to feel negative about it.
3. I can learn a new way to minimize the perceived negativity stemming from my thinking and view others in relation to their thinking before judging their behavior.

Variations From the Standardized Case: A Divorced Family

Under faulty assumptions, many people have stepped into muddy situations involving emotional disputes with their loved ones. When couples move away from mutual understanding, both inside their minds and as a result of communication problems, they face emotional separation issues. In this variation, Joe and Mary have reached a stage where they have grown apart and are contemplating divorce.

***

Joe and Mary have been married for 19 years. Recently, they have been fighting constantly and realize that they can no longer go on pretending that their marriage is fine. They have decided to get a divorce. Although both Joe and Mary feel that the divorce is the right choice, their kids, Ami, 16, and Kevin, 8, are angry. Ami has become defiant and is staying out past her curfew on weekends. She has also started to talk back to Mary. At one point, Ami blamed her mother for the impending divorce. Kevin, who is considered the "jokester" of the family, has been keeping to himself and now remains in his room most of the time when he is home. Mary recently received a phone call from Kevin's teacher, who said she's worried about Kevin because he has been isolating himself from the class and from group activities.

Joe and Mary feel additional stress right now. The lawyers have just called a meeting with all parties involved.

Mary:	I feel so responsible for the way the kids are feeling right now.
MC:	How do your kids feel?
Mary:	They don't even talk to me. If they talk at all, they seem to have an attitude. They're probably angry at me for not wanting to stay with their father.
MC:	Where did you get this idea? Did they tell you this?
Mary:	No, they didn't come out and say that exactly. I can't get them to talk about their feelings.
MC:	Who's responsible for not sharing their feelings?
Mary:	I think I am.
MC:	How about Joe? How about your kids themselves?
Mary:	I see what you're saying, but I still feel responsible.
MC:	So, of the four of you, do you think you're responsible for one-fourth of their feelings?
Mary:	Oh, I don't know. I'm confused.
MC:	You're confused because you think you have to do well all the time.
Mary:	You might be right, but I've sure failed this time.
MC:	Mary, that still doesn't make you a failure.
Mary:	I'm a failure in my marriage.
MC:	You keep mentioning that you're a failure because you aren't doing everything well. You probably think this shouldn't be happening to you, right?
Mary:	Yes.
MC:	Mary, this doesn't make you a failure. Your feelings about being a failure are irrational beliefs. In your mind, you always think you *should* be the best wife and mother. When you feel you aren't achieving this, you feel sad. Is that how you feel now?
Mary:	Yes, I think that pretty well describes how I feel.
MC:	Mary, try to give yourself some credit for the things you're able to do, and start talking to your kids about your feelings. Now, I don't mean the irrational feelings about what you *should* be, but the true feelings about how much you care about them.

Experts Say...

Divorce is a not an outcome. It is a process that involves handling intense feelings. Blaming is common among members of divorced families because divorce is an outcome of mishandling of interpersonal relationships. After trust and love have been lost, communication becomes exhausting in that negativity eats up the energy of both parties and irrationality becomes the dominant force that dictates everyone's thinking and feeling. In some cases, even the idea of being in the same room together stirs within each of them a reservoir of stinging emotion. Social work professor Dr. Camille Hall (2006), University of Tennessee, comments that any analyses of divorce cases should address societal and cultural factors, particularly the sociocultural differences between the couple.

Contact: During the course of divorce, children are separated and the family may split into two or more households. The family seems to separate into several parts. As a result, divorce may have detrimental effects on behavior and give rise to adjustment problems in the children. They perceive different parenting and attachment styles, which vary depending on the children's sex, age, and the social support they perceive from their environment. These negative outcomes of divorce can be alleviated through favorable conditions offered to the children in the post-divorce period (Ozen, 2003).

Assessment: In this case of divorce contemplation, the mother seems to be isolated. It is important to address the mother's role as support for the kids so they do not blame themselves for what has taken place between their parents. Within a multicultural environment, this support may involve a cultural mediator such as a respectful family member to help the family address various issues. According to Al-Krenawi & Graham (2001), a cultural mediator has a high social status within the family network and can help promote the role of the practitioner in a system that has limited experience with that professional. In this case, Kevin's teacher seems to be an appropriate individual to provide support to the family. Another person within the family network could be identified to serve this role if the family can provide additional information.

Intervention: Children in general do not relate rationally to their parents' divorce. They tend to place the blame on themselves. This requires special attention. In this case, the younger child, Kevin, has withdrawn after first displaying anger. The older child, Ami, is angry and defiant. Interventions in this family, as in any divorced family, should focus on changing family members' irrational thinking about the causes of divorce, the new family composition, and the outcome of divorce.

Evaluation: All family members must be included in preparing a new format for the family, allowing time for them to process their feelings and identify their new roles. Evaluating their participation is a must.

Termination: After all the issues have been addressed, this family should be encouraged to return to their daily routine, work, or study. Practitioners should be sensitive about the timing of closing the case to avoid family members' feeling abandoned.

Best Practice Evaluation

Evaluation Stage 9: Identify Family Thinking Patterns

Following the eighth stage of addressing stress in the family from chapter 11, the practice–evaluation integration in this chapter focuses on the ninth stage of identifying faulty thinking patterns within the standardized family. We use a time-series design to demonstrate how to assess the irrational/rational thinking of family members. Here, data are taken from Joe to address the evaluative results.

Suggested evaluation tool: Shortened General Attitude and Belief Scale (SGABS) (Lindner, Kirkby, Wertheim, & Birch, 1999)

Description: The SGABS was originally derived from the 55-item General Attitude and Belief Scale (GABS) (Bernard, 1998). The intent of the GABS is to measure irrational/rational thinking. Lindner and colleagues (1999) compared the SGABS with a 26-item version of the GABS and found that the two forms of the instrument were highly correlated. They showed that the Total Irrationality scores from SGABS accounted for 96% of the variance of Total Irrationality scores from the GABS. They also found that the two forms of the instrument served the same purpose to assess irrational and rational thinking in that the SGABS scores correlated moderately with scores on the same subscales of the GABS.

The subscales include: Need for Achievement, Need for Approval, Need for Comfort, Demand for Fairness, Self-Downing, Other Downing, and Total Irrationality. The SGABS requires approximately 4 minutes to complete compared to 10 minutes for the 55-item GABS. In addition, the SGABS total irrationality scores were statistically correlated with the Irrational Belief Scale (IBS) scores.

How to use the tool: The GABS can be obtained from Dr. Helen Lindner, School of Psychological Science, George Singer Building, La Trobe University, Bundoora, Australia 3083 or via e-mail at H.Lindner@latrobe.edu.au. A full description of the psychometric properties of the GABS is available at the following article: Lindner, Kirkby, Wertheim, and Birch (1999), The Shortened General Attitude and Belief Scale. *Cognitive Therapy and Research,* 23(6), pp. 651–663, provides a brief assessment of irrational thinking. This 26-item measure uses a 5-point Likert-type scale with the following responses, 1 = strongly disagree, 2 = disagree, 3 = neutral, 4 = agree, and 5 = strongly agree. The rationality subscale score is equal to the sum of items 4, 9, 19, and 24. The Self-Downing subscale score is equal to the sum of items 7, 10, 13, and 22. The Need for Achievement subscale score is equal to the sum of items 1, 11, 18, and 20. The Need for Approval subscale score is equal to the sum of items 6, 23, and 25. The Need for Comfort subscale score is equal to the sum of items 3, 5, 17, and 16. The Demand for Fairness subscale score is equal to the sum of items 2, 12, 14, and 21. The Other Downing subscale score is equal to the sum of items 8, 15, and 26. Finally, the Total Irrationality score is equal to the sum of the six subscale scores (Self-Downing, Need for Achievement, Need for Approval, Need for Comfort, Demand for Fairness, and Other Downing). High scores indicate high levels of irrational thinking.

How to evaluate the outcomes: As discussed in chapter 3, six evaluation steps are used to assess irrational thinking using the single-system research design. These steps are demonstrated with a time-series design with Joe after the divorce, with a specific focus on Joe's irrational thoughts.

1. *Define the service target or problem (intake and case assessment):* Irrational thinking has been affecting Joe's work productivity. It was found that Joe thinks that Mary is overpowering him during their child custody dispute.
2. *Define (or formulate) goals and objectives:* To reduce the number of Joe's irrational thoughts.
3. *Identify constraints and resources and select a treatment:* Constraints include emotional distress and lack of trust resulting from the divorce. Resources include the parents' willingness to seek help and the children's respect for their parents' decision.
4. *Measure the monitoring actions (monitor progress):* Joe has not been feeling good about himself. He is willing to participate in cognitive–behavioral therapy to identify his thinking patterns. He is asked to complete the SGABS each week for 7 weeks prior to treatment. He is also asked to complete the same scale immediately after treatment has started, for 7 weeks. The practitioner records the score once a week. The scores are plotted in Figure 12.1. (Mary is treated separately, and her data are not provided here.)
5. *Analyze data:* The Total Irrationality scores in the first 7 weeks are much higher than the ones in the remaining 7 weeks. The trend indicates that the irrational thinking is reduced significantly after treatment.

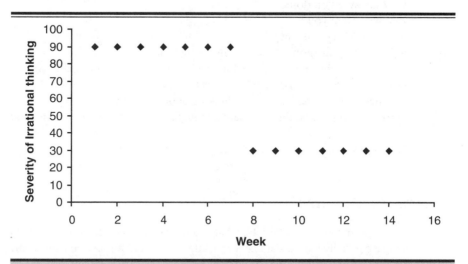

Figure 12.1
Shortened General Attitude and Belief Scale: Total Irrationality Score

6. *Report results and make recommendation:* The results suggest that the cognitive–behavioral therapy has been effective in helping Joe reduce his irrational thinking patterns. Joe is examining his willingness to listen to others in the family, including Mary's reason for seeking custody of the children.

Multicultural Practice Exercises

1. A three-set problem-solving mindset:
   a. My problem is: _____
   b. Name two negative feelings aroused by this problem:

      _____, _____
   c. How can I change these feelings to positive feelings?

      _____

2. Disputing Irrational Thoughts
   - My thought: I must succeed at all times.
   - Dispute: Who can be successful all of the time? Why can't I accept my mistakes and learn from them?

3. Thought Record
   After the client talks about the situation that contains negative thoughts, ask him or her to answer to the following questions:
   - Who else was there when this happened?
   - What were you doing?
   - Where were you?
   - When did this take place?
   - Describe your mood then and rate its intensity.
   - What went through your mind just before you started to feel this way?
   - What evidence would disprove your thought?
   - What is an alternative way of thinking about this situation?
   - How do you make this alternative thought process become your thought now?
   - Describe your mood now and rate its intensity.

Topics for Discussion

1. When disputing irrational beliefs, what could a practitioner do or say to avoid making a culturally biased statement about the client's definition of the problem?
2. What are the similarities and differences between cognitive–behavioral theory and behavioral theory when providing support in a counseling session?
3. Identify the most recent literature attesting to the validity of cognitive–behavioral theory in working with culturally diverse populations.

4. Barker (1999) comments that CBT is not measurable because a client's thoughts, fantasies, or cognitive images cannot be seen. What is your reaction to Barker's statement? How can the practitioner measure practice effectiveness if the target behavior is not measurable? Can thoughts be seen as behaviors? If so, how are thoughts measured to evaluate the client's progress?

Feminist Perspective With an Empowerment Focus

This chapter focuses on using the feminist perspective to empower clients to utilize their personal strengths and help themselves. Practitioners should be aware that the feminist perspective can be appropriate for use with all clients, not just women, because of its emphasis on strengths. The perspective aims to encourage clients to accept their individual differences, appreciate diversity in society, and utilize their strengths to overcome barriers and resolve difficulties (Jaggar & Rothenberg, 1993).

With this case approach, the standardized case will present the following three issues to illustrate application of the feminist/empowerment perspective to practice: (1) gay and lesbian issues, (2) nontraditional student issues, and (3) issues surrounding alternative healing methods. The case is then changed to a situation in which a lesbian couple with children is facing discrimination. The best practice evaluation process targets how to measure perceptions of power and how to evaluate the effectiveness of feminist therapy with an empowerment focus.

Confronting Oppression

Feminist theory is unique because it considers not only interpersonal origins of problems but also their sociopolitical sources. These sources include cultural heritage, historical events, contextual and environmental factors, social and personal identity, as well as family, religious, economic, and power factors (Fouad & Arredondo,

Feminist Empowerment Perspectives in Brief

Importance to Multicultural Practice:

- Encourages using clients' strengths to deal with external obstacles.
- Addresses clients' perception of unfair societal treatment
- Promotes the concept of social justice.

Major Figures:

- Ami B. Anthony: Feminist Theory
- Elizabeth Stanton (1815-1902): Feminist Theory
- Social workers practicing with an empowerment focus

Assumptions:

- Clients' difficulties have sociopolitical sources.
- Social change is the aim, not necessarily individual adjustment.
- Clients have strengths.

Therapeutic Process:

- Avoid labels.
- Emphasize current concerns, especially those related to oppression and discrimination.
- Understand clients' realities.
- Assess the social context and environmental impacts.
- Assess clients' devalued qualities.
- Evaluate current societal conditions.

Goals:

- To encourage clients to uncover social forces that have an impact on their lives and prohibit productive changes.
- To encourage social action that promotes public awareness of existing problems.
- To use a three-phase approach (exploration, action, termination) in the process.

Multicultural Practice Techniques:

- Universalization
- Self-disclosure for the client's best interest
- Present-focus, although includes past materials to facilitate understanding
- Questioning techniques directed at external forces and pressures
- Emphasis on strengths, especially those that society devalues
- Realistic role modeling
- Social action
- Support group

2007; Moodley, 2007). Feminist theory focuses on the important factors in the clients' psychological development that may be affected by traditional, social, and political definitions or standards. Practitioners who use this theory are continually aware of the social context in which their clients live, including the oppression and discrimination that may impact clients' lives. Feminist practitioners attempt to understand the intricacies of clients' lives by active listening and by encouraging them to use narrative formats. The narrative approach is widely used when working with people with little or no power, either politically or economically (Lott & Bullock, 2007). The description of past events stresses not only economic or political struggles but also portrays an understanding of how family history and cultural or ethnic identity impacts the way a person sees or does things. Through the clients' narratives, the practitioner is able to identify whether the clients' culture has been viewed as an enhancer or a barrier to solving this person's problem (Frosh, 2002). Feminist theory does not stress personal adjustment when such a change hinders clients' development but, instead, focuses on personal and political change. Feminist practitioners are particularly concerned with how power differentials and adhering to gender roles (or other traditional roles) restrict individuals from realizing their personal potential.

Applying feminist theory to counseling involves learning about clients' experiences and the realities of diverse multicultural and racial groups, being sensitive to the socioeconomic context in which the clients live, emphasizing the reduction of power differentials, and advocating for political change through clients' strengths, especially those strengths that society devalues. Clients are encouraged to take responsibility for their lives while maintaining awareness that societal conditions may hinder or enable their progress (Enns, 2004).

On the Multicultural Stage: A Family Experiencing Life Changes

Feminist practitioners do not consider themselves "experts." Instead, they view themselves as simply sharing their knowledge with clients in a collaborative effort to reduce barriers to communication and enhance personal potential (Collins, 1998). The empowerment process starts with respectful acknowledgement of clients' cultures and values while recognizing that the impact of past and current sociopolitical and socioeconomic structures may have had great influences on clients' lives.

A family does not experience diversity at one particular time in life. Instead, this is a stage when multiple demands overtly impact clients' perspectives on defining who they are. During the assessment and intervention process, practitioners must analyze the elements that describe human diversity issues as well as the needs and developmental issues that affect clients' perspectives toward themselves and others.

The Case Approach

The following examples illustrate that social support is an empowerment tool for those who feel belittled or socially isolated by others. Three issues are discussed with the client' family: (1) views on gay and lesbian adolescents, (2) the role of being a nontraditional student, and (3) perceptions on healing and naturalistic practices.

Issue #1: Supporting Gay and Lesbian Issues

When an individual lives in an environment that rigidly adheres to a certain set of customs, traditions, and beliefs, he or she often has difficulty being supportive of people who have a perspective or set of values that is different from theirs. Even though this multicultural blindness is not intentional, most people feel more comfortable with familiar situations than with unknowns.

     Feminist therapy expands individuals' comfort zones to accommodate additional input and thereby enhance communication. In this individual session, Mary reluctantly discloses her daughter's sexual orientation, which is affecting Mary's emotional state. The practitioner approaches the situation with a learning attitude—which means learning from the client's perspective and attempting to understand the origins of the client's definition of sexual orientation.

Mary: I'm here because of my daughter, Ami. Well, sort of—I mean, I'm here for myself, but my daughter kind of pushed me into it. I hope this session will help.

MC: Can you tell me more…. Exactly what are you referring to?

Mary: I've gone through a lot of changes in the past. Lately I've been thinking about myself—I mean *more* about myself. If it sounds confusing to you, it's confusing to me, too.

MC: Take your time. I'm listening.

Mary: I must be doing something wrong, because I don't really know what's going on with my daughter.

MC: What do you think is going on?

Focusing on External Forces

Mary: Recently Ami told me out of the blue that she likes girls better than boys. You know — (silence)

MC: Go on, please.

Mary: She wants me to be receptive and open about her new … preference.

MC: So you understand what she means.

Emphasis on Self-Power

Mary: Yes. But I'd like to know more about what she's going through. It's not easy.

MC: What isn't easy?

Societal Expectations

Mary: These people resist the idea of letting kids make their own choices about those kinds of things.

MC: Who are "these people?"

Mary: Well, my friends, for example. They say that gays aren't "normal."

MC: What do you think about that?

Mary: I know it's not true, but I don't want Ami to share her new … preference with others.

MC: Okay, so one part of you thinks, "Ami, don't tell." The other part of you says, "Ami, tell me more."

Mary: Yes…. I know that sounds crazy.

MC: Not at all. Society sometimes tells us that we only have one choice for intimate relationships—people of the opposite sex.

Societal Expectations

Mary: Isn't that what people think?

MC: It's okay to have traditional thoughts and beliefs if you feel comfortable with it, but it seems that you aren't comfortable with your reaction to Ami's disclosure.

Sources of Client's Difficulties

Mary: You're right—I'm not comfortable with it.

MC: Did Ami tell you exactly what she means by being "open" about her preference?

Mary: No. I asked her not to talk about it.

MC: So how can you know what she's referring to? Are you making the assumption that she's talking about her sexual preference?

Mary: I sensed it.

MC: In your family, who would say it's wrong to discuss sexual preferences with your children?

Mary: My father. I don't feel comfortable talking with him about anything.

MC: What can you do to feel comfortable talking with Ami?

Empowering the Client

Mary: I don't know.

MC: What would you like to accomplish here?

Mary: I just want to get your support.

Mary: You'll get my support, but how would you like to use it?

Initiating Action

Mary: I have to think about that.

MC: I'm glad to hear that you're thinking. That means you can think about what this support means to you. You also don't have to accept any view that is *supposed* to determine what is right or wrong when you personally have some doubt. What you just said has a lot of meaning to me.

Client's Perspectives

Mary: Yes, I think you're right. Ami is upset about my reaction because she thought I would understand her.

MC: Okay—and why would she think that?

Women's Experience

Mary: I guess because I'm a woman and her mother.

MC: As a woman and mother, maybe you don't know what to say to show your understanding.

Mary: What do you mean?

MC: I mean that your own experiences and traditional expectations may have blocked you from reacting supportively.

Societal Expectations

Mary: I never thought of it that way.

Issue #2: Becoming a Nontraditional Student

This session describes the issue of Mary's returning to college as a full-time student. After struggling with her decision to pursue a graduate degree, Mary faces the family's opposition, as well as multiple demands on her personal time. Both Mary and Joe are attending this session.

Joe: I don't understand what Mary is having problems with. She doesn't need to change herself.

MC: What if she hasn't been her complete self all along? What if she's longing for more and has been holding back because she needed to be a wife and mother?

Joe: I don't know what else she wants besides this going-to-graduate school thing.

MC: Let's talk about graduate school.... Mary, can you elaborate to Joe why you want to do this for yourself and how you perceive your family's reaction?

Social or Family Support

Mary: It's something I'm really interested in to better myself. The kids are old enough, and they'll be leaving home soon, and I don't want to be hanging around the house all day with nothing to do. Boring!

MC: Joe, what's your reaction to that? Do you think she's being rational?

Joe: I guess so, but she can't stop being a wife and mother.

Mary: Of course not. I never said that was going to stop.

MC: What makes you think that if she goes back to school, she will stop performing her other roles?

Sources of Client Difficulties

Joe: There's is a part of me that thinks she'll be too busy and put school ahead of us.

Mary: I really think I'll be able to manage everything with a little help. I'd like to have my family's support by helping me out from time to time. It seems like they just want me to be there for them all the time because that's what I'm supposed to do as a woman.

Joe: I know that's kind of an issue with me. I grew up in a family where my mom stayed home all the time.

MC: And that's fine. But times have changed. Now there are people who choose to stay in traditional roles, and there are others who choose to branch out of the "norm," so to speak. It depends on what the person, as an individual, wants. It seems that Mary is no longer comfortable in her role, and she should be given the opportunity to further her options. This situation is going to take some getting used to for the family because it's not how either of you were brought up. But it sounds like now may be the time for a change.

Initiating Action

Mary: The other thing is that I don't feel like Joe has faith in me to succeed. As I told you before, my whole family thinks I'm silly for wanting to do this, and I feel like they think I'll fail because I'm too old.

Joe: This must go back to how I was brought up, too. It's kind of like she should have passed that stage already. School is for younger people.

MC: Joe, age doesn't matter. A person keeps learning all throughout life. Many people—men and women—are doing this. I think it will be beneficial if you look at how your wife's goals will affect your family. By your wife going back to school, it will give her more knowledge and experience—and maybe a better job down the road. Can you see how this might help your family?

Societal Expectations

Joe: Well, yes. And that will be great in the long run. But it's going to take a long time for her to finish.

MC: This is something that Mary is capable of doing, especially since she has the self-motivation and desire to follow through. Mary, can you tell Joe how you feel about your decision to pursue a graduate education?

Empowering the Client

Mary: Joe, it's not going to all happen overnight. I know it's going to be hard. I just want the kids, and especially you, to believe in me.

Issue #3: Perceptions on Healing

The definition of healing varies from one person to the next based on personal experiences and cultural backgrounds. In many cultures, natural healing methods are widely used and accepted, including acupuncture, cupping, herbal healing, homeopathy, meditation, and sorcery (see Farooqi, 2006; Portman & Garrett, 2006; Weiner & Ernst, 2004). The use of naturalistic practices is said to sooth anxiety and connect the body to the mind. Some people do not consider natural healing methods helpful, but those who would like to try natural healing methods should be encouraged to observe changes following the elected treatments (Moodley, 2007). This empowers the person to check the validity of the method and also encourages him or her to identify whether and what alternatives should be considered. An example is illustrated here with a focus on Joe's anxiety and Mary's definition of support.

Joe: I feel nervous and anxious for no apparent reason. It's interfering with my sleep, and I know Mary can't sleep when I'm tossing and turning all night.

Mary: He's right! Because of him keeping me awake, I'm having trouble concentrating on my work. I go to work feeling tired because Joe doesn't let me sleep at all.

MC: Mary, let's concentrate on the experience and not put the blame on anyone.

Mary: I'm not blaming. I just want him to know how I feel.

MC: Okay. Let's talk about feelings…. Joe, I know this is causing you undue stress. How do you feel about what Mary just said?

Joe: I shouldn't be disturbing her sleep. I understand why she feels this way, but it hurts.

MC: It sounds like you may feel responsible for Mary's work performance, but you're important, too. Don't put yourself in a less important role. Think back to what you've done to lessen your anxiety in the past. And what do your friends do to relieve their anxiety?

Gaining a New Perspective From Friends

Joe: My friends don't talk about this sort of things. Sam, my next-door neighbor, asked me two Sundays ago if I would go to his temple with him. We walked to the new temple, which is about a mile from our house.

MC: How did you feel afterwards?

Joe: I noticed that after I'd walked, I was able to sleep better at night. As to the temple, I was curious about it at first. I found myself relaxing there. But I think it was the walk that made me feel like my burden had been lifted a little. Later I felt relieved because Mary was able to sleep that night without me tossing and turning. I went with Sam and his wife two more times, but I don't think I'll go all the time, because I want to spend as much time as I can with my family.

MC: Mary, it appears that Joe is concerned not only about his anxiety but also about your rest, work, and spending time with you when you're home.

Search for Exceptions

Mary: I never thought it mattered. He always does whatever he wants whenever he wants. He doesn't seem to care about me.

Joe: That's not true. I worry about you all the time.

MC: Mary, why do you think Joe doesn't care?

Mary: Well, I thought he didn't want to be around me and that was why he started to walk at just the time when I came home from work. I didn't know that it helped him relax.

Joe: I know you'd like me to be there all the time, but walking helps me relax and think about things, and sometimes I need to be by myself. It makes me feel healthier—like I'm regaining power and energy.

MC: Good. There's something about power in your exercise. Let's do something to analyze power. Joe and Mary, would you each complete the following (gives paper to Mary and Joe), "I feel powerful when _____?"

Power Analysis

Joe: (Writes)

MC: Would you please share what you have written?

Joe: I feel powerful when I go on my walk every day. But I would like to have something else besides walking to help me relax. I know the weather will turn colder soon and I won't be able to walk as much.

MC: Mary, how about you?

Mary: I feel powerful when I can make major decisions.

MC: Give an example of a major decision.

Mary: Deciding where to go and what to do.

MC: How about deciding the time for an activity that the two of you can do together?

Mary: Sure.

MC: Joe and Mary, in your culture, what ways do people use to relax?

Analyzing Client's Perspectives

Mary: My culture emphasizes patience. Sometimes we take deep breaths.

Joe: I sigh.

MC: Mary, would you demonstrate first?

Mary: (Breathes deeply)

MC: How about you, Joe?

Joe: (Takes a deep breath and sighs)

MC: That was good. You both use similar techniques to exhale your anxiety. Many people use deep breathing to relax. I'm going to add to your techniques something for the two of you to do at home. Let's try it and

---

Feminist Theory with an Empowerment Focus: Techniques

Analyzing Client's Perspectives: Analysis of the origin of client's perspectives, such as past experiences, peer influences, and/or societal expectations.

Empowering the Client: Encouragement based on the client's strengths and potentials.

Focusing on External Forces: Shifting the focus from a person's feelings about a problem in order to address what other people have said or to analyze what other external factors may have contributed to the issue.

Initiating Action: A plan of action that is initiated from the client's own view or perspective.

Making Suggestions Based on Culture/Values: Use of analysis of the family values and culture in order to gain perspectives on finding an alternative solution to the problem.

New Perspective: Identification of opinions that differ from friends, relatives, family members, or someone close to the client.

Power Analysis: Use of an incomplete statement such as, "I feel powerful when…," to help the client identify sources of power and strength.

Search for Exceptions: Analysis of alternative events or persons that the client can focus on instead of solely on the problem.

Social/Family Support: Identification of resources and support from the surrounding environment, including from the family system.

Societal Expectations: Analysis of a client's perception of the expectations from society and/or cultural upbringing.

Sources of Client Difficulties: Identification of the source of perceptual difficulties.

Women's (or Men's) Experiences: Analysis of clients' view of gender issues based on their own experience as women (or men).

see if you like it: Close your eyes and take a few deep breaths…. Now, at the same time, tense your fists as hard as you can. (demonstrating) Slowly open your hands and relax while exhaling. Try it once more. (doing the exercise again) You can repeat this exercise several times a day—say ten times—or until you feel the anxiety leaving your body.

Making Suggestions Based on Culture and Values

Joe: Is it better if we do it together?

MC: Yes, it's a simple exercise that both of you can do together. Now you can decide when you want to do it.

Joe: How about after dinner?

Mary: Now that I'm in graduate school, I have a lot of work after dinner.

MC: How about breathing and sighing only ten times? It shouldn't take more than a minute.

Mary: Okay. I'll do it every day after dinner.

MC: Remember to do this breathing exercise together. Joe, you seem to like to walk. Mary, would you like to walk, too?

Mary: Not really.

MC: Joe, can you walk at least three times a week?

Joe: I'd like to do it every day.

MC: Mary, this is decision time. It would be best if you could support Joe on this.

Mary: Whatever you say.

MC: How about saying something positive about this support?

Empowerment

Mary: I'll support you, Joe.

MC: That's a good decision. You should feel powerful about it.

Multicultural Practice Applications

In this chapter the family has been changed in terms of its composition. It is portrayed as a lesbian couple who have a daughter from a previous marriage and another child conceived through artificial insemination. Although children in lesbian families often adjust to their family identity through strong parental support, the prevalent societal judgment and biased attitudes place unjust pressure on these children and their families (Ainslie & Feltey, 1991). This case example highlights discriminatory issues and considers that issues faced by lesbian-headed families are similar in many ways to those faced by heterosexual couples.

   All couples with children need to learn solution-focused techniques to examine relationship problems and parenting issues. As in other case scenarios, this case is described based on composite information from lesbian couples who come forward for help when they face family problems. This case scenario serves as an example for discussion purposes only, not for generalization.

Variations from the Standardized Case: A Lesbian Couple With Children

Many gay and lesbian couples have demonstrated their ability to be parents, not only by disputing the stereotypical image about their suitability to become parents but also through their strong motivation to change the public's view about same-sex marriage. To illustrate the composition of this family, the case now involves Jo and Mary. A name similar to Joe is used as a replacement to maintain familiarity with the standardized case used throughout this book.

***

Jo (42) and Mary (38) have been a couple for 7 years. They have a 6-year-old boy named Kevin, whom Mary conceived through artificial insemination, and they also care for Jo's 16-year-old daughter from a previous marriage, Ami. Jo and Mary recently moved to the suburbs to find a more reputable school district for Kevin to attend, and Kevin has started attending a new elementary school in their neighborhood.

At the first PTA meeting, Jo and Mary noticed some surprised and disapproving looks from other parents. Although they have been subjected to various manifestations of hostility before, Jo and Mary are concerned about how their relationship might affect Kevin negatively in his new environment. They soon noticed that Kevin was having trouble concentrating on his schoolwork and was not making friends. Kevin recently had a homework assignment to complete a family tree worksheet, and ever since, he has been reluctant to return to school, often complaining of stomachaches in the morning and before school events.

During individual therapy sessions, Jo has complained about inconsistent parenting styles between her and Mary, as well as her disagreement with how Mary handles the family's finances, including what she sees as unreasonable spending on Kevin. At the same time, Mary has presented symptoms of emotional distress with no recognized physical cause. Ami and Kevin are upset with the couple's constant arguments. Ami is also concerned about her peers' views of her own sexual orientation because no one has asked her to the upcoming school dance.

In a session when Ami discloses her perception about her mom's orientation, the therapist tries to empower her to view herself and her family positively.

Ami:	I'm confused about the whole situation. I can't seem to understand why it happened to me.
MC:	What has happened to you lately that disturbs you?
Ami:	I feel upset about not being asked to go to homecoming.
MC:	Do you want to talk about homecoming or your upset feeling?

Ami:	(Sign) You know why I'm upset. I can't understand my mom. Why would she want to be lesbian?
MC:	What do you think she wants to do?
Ami:	She wants to be with someone she feels most comfortable with.
MC:	What would you share with your mom if she's not happy with life?
Ami:	I'll comfort her, telling her that she has me. I really think that she's taken a wrong route.
MC:	What is a wrong route?
Ami:	A route that nobody would take.
MC:	Do you really think your mom took the route nobody has taken?
Ami:	Not really! I just want her to be happy. But she has made me unhappy.
MC:	How did *she* make you unhappy? Was it your mom who made you unhappy or other things?
Ami:	It's the gossip. I'm sick and tired about it.
MC:	Your mom didn't take the *wrong* route; she took the different route, an unusual or unique route. What would you do to make yourself comfortable if the route wasn't wrong?
Ami:	I'd relax and learn about this route.
MC:	That's it! You have the power to ignore or change your perception of how other people have said about you and your mom, even if it was coming from your family members, or friends.
Ami:	I can't change them.
MC:	But you can change yourself. Changing your view is the first step.

Experts Say...

According to Ms. Ann McFarland, Director of the Office of Community Projects at the University of Houston, there are no substantial differences between working with this family and other families of cultural diversity, gay or straight. Like many couples, this couple is facing relationship and parenting issues. Suggestions for assessment and intervention are listed as follows:

- Professionals must take care not to make any assumption about Kevin's need to have a male figure in this family.
- This case doesn't provide enough information regarding the culture or ethnicity of the parents. It would be important to know the cultural backgrounds of both Jo and Mary to be able to understand their issues with their families-of-origin and their current family.
- The process of working with this family is similar to working with any other family.

- Professionals must address the stereotypical reactions they may have when first encountering this case.
- The couple can be encouraged to join a parenting group, probably with mostly gay and lesbian parents, men and women, to learn parenting skills and share frustrations they encounter in the parenting process.
- Evaluation in cases of this nature may address family-of-origin issues, such as cultural expectations, lack of family support and resources, decisions to bear a child, how divorce affects an older child, and sibling relationships in a reconstituted family.

Best Practice Evaluation

Evaluation Stage 10: Measure Perception of Power

This chapter's practice–evaluation integration focuses on the tenth stage of measuring an individual's perception of power. We use a time-series design with a comparison group to demonstrate how to measure empowerment in a family.

Suggested Evaluation Tool: Family Empowerment Scale (FES) (Koren, DeChillo, & Friesen, 1992)

Description: The FES is a 34-item rating scale to measure empowerment levels in families with children who have emotional, behavioral, or mental disorders. This scale has two conceptual definitions of empowerment: (1) power perceived from family, service system, and community/political empowerment activities; and (2) power expressed through attitude, knowledge, and behaviors. The subscale for Family includes items 2, 4, 7, 9, 16, 21, 26, 27, 29, 31, 33, and 34. The subscale for Service System includes items 1, 5, 6, 11, 12, 13, 18, 19, 23, 28, 30, and 32. The subscale for Community/Political Empowerment activities includes items 3, 8, 10, 14, 15, 17, 20, 22, 24, and 25. The scale has achieved excellent internal consistency with alphas of .88, .87, and .88 for the Family, Service System, and Community/Political subscales, respectively. The scale has also obtained excellent test–retest reliability coefficients of .83, .77, and .85 for the three subscales, respectively. And it has demonstrated appropriate content validity.

How to use the tool: Users may contact the Research and Training Center on Family Support and Children's Mental Health at 1600 SW 4th Avenue, Suite 900, Portland, OR 97201 (Phone: 503-725-4040) for a copy of the scale or send an email to RTC Publications office at rtcpubs@pdx.edu for the scale information. Readers may also find the scale at the following website: http://www.tacommunities.org/ev.php?ID=4752_201&ID2=DO_TOPIC. This 34-item measure uses a 5-point Likert-type scale with the following responses, 1 = not true at all, 2 = mostly not true, 3 = somewhat true, 4 = mostly true, and 5 = very true. Higher scores indicate that the family has perceived a higher level of empowerment. The subscale scores can be computed based on the sum of scores for the respective items. The Family and Service System subscale scores range from 12 to 60; the Community/Political subscale scores range from 10 to 50.

How to evaluate the outcomes: Following the six evaluation steps toward measuring practice effectiveness, a time-series design with comparison group is used to demonstrate how to measure outcomes from working with Jo and Mary's family:

1. *Define the service target or problem (intake and case assessment):* Mary feels disempowered because of Jo's disinterest in her recent accomplishments.
2. *Define (or formulate) goals and objectives:* To increase Mary's level of empowerment.
3. *Identify constraints and resources and select a treatment:* Constraints include disapproving and surprise looks from Jo, and Kevin's inability to concentrate on school homework. Resources include family support and willingness to discuss the issues with the child.
4. *Measure the monitoring actions (monitor progress):* Mary is referred to the practitioner for feminist therapy. From a research point of view, she represents the experimental group. From a clinical perspective, she is the identified patient who is empowered to reframe family problems. Mary is asked to complete the FES each week for 7 weeks prior to the therapy. She completes the FES immediately after treatment has started, for 7 weeks. The practitioner records the score each week. The scores are plotted in Figure 13.1. A parent from another family, Ann, who faces similar family issues, chooses not to participate in the treatment program because of her lack of interest in the therapeutic format. Ann has agreed to fill out the FES during the same 7-week period. Ann is regarded as the comparison group because she is not receiving the treatment. The scores for Ann are plotted in Figure 13.2.

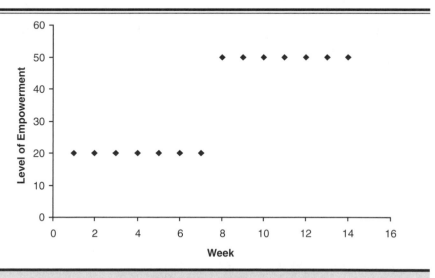

Figure 13.1
Family Empowerment Scale: Experimental Group

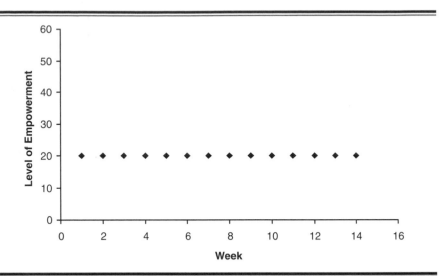

Figure 13.2
Family Empowerment Scale: Comparison Group

5. *Analyze data:* During the intervention period, Mary's FES family subscale average score (50) is higher than Ann's (20), which indicates that Mary is more empowered than Ann. Because both Mary and Ann received the same scores before treatment and the scores during treatment have changed, it provides evidence that the empowerment effect may be related to treatment if extraneous factors are controlled.

6. *Report results and make recommendations:* The results suggest that the feminist therapy has been effective in empowering Mary to address her concerns. The time-series design with comparison group has controlled for most of the confounding factors that might skew the findings.

Multicultural Practice Exercises

Questioning Techniques

Asking questions that may show the connection between a client's behaviors and attitudes and the environmental factors that may have influenced them:

e.g., "What do your friends think about this issue?"

"How did your family handle this issue when you were a child?"

"What movies have you seen or what books have you read dealing with this issue?"

Ethical Guidelines for Feminist Therapists

I. Cultural Diversities and Oppressions

   A. A feminist therapist increases her accessibility to and for a wide range of clients from her own and other identified groups through flexible delivery of services. When appropriate, the feminist therapist assists clients in accessing other services and intervenes when a client's rights are violated.

   B. A feminist therapist is aware of the meaning and impact of her own ethnic and cultural background, gender, class, age, and sexual orientation, and actively attempts to become knowledgeable about alternatives from sources other than her clients. She is actively engaged in broadening her knowledge of ethnic and cultural experiences, non-dominant and dominant.

   C. Recognizing that the dominant culture determines the norm, the therapist's goal is to uncover and respect cultural and experiential differences, including those based on long term or recent immigration and/or refugee status.

   D. A feminist therapist evaluates her ongoing interactions with her clientele for any evidence of her biases or discriminatory attitudes and practices. She also monitors her other interactions, including service delivery, teaching, writing, and all professional activities. The feminist therapist accepts responsibility for taking action to confront and change any interfering, oppressing, or devaluing biases she has.

II. Power Differentials

   A. A feminist therapist acknowledges the inherent power differentials between client and therapist and models effective use of personal, structural, or institutional power. In using the power differential to the benefit of the client, she does not take control or power which rightfully belongs to her client.

   B. A feminist therapist discloses information to the client which facilitates the therapeutic process, including information communicated to others. The therapist is responsible for using self-disclosure only with purpose and discretion and in the interest of the client.

   C. A feminist therapist negotiates and renegotiates formal and/or informal contacts with clients in an ongoing mutual process. As part of the decision-making process, she makes explicit the therapeutic issues involved.

   D. A feminist therapist educates her clients regarding power relationships. She informs clients of their rights as consumers of therapy, including procedures for resolving differences and filing grievances. She clarifies power in its various forms as it exists within other areas of her life, including professional roles, social/governmental structures, and interpersonal relationships. She assists her clients in finding ways to protect themselves and, if requested, to seek redress.

(continued)

Ethical Guidelines for Feminist Therapists *(continued)*

III. Overlapping Relationships

A. A feminist therapist recognizes the complexity and conflicting priorities inherent in multiple or overlapping relationships. The therapist accepts responsibility for monitoring such relationships to prevent potential abuse of or harm to the client.

B. A feminist therapist is actively involved in her community. As a result, she is aware of the need for confidentiality in all settings. Recognizing that her client's concerns and general well-being are primary, she self-monitors both public and private statements and comments. Situations may develop through community involvement where power dynamics shift, including a client having equal or more authority than the therapist. In all such situations a feminist therapist maintains accountability.

C. When accepting third party payments, a feminist therapist is especially cognizant of and clearly communicates to her client the multiple obligations, roles, and responsibilities of the therapist. When working in institutional settings, she clarifies to all involved parties where her allegiances lie. She also monitors multiple and conflicting expectations between clients and caregivers, especially when working with children and elders.

D. A feminist therapist does not engage in sexual intimacies or any overt or covert sexual behaviors with a client or former client.

IV. Therapist Accountability

A. A feminist therapist is accountable to herself, to colleagues, and especially to her clients.

B. A feminist therapist will contract to work with clients and issues within the realm of her competencies. If problems beyond her competencies surface, the feminist therapist utilizes consultation and available resources. She respects the integrity of the relationship by stating the limits of her training and providing the client with the possibilities of continuing with her or changing therapists.

C. A feminist therapist recognizes her personal and professional needs and utilizes ongoing self-evaluation, peer support, consultation, supervision, continuing education, and/or personal therapy. She evaluates, maintains, and seeks to improve her competencies, as well as her emotional, physical, mental, and spiritual well being. When the feminist therapist has experienced a similar stressful or damaging event as her client, she seeks consultation.

D. A feminist therapist continually re-evaluates her training, theoretical background, and research to include developments in feminist knowledge. She integrates feminism into psychological theory, receives ongoing therapy training, and acknowledges the limits of her competencies.

(continued)

Ethical Guidelines for Feminist Therapists *(continued)*

E. A feminist therapist engages in self-care activities in an ongoing manner outside the work setting. She recognizes her own needs and vulnerabilities as well as the unique stresses inherent in this work. She demonstrates an ability to establish boundaries with the clients that are healthy for both of them. She also is willing to self-nurture in appropriate and self-empowering ways.

V. Social Change

A. A feminist therapist seeks multiple avenues for impacting change, including public education and advocacy within professional organizations, lobbying for legislative actions, and other appropriate activities.

B. A feminist therapist actively questions practices in her community that appear harmful to clients or therapists. She assists clients in intervening on their own behalf. As appropriate, the feminist therapist herself intervenes, especially when other practitioners appear to be engaging in harmful, unethical, or illegal behaviors.

C. When appropriate, a feminist therapist encourages a client's recognition of criminal behaviors and also facilitates the client's navigation of the criminal justice system.

D. A feminist therapist, teacher, or researcher is alert to the control of information dissemination and questions pressures to conform to and use dominant mainstream standards. As technological methods of communication change and increase, the feminist therapist recognizes the socioeconomic aspects of these developments and communicates according to clients' access to technology.

E. A feminist therapist, teacher, or researcher recognizes the political is personal in a world where social change is a constant.

© Copyright 2000, Feminist Therapy Institute, Inc.
From: Marcia Chappell, 912 Five Islands Rd., Georgetown, ME 04548 or info@feministtherapyinstitute.org

---

Source: Feminist Therapy Institute. (2005). *Feminist therapy code of ethics* (Revised, 1999). Retrieved May 10, 2005, from http://www.feministtherapyinstitute.org/ethics.htm

Asking questions that bring out the client's strengths (paying attention to those that may be devalued by the society):

e.g.   "Have you ever noticed that you can clarify your goals well?"

"Have you ever thought of your assertiveness as a plus in your life?"

Challenging the Clients

Empower each person in the family to suggest new ways of relating, behaving, and thinking, and then discuss what implications these changes have on the family in the context of societal pressures.

Discuss alternative actions that directly or indirectly address the question: "What does this cost you?"

Topics for Discussion

1. What techniques do the helping professionals use to integrate traditional interventions with empowerment-based interventions in order to help clients address personal/familial issues affected by society?

2. The uniqueness of the empowerment-based feminist approach lies in the "personal is political" philosophy that "personal problems are often connected to or influenced by the political and social climate in which people live" (Enns, 2004, p.11). How is this philosophy helpful when the client's decision is influenced by his or her culture, rather than the current political environment in the society?

3. In what ways do practitioners utilize clients' strengths if clients do not recognize their own strengths? What steps should be taken if clients cannot list any of their strengths even after using empowerment techniques? Is the reframing technique helpful in conjunction with an empowerment approach? Why or why not?

CHAPTER FOURTEEN

Solution-Focused Approach

In this last chapter on theory applications in cross-cultural situations, practical use of the solution-focused approach demonstrates how to address clients' strengths. The chapter begins by describing the purpose behind the use of narratives and explains how events-telling can help practitioners identify clients' solution-focused language. Goal-oriented techniques highlight the importance of eliciting clients' own solutions. From the multicultural perspective, the task of grandparenthood is described as a learning process for families with children and grandchildren. The family stage of grandparenthood reveals issues related to intergenerational conflict and the role of family caregivers. Regardless of whether or not the family is going through the grandparenthood stage, this chapter addresses issues related to individual perceptions concerning significant changes in life. Stage 11 of the Best Practice Evaluation provides direction on how to map out solutions and alternatives.

Solution-Focusing To Find Solutions

The philosophy behind the solution-focused approach is to maintain a positive attitude while identifying a solution or an exception to the problem. If a problem has an identifiable solution, individuals should be able to reconstruct the solution by examining what has worked previously in similar situations. According to Steve de Shazer

(1997), therapeutic work starts with the client's description of what has worked in the past as an indication of what can be helpful in the future. All solutions are embedded in contexts and patterns that can be recovered or uncovered from clients'

Solution-Focused Theory in Brief

Importance to Multicultural Practice:

- There are no specific cultural boundaries when searching for exceptions to the problem.
- This approach helps clients feel important.
- Culturally relevant alternatives can be generated to reach a solution.

Major Figures:

- George Kelly (1905-1967)—Founder of Solution-Focused Theory
- Steve de Shazer (1940-2005)—Clinical Applications and Brief Therapy
- Insoo Kim Berg (1935-2007)—Brief Therapy with Multicultural Families

Assumptions:

- Individuals can construct a new worldview.
- The central aim is on solutions rather than on problems.
- Anxiety is a symptom of a problem-saturated self-description.

Therapeutic Process:

- Clients are considered the experts, especially related to their own social interactions with others.
- Clients' use of language and concepts should be assessed to construct past and present meanings.

Goals:

- To construct new realities that allow clients to make productive choices.
- To identify clients' strengths and resources.

Multicultural Practice Techniques:

- Search for alternatives to a complaint
- Augment clients' suggestions for solutions
- Clarify goals for change
- Use solution-focused language
- "Miracle Question": How do you envision life without this problem?
- "Backward/Fast-Forward Questions": What was life like before this problem existed? What would be the first thing you would notice if this problem were to disappear? What would your life be like 5 years from now without this problem?

own narratives. As such, encouraging clients to tell their stories through narratives is the key to the success of this approach.

Solution-focused therapy emphasizes the client's own personal descriptions to justify one of three possible types of conclusions, by means of (1) *progressive narratives* that justify the conclusion that people and situations are progressing toward their goals, (2) *stability narratives* that justify the conclusion that life is unchanging, and (3) *digressive narratives* that justify the conclusion that life is moving away from goals (de Shazer, 1985, 1997; Riley & Malchiodi, 2003; Strand, 1997). Storytelling strategies are used to highlight past events that may bring about one of these possible conclusions so that the client can clearly see what he or she has done to bring about changes in the past. Questions such as "what have you done in the past to solve this kind of problem?" and "how did you reach this point of understanding of the problem?" help the client realize the strengths he or she used to understand or solve problems in the past. By means of these strengths, the client can then find solutions to the current situation.

These descriptions stress alternatives and exceptions, not the problem itself. The underlying principle simply states, "We tend to get what we notice, so we need to notice what we want to get!" (Cottrell, 2000). If the problem or the client's resistance is the central concern, a solution is less likely to be generated. One of the tasks is to analyze potential possibilities that might work. Once a solution has been identified and the client is demonstrating improvement, the emphasis should be on continued implementation of that solution. Although the past is not considered to be an important analytical element in the solution-focused approach, it is utilized as an instrument to inform action in the present and the future. In sum, the solution-focused approach is a cooperative intervention, not expert-led or diagnostic. The therapist's role is to facilitate and co-construct solutions with the client.

The solution-focused therapeutic approach utilizes techniques that yield results, validate clients' experiences, and expand clients' views to accept potential options. In solution-focused therapy, the goals that are set should be

1. directed initially to small tasks;
2. relevant to the client's cultural expectations;
3. observable, measurable, and concrete;
4. described as the commencement of an expectation;
5. treated as incorporating new behaviors; and
6. achievable, practical, and within reach in clients' lives.

In summation, the solution-focused approach is a cooperative intervention, not expert-led or diagnostic. The therapist's role is to facilitate and co-construct solutions with the client. This approach focuses on clients' strengths, goals accomplished in the past, changes based on action, and the clients' own statements that contain possible solutions or answers to the problem.

On the Multicultural Stage: Becoming Grandparents

Grandparenthood is a stage in life that many families find enjoyable and rewarding. The number of grandparents is increasing as family dynamics begin to shift and grandparents are living longer. As challenges and change are incorporated into every step in the next generation, family structures and relationships form resourceful ways of coping. In multicultural counseling the dynamics of all family systems must be considered because each generation impacts the others in different ways depending on culture, traditions, and levels of acculturation. For example, "First-generation elderly immigrants find that what they expected from their offspring within the cultural framework of their original home is challenged by the cultural milieu and material demands of the family's new place of residence" (Dressel, 1996, p. 5). Among the factors that influence grandparenting are culture, ethnicity, gender, race, family traditions, family structure, and personal history (Holmes, 2001). Intergenerational issues need to be explored with participation by the children and grandchildren. The younger generations can review their perspectives while the elderly parents can also share their views. The solution to a specific conflict may not be taking that conflict away; it may be about understanding each other's perspective.

The role of grandparents is changing as more and more grandparents are becoming primary caregivers for their grandchildren. Currently, grandparents are the largest group providing foster care, as well as adopting their own grandchildren (DelCampo, 2003). Other issues that grandparents face today include dealing with divorce and remarriage of their own children. All of the unique grandparenting roles, including the traditional grandparent, step-grandparent, or a grandparent raising a grandchild, are significant in the grandchild's life.

The Case Approach

The use of solution-focused approach is demonstrated through the modified case content related to grandparenting. Three issues are addressed: 1) what to do when a grandparent has decided to move in with the family, 2) how to accept changes in the caregiver role, and 3) how to resolve conflict.

Issue #1: Grandparent Moving In

In the following scenario, Mary addresses her mother about wanting to move into her household. Mary welcomes this possibility because she is starting a new job. However, she is upset about how her mother handled Ami's misbehavior when she came home around 4:30 a.m. The dialogue takes place in the middle of a session with Mary and her mom.

Mary: Mom, I just want you to know that I should be the one who takes care of Ami's behavioral problems.

Grandmother:	I just want to help.
Mary:	I know, and you've been helpful, but I don't want Ami to be over-protected by you.
MC:	This sounds like a very emotionally charged topic. I'd like for each of you talk about your perception of the problem.
Mary:	I'd like to start because I want an answer!
MC:	Okay, Mary, go ahead.
Mary:	Last Friday night the soccer team was having their end-of-the year party at the coach's house. Ami told me she'd be at the party for a couple of hours. She was expected home at 10 o'clock p.m. since that's her curfew. I was *so* worried.
Grandmother:	Ami called me in the middle of the night, telling me her mom and dad were about to kill her.
MC:	It appears that you all had a difficult weekend. Tell me more about what happened after that phone call.
Grandmother:	I went to their house and tried to help out.
MC:	Mary, what happened to you before Ami came home?

Backward Question

Mary:	Before Ami came home, I started calling Ami's teammates, but they didn't know where she was. I tried the coach's house, but no one answered. I woke Joe up to call the police. While he was on the phone with the police, I heard Ami coming in. We had to explain to the police that she was home. How embarrassing!
Grandmother:	I told you before that you didn't have enough time to be with your family.
Mary:	Mom, I'd like you to move in even tomorrow. But, I don't think it'd help to reduce my anxiety.
MC:	Mary, what do you mean?
Mary:	I was worried that Ami *slept* with the coach's son. I don't know if she used protection. What if she got pregnant? What if she got a disease?
MC:	Calm down. You know Ami is capable of knowing the consequences of her actions.

Reinforcing/Complimenting

MC:	It wasn't about Ami; it is about yourself, right?
Mary:	I don't think I was ready to be a grandmom.
MC:	Mary, what do you think would help turn this situation around?

Using the Client as the Consultant

| Mary: | I don't want her staying out all night! We do have rules in our house. |

Grandmother:	I agree. I definitely don't want her staying out late either. Mary, let me try to help.
Mary:	Mom, I just don't want you to intervene in what I do with Ami.
Grandmother:	I know … but Ami needs someone to listen to.
Mary:	Mom, I know you want to come to help. I just want to make sure things are under control.
Grandmother:	I want to move in not only because of Ami. I want you to know I want to help you.
MC:	What did you hear, Mary?
Mary:	Mom wants to be a good grandmother and a good mother at the same time.
MC:	That's a start. Now let's talk about communication. How will you know if your family is communicating well in the future—say ten years from now?

Fast-Forward Question

Mary:	Hmm. By then, I might be spending a lot of time talking to Ami … finding out what's going on in her life.
Grandmother:	Ten years? I think I'll play with my great-grandchildren.
Mary:	I don't think I want to be a grandmom that soon.
Grandmother:	I was grandmom when I was your age.
MC:	Mary, what do you think about what your mom just said?
Mary:	I don't know. Mom, I understand where you're coming from, but this is a different age.
MC:	Mary, what do you see when you compare what's taking place now and what it will be ten years in the future?
Mary:	I'm not exactly sure, but I definitely see your point.

Issue #2: Accepting Changes in the Caregiver Role

This first session is with Mary alone. The main reason for her seeking therapy is to evaluate some changes she is contemplating in her life and the possible negative reactions she perceives from her family members.

Mary:	At this time in my life I'd like to do something for me, but I'm not sure how my family will react to changes in my role. What if I make changes that nobody likes?
MC:	So you're considering changes that the others may not like? Tell me more.

Focusing on Solution-Oriented Language

Mary: Well, I want to break free from the roles I've always had—wife and mother and homemaker—but I don't know how to begin. And I'm not even sure of what I would do—or even if I would do anything at all. I've never thought of myself as a selfish person, but there are times when I don't take care of my own needs because my family depends on me completely.

MC: Has there ever been a time when you expanded your roles beyond the ones you just described? What you call "being selfish?"

Seeking Exceptions to the Complaint

Mary: Well, yes.... Taking college courses a while back was a different role for me. Boy did that ever cause a stir! Everyone in my family panicked and thought I was abandoning them! Imagine teenagers and adults having to do their own cooking and laundry! Their response should have made me feel needed, and it did to a certain extent, but I also felt disappointed. Maybe that's why I'm thinking about going back to college, regardless of whether anyone approves of it or not. But I've almost decided to do it only part-time because I can't bear the thought of deserting my family entirely!

MC: What do you think it says about you that you were able to venture out on your own before and expand your roles and life experiences without compromising your need to be needed—even in the face of disapproval from others?

Using Questions to Focus on Client's Strengths

Mary: Hmm.... I've never thought of it that way. I suppose it says at least that at one time I was able to be my own person and still find a way to keep my family together—something I value.

MC: Is that what you want now, Mary—to find a way to be your own person and still keep your family together?

Identifying and Clarifying Client's Goals

Mary: Yes, I think so. But I haven't been able to imagine how to do that now.

MC: Help me get a better picture of what you're looking for in the way of changes. If you were to wake up tomorrow and all of your problems were gone, how would you know that these problems had disappeared? What would that day be like?

The Miracle Question

Mary: Wow! I don't think I've ever even imagined what it would be like. Let me think.... (pause) ... um ... well, for one thing, I'd get up and get dressed in the morning because I'd have somewhere to go! I'd have somewhere to go to be productive and to be creative. I'd be doing something *I'm* interested in instead of helping everyone else do what *they're* involved in.

MC: What else would be different?

Solution-Seeking Language

Mary: My husband would … (pause) accept … no, he would *enjoy* that I'm feeling fulfilled and happy. He'd even share some of the responsibility around the house—which isn't even that big of a deal any more since the kids are almost on their own.

MC: Has there ever been a time when he did help take care of the home?

Searching for Exceptions to the Complaint

Mary: Yes, he sure did! It was back when I was taking some evening classes at the college. He would cook for the kids and wash the dishes. He didn't complain at all after things were set up and we had a routine.

MC: What's different between then and now? How were you able to make the situation work so well back then?

Focusing on Client's Own Solution

Mary: Ha! I'm not used to seeing myself in control of things like that! I never thought of myself as *making* things work out. I guess one difference was that I knew exactly what I wanted to do—get more education and eventually a degree. I was sure of it. I had no doubts. After that, the rest was inevitable. At first it was hard and scary, but then it got better….

MC: How can you relate that stage in your life to how you feel now?

Mary: I'm beginning to see some similarities. I haven't made up my mind for sure because it's so hard for me to risk disapproval from my family.

MC: It seems that you can appreciate your own achievement and begin to understand how other people react to it.

Amplifying Change and Client's Strengths

Mary: All this doesn't change the fact that I'm worried and afraid about my marriage and what my kids will think. How will they handle a change in me?

MC: You're pinpointing the next element necessary for a solution. During the week before our next session, I'd like you to record the times your family reacts positively toward you and shows approval and appreciation. Each day, describe the surrounding events and the family member's behaviors. This may give us useful information for determining the next step toward a solution.

Prescribing More of What Works

Mary: I'll give it a try.

Issue #3 Conflict Resolution

This is the fourth session that Mary and Joe have attended to explore their relationship issues. After the recent hospitalization of Joe's mother, the family has reminisced about past events that solidified the family members.

MC: It's been a couple of weeks since our last session. What's changed since we last met?

Solution-Oriented Language

Joe: Actually, everything has been pretty good. Ami and I have gotten closer because we talk on our way to see Grandma. Ami looks forward to those talks and the visits.

MC: How about you, Mary?

Mary: School has been good. I was able to study a lot this past week while Joe visited his mom. I got 2 As—on an assignment and a test in class. I feel less stressed when I can get my homework done and do well in school. I still feel guilty about this sometimes, though—that I should be more of a wife and mother. Sometimes I don't think they understand just how important it is for me to be going to college.

MC: Are you feeling like your family isn't being supportive of you and giving you the time you need for your education?

Mary: Well, I guess so.

MC: Has there ever been a time when you were studying and felt that your family was supportive of you?

Seeking Exceptions to the Complaints

Mary: Now that you mention it—a couple of times Joe has grilled something for dinner without my asking him to. That way I can just eat and get right back to studying. The kids are helping out with the cleaning, too, once in a while, so I guess you can call that being supportive. But it doesn't happen very often.

Reframing

Joe: Mary, how you can say that? I don't understand where this is coming from. Have I ever complained? Have the kids? (Looks at therapist) Do you see how she is? This is exactly what I mean.

Mary: Joe ... don't be like that. All I'm saying is that I'm starting to realize that I *do* have your support after all. Maybe I'm not more appreciative because I feel guilty that I can't do everything I used to.

MC: That's great, Mary! Not everyone has that much insight!

Focusing on the Positive

MC: Mary, do you remember the early session when I asked you to keep a log on times when you felt the family was supportive? How has that been going?

Solution-Seeking Language

Mary: Like I said, it's been pretty hectic, and I didn't keep up with the log after a while, especially when I didn't feel supported. Like the time Ami complained when I didn't have her soccer uniform washed, and then another time Joe complained when he had to work late and dinner wasn't ready for him or the kids when he got home at eight p.m. I was studying for a big test the next morning, and time got away from me. Sometimes the log just made me feel worse.

Joe: Mary, every time you've told me you needed help, we've helped out! Do you remember that I picked up the dry cleaning and took the kids to soccer practice? And that's just part of it. I do *a lot* more! You have to let me know what you need from me because I can't read your mind.

Mary: (Looking at MC) He's right. Come to think of it, things do run pretty smoothly when I communicate what's going on with me.

MC: That's good, Mary. It's important to realize that communication within any family is vital, especially in one as busy as yours.

Solution-Seeking Language

MC: Between now and your next session, why don't you communicate with Joe and your children in advance when you need time to study? And go back to keeping a log about how well that works. Journaling will help you visually see what works best for your family. And— don't laugh—how about going on a "date" with just the two of you—no children—to give you a break and a chance to rekindle your communication?

(Next session)

Prescribing More of What Works

MC: Sounds like you've been very busy. Let's talk about how your assignments from last week went.

Mary: Well, last Saturday I'd been studying all day. Joe asked me out to dinner that evening, and I hesitated to go because I was so busy. I had an exam coming up, but Joe convinced me to take a break.

Joe: Yeah, at first it seemed like she didn't want to go, but she'd been working so hard that I wanted her to take a break so we could enjoy some time together.

Mary: I told myself that things would never get better in our relationship if I didn't try.

MC: Tell me—how did it go?

(Mary and Joe gaze at each other and giggle)

Joe: You tell her, Mary.

Mary: Well, we started to go to a new restaurant in the city, and on our way there (looks at Joe) … this is really silly. Anyway, on our way there, we saw an announcement in the window of the Hilton for a new dance club that plays 70's and 80's music. We both had flashbacks of our high school days and thought it would be fun to check it out.

Joe: I was surprised that she agreed. Mary's usually more reserved than that.

(Mary giggles)

MC: Go on.

Mary: They had this buffet at the hotel, so we had dinner and then made our way out to the dance floor.

Joe: … That was a few margaritas later.

(Mary giggles and covers her face with her hands)

Mary: You finish the story, Joe.

Joe: It was great fun. We danced all night … and we hadn't done that since before the kids were born. We found ourselves laughing and being silly. We closed the place down! Since it was so late, it only made sense to get a room at the hotel.

Mary: I didn't even have a bag packed. We had to get toothbrushes from a machine in the lobby. We called and woke up the kids to tell them where we were. Then we went back to the room, and, needless to say, one thing led to another, and my wild side took over. He's has been quite the tiger ever since. (Mary blushes and giggles)

MC: Am I to assume there's more intimacy in your relationship now?

(Mary and Joe nod yes.)

MC: At our last session before the dating assignment, you both rated your relationship as a 4 on a scale of 1 to 10, with 10 being the best. How would you rate your relationship now?

Scaling Progress

Joe: These past few weeks have been quite exciting. I'd rate it at least a 7.

Mary: I agree.

MC: When you move upward from there, what will be different?

Mary: When Joe asks me out on a date, I won't hesitate like I did the last time. Who knows—maybe I'll even ask Joe out on a date!

Joe: Sounds good to me!

MC: Now that there's more intimacy between the two of you, what's different between you and Joe?

Finding the Difference

Solution-Focused Techniques

Amplifying or Focusing on Strengths: A way to identify solutions by drawing clients' attention to the their strengths.

Clarifying the Client's Goals: Developing goals by analyzing or highlighting client's own goal-oriented statements.

Fast-Forward Questioning: A way to check perceptions by moving the situation a few years ahead.

Finding the Difference: Identifying perceived differences after a certain action has been taken.

Focusing on Change: Identifying what change the client has noticed when comparing circumstances before and after he or she implemented an action.

Focusing on Client's Own Solutions: Pointing out the client' contributions in the process of developing or trying solutions.

Focusing on the Positive: A technique to raise clients' awareness about using positive energy to find solutions.

Focusing on Solution-Oriented Language: Encouraging clients to think about making changes or planning solutions.

Prescribing More of What Works: Assigning a task or homework activity that has worked in the past.

Reframing: A technique that redefines a worry or concern into something positive or that recognizes that the concern is out of the client's control.

Reinforcing or Complimenting: Praising the client for the successful identification of solutions.

Scaling Progress: Using a rating scale to help clients identify observable steps toward solving problems.

Searching for Exceptions to the Complaint: A questioning technique to help a client recall a past event when the problem was not present so the surrounding factors involved can be identified to help avoid recurrence of the same issue.

Solution-Seeking Language: Emphasizing the future rather than the past, and on the solution rather than the problem.

Miracle Question: What would life be like without the problem?

Using the Client as Consultant: A positive way to maximize the client's belief that he or she is aware of a possible solution.

Mary:	We're more affectionate with each other.
MC:	What do you mean by "more affectionate?" Can you give an example?
Mary:	We watched a movie after midnight and held hands.
MC:	Mary, continue to recall some of these examples and write them down.... Joe, what about you?
Joe:	I feel like I'm getting my old Mary back.
MC:	What else is different at your house?
Joe:	The kids are wondering what's up with us. You know how teenagers are. They were surprised when we told them were staying overnight at the Hilton, and they've been curious ever since.
MC:	What does all this tell you about your relationship?
Mary:	It tells me that our relationship isn't in as serious trouble as I thought it was.
MC:	How did you figure that out?
Mary:	This last assignment made me realize that in order to keep intimacy alive in a relationship, it takes work.
MC:	It sounds like in the few weeks since we've been seeing each other, you've all been working very hard. How will you know when it's time to stop seeing me? What will be different?
Mary:	I was leery about coming to a therapist for what I thought was a relationship problem, but you helped us realize that what we need to do is to work on our relationship. While I don't think we need to continue seeing you on a regular basis, I think both of us are definitely more aware of what we need to do for each other. Eventually, what will be different is that I won't be questioning Joe's love for me. I just wish my relationship with Ami was improving as well.
MC:	This sounds like a good time to start our family sessions.
Mary and Joe:	(nod in agreement.)

Multicultural Practice Applications

In this case discussion, poverty is selected as a target variable. Poverty is an aspect of a society with economic and political imbalance; unjust treatment toward the "have nots"; unresolved inequalities stemming from classism, racism, and sexism; and other discriminatory behaviors or actions against those who are differently abled. Among all of the different issues we address in clinical situations, poverty is one of the most complex, but at the same time it is a concrete and up-front issue. Poverty is a critical issue because of its economic implications for a family's growth and development, and its outcomes seem to be approachable given an optimistic view of societal care and concerns.

Unfortunately, numerous studies show that many racial minorities continue to live in the stark conditions of poverty as a result of racism and discrimination (Snowden, 2005) and gender biases (Limbert & Bullock, 2005). People who lack financial resources are most likely to have poor and unfavorable housing, employment, education, recreation, health care, and mental health—all factors that constitute a basic quality of life. Many people who live in poverty are not aware of alternative ways of living because they lack education or access to other parts of society, they cannot access resources, or they do not know how to access societal support.

An intervention based on empowerment aims to help individuals become more proactive and involved in society, gain greater access to information and resources, and report their difficulties without shame. Eight basic principles guide solution-focused practices (Pichot & Dolan, 2003, p.13):

1. If it isn't broken, don't fix it.
2. If something is working, do more of it.
3. If it's not working, do something different.
4. Small steps can lead to large changes.
5. The solution is not necessarily directly related to the problem.
6. The language requirements for solution development are different form those needed to describe a problem.
7. No problem happens all the time. There are always exceptions that can be utilized.
8. The future is not created and negotiable.

In solution-focused interventions, the practitioner examines the client's current situation and encourages the client to search strengths and resources that the client possesses and can access. With a focus on the client's positive attitude toward self and others, the practitioner can help the client mobilize resources and utilize strengths to solve his/her immediate concerns.

Variations From the Standardized Case: A Family in Poverty

Because solution-focused techniques are designed for a broad range of families, this chapter chooses a family in poverty to illustrate the solution-focused approach. This case involves demographic variations including living arrangements, employment and financial status, and household composition to help practitioners examine whether solution-focused strategies are appropriate in working with many types of family systems issues.

***

Mary and Joe usually arrive home from work around the same time. Mary's mother stays at their home with the two children and usually has started cooking dinner by the time Mary and Joe arrive home. One night the electricity suddenly goes off in their two-bedroom apartment. When Mary asks Joe if he paid the electric bill, Joe explains that there was not enough money to pay the bill that month, but that he had talked to somebody at the electric company who told him that he could pay double next month.

Upon hearing this, Mary's mother whispers to Mary that it was a bad idea for her to have married Joe because he can't support the family. Joe hears the remark but ignores it and looks for the telephone number for the electric company. Then Joe collects some change and leaves to use the phone next to the manager's office. When he gets to the manager's office, a teenage boy is sitting on the floor using the phone, seemingly chatting with a girlfriend. Joe waits his turn to use the phone.

When Joe finally arrives back at the apartment, he discovers that Mary, her mother, and the two children have packed some bags. Mary tells him that they are going to stay with her mother until the electricity is turned back on. After some discussion, Joe agrees this is the best solution, and he helps move some essential items to their car. The whole family squeezes into the car with the belongings, but the car fails to start. Joe knows that the battery has to be replaced, but doesn't have enough money to purchase a new one. He had hoped the battery would make it until the next paycheck.

Mary's mother gets out of the car and tells the children to follow her to the bus stop. Joe starts to argue with Mary's mother, telling her it is too late in the evening and too dangerous to be out on the streets. Mary's mother tells him that he should have thought about that before he "chose" not to pay the bills.

After getting in an emergency shelter, Mary and Joe discussed their problem to a social worker:

Joe: I really didn't know the car would break down. My family couldn't live on the street.

MC: I understand. You said you had a fight with your mother-in-law and couldn't stay in her place.

Mary: Yes, it'd be hard. My mom was helpful but she couldn't accept Joe.

Joe: She hated me because I didn't have money. I really don't want to ask for her to help again.

Mary: No, she didn't hate you. She was frustrated. That's all.

MC: Frustrations came from our perception of the situation. Please tell me what you can do to get yourself out of this situation.

Joe: I just need to take care of my household. My mother-in-law indeed is very helpful. She helps us whenever we need her. We couldn't work if she weren't there to look after our children.

Mary:	Joe, mom wants to help. Please take care of the electricity and call her back.
MC:	It seems that you have a great resource.
Joe:	I admit that she's been very helpful. I don't know how to ask her.
Mary:	Let me do the work. I just want you to appreciate her.

Experts Say...

Based on the analysis from experts in poverty such as Dr. Joe Rubio, Catholic Charities, Archdiocese of Galveston-Houston, and Mrs. Anne Rubio, Galveston Interfaith, this family has interpersonal relationship problems similar to those faced by most families. For the fragile group of people in poverty, however, issues of cohesion, communication, allocation of resources, boundaries, and roles are magnified to such an extent that members are in serious crisis and have come to a juncture. The family will either proceed in a new direction and survive as a unit or will begin to fall apart because of its inability to deal with both internal and external struggles, posed largely by financial barriers. The solution-focused approach seems to be appropriate in helping each individual think about what has worked in the past and what can be done in the future. Emotional connections to the family's current financial circumstances are to be processed before each person gets into a heated discussion about what they can do together.

Assessment: The good news is that, surprisingly, these individuals are already in therapy. It would be interesting to know how they arrived at the therapist's door. Tendencies toward isolation and passivity, such as theirs, do not easily lend themselves to outside intervention. When all parties are desperate for relief, however, positive change is possible.

Interventions: The presenting problem is communication with the grandmother, and the intervention should focus on concrete needs. Upon a closer look, systemic family tensions will surface. The practitioner uses a strength-based approach to help clients face their problems while supplying them with resources. One strength is the hopefulness expressed in the family's wish, voiced in their individual sessions, to address their need for structure and clear communication in a safe family therapeutic setting. Second, the parents both maintain jobs that provide the family with two incomes, which can be managed more prudently.

The areas in need of improvement in this case scenario are numerous. The father sees himself as powerless, not only within his own family but also in the larger social system. An assessment of his social intelligence and emotional health would be revealing. The mother's powerlessness in the face of strong forces—her husband, her mother, and her children—likely contributes to her internalized emotions and resulting symptoms of stress. The children are responding to the family dysfunction with fairly common challenges to authority. One of the primary concerns about the children is their risk for poor school performance. The grandmother's role is pivotal in this scenario. Even though she is providing some assistance by cooking and caring for the children, her level of authority within the household is disproportionate. Her judgmental statements, aimed at subverting the parents' authority, may create a pathological effect to the extent that the parents cannot function. It would be best to communicate with the grandmother to allow her to see her strengths, as well as the family's strengths, so that she will not be critical about the way the family's concrete needs are met, but instead focus on the family's emotional support provided by both parents and the grandparent.

Applying a strength-based approach, the practitioner likely would point to the adverse aspects of this emotional tinder box: inability to communicate appropriately, limited social outlets, poorly defined roles and boundaries, possibly crowded sleeping arrangements, symptoms of depression, and risks that the children will seek harmful social outlets outside the family. A positive intervention will reach beyond the presenting problem with a goal of strengthening the family unit. Optimally, through culturally sensitive family therapy and the prudent use of community resources, family members will be empowered to communicate clearly in a manner congruent with their cultural framework, define roles and responsibilities for each family member (including the grandmother), understand and provide for the children's social and educational needs, and implement basic financial management strategies.

Best Practice Evaluation:

Evaluation Stage 11: Map out Solutions and Alternatives

Following the tenth stage of measuring perception of power, this chapter's practice–evaluation integration focuses on the last stage of mapping out solutions and alternatives. We use a time-series design with a comparison group to demonstrate how to measure family coping.

Suggested Evaluation Tool: Family Crisis Oriented Personal Evaluation Scales (F-COPES) (McCubbin, Larsen, & Olson, 1982)

Description: The F-COPES is a 30-item rating scale designed to measure family coping. This scale contains five subscales: Acquiring Social Support (items: 1, 2, 5, 8 10, 20, 25, and 29); Reframing (items: 3, 7, 11, 13, 15, 19, 22, and 24); Seeking Spiritual Support (items: 1, 4, 23, 27, and 30); Mobilizing Family to Acquire and Accept Help (items: 4, 6, 9, and 21); and Passive Appraisal (items: 12, 17, 26, and 28). McCubbin and associates (1982) reported that the reliability coefficients for the subscales involving acquiring social support, reframing, seeking spiritual support, and mobilizing the family to acquire and accept help were .83, .82, .80, and .70, respectively. Plunkett, Carolyn, and Knaub (1999) obtained a similar internal consistency reliability coefficient for the four subscales.

According to McCubbin and colleagues, the norms of the subscales were: total score mean = 93.3, Acquiring Social Support mean = 27.2, Reframing mean = 30.2, Seeking Spiritual Support mean = 16.1, Mobilizing Family to Acquire and Accept Help mean = 11.96, and Passive Appraisal mean = 8.55. In terms of validity, the

F-COPES has an excellent concurrent validity as it correlates with other family scales such as Parenting Stress Index (PSI) (see Barnett, Hall, & Bramlett, 1990).

How to use the tool: Permission to use the instrument is obtained by purchasing the book: McCubbin, Thompson, and McCubbin (1996), *Family assessment, resiliency coping & adaptation: inventories for research & practice.* The book is available at the University of Wisconsin, University Book Store at 711 State Street, Madison, WI 53703 (Phone: 1-800-993-2665 x344). This 30-item measure uses a 5-point Likert-type scale with the following responses, 1 = strongly disagree, 2 = moderately disagree, 3 = neither agree nor disagree, 4 = moderately agree, and 5 = strongly agree. Higher scores indicate that the family is coping with the problem more effectively. The total score can be obtained by summing all items. (Note: Scores for items 12, 17, 26, and 28 are to be reversed.) The subscale scores can be computed by summing all the individual subscale items.

How to evaluate the outcomes: As discussed in chapter 3, six evaluation steps are used to measure whether the family is able to cope with the problem using the time-series single-system design with a comparison group. These steps are demonstrated with Joe and Mary's family in poverty.

1. *Define the service target or problem (intake and case assessment):* Joe lacks effective problem-solving skills and has displayed a negative attitude and behavior in responding to difficult or problematic situations, especially those related to his wife, Mary.
2. *Define (or formulate) goals and objectives:* To increase Joe's coping abilities, especially when communicating with his family.
3. *Identify constraints and resources and select a treatment:* Constraints include the problem of poverty and lack of financial support. Resources include support from the mother-in-law and the wife.
4. *Measure the monitoring actions (monitor progress):* Joe is referred to the practitioner to discuss his issues with solution-focused skills. From a research point of view, Joe represents the experimental group. From a clinical perspective, he is the client in need of help to reframe family problems so he will gain a new and positive perspective. Joe is asked to complete the F-COPES each week for 7 weeks prior to his participating in solution-focused therapy. He is also asked to complete the F-COPES immediately after treatment has started, for 7 weeks. The practitioner records the score each week. The scores are plotted in Figure 14.1.

   A father from another family, John, who faces similar family issues, cannot participate in the treatment program because of his busy schedule. John has agreed to fill out the F-COPES in the same 14-week period and may consider joining the treatment at a later time. John is regarded as the comparison group because he is not receiving the treatment. John's scores are plotted in Figure 14.2.
5. *Analyze data:* Joe's F-COPES average total score during the intervention period (120) is higher than that of John's (40), which indicates that Joe has

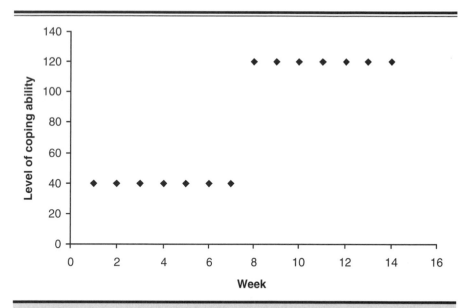

Figure 14.1

Family Crisis-Oriented Personal Evaluation Scale: Experimental Group

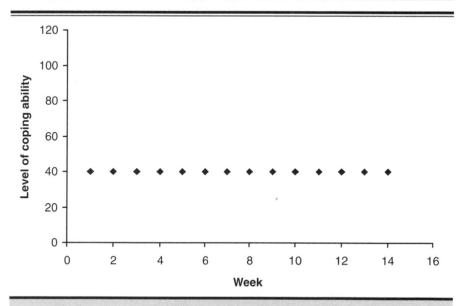

Figure 14.2

Family Crisis-Oriented Personal Evaluation Scale: Comparison Group

better coping skills than John does. It is important to note that Joe and John had similar scores during the week before treatment, which suggests that the experimental and comparison groups are equal in their coping difficulties during the nonintervention period.

6. *Report results and make recommendations:* The quantitative results suggest that the solution-focused therapy has been effective in helping Joe to develop problem-solving skills and to use appropriate behaviors to deal with his family issues. The time-series design with a comparison group has controlled for most of the confounding factors that might have skewed the findings. Additional qualitative data, such as narrative data from Joe and Mary are helpful to support the results before additional recommendations are made. The practitioner uses the Solution-Focused Assessment to help the couple understand more about each other's strengths and expectations (see Figure 14.3).

Multicultural Practice Exercises:

1. Finding the exceptions
   Think about the best day or the best part of the day.

   ■ Please describe what happens when _____.
   ■ Think about the difference when _____.
   ■ How did you get this exceptional situation to happen?
   ■ How is this _____ (exception) different from the way you handled it a week (month) ago? How did you do that?
   ■ Who else noticed this _____ (exception)? How did they respond? How do you know they noticed?

2. Using solution-focused (rather than problem-focused) language

   ■ Tell me what you would like to change.
   ■ Observe what is going on when _____ is changed.
   ■ You seem to think a lot about this situation. You must have thought about a possible solution. What is it?

3. Amplifying the client's spontaneous suggestion for solutions

   ■ Mary: "I'd like to make changes only if my kids would listen."
   ■ MC: "Are you considering making changes with your kids together?"
             or "How would this change help?"

4. The Miracle Question:

   ■ How would life be different without this problem?
   ■ Have there been times in the recent past when the problem seemed to have disappeared?

Name: _____Date: _____

Directions: Write your first brief response to each question. You can review all of the questions with more reflection later. You may also choose to talk about these questions or responses with the clinician.

1. In your family, who has been ventilating feelings recently? _____
   What is the issue?_____

2. Are you the one who talked about the issue? _____
   _____Yes (Who else? _____)
   _____No (If not, Who _____)

3. Are you someone who wants to do something about this issue?
   _____Yes   _____No   (If not, Who _____)

4. Has there been a time when you or your family worked on this issue so it went away?
   _____Yes   _____No   If so, When? _____

5. Has there been a time when this issue did not seem to be as bothersome as it is now?
   _____Yes   _____No   If so, When? _____

6. What was the *best* time or period in your life thus far?_____

7. How do you see yourself *now*? _____
   _____

8. What are *three* things you'd most like to change about yourself?
   (a) _____
   (b) _____
   (c) _____

9. What are *three* things you'd most like to change about your family members?
   (a) _____
   (b) _____
   (c) _____

10. If you could have a magic wand to make all your worries or problems go away, what three changes would you make in your life? Who would have to make the greatest change? _____
    _____

11. What has been preventing you from changing these things or people? _____
    _____

12. What would you like to see yourself doing 5 years from now? _____
    _____

13. What are you doing now to ensure that you accomplish this 5-year goal?_____
    _____

14. When making changes in your life, what are some things that you need to take into consideration (such as your family values, culture, social, economic, and/or personal factors)? _____
    _____

Figure 14.3
Solution-Focused Assessment

■ Can you predict what you would do during the first evening after your problem disappeared?

Topics for Discussion

1. The solution-focused approach assumes that clients are aware of solutions or have attempted successful solutions in the past. How do you apply the principle that all clients have the potential to identify their own solutions without tracing back the causes of the problem?
2. What concerns would a practitioner have about the ripple effect that change in one area of a client's life may affect other areas?
3. In what kind of situation would the solution-focused approach be beneficial? What are the limitations of solution-focused therapy in cross-cultural counseling and practice?

Multicultural Competency

In Part Two, Mary and Joe's family was used as a constant standardized case in which practitioners applied a variety of theoretical approaches to examine the usefulness of these approaches to a given situation. Part Two also identified variations of the case, with additional input from experts for a better understanding of cultural sensitivity issues and the relevance of various assessment and treatment methods to multicultural practice. In Part Three we discuss an important practice principle: An integrated approach is more useful than any one single approach.

Culturally competent practitioners who have read the standardized case may ask: What if Mary and Joe's family is different from what we expected? What if the family has experienced unemployment, members were separated as a result of military deployment, or their home was destroyed by a natural disaster or a terrorist attack? What skills or techniques would be helpful in providing human services if the family has no children but wants to have a child, or if the parents have more children than they wish for? In considering adoption, what if the family has first provided foster care but found significant problems with a foster child? Variations within the family structure, such as two or three generations living in the same household or a family member being recruited as a therapeutic foster parent for a defiant child, can change the function of the family or the role of each individual member.

As a practice exercise, the standardized case can be modified in terms of its nature, roles, responsibilities, structure and composition, living conditions, and other environmental characteristics. Through a variety of exercises, the practitioner will learn what multicultural practice really means. Needless to say, multicultural practice involves much more than working with people from various cultures. It is a dynamic application supported by a strong theoretical base with a variety of theories and a great sense of flexibility based on human diversity.

Social workers and mental health and counseling practitioners have been placing more emphasis on values and ethics training, with an aim to improve multicultural competencies and to encourage the use of an interdisciplinary approach to measure professionals' attitudes toward human diversity. In a study of 344 social workers, Green and associates (2005) concluded that helping professionals should conduct self-assessments regularly to evaluate their knowledge, skills, and attitudes to find ways to improve their practice when working with multicultural clients. Similarly, Holcomb-McCoy (2005) conducted a study of 209 professional school counselors and discovered that counselors want to assess multicultural competencies systematically through educational or ongoing training programs as their perceived competencies cannot be used without evaluating their effectiveness in practice.

Beyond demonstrating the importance of continuous self-assessment to multicultural competencies in terms of attitudes, skills, and knowledge (ASK), researchers have contributed significantly to the development of multicultural practice principles. Research findings stress the following principles:

1. Diversity is the norm (Daughtry, Twohey, & Whitcomb, 2005).
2. Self-awareness is a prerequisite to practice (Constantine & Sue, 2005).

3. Multidisciplinary and collaborative consultation is important (Horne & Mathews, 2004).
4. A professional code of ethics is required (Pettifor, 2001).
5. Social justice is the key to open a truly multicultural environment (Goodman, Liang, & Helms, 2004; Hage, 2005).

These principles further affirm the role of multicultural ASK development—that is, practitioners continue their commitment by identifying areas for improvement in *attitudinal change*, *skill building,* and *knowledge development* to enhance our work with multicultural populations. Research-based information is provided to help practitioners integrate theories into practice, identify strengths and limitations of various theoretical approaches, and appreciate research findings as a basis for developing multicultural competencies in working with the diverse populations in our society.

Developing Multicultural Competency

This chapter integrates the theoretical foundations from previous chapters and incorporates the competencies of multicultural practice for personal awareness, integrated practice, and evaluation. First, attaining self-awareness, one of the most important domains of multicultural practice, is possible through self-practice with scenarios and self-evaluation. Next, practice theories connect practice to multiculturalism. A critical piece of this chapter lies in the awareness gained by examining personal approaches and how this affects all parts of multicultural practice. The tables in this chapter summarize the theories of multicultural practice and provide synopses of research-based data on multicultural practice.

Integrated Practice

Practice and evaluation are inseparable. Through an eco-strengths perspective, integration must assess environmental support in the helping process (Viramontez Anguiano & Harrison, 2002). This perspective, which is inclusive of the environment, works well with clients from different cultural backgrounds. The basic premises of "client's best interest, value-based practice, goal-directed practice, accountability, and commitment to scientific standards of practice" support the evidence-based practice of social work (Zlotnik & Galambos, 2004, p. 259). Evidence-based practice allows for integration of the therapist's clinical experience along with other external values and evidence presented by the client for a more systematic approach to the intervention.

Practice Philosophy: Experiential, Existential, Equilibrium

Major practice principles in multicultural counseling are exemplified through the 11 theories demonstrated with the case approach. These demonstrations represent the foundation of multicultural practice because many other theories, such as motivation theory and theories of cultural identity development, can be incorporated if practitioners integrate them in practice with their multicultural principles.

In this book three major principles describe and demonstrate the usefulness of the case approach:

1. The *experiential* principle illustrates the learning process. Kim and Lyons (2003) suggest that experiential learning is one of the most important components in multicultural practice because it helps practitioners identify strengths and insights through their attitude, knowledge, and skill development. Running Wolf and Rickard (2003) use an innovative approach to attest that a fruitful process of experiential learning requires genuine understanding and appreciation of cultural similarities and differences.
2. The *existential* principle identifies a need to understand each other further in terms of the meaning of life and the presence of interpersonal relationships. For example, the existential theoretical approach is based on the foundation that all cultures experience universal issues of love, death, anxiety, and crisis (Evans & Valadez, 2003). The existential approach involves the individual and his or her environment, interpersonal relationships, intrapsychic events, and biological contributions, all of which have an effect on the individual's experience (Bauman & Waldo, 1998). This approach has practical use for promoting a multicultural setting because it takes into account the individual's overall wellness and does not focus only on the symptomatic issues.
3. The *equilibrium* principle demonstrates the importance of systemic and holistic thinking during assessment and intervention.

A comprehensive assessment leads to a better understanding of where the client is within the immediate environment, the social systems, and society at large.

Although the objective in educating practitioners about multicultural practice is evident, the means to achieve this goal can be multifaceted. Simply communicating information about diverse cultures has proven to be insufficient in preparing individuals for cross-cultural practice (Thornton & Garrett, 1995). Instead, adopting the experiential, existential, and equilibrium practice principles allows for the integration of self-awareness, environmental factors from the past and present that affect the client's future, and the application of various theories to multicultural practice.

Evaluative Questions on Multicultural Competency

The experiential principle of multicultural practice exemplifies the importance of enhancing the image of cultural diversity through education and professional training so everyone will appreciate the value of human diversity. To achieve this appreciation, all helping professionals must believe in this principle firmly and pass along this value to others. According to Liu, Sheu, and Williams (2004), a multicultural environment coupled with self-efficacy and training will enhance the value of multiculturalism in society. In addition to this principle and the ASK competencies in working with diverse populations described in chapter 3, practitioners in human services should evaluate their competencies regularly when working with families in the following five areas as proposed by the University of Kentucky (1989):

Do I continuously exhibit competencies as a helping professional?
Do I possess the following competencies before I work with diverse populations?

1. Informational competencies: General knowledge or knowledge about
   - growth and development of children, adolescents, and adults;
   - personality patterns and behaviors;
   - emotional/behavioral disorders in children, adolescents, and adults;
   - causes of dysfunctional relationships and emotional disturbances and their effect on children, adolescents, families, and communities;
   - theories, principles, and methods of interpersonal communication in helping relationships;
   - a wide range of treatment and intervention approaches;
   - system of care (agencies and programs designed to help);
   - psychosocial assessment;
   - community resource development and advocacy; and
   - characteristics of special populations and families and their implications for assessment and interventions.

2. Intellectual competencies: Knowledge application or knowing how to
   - determine the information required to assess the needs and problems of children, adolescents, and their families;
   - obtain enough information about clients and their situations to process with one's professional knowledge base to determine the clients' needs and appropriate intervention approaches;
   - record and report client-related data and information in written form which meets all legal and professional standards;
   - analyze and interpret data about the client's problems, family, history, environment, and resources;
   - make priority decisions while allowing family or child to make own decisions whenever possible;

■ negotiate action plans; and

■ implement intervention plans and revise as needed.

3. Interpersonal competencies: Relationship skills or being able to communicate

■ warmth in relationships with children, adolescents, and their family members, including those who are emotionally disturbed, hostile, or resistant;

■ empathy with children, adolescents, and their families;

■ positive regard for children, adolescents, and their families, regardless of their problems, behavior, or attitudes;

■ a desire for rapport (a positive, harmonious relationship) with children, adolescents, and their parents;

■ nonthreatening disagreement with children, adolescents, or their parents, sincerely and realistically; and

■ appropriate assertiveness with children, adolescents, and family.

4. Intrapersonal competencies: Qualities and character or being personally and deeply committed to

■ working directly with children, adolescents, and their families on a wide variety of problems and across a broad range of severity;

■ working at the system level on behalf of children, adolescents, and families needing help and services;

■ being flexible in adapting to changing requirements or circumstances;

■ maintaining objectivity and personal emotional control;

■ serving as an advocate and proponent for children, youth, and their families

■ being tolerant of "different" individuals and lifestyle variations; and

■ continuing learning and growing as a professional and as a person.

5. Intervention competencies: Change agent skills or possessing skills necessary for performing

■ assessment (interviewing) with key individuals in the system;

■ observations, recording, and reporting—with accuracy, objectivity, relevancy, and thoroughness; and

■ crisis identification or crisis anticipation and avoidance with children, adolescents, and their families.

With practice competencies at the core when working with diverse populations, multicultural competence can be defined as a process of gaining and expanding knowledge and skills and developing positive attitudes and values toward working in a variety of situations involving human diversity. Without diversity, all practice skills would become a rule rather than an application. Without variations, all cases would be the same, with no challenges. Without critical examination of practice theories, practitioners would not be able to deliver evidence-based practice. As a general principle, social justice provides the background and foundation of practice, and theories are the supports to identify, assess, and help practitioners work through diverse issues in life.

Integration and Application of Techniques: Families With Variations

Theories that outline a rigid, step-by-step application to all clients are not regarded as multicultural practice theories because of their lack of sensitivity to variations. As a practice principle, we must consider theory application as a process of integrating assessment and intervention skills based on theories that have been tested to be effective in practice with diverse populations. Table 15.1 provides a summary of all the theories described in this book. This brief summary aims to help practitioners integrate the essentials of various approaches to achieve efficiency and effectiveness, as well as flexibility in practice. Although describing a theory in a few words may not help us to understand it in its entirety, it will assist practitioners to gain insight into the process of forming a flexible and integrative approach for practice. These basic theoretical concepts are incorporated in this summary to illustrate the way all of these concepts may be integrated into a variety of helping relationships with people from all cultures. For this purpose, the last theory is integrated for the practitioner to identify the best-fit description for his or her own practice.

Before applying any theory to multicultural practice, practitioners should study the assumptions of the theory, its applications for diverse populations, its strengths and limitations. Table 15.1 provides the basic premises of each theory, and Tables 15.2 and Table 15.3 summarize the applicability and the strengths and limitations of each theoretical approach, respectively. Table 15.2 describes the theoretical focus, multicultural applications, and limitations of each theory or approach. The culturally skilled practitioner should establish a conceptual outlook for understanding the strengths and weaknesses of the self while studying each practice theory and analyzing the role of each theory in multicultural practice. Table 15.3 presents both strengths and weaknesses that explicate how to build a starting ground to incorporate theories into practice with specific clients.

In choosing a theoretical approach that is appropriate for a family, the practitioner must assess the family's background and cultural values as a first step. Then the practitioner will focus on the family's strengths and utilize the strengths of the practice approaches to plan interventions that address and meet clients' unique cultural needs. Extensive knowledge about both strengths and limitations of each theory allows the practitioner to integrate a variety of approaches in practice. Applicability of each theory will then be enhanced and linked to evaluation of practice effectiveness.

To enhance practice–evaluation integration, practitioners have the responsibility to stay abreast of current research that identifies cultural factors and application of theory with various populations. Table 15.4 provides data with an emphasis on trends and multicultural practice considerations. It summarizes literature that describes the cultural values and factors as they relate to practice. This table also includes multicultural practice considerations based on research-based results.

Table 15.1

Theoretical Approaches in Brief

Theory	Description
Psychoanalytic	Emphasizes root causes, with the assumption that unconscious motivation in early life can affect later development of personality; patients receive in-depth analysis of life experiences.
Adlerian	Family constellation, lifestyle assessment, and challenging faulty assumptions can help us evaluate our views of human nature.
Person-Centered	Acceptance, active listening, and reflective techniques guide clients to find their potential, capabilities, and destinations.
Gestalt	The body–mind connection within a here-and-now environment stimulates clients to think about and look for personal growth.
Behavioral	Self-directed learning can lead to modifications in behavior.
Cognitive–Behavioral	Challenging our cognitive distortions is a means to help us fully recognize the underlying causes of malfunctioning personal relationships.
Feminist Approach	Major socioeconomic forces affect men and women, and we can utilize our own strengths to evaluate the personal, social, and political conditions surrounding a given problem.
Solution-Focused	Searching for exceptions and solutions is a major goal.
Family System	Relationship problems are caused by rigidity of structure, functions, and roles within a family, as well as lack of interconnectedness among the family members.
Structural	Restructuring takes place when clients find that their problems are manifested from the rules and structure enforced in the family.
Strategic	Symptoms are the center of attention, and the use of experiential strategies is the method for breaking through these symptoms.

What is your integrated approach to multicultural practice?

Describe it in a sentence or two: _____

_____

Table 15.2

Applicability of Selected Theories in Multicultural Practices

Theory	Theoretical Focus	Multicultural Applications	Limitations in Multicultural Practices
Psychodynamic Theory	"The novelty of Freud's approach was in recognizing that neurotic behavior is not random or meaningless but goal-directed. Thus, by looking for the purpose behind so-called 'abnormal' behavioral patterns, the analyst was given a method for understanding behavior as meaningful and informative, without denying its physiological aspects." (Quigley, 1998, para. 1)	The theory recognizes that in addition to actual lived experiences, cultural material infuses our intrapsychic lives, shaping our desires, reframing our fantasies, and becoming part of preconscious mental content. Personal change through psychoanalysis works in conjunction with newly formed dreams, which are constructed through self-generated or borrowed cultural background (Person, 2004).	Psychoanalysis is enmeshed in white Western cultural values, and its practice in non-Western cultures is questionable. Individualistic and introspective bias can make this practice unsuitable for some cultures (Innis, 1998).
Adlerian Theory	Individual psychology is based on the relationship of the individual with the outside world (Adler, 1982). "Modern Adlerian approaches focus on an understanding of individual lifestyle, his or her socially constructed pattern of living." (Bitter & Nicoll, 2000, p. 31)	Cultures that stress the welfare of the collective group and emphasize the role of the family will find this theory's focus on social interest to be in line with their values. The emphasis is on the person in the social context (Corey, 2005). For multicultural applications, especially when used in brief modality situations, three Adlerian principles are particularly helpful: purposiveness, lifestyle, and social embeddedness (Nicoll, Bitter, Christensen, & Hawes, 2000).	In his study with a Navajo boarding school, Salzman (2002) found six Adlerian principles to be of importance: social equality, belonging, mutual respect, social interest, democratic practices, and the demands of reality as ultimate authority and teacher. In a study of Latin culture, Frevert and Miranda (1998) suggested that lifestyle analysis should focus on how acculturation may influence a

(continued)

Table 15.2 *(continued)*

Theory	Theoretical Focus	Multicultural Applications	Limitations in Multicultural Practices
			person's mental health, both from the individual perspective and from collective influences. Because this approach centers more on the individual or self, additional principles from the culture should be considered when working with a culture of a collectivist nature.
Family Systems Theory	"Theory of human behavior that views the family as an emotional unit and uses systems thinking to describe the complex interactions." (Bowen Center for the Study of Family, 2004, para. 1)	"A core assumption is that an emotional system that evolved over several billion years governs human relationship systems. People have a 'thinking brain,' language, a complex psychology and culture, but people still do all the ordinary things other forms of life do. The emotional system affects most human activity and is the principal driving force in the development of clinical problems. Knowledge of how the emotional system operates in one's family, work, and social systems reveals new and more effective options for solving problems in each of these areas." (Bowen Center of the Study of Family, 2004, para. 4)	This theory is grounded in Western ideas and experiences (Rothbaum, Rosen, Ujiie, & Uchida, 2002). The therapist should be aware of this bias and know that family stages/ patterns may be different in other cultures.

(continued)

Table 15.2 *(continued)*

Theory	Theoretical Focus	Multicultural Applications	Limitations in Multicultural Practices
Structural Theory	"Structural social work is so called because social problems are inherent in our present social order and therefore the focus of change should be mainly on social structures not individuals. Structural social work is inclusive because it is concerned with all forms of oppression." (Payne, 2005, p. 237)	Minuchin (1974) emphasizes that the structural approach to family therapy is directed to the family as a unit rather then to the individual, and therefore may be more effective with cross-cultural counseling.	Structural family therapy works by placing pressure on one family member, thereby forcing a change throughout the entire system. Minuchin's approach has been criticized by feminists, who point out that he favors "unbalancing" the mother while elevating the father. Therapists must avoid gender bias and make sure that their own personal biases are not influencing what is important for the family (Navarre, 1998).
Client-Centered Theory	"[Rogers] proposed that a therapist's role is to listen to clients, be empathetic, and accept them for who they are rather than offer deep interpretations of unconscious material" (Hill & Nakayama, 2000, p. 861).	The focus on the client's present situation enables this approach to work well with clients from different backgrounds. Culture and traditions can easily become a part of the therapeutic work. In addition, client-centered therapy is respectful of individuality while identifying the commonality between the client and the therapist (Freeman, 1993).	Some individuals think this non-directive therapy lacks sufficient structure for healing purposes. In addition, the emphasis on individual potential to discover one's own solutions may not be seen as effective by those from some cultures. For example, this form of therapy may not be seen as appropriate by those whose cultures are oriented more on the external than internal locus of control (Hill & Nakayama, 2000).

(continued)

Table 15.2 *(continued)*

Theory	Theoretical Focus	Multicultural Applications	Limitations in Multicultural Practices
Gestalt Theory	"Perceptions of objects, events, and behaviors are experienced as wholes." (Rhyne, 1990, p. 2)	This approach, when timed appropriately, allows therapists to concentrate not only on the cognitive aspect of the presenting problem but also on the emotional, physical, and spiritual components (Ikehara, 1999). Its application is appropriate for individuals from different cultures because it focuses on how the individual feels about his or her own situation, including his or her culture.	The ability to express emotion is viewed as an imperative component in this theory (O'Leary, Sheedy, O'Sullivan, & Thoresen, 2003). When working with individuals whose culture emphasizes reserved emotions, therapists should explain the techniques thoroughly.
Strategic Theory	"Strategic therapy is a term that has come to denote a problem-focused, directive approach to the treatment of symptomatic behavior." (Dammann & Jurkovic, 1986, p. 556)	Strategic theory or, more specifically, brief strategic family therapy, operates at the content level to work through cultural issues while also working at the process level to modify the manner in which family members relate to each other (Santisteban, Coatsworth, Perez-Vidal, Mitrani, Jean-Gilles, & Szapocznik, 1997).	Most studies involving the brief strategic family therapy model have been conducted with African Americans and Hispanics (Brown University Child & Adolescent Behavior Letter, 2002). More formalized studies have to be conducted with families of other cultures and backgrounds.
Behavioral Theory	"Early major American forces in behaviorism were Watson, Hull, and Skinner, all of whom believed only observable behavior [is] important	When planning behavioral interventions, the therapist examines the sociocultural background of clients to better understand the sources of behaviors. The	Behavior therapists have not been concerned enough with issues of race, gender, ethnicity, and sexual orientation (Iwamasa & Smith, 1996).

(continued)

Table 15.2 *(continued)*

Theory	Theoretical Focus	Multicultural Applications	Limitations in Multicultural Practices
	and [it] dismiss[es] inner consciousness." (Hill & Nakayama, 2000, p. 863)	learning process is tied to characteristics of the client's culture or structural background (Labovitz & Hagedorn, 1975).	Additional research should be conducted to ensure applicability.
Cognitive–Behavioral Theory	A major goal is to "show people how to change their feelings, in emotional and behavioral ways" (American Psychological Association, 2002, para. 6).	This approach acknowledges the impact of environment and cognitive processes on behavior (Waldron & Kaminer, 2004), thereby encouraging the therapist to be fully aware of the client's cultural background.	Before a therapist can challenge individual beliefs and behaviors, he or she must have some understanding of the cultural background of clients and be sensitive to their struggles (Corey, 2005).
Feminist Theory/ Empowerment Theory	Jean Baker Miller (1976) writes, "Unlike other groups, women do not need to set affiliation and strength in opposition one against the other. We can readily integrate the two, search for more and better ways to use affiliation to enhance strength—and strength to enhance affiliation." (p. 96)	The empowerment theory with a feminist perspective examines how oppression, discrimination, and racism are sources of many issues that individuals face today (Carr, 2003). This integrated approach is helpful for those who work collectively, as "empowerment is an inherently interpersonal process in which individuals collectively define and activate strategies to gain access to knowledge and power." (Carr, 2003, p. 18)	Empowerment theory and feminist theory both are subjective to the individual client (Carr, 2003). Before utilizing this approach, the therapist must take into account the client's definition of empowerment.

(continued)

Table 15.2 *(continued)*

Theory	Theoretical Focus	Multicultural Applications	Limitations in Multicultural Practices
Solution-Focused Theory	This theory focuses on "utilizing what the client brings with him to meet his needs in such a way that the client can make a satisfactory life for himself" (de Shazer, 1985, p. 6). The theory notes that "it does seem that *any* really different behavior in a problematic situation can be enough to prompt a solution and give the client the satisfaction he seeks from therapy" (de Shazer, 1985, p.7).	"The distinctiveness of solution-focused therapy involves both the practical strategies that solution-focused therapists use in interacting with clients, and the intellectual traditions that they draw upon in orienting to personal troubles and change in therapy" (Miller & de Shazer, 2000, p. 5). This approach works well with the underlying premises of multiculturalism (Corey, 2005). It takes into account the client's cultural background and traditions when solutions are discovered or created.	The solution-focused perspective is essentially interactional (Lethem, 2002), and the client is looked at as the expert (Corey, 2005). This approach may have to be explained in detail when used with clients of cultures that value the authority of the therapist (Corey, 2005).

Table 15.3

Strengths and Weaknesses of Various Practice Approaches

Theory	Strengths	Weaknesses
Psychodynamic	• Breaks through defensive wrangling. • Blocks argument by exploring feelings of each individual. • Fosters insight and understanding. • Holds clients accountable for behavior. • Provides a conceptual framework to examine behavior with an understanding of the origins and functions of the symptoms. • Understands resistance. • Analyzes inner conflict. • Understands the value and role of transference and countertransference. • Understands how the overuse of ego defenses affects the counseling relationship and daily life.	• Depends on subjective clinical judgment. • Does not support evaluation based on empirical standards. • Does not document, or has questionable benefits. • Poses questions regarding adequate training. • Requires long-term commitment. • Limits its applications to certain client populations. • Does not work well with severely disturbed clients who lack the level of ego strength needed for this treatment. • Focuses on internalizing problems that may be in conflict with cultural values, which causes stress.
Adlerian	• Helps clients identify and change their mistaken beliefs about life. • Helps clients become aware of their behavioral patterns. • Assists clients in making basic changes from beliefs and thinking to how they feel and behave. • Focuses on social interest, doing good for society, importance of family, goal orientation. • Strives for belonging that is congruent with Eastern cultures. • Focuses on person-in-environment that allows for cultural factors to be explored. • Is resourceful in drawing on many methods. • Provides flexibility for counselors by not following a specific procedure. • A holistic approach that encompasses the full spectrum of human experience.	• The contributions of Adler to contemporary therapeutic practice are difficult to estimate. • Accepts the same theoretical concepts as psychodynamic theory but does not have a monolithic view of the therapeutic process. • Gives rise to conflict between carrying out detailed interviews about one's family background and cultures that have injunctions against disclosing family matters. • Methods of assessment and treatment differ substantially. Some Adlerians are highly directive, and others are nondirective.

(continued)

Table 15.3 *(continued)*

Theory	Strengths	Weaknesses
Family Systems	• Provides techniques for resolving an individual's relationship with other people. • Places individual problematic behavior within the context of the environment. • Provides a new perspective on a person's relationship with the family system. • Explores family-of-origin; increases opportunities to resolve other relationship conflicts. outside of the family. • Places value on extended family and kinship networks. • Empowers clients' use of family as a resource. • Uses a variety of techniques.	• Does not address issues at the organizational and societal level. • May not be effective with cultures in which independence and autonomy are not the top values. • Potential problems in recalling details about all family members. • Some family members may resist changing the structure of the family system. • The therapist rests on value assumptions that are not congruent with the values of clients from some other cultures. • In some cultures, admitting problems with the family is shameful. The value of "keeping problems within the family" may make it difficult to explore conflicts openly.
Structural	• Pays special attention to the structure of family relationships in relation to the focal issue. • Focuses on concrete issues and chronic situations by intensifying a conflict within a family by drawing attention to disagreement. • Stresses the present and views the past as "manifest in the present and available to change by interventions that change the present." • Centers the therapeutic process on resources and power of clients to grow and change, within themselves and/or their family and community. • Engages actively with the family to impede old, pathological transactional patterns while working with the family's strengths to build new, positive patterns of interaction.	• Therapists' spiritual biases will influence what they consider healthy and pathological attitudes and behaviors. • Therapists should pay special attention to clients' psychological struggles that may be related to family-of-origin themes. • Therapists must be aware of the value learning that clients bring to the therapeutic relationship.

(continued)

Table 15.3 *(continued)*

Theory	Strengths	Weaknesses
Client-Centered (Based on Rogers)	• Makes significant contributions to breaking cultural barriers and facilitating open dialogue among diverse cultural populations. • Emphasizes respecting clients' values, active listening, welcoming differences, nonjudgmental attitude, understanding, willingness to allow clients to determine what will be explored in sessions, and prizing cultural pluralism. • Allows for diversity and doesn't foster practitioners to become mere followers of a guru.	• Lack of leader direction and structure are unacceptable to clients who are seeking help and want immediate answers from a knowledgeable leader. • Some of the core values of this approach may not be congruent with the client's culture. • Practitioners are advised to avoid becoming too loyal to a method, a school of thought, or a technique, as this could have a counterproductive effect on the counseling process.
Client-Centered (Based on Satir)	• Builds self-esteem in each family member. • Emphasizes the uniqueness of each individual. • Helps family members recognize individual differences. • Helps family accept disagreements. • Helps family members interact with each other. • Each person has the right to express his or her own views.	• Depends too much on techniques to elicit feelings. • Focuses heavily on self-actualization and little on intrapersonal psychological barriers. • Fosters a dichotomy between the individual and the family: "bad" families repress people; "good" families leave them alone. • Lacks interest in verifying theories or their results. • Doesn't believe that every family member must change overtly to validate each others' efforts. • Is difficult to measure small changes related to family communication.
Gestalt	• Works with issues that are obstructing current functioning. • Employs nonverbal expression, which is congruent with cultures that look beyond words for messages. • Pays attention to obvious verbal and nonverbal cues that lead clients to approach a counseling session.	• Emphasizes confrontation. • Deemphasizes cognitive factors of personality. • Has a potential danger for abusing power. • Culturally conditioned clients who are emotionally reserved may not embrace gestalt experiments.

(continued)

Table 15.3 *(continued)*

Theory	Strengths	Weaknesses
	• Heightens client's present-centered awareness (thinking, feeling, and doing). • Moves clients from talk to action and experience. • Values each aspect of the individual's experience equally.	• Ready-made techniques can damage client–worker relationship. • Some clients may not see how "being aware of present experiencing" will lead to a solution to their problems.
Strategic	• Understands symptoms as a part of rigid repeating patterns among intimates. • Gives directives that lead to enlightenment. • Devises a unique plan for each individual to fit his or her specific problem. • Assumes that clients will respond positively when the therapist is clearly taking a personal interest in them.	• All directives require a leap of faith. • Causal relationships are not yet understood regarding how and why symptoms actually develop and what actually occurs when a person is able to change. • Directives don't cause change; they trigger a process. • Its free association method is often hard to follow, e.g., pretending to be six years old, sitting next to a parent, and yelling at the imaginary parent. • Clients feel weird when they are asked to repeat certain behavior in therapy. • It assumes if the presenting problem is resolved, the client will never have this problem again.
Behavioral	• Focuses on behavior rather than on feelings—which is compatible with many cultures. • Aims at behavioral changes and cognitive restructuring based on behavioral and learning principles. • Contributes to the counseling field with a focus on specifics and on a systematic way of applying therapeutic techniques. • Assists clients in formulating a plan of action for changing behavior. • Emphasizes research on assessment of treatment outcomes.	• May change behaviors but doesn't change feelings. • Clients need help to assess possible consequences of making behavioral changes. • Clients' newly acquired assertive style may not be congruent with their cultural values, so clients must cope with resistance from others. • Places less emphasis on other relational factors in therapy. • Doesn't stress therapeutic insight.

(continued)

Table 15.3 *(continued)*

Theory	Strengths	Weaknesses
	• Suggests examination of effectiveness, generalizability, meaningfulness, and durability of change. • Is ethically neutral in that it doesn't dictate whose behavior or what behavior should be changed. • Is suitable for all cultural and ethnic backgrounds in that it stresses changing specific behaviors and developing problem-solving skills.	• Treats symptoms before analyzing causes. • Involves control and manipulation by the therapist. • Uses techniques in narrowly treating a specific behavioral problem. • If concentrating on problems within the individual, which may overlook significant environmental issues, practitioners are not likely to bring about beneficial changes for ethnic clients.
Cognitive–Behavioral	• Uses a variety of diverse methods. • Offers clients opportunities to express concern. • Emphasizes a comprehensive and eclectic therapeutic practice, including cognitive, emotive, and behavioral techniques. • Offers an openness to incorporate techniques from other approaches. • Observes what happens and then measures change. • Provides a methodology for challenging and changing faulty thinking. • Develops a wealth of reliable and valid assessment methods and applies them to initial evaluation, treatment planning, and monitoring progress and outcome. • Moves gradually from eliminating or reinforcing discrete "marker" behaviors to teaching general problem-solving, cognitive, and communicational skills. • Targets behavior improvement. • Explores cultural conflicts and teaches new behavior. • Emphasizes teaching and learning to avoid the stigma of mental illness.	• Challenges clients when questioning their basic cultural values and beliefs. • Defines appropriateness to solve problems for clients, which may not be culturally relevant. • Tends to accept the family's definition of one person (or couple) as the problem. • Rarely discusses the role that children or extended family members play in marital distress. • Hardly ever treats whole families.

(continued)

Table 15.3 *(continued)*

Theory	Strengths	Weaknesses
	• Uses methods that are active, directive, time-limited, present-centered, and structured. • Offers impressive techniques for treating problems with children and troubled marriages. • Modular treatment interventions are organized to meet the specific and changing needs of the individual and the family.	
Feminist	• Paves the way for gender-sensitive practice. • Brings attention to the use of gender power in relationships. • Encourages women and men to question gender stereotypes and to reject limited views of what a woman or man is expected to be. • Brings about empowerment, collaborative relationships, and self-determination. • Helps clients to recognize the impact of social, cultural, and political factors on their lives. • Helps clients to transcend limitations resulting from gender stereotypes. • Recognizes the extent to which individual behaviors may reflect internalization of harmful social standards. • Includes gender-role analysis as a component of assessment. • Helps clients to develop and integrate traits that are culturally defined as "masculine" and "feminine." • Develops collaborative counselor–client relationships.	• Imposes a new set of values on clients—such as striving for equality, power in relationship and defining oneself, freedom to pursue a career outside the home, and the right to an education. • Takes risks by assuming sameness among families that share a common cultural background.
Empowerment	• Understands the dynamics and effects of stratification, discrimination, and oppression, which are central to our knowledge of human behavior.	• Ignores the importance of biological factors in human development, which also may neglect the biological differences and similarities among people.

(continued)

Table 15.3 *(continued)*

Theory	Strengths	Weaknesses
	• Aims to reduce the powerlessness that has been created by negative valuations based on membership in a stigmatized group. • Recognizes that empowerment has both objective and subjective dimensions. • Helps people to overcome oppression and affiliate with people who share common obstacles. • Helps individuals and groups develop the knowledge and skills needed to recognize and affect political processes. • Focuses on social, cultural, economic, and political forces that produce inequality and oppression, as well as opportunities for liberation. • Connects micro, mezzo, and macro levels of social systems, which connects personal problems and structural barriers. • Focuses on the value of multiculturalism, fosters wellness of people, and stresses its relevance to issues of diversity.	• Places little emphasis on developmental life stages because of overgeneralized assumptions about culture, gender stereotypes, and the heterosexism inherent in life-stage theories. • Emphasizes situation-specific understandings of oppression and liberation, which implicitly suggests that only those who actually experience oppression can understand the problem.
Solution-Focused	• Creates well-defined goals and develops solutions based on exceptions. • Offers feedback to clients at the end of each solution-building conversational session. • Empowers clients to examine outcomes. • Concludes therapy within a few sessions of solution-talk.	• Appears too simplistic and brief. • Relies heavily on clients' suggestibility and neglects the therapist's power. • Does not assess long-term gains or effectiveness. • Provides a formulaic approach to deal with a variety of problems.

Table 15.4

Research-Based Information for Multicultural Practice

Type or Form of Families	Trends and Basic Facts	Cultural Values and Factors	Research-Based Considerations for Theory Applications
African American	• In March 2002, there were 36 million African American people in the United States, which constituted 13% of the civilian noninstitutionalized population (McKinnon, 2003). • In March 2002, the unemployment rate for African Americans was twice that for Caucasians (McKinnon, 2003). • African Americans accounted for about one quarter (8.1 million) of the population in poverty in 2001 (McKinnon, 2003).	• History of oppression • Collectivist perspective • Emphasis on community • Role flexibility in family structure • Support from extended family network and kinship system • Increasing number of female-headed households • Negative male/father stereotypes • Negative environmental influences • Importance of spirituality	• Theories of parentification do not take into consideration the past or the contemporary experiences of people of African descent Anderson (1999).
Asian American	• In March 2002, 12.5 million Asians were living in the United States, representing 4.4% of the civilian noninstitutionalized population (Reeves & Bennett, 2003). • Immigration contributed greatly to the growth of the Asian population after the passage of the Immigration and Nationality Act of 1965 (Chang, 2003, p. 79). • In 2001, 10% (1.3 million) of Asians lived below the poverty level (Reeves & Bennett, 2003).	• Emphasis on group and family values, academic achievement and education, and respect • History of discrimination • Collectivist perspective • Gender-role issues • Stereotype as a model minority • Reluctant to seek help for mental issues	• The beginning point is practitioners' self-exploration and awareness (Kao, 2005).

(continued)

Table 15.4 *(continued)*

Type or Form of Families	Trends and Basic Facts	Cultural Values and Factors	Research-Based Considerations for Theory Applications
Latino American	• In 2002, there were 37.4 million Latinos in the civilian, noninstitutionalized population of the United States, representing 13.3% of the total (Ramirez & Patricia de la Cruz, 2003). • Among the Hispanic population, two-thirds (66.9%) were of Mexican origin and 40.2% were foreign born (from Mexico, Central America and South America (Ramirez & Patricia de la Cruz, 2003). • In 2002, 21.4% of Latinos were living in poverty, constituting 24.3% of the population living in poverty (Ramirez & Patricia de la Cruz, 2003).	• Collectivist perspective • Strong familism • High value on interpersonal relationships • Emphasis on courtesy and manners • Desire for personal relationship with helpers • Emphasis on gender roles • Use of native language • Importance of spirituality	• The pitfalls of earlier theories in understanding various Latino groups should be avoided and the ramification of Latino families' diversity should be considered at the core of family theory (Baca Zinn, 1995; Baca, Zinn, & Wells, 2000).
Native American	• Native Americans consist of approximately 2.3 million self-identified people with a population that is steadily growing (Garrett, 2003). • Only 52% of Native American youth finish high school, and only 4% graduate from college (Russell, 1998). • 75% of the Native American workforce earns less than $7,000 per year, and 45% live below the poverty level (Russell, 1998).	• Communal perspective • Importance of spirituality • Emphasis on balance and harmony • Respect for elders • Alcohol-abuse issues • Reluctance to seek mental health assistance	• Examination of Native Americans' historical legacy of trauma is an essential component of assessment and intervention (Brave Heart, 2004; Edwards, 2002).

(continued)

Table 15.4 *(continued)*

Type or Form of Families	Trends and Basic Facts	Cultural Values and Factors	Research-Based Considerations for Theory Applications
Adoptive	• There were 2.1 million adopted children in 2000, including 1.6 million under age 18 and 473,000 over the age of 18 (Kreider, 2003). • Of the 45.5 million households in 2000 that contained children of any age, 1.7 million households included adopted children within their residence (Kreider, 2003). • Since 1987, the number of annual adoptions has remained relatively constant, ranging from 118,000 to 127,000 (ACF, 2007).	• Perception that family type is considered inferior to having a biological child • Children with multiple problems • Attachment issues • Stereotypes of birth parents	• For adoptees to form personal and ethnic identity, their historical and cultural context must be considered (especially in transracial adoptions) as well as facilitating familiarity with the birth parents and, thus, open adoption should be encouraged (Hollingsworth, 1998b).
With Drug Problems	• Among youths aged 12 to 17 in 2003, 2.8 million were current illicit drug users, 2.7 million were current binge drinkers of alcohol, and 3.6 million people reported current (past month) use of a tobacco product (SAMHSA, 2007). • The corresponding numbers for adults aged 18 or older were, respectively, about 16.7 million, 51.1 million, and 67.1 million (SAMHSA, 2007).	• Stereotype about black Americans and drug abuse issues • Stereotype about Native Americans and alcohol abuse issues	• Interactional theory lacks differentiated conceptualization of acculturation and cultural meaning of individual behaviors (US DHHS, 2001). • The sample used in testing the stage theory was not large enough or ethnically diverse. The explanation for

(continued)

Table 15.4 *(continued)*

Type or Form of Families	Trends and Basic Facts	Cultural Values and Factors	Research-Based Considerations for Theory Applications
	• Among all the illicit drugs, marijuana is most commonly used, with an overall number of 14.6 million and a number of about 2 million among youths aged 12 to 17 in 2003 (SAMHSA, 2007).		the use of multiple substances is also lacking (US DHHS, 2001).
Single-Parent	• As of 2000, 13.5 million single parents had custody of 21.7 million children under the age of 21 years whose other parent lived elsewhere (Parents Without Partners, 2005). • Single-mother families increased from 7 million in 1990 to more than 10 million in 2000 (Parents Without Partners, 2005). • In 2000, an estimated 13.8 million children under 15 years of age (23% of total) were living with single mothers, while 2.7 million (5%) were living with single fathers (Parents Without Partners, 2005).	• Father absence may be a causative factor of children's multiple problems • Stereotype of single mothers' dependency on welfare	• Family stress theory identifies social support and neighborhood factors as important elements in developing positive parenting style in African American single mothers (Kotchick, Dorsey, & Heller, 2005).
With Domestic Violence	• In 2001, women accounted for 85% of victims of intimate partner violence, and men accounted for approximately 15% of the victims (US DOJ, 2003). • 4 million American women experience a serious assault by an intimate partner	• A critical problem associated with unhealthy individual and family functioning • Special issues with immigrant women who suffer from domestic violence	• Psychoanalytic theory can be applied to explain only male-perpetrated violence (Sommer, 1994). • Family systems perspective has a bias that only women

(continued)

Table 15.4 *(continued)*

Type or Form of Families	Trends and Basic Facts	Cultural Values and Factors	Research-Based Considerations for Theory Applications
	during an average 12-month period (APA, 1996, p. 10). • Nearly one-third of American women (31%) report being physically or sexually abused by a husband or boyfriend at some point in their lives (Collins, Schoen, Joseph, Duchon, Simantov, & Yellowitz, 1999).		are victims of domestic violence (Sommer, 1994).
Interracial Couples	• 7% of married couples had spouses of a different race or origin, and unmarried partners consistently had higher percentages of partners of different races or origins (Simmons & O'Connell, 2003). • The numbers of unmarried and married interracial male–female couples in March 2000 were 165,000 and about 1 million, respectively, and for Hispanic origin difference, the numbers were 222,000 and about 1.7 million, respectively (Fields & Casper, 2001). • The number of children in interracial families grew from less than 1.2 million in 1970 to about 2 million in 1990 (Bentley, Mattingly, Hough & Bennett, 2003, p. 4), and the number of multiracial babies born	• Interracial dating often is considered unfavorable by members of different races • Interracial marriage can destroy family traditions, lead to problems for the couple and children, and result in loss of racial purity • Stereotype about individuals who marry outside of their race • Negative image about biracial or multiracial children	• Some racial groups are not willing to disclose their feelings to therapists. • The value sets of feminist therapists may conflict with those of women in some racial groups.

(continued)

Table 15.4 *(continued)*

Type or Form of Families	Trends and Basic Facts	Cultural Values and Factors	Research-Based Considerations for Theory Applications
	since the 1970s has increased more than 260%, compared to 15% of single-race babies (Wardle, 2001).		
With Divorce Issues	• The 2002 provisional estimate for the annual U.S. divorce rate is 0.40% per capita (Sutton, 2003). • 43% of first marriages end in separation or divorce within the first 15 years of marriage (Bramlett & Mosher, 2001). • 50% of individuals now in their early forties divorced from their first marriage (Kreider & Field, 2002).	• Reflects a breakdown in the moral order of our society • Children are portrayed as victims • Stereotype of divorced parents • Parents may refuse to divorce for the sake of the children	• Family systems therapy may be limited in working with divorced families, as involving all family members in therapy may be difficult.
Gay/Lesbian Couples	• There are approximately 1 to 5 million lesbian mothers (Falk 1989, Gottman, 1990) and nearly 1 to 3 million gay fathers (Gottman, 1990). • Gay/lesbian parenting is on the rise in the United States, with an estimate that 5,000 to 10,000 lesbians have given birth after coming out (Lambert, 2005). • In addition, gay men and lesbians are not only adopting but also becoming foster parents.	• Stereotype about fitness to be parents because of mental illness, less maternal (lesbian mothers), and little time for interaction with children • Gender role behavior issues • Perception that children will become gay or lesbian • Children may face difficulties in personal development and peer relationships	• Do not practice with rigid stage models of family development and other theories of family therapy that may convey a message that heterosexuality is the only legitimate form of sexual identification and any other type of relating is deviant (Adams, Jaques, & May, 2004).

(continued)

Table 15.4 *(continued)*

Type or Form of Families	Trends and Basic Facts	Cultural Values and Factors	Research-Based Considerations for Theory Applications
			• The broader social context must be considered when counseling gay and lesbian families (Adams, Jaques & May, 2004).
In Poverty	• Of all 76.2 million families in 2003, the family poverty rate is 10%. • The poverty rate of married-couple families, male householder with no wife present, and female householder with no husband present in 2003 are, respectively, 5.4%, 13.5%, and 28.0%.	• Negative stereotype about people in poverty • Perception that people are poor because of lack of motivation or other intrinsic reasons • Varying attitudes toward the poor and attributions of poverty	• Families in poverty may have difficulty identifying their personal meaning of life before their basic needs are satisfied (Corey, 2005). • Person-centered approach was not intended to address poverty issues (Weinrach, 2003).

Table 15.5

Assessing Cultural Competence for Working With Families

Self-Assessment Date: _____

• Check your cultural competence with this 3 point scale:

Competent	Needs improvement	Not competent
2————————————————1————————————————0		

When working with families,

☐ I have specific knowledge about my own culture and its influence.

☐ I am aware of my own biases and their potential impacts on my intervention style.

☐ I understand and respect differences in values, norms, and beliefs among families.

☐ I understand the influence of culture on family structure, family functioning, and values and behaviors of its members.

☐ I am knowledgeable about the cultures of the families I am working with.

☐ I develop effective strategies to work with families of different cultures based on their values, beliefs, communication styles, etc.

☐ I am aware of my limitations in applying certain techniques and instruments with families of different cultures.

☐ I understand the issues of oppression, racism, sexism, classism, and their impact on families.

☐ I continue to increase my skills in working with families of different cultures through education, literature, networking, and learning from my clients.

☐ I apply the following principles in my family practice:

1. Continue to increase my awareness of my own cultural heritage
2. Continue to increase my knowledge and understanding of other cultures
3. Am aware of my stereotypes and biases
4. Am open to differences
5. Develop culturally appropriate and sensitive strategies to work with families
6. Am aware of differences even within a family or culture
7. Am willing to learn
8. Take care of myself

Through this research effort, we discovered that few studies have focused on applications of theory with selected culturally diverse families. Nevertheless, this limited information identifies a need for practitioners to pursue evaluative research that will verify the applicability of theories and cultural considerations. This continuous commitment to practice–evaluation integration will guide helping professionals to engage multicultural practice in an evidence-based learning process. We can gain extensive knowledge from clients about who they are, when they need services, what their cultural values are, and how cultural considerations influence their engagement in mental health services or social support.

Exercises for Multicultural Practice

To polish their multicultural practice skills, we suggest that practitioners engage in the following exercises and participate in discussions with the following questions in mind:

1. Which theories and techniques does this case demonstrate?
2. Which multicultural practice issue is present in this case?
3. Which techniques would a practitioner use to establish a good working relationship with this client?
4. What further assessment should I conduct to obtain additional information to achieve practice effectiveness?
5. What are the strengths and limitations of the selected approaches I use?

Case 1: Working with Families in Separation

Client: 25-year-old female

Client:	I don't understand why Jimmy—my five-year-old—still wants to see his dad…. He was very abusive to us in the past.
MC:	Have you ever heard the term "family attachment?"
Client:	It sounds like my son wants to be just like his dad to show his loyalty.
MC:	Where did you get this idea?
Client:	Do you mean why my son wants to be just like his dad? Or why he wants to be loyal?
MC:	How about starting with "your son wants to be like his dad."
Client:	I guess every child wants to model after his parents.
MC:	Which part of his dad is he modeling after?
Client:	I'm not sure.
MC:	Which part of you do you think your child is modeling?
Client:	He talks like me. He's not shy.

MC: Can you find a friend tonight and talk to her about how glad you feel that your boy is learning many things from you?

Client: You mean brag about him?

MC: Would your friend listen?

Client: Yes, I think so. I could also tell her that I need someone to listen to.

MC: We still have the second part of the idea of family loyalty. Where did you get the idea that "Jimmy wants to be loyal?"

Client: I guess that came from the expectations of society.

MC: Who in society gave him this idea?

Client: From me, I guess.

Theories Used: _____

_____

Techniques Demonstrated: _____

_____

Multicultural Issues: _____

_____

Critical Issues to be Further Assessed: _____

_____

Strengths and Limitations of the Theories or Techniques Used: _____

_____

Case 2: Working with Cohabiting Adults

Client: 23-year-old female

Client: I've been feeling really stressed lately because my boyfriend, Greg, isn't feeling comfortable around me.

MC: Not comfortable around you? How do you know?

Client: Well, like last night—he came home late and didn't want to talk about his work.

MC: When did this behavior start?

Client: About a month ago.

MC: Did you notice that anything was different before or after this happened?

Client: Well, last month he went home for his dad's birthday, and when he came home, he had sort of a strange attitude.

MC: Tell me about this attitude.

Client: He didn't want to talk about his dad when I asked him about his dad's birthday.

MC: Did you ask him about his feelings or the event?

Client: I tried to ask about the event, but he just didn't want to talk.

MC: So he seemed to feel distressed over something that happened during this birthday party? Did he or his family invite you to attend this party?

Client: No. They don't invite me places. I'm really not part of his family.

MC: Do you have a close friend?

Client: Yes—Jennifer.

MC: What would Jennifer say if you told her about this "not really part of his family" feeling?

Client: She probably would say, "Just forget about them!"

MC: Can you forget?

Client: No. I feel hurt.

MC: Did you share this feeling with Greg?

Client: I don't want to overburden him with my emotions. He's already stressed about it.

MC: What can you do now?

Client: I really don't know.

MC: How about addressing his overburdened feeling first?

Client: That's a good idea. Do you think he would say I'm being too nervous about this whole thing?

MC: I guess he could. But if he did, could you let him know that you do feel anxious not because of his family but because you see that he's unhappy.

Theories Used: _____

_____

Techniques Demonstrated: _____

_____

Multicultural Issues: _____

_____

Critical Issues to be Further Assessed: _____

_____

Strengths and Limitations of the Theories or Techniques Used: _____

_____

Post-Test on Multicultural Competency

Continuing with multicultural assessment on self-learning is important. As a practice exercise on how to conduct single-system practice evaluation, we suggested the use of ASK, in chapter 3. Follow these steps to conduct your post-test and data analysis on your own multicultural skill development.

Step 1:   Read chapters 3–14. After reading each chapter, complete the ASK Scale in chapter 3, write down your ASK score on Chart 3.1 and plot the data on Graph 3.2

Step 2:   Now complete the ASK Scale again and plot your data.

Step 3:   Compute your average scores from week 2 to week 14.

Step 4:   Now compare your three scores: pre-test score for chapter 3, average scores for chapters 4–14, post-test score for chapter 15 (this chapter).

Keep in mind that you may overestimate your multicultural competencies at the pre-test stage because of your perceived readiness to be a professional. Critically reviewing various practice approaches and incorporating those into practice, however, can result in a more critical self-evaluation, as self-awareness reminds us of our limitations in certain practice areas. As a result, if your score on the post-test is not as high as your pre-test score, do not think that you are less competent. In fact, you may actually be more sensitive to your own practice needs and score yourself lower on the scale after carefully considering all aspects of learning.

An additional tool is included in this chapter to assist practitioners in evaluating their cultural competence when working with families (Table 15.5). This tool assesses the values of understanding and respect, knowledge and skills in performing the work, and the examination of the practitioner's strengths and limitations. Eight principles must be kept in mind:

1. Continue to increase my awareness of my own cultural heritage.
2. Continue to increase my knowledge and understanding of other cultures.
3. Be aware of my stereotypes and biases.
4. Be open to differences.
5. Develop culturally appropriate and sensitive strategies to work with families.
6. Be aware of differences even within a family or culture.
7. Be willing to learn.
8. Take care of myself.

Using this tool on a regular basis will help practitioners achieve total quality improvement in practice, as well as provide data for future practice.

Future Visions for Multicultural Practice

As globalization becomes a way of life in the United States, multicultural practice is becoming ingrained in all of the helping professions, including counseling and social work. "No longer can multiculturalism be relegated to one course, mentioned as a passing comment in a presentation or publication, or avoided by educators and administrators who may see the domain as too much of a bother to debate its merits" (Arredondo, Rosen, Rice, Perez, & Tovar-Gamero, 2005, p. 160). Promoting gender, ethnic, and social equality will remain at the forefront of counseling and social work ethics. As practitioners have become more aware of multicultural practice, self-examination concerning cultural sensitivity has become a key ingredient, especially when the constant caseload or service targets are related to working in cross-cultural situations (Vontress & Jackson, 2004). Learning from clients and effecting changes in the socio-political system are two major goals for practitioners to advance human equality and respect on both the micro and macro levels.

A current trend in counseling and social work practice lies in the emphasis in evidence-based practice. Research-based data must be incorporated into the selection process of theories and techniques. Constant evaluation of practice becomes our practice foundation to provide data to improve our service delivery system.

A Final Note About Self-Awareness

This book establishes a link between multicultural practice and self-awareness, the need for integrated practice, and practice evaluation. Multicultural competencies have become a necessity in counseling and social work education and practice. The goal of practicing multiculturalism when providing therapy and counseling is to increase clients' retention and enhance treatment outcomes. The integration of practice utilizing the principles of experiential, existential, and equilibrium allows for the ability to gain self-awareness.

We must continuously examine our integrated "self," which includes our *personal self*—such as prejudicial attitude and biases, history and family-of-origin issues—and our *professional self*—our skills and knowledge and commitment to evidence-based learning and self-care. Through this self-examination the practitioner is able to gain insight when working with diverse populations and to employ a varied style of valid approaches to healing. We firmly believe that flexibly employing various practice theories will provide the medium to incorporate multiculturalism into everyday practice.

APPENDIX A

Intake Form for a Minor Patient

Please note: A parent, caretaker, or legal guardian of a patient who is under the age of 18 will complete Part I of this form. The minor patient will complete Part II on the last page.

Part I. To Be Completed by the Parent or Guardian

A. Parent/Guardian Information

In order to better assist you and your child, please complete the following questions. All information is considered confidential within the limits of the law (i.e., professionals must report to the related authority child abuse, harmful acts or intents). If you choose not to answer any question in writing at this time, it can be discussed during our session.

Parent/Guardian's name: _____ Age:_____ Sex: _____

Birth Date: _____ Place of Birth: _____

Immigration Date (if applicable): _____

Address (Parent/Guardian): _____

     City _____ State _____ Zip_____

Phone: Home (   ) _____

            Work (   ) _____

Marital Status: Single____ Married____ (since_____) Widowed____ (since_____)

                Divorced/Separated____ (since_____)

Language(s) Spoken: _____ Language Preferred:_____

Occupation: _____ Income: _____

Name of Spouse or Significant Other:_____

Any prior marriage/relationship? Yes____ No____ What years? _____

B. Child Information (To be completed by parent/guardian)

Name of child: _____ Nickname: _____

Age:_____ Sex:_____ Birth Date:_____Place of Birth: _____

Immigration Date (if applicable): _____

Child's address (if different): _____

      City _____ State _____ Zip_____

Language(s) Spoken: _____ Language Preferred:_____

Occupation: _____ School (attending/last attended): _____

Special education: Y/N (type:_____ Alternative school: _____

Education: No. of years completed_____ Grade/Level: _____

Child's father name: _____

Child's mother name:_____

Household members:_____

Name	Age	Education	Relationship with child

Primary Physician: _____ Phone: _____

In case of emergency, contact: _____ Phone: _____

Relationship:_____

Insurance Provider:_____

Policy or group number:_____

Referred by: _____

C. Information for Counseling Purposes
(To be completed by parent or guardian)

1. When was the child's last medical examination? _____

2. Does the child have a history of alcohol or drug problems? Yes___ No___

   (What type? _____)

3. Is there a history of alcohol or drug problems in the child's family?

   Yes___ No___

4. Has the child ever been hospitalized? Yes___ (reasons _____)

   No___

5. Has the child had any serious injuries or surgeries? Yes___ No___

6. List illnesses or symptoms that may require medical attention:

   _____

   _____

7. List any prescribed and over-the-counter medications the child is taking and

   their purpose:

   _____

   _____

8. Is the child on a special diet? Yes ___ No___

   Purpose of the diet: _____

   _____

9. Is there any family history of psychiatric treatment? Yes___ No___

   Who: _____ Relationship: _____

10. Please identify several people who give the child emotional support:

    _____

    _____

11. Reasons for Seeking Counseling:

    What changes would you or the child like to see or make?

    _____

    _____

    _____

    _____

    _____

    _____

12. Previous Counseling Experience

   Has the child ever been in counseling before? Yes____   No____

   Dates and duration of counseling: _____

   Where did the child seek counseling? _____

   What was helpful to the child in that counseling? _____

   _____

13. Cultural Expectations

   What would you like the therapist to know regarding the child's cultural
   background, values, beliefs, and/or expectations?

   _____

   _____

   _____

   _____

14. List three of the child's strengths:

   1. _____

   2. _____

   3. _____

Please check any recurrent feelings, thoughts, or experiences expressed by the
child or observed by others:

____ appetite increase/decrease

____ accelerated heart rate

____ avoidance of things related to the traumatic event

____ abuse

____ bed wetting

____ chest pain or discomfort

____ decreased need for sleep

____ dizziness or faintness

____ de-realization (feelings of unreality)

____ de-personalization (feeling detached from self)

____ fatigue/loss of energy

____ feelings of detachment from others

____ feelings of guilt/shame

___ fear of dying

___ fear of going crazy or losing control

___ feeling "on edge"

___ hopelessness/helplessness

___ hearing voices/hallucinations

___ hypersomnia (too much sleep)

___ irritability

___ insomnia (can't sleep)

___ intense fear or discomfort

___ inability to think

___ impaired functioning (at home/work/school)

___ inability to recall important details of the traumatic event

___ intense psychological distress when reminded of the traumatic event

___ loss of interests or pleasure

___ low self-esteem

___ loss of concentration

___ lack of emotional responsiveness

___ more talkative than usual

___ mind going blank

___ muscle tension or soreness

___ numbness/tingling feeling

___ nausea or abdominal distress

___ outbursts of anger

___ persistent re-experiencing of the trauma (flash-backs, intrusive thoughts)

___ restless, unsatisfying sleep

___ racing thoughts

___ recurrent distressing dreams

___ restricted range of emotions/feelings

___ sadness/depressed mood

___ sleep interruption

___ sense of worthlessness

___ shortness of breath

___ sweating

___ symptoms of increased arousal

___ suicide ideation

___ self mutilation

___ trembling or shaking

___ thinking about death

___ unplanned weight gain/loss

___ violent episodes

___ others (specify:_____)

___ others (specify:_____)

___ others (specify:_____)

___ others (specify:_____)

15. Other Concerns or Comments:

_____

_____

_____

_____

_____

_____

Completed by: _____Date:_____

Relationship to the Minor: _____

Part II. To be Completed by a Minor: Intake Information

In order to better assist you and your family, please complete the following questions. All information is considered confidential within the limits of the law (i.e., professionals must report to the related authority child abuse, harmful acts or intents). If you choose not to answer any question in writing at this time, it can be discussed during our session.

Name: _____ Name you like to be called: _____

1. What is your favorite subject in school?_____

2. List the first names of 3 of your closest friends:

_____   _____   _____

3. What indoor/outdoor activities do you enjoy?

_____

4. Name a favorite food: _____

5. Name a favorite singer and song: _____

6. Name a person you admire the most: _____

7. Name your favorite person in your family: _____

8. What is one of your dislikes? _____

_____

9. How do you describe your personality? _____

_____

10. How do other people see you? _____

_____

11. Use 3 adjectives or words to describe yourself or your feelings now.

_____   _____   _____

12. Describe your current living arrangement and conditions. _____

_____

_____

13. Have you ever been abused by others, either physically, emotionally, or sexually?   Yes___   No___

If Yes, When: _____ Who knew about it? _____

What kind of abuse: _____

14. Have you ever been hospitalized? Yes___   No___   When: _____

Reason: _____

15. Have you ever used substance such as cigarettes or alcohol?

Cigarettes_____   Alcohol_____   Neither_____   Both_____

Other Substance _____

16. List three of your wishes:

1. _____

2. _____

3. _____

Completed by: _____ Date: _____

APPENDIX B

Consent to Treat a Minor

I, the undersigned, agree that my child _____ (Child's Full Name) (Birth Date: _____) will receive psychotherapy and related services from the psychotherapist or social worker named below (thereafter "the clinician") and his/her clinical team of interns and associates at the _____ (Agency Name).

I understand that information revealed in my child's individual sessions may not be shared with me, unless it is essential for treatment purposes, in the best interest of the child, with my prior request, and/or required by the law. I acknowledge that psychotherapy and counseling are not an exact science and that no guarantees have been made as to the results of the treatment hereby authorized.

In an emergency situation, such as a suicide attempt or an acute mental health problem, if the clinician or associates are not available for consultation, I will contact the police or a hospital emergency room for my child's treatment.

Because of the unique nature of each psychotherapy treatment, I agree that the treatment contents may be used for training and/or educational purposes with strict confidence. I also understand that the clinician reserves the right of publication related to the treatment process in order to provide research data to support practice methods. I understand that personal identification such as my name or my child's name will *not* be revealed if any materials are to be used for such purposes.

I will be responsible for the co-payments and any uncovered payments according to the insurance fee schedule. I also agree that psychotherapy progress regarding my child and my family can be released to the insurance company for insurance claims and to the clinician's associates for treatment and follow-up purposes, unless otherwise indicated by me in writing.

Signed by:

_____ Parent   _____Date

Address: _____

Clinician: Psychotherapist/Social Worker:

_____   _____

                                                              Date

License # _____ State: _____

Special Note: _____ (Licensing Board) is a regulatory state agency authorized by state law. Its mission is to protect the health and safety of the general public of the state by ensuring that only qualified persons are providing social work/counseling services and by regulating licensed social workers/counselors. The Consumer Complaint Hotline is _____.

APPENDIX C

My Family

Draw, write or symbolize any thing come to your mind about your family.

REFERENCES

Ackerman, N. W. (1966). *Treating the troubled family*. New York: Basic Books.

Adams, J. L., Jaques, J. D., & May, K. M. (2004). Counseling gay and lesbian families: Theoretical considerations. *The Family Journal: Counseling and Therapy for Couples and Families, 12*(1), 40–42.

Adler, A. (1926). A quote on encouragement from a new translation of Individual Psychology, *Psychotherapie und Erziehung,* in the *AAISF/ATP Archives.* Retrieved May 18, 2005, from http://ourworld.compuserve.com/homepages/hstein/qu-encou.htm

Adler, A. (1964). *Social interest: A challenge to mankind.* New York: Capricorn.

Adler, A. (1982). The fundamental views of individual psychology. *Individual Psychology: The Journal of Adlerian Theory, Research, and Practice, 38*(1), 3–7.

Administration for Children & Families. (ACF, 2007). Latest U.S. adoption statistics show increase in public agency adoptions, while total numbers remain constant. Retrieved October 1, 2007, from http://cbexpress.acf.hhs.gov/articles.cfm?article_id=881&issue_id=2004-12

Ahmeadi, N. (2003). Globalization of consciousness and new challenges for international social work. *International Journal of Social Welfare, 12*(14), 14–23.

Ainslie, J., & Feltey, K.M. (1991). Definitions and dynamics of motherhood and family in lesbian communities. *Marriage and Family Review, 17*(1/2), 63–85.

Alessandria, K. P. (2002). Acknowledging white ethnic groups in multicultural counseling. *Family Journal, 10*(1), 57–60.

Alexander, D. (2003). A marijuana screening inventory (experimental version): Description and preliminary psychometric properties. *American Journal of Drug and Alcohol Abuse, 29*(3), 619–645.

Alexander, D., & Leung, P. (2004). The marijuana screening inventory (MSI-X): Reliability, factor structure, and scoring criteria with a clinical sample. *American Journal of Drug and Alcohol Abuse, 30*(2), 321–351.

Ali, S. R., & Saunders, J. L. (2006). College expectations of rural Appalachian youth: An exploration of social cognitive career theory factors. *The Career Development Quarterly, 55*(1), 38-51.

American Counseling Association. (2005). *ACA codes of ethics and standards of practice*. Retrieved March 28, 2005, from http://www.counseling.org/resources/ethics.htm#ce

American Psychological Association. (1996). *Violence and the family*. Washington, DC: American Psychological Association, Presidential Task Force on Violence and the Family.

American Psychological Association. (2002). *Guidelines on multicultural education, training, research, practice, and organizational change for psychologists*. Retrieved April 11, 2005, from http://www.apa.org/pi/multiculturalguidelines.pdf

American Psychological Association. (2005). *Ethical principles of psychologists and code of conduct*. Retrieved March 28, 2005, from http://www.apa.org/ethics/code 2002.html#principle_e

Americans for Divorce Reform. (2007a). *Divorce rates*. Retrieved May 27, 2005, from http://www.divorcereform.org/rates.html

Americans for Divorce Reform. (2007b). *Your real chance of divorce*. Retrieved May 27, 2005, from http://www.divorcereform.org/real.html

Amin, R., Browne, D. C., & Ahmed, J. (2006). A study of an alternative school for pregnant and/or parenting teens: Quantitative and qualitative evidence. *Child & Adolescent Social Work Journal, 23*(2),172-195.

Anderson, C. (2003). The diversity, strength, and challenges of single-parent households. In F. Walsh (Ed.), *Normal family processes: Growing diversity and complexity* (3rd ed.) (pp. 121–152). New York: Guilford Press.

Anderson, L.P. (1999). Parentification in the context of the African American family. In N.D. Chase (Ed.), *Burdened children: Theory, research, and treatment of parentification* (pp. 154–170). Thousand Oaks, CA: Sage Publications.

Anderson, S. A. (1984). The Family Environment Scales (FES): A review and critique. *American Journal of Family Therapy, 12*, 59–62.

Aquilino, W. S. (2005). Impact of family structure on parental attitudes toward the economic support of adult children over the transition to adulthood. *Journal of Family Issues, 26*(2), 143–167.

Aramony, William (1982). *Needs assessment*. Alexandria, VA: United Way of America.

Arredondo, P., & Perez, P. (2003). Counseling paradigms and Latina/o Americans. In F. Harper & J. McFadden (Eds.). *Culture and counseling: New approaches* (pp. 115–132). Boston, MA: Allyn & Bacon.

Arredondo, P., Rosen, D., Rice, T., Perez, P., & Tovar-Gamero, Z. (2005). Multicultural counseling: A 10-year content analysis of the Journal of Counseling and Development. *Journal of Counseling and Development, 83*, 155–161.

Asay, T.P., & Lambert, M.J. (1999). The empirical case for the common factors in therapy: Quantitative findings. In M.A. Hubble & B.L. Duncan (Eds.), *Heart and soul* of change: What works in therapy (pp. 23–55). Washington, DC: American Psychological Association.

Association for the Advancement of Gestalt Therapy. (2007). The theory of Gestalt therapy. Retrieved August 27, 2007, from http://www.aagt.org/html/character__psy chopathology__an.html

Atkinson, D., Morten, G., & Sue, D. (1989). *Counseling American minorities: A cross-cultural perspective.* Dubuque, IA: Wm. C. Brown Publishers.

Baca Zinn, M. (1995). Social science theorizing for Latino families in the age of diversity. In R. E. Zambrana (Ed.), *Understanding Latino families: Scholarship, policy, and practice* (pp.177–189). Thousand Oaks, CA: Sage Publications.

Baca Zinn, M., & Wells, B. (2000). Diversity with Latino families: New lessons for family social science. In D. H. Demo, K. R. Allen, & M.A. Fine (Eds.), *Handbook of family diversity* (pp. 252–273). London: Oxford University Press.

Ballard, S., & Morris, M. (2003). The family life education needs of midlife and older adults. *Family Relations, 52*(2), 129–137.

Bandura, A., & Walters, R.H. (1967). *Social learning and personality development.* New York: Holt, Rinehart & Winston.

Barbarin, O. (1993). Coping and resilience: Exploring the inner lives of African-American children. *Journal of Black Psychology, 19,* 478–492.

Barber, C. (1989). Transition to the empty nest. In S. J. Bahr & E. T. Peterson (Eds.), *Aging and the family* (pp.15–32). Lexington, MA: Lexington Books.

Barker, R.L. (1999). *The social work dictionary.* Washington, DC: NASW Press.

Barners, S.L. (2001). Stressors and strengths: A theoretical and practical examination of nuclear, single-parent and augmented African American families. *Families in Society, 82*(5), 449–460.

Barnes, G.G. (2005). Divorcing children: Children's experience of their parents' divorce. *Child & Adolescent Mental Health, 10*(1), 47.

Barnes, H.L., & Olson, D.H. (1982). Parent–adolescent communication scale. In D.H. Olson (Ed.), *Family inventories: Inventories used in a national survey of families across the family life cycle* (pp. 33–48). St. Paul: University of Minnesota, Family Social Science.

Barnes, P. (1998). It's just a quarrel. *American Bar Association Journal, 84,* 24–25.

Barnett, D.W., Hall, J.D., & Bramlett, R.K. (1990). Family factors in preschool assessment and intervention: A validity study of parenting stress and coping measures. *Journal of School Psychology, 28*(1), 13–20.

Barth, R.P., Brooks, D., & Iyer, S. (1995). *Adoptions in California: Current demographic profiles and projections through the end of the century.* Berkeley, CA: Child Welfare Research Center.

Bauman, S., & Waldo, M. (1998). Existential theory and mental health counseling: If it were a snake, it would have bitten. *Journal of Mental Health Counseling, 20*(1), 13–28.

Beauvais, F. (1998). American Indians and alcohol. *Alcohol Health & Research World, 22*(4), 253–259.

Becker, D., & Liddle, H.A. (2001). Family therapy with unmarried African American mothers and their adolescents. *Family Process, 40*(4), 413–427.

Bentley, M., Mattingly, T., Hough, C., & Bennett, C. (2003). *Census quality survey to evaluate responses to the census 2000 question on race: An introduction to the data.* Washington, DC: U.S. Census Bureau.

Bernard, M.E. (1998). Validation of the General Attitude and Belief Scale. *Journal of Rational Emotive and Cognitive Behavior Therapy, 16*(3), 183–196.

Betz, N. E. (2006). Women's career development. In J. Worell & C. D. Goodheart (Eds.), *Handbook of girls' and women's psychological health: Gender and well-being across the lifespan* (pp. 312-320). New York: Oxford University Press.

Billingsley, A. (1968). *Black families in America.* New York: Carroll and Graf.

Billingsley, A. (1969). Family functioning in the low-income black community. *Social Casework, 50,* 563–572.

Bitter, J.R. (2004). Two approaches to counseling a parent alone: Toward a Gestalt–Adlerian integration. *Family Journal: Counseling and Therapy for Couples and Families, 12*(4), 358–367.

Bitter, J.R., & Nicoll, W. (2000). Adlerian brief therapy with individuals: Process and practice. *Journal of Individual Psychology, 56*(1), 31–45.

Blender, N.J., & Sanathara, V. (2003). Outcomes and incomes: How to evaluate, improve, and market your psychotherapy practice by measuring outcomes. *Bulletin of the Menninger Clinic, 67*(4), 367–368.

Bloom, M., Fischer, J., & Orme, J.G. (2003). *Evaluating practice: Guidelines for the accountable professional.* Boston: Allyn & Bacon.

Bloomquist, M.L., & Harris, W.G. (1984). Measuring family functioning with the MMPI: A reliability and concurrent validity study of three MMPI scales. *Journal of Clinical Psychology, 40,* 1209–1214.

Borland, D.C. (1982). A cohort analysis approach to the empty-nest syndrome among three ethnic groups of women: A theoretical position. *Journal of Marriage and the Family, 44,* 117–129.

Bowen, M. (1978). *Family therapy in clinical practice.* New York: Jason Aronson.

Bowen Center for the Study of the Family. (2004). *Bowen theory: Murray Bowen, M.D.* Retrieved May 11, 2005, from http://www.thebowencenter.org/pages/murray bowen.html

Brack, G., Hill, M.B., Edwards, D., Grootboom, N., & Lassiter, P.S. (2003). Adler and Ubuntu: Using Adlerian principles in the New South Africa. *Journal of Individual Psychology, 59*(3), 316–326.

Bramlett, M., & Mosher, W. (2001). First marriage dissolution, divorce, and remarriage: United States. *Advance Data from Vital and Health Statistics, 323.* Hyattsville, MD: National Center for Health Statistics.

Brave Heart, M. Y. H. (2004). The historical trauma response among Natives and its relationship to substance abuse: A lakota illustration. In E. Nebelkopf & M. Philips (Eds.), *Healing and mental health for Native Americans: Speaking in red* (pp. 7–18). Walnut Creek, CA: AltaMira Press.

Brendel, J. M., & Sustaeta, C. M. (2003). Counseling Hispanic Americans. In N.A. Vacc, S.B. DeVaney, & J.M. Brendel (Eds.), *Counseling multicultural and diverse populations: Strategies for practitioners* (pp. 93–115). New York: Brunner-Routledge.

Briggs, H.E., Feyerherm, W., & Gingerich, W. (2004). Evaluating science-based practice with single systems. In H.E. Briggs & T.L. Rzephnicki, *Using evidence in social work practice: Behavioral perspectives* (pp. 323–342). Chicago: Lyceum Books.

British Broadcasting Corporation News (BBC). (2007). *Factlife: Global migration.* Retrieved September 21, 2007, from http://news.bbc.co.uk/2/shared/spl/hi/world/04/migration/html/migration_boom.stm

Brooks, L.J., Haskins, D.G., & Kehe, J.V. (1999). Counseling and psychotherapy with African American clients. In T. Smith (Ed.), *Practicing multiculturalism: Affirming diversity in counseling and psychology* (pp. 145–166). Boston: Pearson.

Brown University Child & Adolescent Behavior Letter. (2002). Brief strategic family therapy. *Brown University Child & Adolescent Behavior Letter, 18*(8), 3–6.

Bryant, W. (2001). The practice of Gestalt therapy within a brief therapy context. *Gestalt Journal, 24*(1), 7–62.

Burston, B.W., Jones, D., & Roberson-Saunders, P. (1995). Drug use and African Americans: Myth versus reality. *Journal of Alcohol & Drug Education, 40*(2), 19–39.

Camarota, S. (2002). *Immigrants in the United States – 2002: A snapshot of America's foreign born population.* Retrieved March 22, 2005, from http://www.cis.org/articles/2002/back1302.html

Carlson, J.M., & Carlson, J.D. (2000). The application of Adlerian psychotherapy with Asian-American clients. *Journal of Individual Psychology, 56*(2), 214–226.

Carr, A. (1998). Michael White's narrative therapy. *Contemporary Family Therapy: An International Journal, 20*(4), 485–503.

Carr, S. (2003). Rethinking empowerment theory using a feminist lens: The importance of process. *Affilia: Journal of Women and Social Work, 18*(1), 8–20.

Carter, B. (1988). Divorce: His and hers. In M. Walters, B. Carter, P. Papp, & O. Silverstein, *The invisible web: Gender patterns in family relationships* (pp. 253–271). New York: Guilford Press.

Carter, B., & McGoldrick, M. (1989). *The changing family life cycle: A framework for family therapy.* Boston, MA: Allyn & Bacon.

Carter, B., & McGoldrick, M. (2005). *The expanded family life cycle: Individual, family and social perspectives* (3rd ed.). New York: Allyn & Bacon.

Casey, J. (2004). Is your nest too full? Retrieved on August 27, 2007, from http://www.medicinenet.com/script/main/art.asp?articlekey=52508

Chalk, R., & King, P.A. (Eds.) (1998). *Violence in families: Assessing prevention & treatment programs.* Washington, DC: National Academy Press.

Chang, C.Y. (2003). Counseling Asian Americans. In N. A. Vacc, S. B. DeVaney, & J. M. Brendel (Eds.), *Counseling multicultural and diverse populations: Strategies for practitioners* (pp. 73–92). New York: Brunner-Routledge.

Chang, J. (1997, November). Contexts of adolescent worries: Impacts of ethnicity, gender, family structure, and socioeconomic status. Paper presented at the NCFR Fatherhood and Motherhood in a Diverse and Changing World, Arlington, VA.

Chatters, L. M., Taylor, R. J., & Jackson, J. S. (1986). Aged blacks' choices for an informal helper network. *Journal of Gerontology, 41*, 94–100.

Cheung, M., & Leung, P. (2006). Culturally appropriate family support practice: Working with the Asian populations. In P. Dolan, J. Canavan, & J. Pinkerton (Eds.), *Family support as reflective practice* (pp. 214-233). London: Jessica Kingsley.

Cheung, M., & Nguyen, M.S. (2001). Parent–child relationships in Vietnamese American families. In N. Webb (Ed.), *Culturally diverse paren–child and family relationships* (pp. 261–282). New York: Columbia University Press.

Child Welfare League of America. (2001). Fact sheet. Retrieved May 27, 2005, from http://www.cwla.org/advocacy/aodfactsheet.htm

Child Welfare League of America. (2007). *Alcohol and other drugs: About the program.* Retrieved May 29, 2007 from http://www.cwla.org/programs/bhd/aod.htm

Clemmens, M. C., & Matzko, H. (2005). Gestalt approaches to substance use/abuse/dependency: Theory and practice. In A. L. Woldt & S. M. Toman (Eds.), *Gestalt therapy: History, theory, and practice* (pp. 279-300). Thousand Oaks, CA: Sage Publications.

Cohan, S. L., Chavira, D. A., & Stein, M. B. (2006). Practitioner Review: Psychosocial interventions for children with selective mutism: A critical evaluation of the literature from 1990-2005. *Journal of Child Psychology and Psychiatry, 47*(11), 1085-1097.

Christian and Missionary Alliance. (2003). *Ethnic populations in the U.S.* Retrieved March 13, 2005, from http://web2.cmalliance.org/ncm/intercultural/population.jsp

Cohen, S., Kamarch, T., & Mermelstein, R. (1983). A global measure of perceived stress. *Journal of Health and Social Behavior, 24,* 385–396.

Coleman, M.N. (2005). *Applying the tripartite model of multicultural counseling competency to the internship training program.* Retrieved April 6, 2005, from http://www.acpa.nche.edu/comms/comm07/feature2-05.HTM

Collins, L.H. (1998). Illustrating feminist theory: Power and psychopathology. *Psychology of Women Quarterly, 22,* 97–112.

Collins, S.S., Schoen, C., Joseph, S., Duchon, L., Simantov, E., & Yellowitz, M. (1999). *Health concerns across a woman's lifespan: The Commonwealth Fund 1998 survey of women's health.* New York: Commonwealth Fund.

Cone, J.D. (2001). *Evaluating outcomes: Empirical tools for effective practice.* Washington, DC: American Psychological Association.

Congress, E. P. (1994). The use of culturagrams to assess and empower culturally diverse families. *Families in Society, 75*(9), 531-540.

Congress, E. P. (2004). Cultural and ethnical issues in working with culturally diverse patients and their families: The use of the culturagram to promote cultural competent practice in health care settings. *Social Work in Health Care, 39*(3-4), 249-262.

Constantine, M.G., & Sue, D.W. (2005). *Strategies for building multicultural competence in mental health and educational settings.* New York: John Wiley & Sons.

Cook, T.D., & Campbell, D.T. (1979). *Quasi-experimentation: Design & analysis issues for field settings.* Boston: Houghton Mifflin.

Corey, G. (2005). *Theories and practice of counseling and psychotherapy* (7th ed.). Belmont, CA: Brooks/Cole.

Corey, G., Corey, M., & Callanan, P. (2003). *Issues and ethics in the helping professions* (6th ed.). Belmont, CA: Brooks/Cole.

Cottrell, S. (2000). *Solution-focused therapy workshop notes.* Retrieved March 26, 2005, from http://www.clinicalsupervision.com/Solution%20Focused%20Therapy%20Workshop%20Notes.htm

Council on Social Work Education. (2001; revised 2004). *Educational policy and accreditation standards.* Retrieved April 11, 2005, from http://www.cswe.org/accreditation/EPAS/epas.pdf

Coven, A.B. (1977). Using Gestalt psychodrama experiments in rehabilitation counseling. *Personnel and Guidance Journal, 56*(3), 143–147.

Coven, A.B. (2004). Gestalt group dreamwork demonstrations in Taiwan. *Journal for Specialists in Group Work, 29*(2), 175–184.

Cozzarelli, C., Wilkinson, A.V., & Tagler, M.J. (2001). Attitudes toward the poor and attributions for poverty. *Journal of Social Issues, 57*(2), 207–227.

Cross, T.L., Bazron, B.J., Dennis, K.W., & Isaacs, M.R., (1989). *Towards a culturally competent system of care* (Vol. 1). Washington, DC: National Center for Technical Assistance Center for Children's Mental Health, Georgetown University Child Development Center.

Crow, G. (1997). *Comparative sociology and social theory: Beyond the three worlds.* London: Macmillan.

Cseh-Szombathy, L., Kock-Nielsen, I., Trost, J., & Weda, I. (1985). *The aftermath of divorce—Coping with family change: An investigation in eight countries.* Budapest, Hungary: Akademiai Kiado.

Curtis, P.A., & McCullough, C. (1993). The impact of alcohol and other drugs on the child welfare system. *Child Welfare, 72*(6), 533–542.

Dagirmanjian, S., Eron, J., & Lund, T. (2007). Narrative solutions: An integration of self and systems perspectives in motivating change. *Journal of Psychotherapy Integration, 17*(1), 70-92.

Dammann, C., & Jurkovic, G. (1986). Strategic family therapy: A problem-focused systematic approach. *Individual Psychology: The Journal of Adlerian Theory, Research, and Practice, 42*(4), 556–567.

Daughtry, D., Twohey, D., & Whitcomb, D.H. (2005). When diversity becomes the norm. In J.L. Chin (Ed.), *Psychology of prejudice and discrimination: Disability, religion, physique, and other traits,* Vol. 4 (pp. 253–281). Westport, CT: Praeger Publishers/Greenwood Publishing Group.

Davey, G. (1987). *Cognitive processes and Pavlovian conditioning in humans.* New York: Wiley.

David, D., Montgomery, G.H., Macavei, B., & Borbjerg, D.H. (2005). An empirical investigation of Albert Ellis's binary model of distress. *Journal of Clinical Psychology, 61*(4), 499–516.

DelCampo, D. (2003). *Grandparenting.* Retrieved August 8, 2005 from http://cahe.nmsu.edu/pubs/_f/F-406.pdf

DeNavas-Walt, C., Proctor, B.D., & Mills, R.J. (2004). *Income, poverty, and health insurance coverage in the United States: 2003* (Current Population Reports, 60–226). Washington, DC: U.S. Government Printing Office.

de Shazer, S. (1985). *Keys to solution in brief therapy.* New York: W.W. Norton & Co.

de Shazer, S. (1997). Some thoughts on language use in therapy. *Contemporary Family Therapy: An International Journal, 19*(1), 133–142.

Devore, W., & Schlesinger, E.G. (1999). *Ethnic sensitive social work practice.* Boston: Allyn and Bacon.

Dowd, E.T., & Milne, C.R. (1986). Paradoxical interventions in counseling psychology. *Counseling Psychology, 14*(2), 237–282.

Dressel, P. (1996). Grandparenting at century's end: An introduction to the issue. *Generations, 20*(1), 5–7.

Duvall, E. M. (1957). *Family development.* Philadelphia: J. B. Lippincott.

Duvall, E. M. (1988). Family development's first forty years. *Family Relations, 37,* 127–134.

Dwairy, M. (2002). Psychotherapy in competition with culture: A case study of an Arab woman. *Clinical Case Studies, 1*(3), 254–267.

Edwards, Y. J. (2002). *Healing the soul wound: The retraditionalization of Native Americans in substance abuse treatment* (Doctoral dissertation, California Institute

Integral Studies, 2002). *Dissertation Abstracts International: Section B: The Sciences & Engineering, 63*(2–8).

Ellis, A. (1996). *Better, deeper, and more enduring brief therapy: The rational emotive behavior therapy approach.* New York: Brunner/Mazel Publishers.

Ellis, A. (2002). *Overcoming resistance: A rational emotive behavior therapy integrated approach.* New York: Springer Publishing.

Ellis, M. L. (2006). Review of sex and sexuality, Winnicottian perspectives. *Psychodynamic Practice: Individuals, Groups and Organisations, 12*(4), 487-490.

Enns, C.Z. (2004). *Feminist theories and feminist psychotherapies.* New York: Haworth Press.

Epstein, N.B., Baldwin, L.M., & Bishop, D.S. (1983). The McMaster Family Assessment Device. *Journal of Marital and Family Therapy, 9,* 171–180.

Evan B. Donaldson Adoption Institute. (1997). *Benchmark adoption survey: Report on the findings.* New York: Evan B. Donaldson Institute.

Evans, M.P., & Valadez, A.A. (2003). Culture-centered counseling from existential perspective: What does it look like and how does it work for an African American client? In G. Roysircar, D.S. Sandhu, & V.E. Bibbins (Eds.), *Multicultural Competencies: A guidebook of practices* (pp. 149–160). Alexandria, VA: Association of Multicultural Counseling and Development.

Ezra, M. (2003). Factors associated with marriage and family formation processes in southern Ethiopia. *Journal of Comparative Family Studies, 34*(4), 509–530.

Falicov, C. J. (1998). *Latino families in therapy: A guide to multicultural practice.* New York: Guilford.

Falk, P. (1989). Lesbian mothers: Psychosocial assumptions in family law. *American Psychologist, 44,* 941–947.

Fang, S.S., & Wark, L. (1998). Developing cross-cultural competence with traditional Chinese Americans in family therapy: Background information and the initial therapeutic contact. *Contemporary Family Therapy: An International Journal, 20*(1), 59–77.

Feminist Therapy Institute. (2005). *Feminist therapy code of ethics* (Revised, 1999). Retrieved May 10, 2005, from http://www.feministtherapyinstitute.org/ethics.htm-

Fernbacher, S., & Plummer, D. (2005). Cultural influences and considerations in Gestalt therapy. In A.L. Woldt & S.M. Toman (Eds.), *Gestalt therapy: History, theory, and practice* (pp. 117–132). Thousand Oaks, CA: Sage Publications.

Fields, J., & Casper, L.M. (2001). *America's families and living arrangements: March 2000.* (Current Population Reports 20-537). Washington, DC: U.S. Census Bureau.

Ford-Gilboe, M. (2000). Dispelling myths and creating opportunity: A comparison of the strengths of single-parent and two-parent families. *Advances in Nursing Science, 23*(1), 41–58.

Fouad, N. A., & Arredondo, P. (2007). *Becoming culturally oriented: Practical advice for psychologists and educators.* Washington, DC: American Psychological Association.

Framo, J. L. (1982). *Explorations in marital and family therapy: Selected papers of James L. Framo.* New York: Springer.

Framo, J. L. (1992). *Family-of-origin therapy: An intergenerational approach.* New York: Brunner/Mazel.

Fraser, J. S., & Solovey, A. D. (2007). Problem formation. In J. S. Fraser & A. D. Solovey, *Second-order change in psychotherapy: The golden thread that unifies effective treatments* (pp. 19-38). Washington, DC: American Psychological Association.

Freeman, S. (1993). Client centered therapy with diverse populations: The universal within the specific. *Journal of Multicultural Counseling and Development, 21*(4), 248–255.

Freud, S. (1959). Fragments of an analysis of a case of hysteria (1905). *Collected papers* (Vol. 3). New York: Basic Books.

Frevert, V.S., & Miranda, A.O. (1998). A conceptual formulation of the Latin culture and the treatment of Latinos from an Adlerian psychology perspective. *Journal of Individual Psychology, 54*(3), 291–309.

Frosh, S. (2002). *Afterwords: The personal in gender, culture and psychotherapy.* New York: Palgrave.

Garcia, C., Baker, S., DeMayo, R., & Brown, G.I. (2005). Gestalt educational therapy. In A.L. Woldt & S.M. Toman (Eds.), *Gestalt therapy: History, theory, and practice* (pp. 301–317). Thousand Oaks, CA: Sage.

Gardner, B. C., Burr, B. K., & Wiedower, S. E. (2006). Reconceptualizing strategic family therapy: Insights from a dynamic systems perspective. *Contemporary Family Therapy: An International Journal, 28*(3), 339-352.

Garrett, M. T. (2003). Counseling Native Americans. In N.A. Vacc, S.B. DeVaney, & J.M. Brendel (Eds.), *Counseling multicultural and diverse populations: Strategies for practitioners* (pp. 27–54). New York: Brunner-Routledge.

Gartrell, N., Banks, A., Hamilton, J., Reed, N., Bishop, H., & Rodas, C. (1999). The National Lesbian Family Study: Interview with mothers and toddlers. *American Journal of Orthopsychiatry, 69,* 362–369.

Geron, S.M. (2002). Cultural competency: How is it measured? Does it make a difference? *Generations, 26(3),* 39–45.

Giannini, A. J., Quinones-Delvalle, R.M., & Blackshear, G. (1990). The use of cognitive restructuring in cross-cultural therapy. *Psychiatric Forum, 15*(2), 30–32.

Gil, E. (2005). From sensitivity to competence in working across cultures. In E. Gil & A.A. Drewes (Eds.), *Critical issues in play therapy* (pp. 3–25). New York: Guilford Press.

Glaserfeld, E. V. (1984). An introduction to radical constructivism. In P. Watxlawick (Ed.), *The invented reality: How do we know what we believe we know?* (pp. 17–40). New York: Norton.

Glass, S. P., & Wright, T. L. (1992). Justifications for extramarital relationships: The association between attitudes, behaviors, and gender. *Journal of Sex Research, 29*(3), 361–387.

Gloria, A.M., Ruiz, E.L., & Castillo, E.M. (1999) Counseling and psychotherapy with Latino and Latina clients. In T. Smith (Ed.), *Practicing multiculturalism: Affirming diversity in counseling and psychology* (pp. 167–189). Boston: Pearson.

Goldenberg, I., & Goldenberg, H. (2004). *Family therapy: An overview* (6th ed.). Pacific Grove, CA: Brooks/Cole.

Goodman, L.A., Liang, B., & Helms, J.E. (2004). Training counseling psychologists as social justice agents: Feminist and multicultural principles in action. *Counseling Psychologist, 32*(6), 793–837.

Gottman, J. (1990). Children of gay and lesbian parents. In F.W Bozett & M.B Sussman (Eds.), *Homosexuality and family relations* (pp.177–196). New York: Harrington Park Press.

Green, R., Kiernan-Stern, M., Bailey, K., Chambers, K., Claridge, R., Jones, G., et al. (2005). The multicultural counseling inventory: A measure for evaluating social work student and practitioner self-perceptions of their multicultural competencies. *Journal of Social Work Education, 41*(2), 191–208.

Greenberg, M., & Rahmanou, H. (2007). *Four commentaries: Looking to the future.* Retrieved September 26, 2007, from http://www.futureofchildren.org/information2827/information_show.htm?doc_id=241583

Guadalupe, K., & Lum, D. (2005). *Multidimensional contextual practice: Diversity and transcendence.* Belmont, CA: Thomson Brooks/Cole.

Gulnar Nugman of the Heritage Foundation (2002). *World divorce rates.* Retrieved May 13, 2005, from http://www.divorcereform.org/gul.html

Hage, S.M. (2005). Future considerations for fostering multicultural competence in mental health and educational settings: Social justice implications. In M.G. Constantine & D.W. Sue (Eds.), *Strategies for building* multicultural *competence in mental health and educational settings* (pp. 285–302). New York: John Wiley & Sons.

Haley, J. (1980). *Leaving home.* New York: McGraw-Hill.

Hall, J. C. (2006). Review of *Divorce and family mediation: Models, techniques, and applications. Clinical Social Work Journal, 34*(1), 133-135.

Hanson, S.M.H. (1986). Healthy single parent families. *Family Relations, 35*, 125–132.

Helburn, S.W., & Bergmann, B.R. (2002). *America's child care problem: The way out.* New York: Palgrave for St. Martin's Press.

Henry, C.S., Peterson, G.W., & Wilson, S.M. (1997). Adolescent social competence and parental satisfaction. *Journal of Adolescent Research, 12*(3), 389–409.

Herie, M., & Martin, G.W. (2002). Knowledge diffusion in social work: A new approach to bridging the gap. *Social Work, 47*(1), 85–95.

Herman, J.L., Morris, L.L., & Fitz-Gibbon, C.T. (1987). *Evaluator's handbook.* Newbury Park, CA: Sage Publications.

Hernandez, D.J. (1993). *America's children: Resources from family, government and the economy.* New York: Russell.

Hill, C., & Nakayama, E. (2000). Client centered therapy: Where has it been and where is it going? *Journal of Clinical Psychology, 56*(7), 861–876.

Hodge, D. (2004). Working with Hindu clients in a spiritually sensitive manner. *Social Work, 49(1),* 27–38.

Hofmann, S. G. (2006). The importance of culture in cognitive and behavioral practice. *Cognitive and Behavioral Practice, 13*(4), 243-245.

Holcomb-McCoy, C.C. (2000). Multicultural counseling competencies: An exploratory factor analysis. *Journal of Multicultural Counseling & Development, 28*(2), 83–97.

Holcomb-McCoy, C.C. (2005). Investigating school counselors' perceived multicultural competence. *Professional School Counseling, 8*(5), 414–423.

Holland, T.P., & Kilpatrick, A.C. (1993). Using narrative techniques to enhance multicultural practice. *Journal of Social Work Education, 29*(3), 302–308.

Hollingsworth, L.D. (1998a). Adoptee dissimilarity from the adoptive family: Clinical practice and research implications. *Child and Adolescent Social Work Journal, 15*(4), 303–319.

Hollingsworth, L.D. (1998b). Promoting same-race adoption for children of color. *Social Work, 43*(2), 104–116.

Holmes, P. (2001). *The role of a grandparent.* Retrieved August 8, 2005 from http://ohioline.osu.edu/ss-fact/0181.html

Horne, S.G., & Mathews, S.S. (2004). Collaborative consultation: International applications of a multicultural feminist approach. *Journal of Multicultural Counseling & Development, 32*(extra), 366–378.

Hudson, W.W. (1997). *The WALMYR Assessment Scales Scoring Manual.* Tallahassee, FL: WALMYR Publishing Company.

Ikehara, H. (1999). Implications of Gestalt theory and applications for the learning organization. *Learning Organization, 6*(2), 63–69.

In Touch. (2005). *Cross cultural cohesiveness.* Retrieved September 28, 2005, from http://www.washington.edu/admin/hr/worklife/carelink/nwsltrs/intouch_vol5issue 3.pdf

Innis, B. (1998). Experiences in difference: An exploration of the usefulness and relevance of psychoanalytic to transcultural mental health work. *Psychodynamic Counseling, 49*(2), 171–189.

International Migration. (2002). Number *of world's migrants reaches 175 million mark.* Retrieved August 22, 2005, from http://www.un.org/esa/population/publica tions/ittmig2002/press-release-eng.htm

Irving, P., & Dickson, D. (2006). A re-conceptualization of Rogers' core conditions: Implications for research, practice and training. *International Journal for the Advancement of Counselling, 28*(2), 183-194.

Iwamasa, G., & Smith, S. (1996). Ethnic diversity in behavioral psychology. *Behavior Modification, 20,* 45–59.

Jackson, A.P., & Turner, S. (1999). Counseling and psychotherapy with Native American clients. In T. Smith (Ed.). *Practicing multiculturalism: Affirming diversity in counseling and psychology* (pp. 215–233). Boston: Pearson.

Jaggar, A.M., & Rothenberg, P.S. (1993). *Feminist frameworks: Alternative theoretical accounts of the relations between women and men.* New York: McGraw-Hill.

Jensen, L.A. (2003). Coming of age in a multicultural world: Globalization and adolescent cultural identity formation. *Applied Developmental Science, 7*(3), 189–196.

Johnson, M., Wall, T., Guanipa, C., Terry-Guyer, L., & Velasquez, R. (2002). The psychometric properties of the Orthogonal Cultural Identification Scale in Asian Americans. *Journal of Multicultural Counseling and Development, 30*(3), 181–191.

Johnson, M.K. (2005). Family roles and work values: processes of selection and change. *Journal of Marriage &* Family, *67*(2), 352–369.

Jones, R. (1983). Increasing staff sensitivity to the black client. *Social Casework, 29,* 419–425.

Kahana, B., & Kahana, E. (1982). Clinic issues of middle age and life. In F.M. Berardo (Ed.), *The annals of the American academy of political and social science: Middle and late life transitions* (pp. 140–161). Beverly Hills: Sage.

Kao, S. (2005). Play therapy with Asian children. In E. Gil & A. Drewes (Eds.), *Cultural issues in play therapy* (pp. 180–193). New York: Guilford.

Kerl, S.B. (2002). Using narrative approaches to teach multicultural counseling. *Journal of Multicultural Counseling & Development, 30*(2), 135–143.

Kim, B.S.K., & Lyons, H.Z. (2003). Experiential activities and multicultural counseling competence training. *Journal of Counseling & Development, 81*(4), 400–408.

Klass, G. (2002). *Presenting data: Tabular and graphic display of social indicators.* Retrieved May 17, 2005, from http://lilt.ilstu.edu/gmklass/pos138/datadisplay/ poverty.htm

Kleist, D. (1999). Single parent families: A difference that makes a difference? *Family Journal, 7*(4), 373–379.

Kocarek, C.E., Talbot, D.M., Batka, J.C., & Anderson, M.Z. (2001). Reliability and validity of three measures of multicultural competency. *Journal of Counseling and Development, 79*(4), 486–496.

Koren, P.E., DeChillo, N., & Friesen, B.J. (1992). Measuring empowerment in families whose children have emotional disabilities: A brief questionnaire. *Rehabilitation Psychology, 37,* 305–321.

Kotchick, B.A., Dorsey, S., & Heller, L. (2005). Predictors of parenting among African American single mothers: Personal and contextual factors. *Journal of Marriage and Family, 67,* 448–460.

Kreider, R.M. (2003). *Adopted children and stepchildren: 2000* (Census 2000 Special Reports). Washington, DC: U.S. Census Bureau.

Kreider, R.M. (2005). *Number, timing, and duration of marriages and divorces: 2001* (Current Population Reports, P70-97). Washington, DC: U.S. Census Bureau.

Kreider, R.M., & Field, J.M. (2001). *Number, timing, and duration of marriages and divorces: Fall 1996* (Current Population Reports, P70–80). Washington, DC: U.S. Census Bureau.

Kuperminc, G.P., Blatt, S.J., Shahar, G., Henrich, C., & Leadbeater, B.J. (2004). Cultural equivalence and cultural variance in longitudinal associations of young adolescent self-definition and interpersonal relatedness to psychological and school adjustment. *Journal of Youth and Adolescence, 33*(1), 13–30.

Labovitz, S., & Hagedorn R. (1975). A structural-behavioral theory of intergroup antagonism. *Social Forces, 53*(3), 444–449.

Lambert, M.J. (2005). Early response in psychotherapy: Further evidence for the importance of common factors rather than "placebo effects." *Journal of Clinical Psychology, 61*(7), 855–869.

Lambert, S. (2005). Gay and lesbian families: What we know and where to go from here. *Family Journal: Counseling and Therapy for Couples and Families, 13*(1), 43–51.

Lantz, J. (1978). *Family and marital therapy.* New York: Appleton-Century-Crofts.

Lanzet, B., & Bernhardt, J. (2000). Moving on: Families of separation and divorce. *Journal of Jewish Communal Service, 76(3),* 236–243.

Laszloffy, T.A. (2002). Rethinking family development theory: Reaching with the systemic family development (SFD) model. *Family Relations: Interdisciplinary Journal of Applied Family Studies, 51*(3), 206–214.

Lawrence, S. (2002). Domestic violence and welfare policy: Research findings that can inform policies on marriage and child well-being. *Research forum on children, families, and the new federalism.* New York: National Resource Center for Children in Poverty.

Lazarus, A.A. (1986). Multimodal psychotherapy: Overview and update. *Journal of Integrative & Eclectic Psychotherapy, 5*(1), 95–103.

Lester, D. (1996). Trends in divorce and marriage around the world. *Journal of Divorce and Remarriage, 25*(1–2), 169–171.

Lethem, J. (2002). Brief solution focused therapy. *Child and Adolescent Mental Health, 7*(4), 189–192.

Leung, P., Cheung, K.M., & Stevenson, K.M. (1994). A strengths approach to ethnically sensitive practice for child protective service workers. *Child Welfare, 73*(6), 707–721.

Lewandowski, D.A., & Jackson, L.A. (2001). Perceptions of interracial couples: Prejudice at the dyadic level. *Journal of Black Psychology, 27*(3), 288–303.

Lewis, R.F. (2005). Using the solving circle with an Adlerian and postmodern twist: Fostering relationships with couples and families. *Family Journal: Counseling and Therapy for Couples and Families, 13*(1), 77–80.

Liaison Committee on Medical Education. (2007). *Functions and structure of a medical school.* Chicago: Author. Retrieved September 12, 2007, from http://www.lcme.org/functions2004oct.pdf

Liberman, R. (1970). Behavioral approaches to family and couple therapy. *American Journal of Orthopsychiatry, 40*(1), 106–118.

Liem, R. (1997). Shame and guilt among first- and second-generation Asian Americans and European Americans. *Journal of Cross-Cultural Psychology, 28*(4), 365–392.

Liggan, D. Y., & Kay, J. (2006). Race in the room: Issues in the dynamic psychotherapy of African-Americans. In R. Moodley & S. Palmer, *Race, Culture and Psychotherapy: Critical Perspectives in Multicultural Practice* (pp. 100-115). Philadelphia: Routledge/Taylor & Francis Group.

Limbert, W. M., & Bullock, H. E. (2005). 'Playing the fool': U.S. welfare policy from a critical race perspective. *Feminism & Psychology, 15*(3), 253–274.

Lindner, H., Kirkby, R., Wertheim, E., & Birch, P. (1999). A brief assessment of irrational thinking: The shorted General Attitude and Belief Scale. *Cognitive Therapy and Research, 23*(6), 651–663.

Liu, F. (2004). From being to becoming: Nüshu and sentiments in a Chinese rural community. *American Ethnologist, 31*(3), 422–439.

Liu, W.M., Sheu, H., & Williams, K. (2004). Multicultural competency in research: Examining the relationships among multicultural competencies, research training and self-efficacy, and the multicultural environment. *Cultural Diversity & Ethnic Minority Psychology, 10*(4), 324–339.

Lobb, M.S., & Lichtenberg, P. (2005). Classical gestalt therapy theory. In A.L. Woldt & S.M. Toman (Eds.), *Gestalt therapy: History, theory, and practice* (pp. 21–39). Thousand Oaks, CA: Sage Publications.

Locke, D. (1992). *Increasing multicultural understanding.* Beverly Hills, CA: Sage.

López, A.G., & Carrillo, E. (2001). *The Latino psychiatric patient: Assessment and treatment.* Washington DC: American Psychiatric Publishing.

Lothane, Z. (2006). Freud's legacy—Is it still with us? *Psychoanalytic Psychology, 23*(2), 285-301.

Lott, B., & Bullock, H. E. (2007). *Psychology and economic injustice: Personal, professional, and political intersections.* Washington, DC: American Psychological Association.

Lum, D. (1999). *Culturally competent practice: A framework for growth and action.* Pacific Grove, CA: Brooks/Cole.

Lum, D. (2004). *Social work practice & people of color.* Pacific Grove, CA: Brooks/Cole.

Lyon, E. (2000). Welfare, poverty and abused women: New research and its implications (Policy and Practice Paper #10). *Building comprehensive solutions to domestic violence.* Harrisburg, PA: National Resource Center on Domestic Violence.

Mageo, J.M. (2001). Dream play and discovering cultural psychology. *Ethos, 29*(2), 187–217.

Maiter, S. (2004). Considering context and culture in Child Protective Services to ethnically diverse families: An example from research with parents from the Indian subcontinent (South Asians). *Journal of Social Work Research and Evaluation, 5(1),* 63–80.

Majercsik, E. (2005). Hierarchy of needs of geriatric patients. *Gerontology, 51*(3), 170–173.

Marger, M.N. (2003). *Race and ethnic relations: American and global perspectives* (6th ed.). Belmont, CA: Wadsworth.

Martain, A. (1982). Learning to hide: The socialization of the gay adolescent. *Adolescent Psychiatry, 10,* 52–65.

Maslow, A.H. (1973). *Dominance, self-esteem, self-actualization: Germinal papers of A. H. Maslow* (edited by Richard J. Lowry). Monterey, CA: Brooks/Cole.

McClurg, L. (2004). Biracial youth and their parents: Counseling considerations for family therapists. *Family Journal: Counseling and Therapy for Couples and Families, 12*(2), 170–173.

McCubbin, H.I., & Patterson, J.M. (1991). FILE: Family Inventory of Life Events and Changes. In H.I. McCubbin & A. I. Thompson (Eds.), *Family assessment inventories for research practice* (pp. 81–98). Madison: University of Wisconsin-Madison Press.

McCubbin, H.I., Larsen, A., & Olson, D.H. (1982). Family Crisis Oriented Personal Evaluation Scales. In D.H. Olson, H.I. McCubbin, H. Barnes, A. Larsen, M. Muxen, & M. Wilson (Eds.), *Family inventories* (pp. 143–159). St. Paul: University of Minnesota Press.

McGoldrick, M., Gerson, R., & Shellenberger, S. (1999). *Genograms: Assessment and intervention* (2nd ed.). New York: W. W. Norton and Co.

McKinnon, J. (2003). *The black population in the United States: March 2002* (Current Population Reports, series 20-541). Washington, DC: U.S. Census Bureau.

McPhatter, A.R. (1997). Cultural competence in child welfare: What is it? How do we achieve it? What happens without it? *Child Welfare, 76(1),* 255–277.

Mears, D.P., & Visher, C.A. (2005). Trends in understanding and addressing domestic violence. *Journal of Interpersonal Violence, 20*(2), 204–211.

Mederos, F., & Woldeguiorguis, I. (2003). Beyond cultural competence: What child protection managers need to know and do. *Child Welfare, 82(2),* 125–142.

MedlinePlus. (2007). *Teenage pregnancy.* Retrieved on May 10, 2007, from http://www.nlm.nih.gov/medlineplus/teenagepregnancy.html#cat1

Menjivar, C., & Salcido, O. (2002). Immigrant women and domestic violence: Common experiences in different countries. *Gender & Society, 16*(6), 898–920.

Metropolitan Community College. (1999). *Multicultural counseling techniques.* Retrieved April 3, 2005, from http://idsdev.mccneb.edu/dcarter/counseli.htm

Miller, G., & de Shazer, S. (2000). Emotions in solution focused therapy: A re-examination. *Family Process, 31*(1), 5–28.

Miller, J.B. (1976). *Toward a new psychology of women.* Boston: Beacon.

Miller, W.B. (2001). *The growth of youth gang problems in the United States: 1970–98.* Washington, DC: Office of Juvenile Justice and Delinquency Prevention. Retrieved August 17, 2005, from http://www.ncjrs.org/pdffiles1/ojjdp/181868-1.pdf

Ministry of Economic Development. (2003). *Population and sustainable development.* Retrieved February 23, 2005, from http://www.med.govt.nz/irdev/econ_dev/population/2003/2003-07.html

Minuchin, S. (1974). *Families and family therapy.* Cambridge, MA: Harvard University Press.

Miocevic, N. (2006). Review of clinical issues with interracial couples: Theories and research. *ANZJFT Australian and New Zealand Journal of Family Therapy, 27*(3), 173.

Mitchell, B.A. (1998). Too close for comfort? Parental assessments of "boomerang kid" living arrangements. *Canadian Journal of Sociology, 23*(1), 21–46.

Moodley, R. (2007). (Re)placing multiculturalism in counselling and psychotherapy. *British Journal of Guidance & Counselling, 35*(1), 1-22.

Mwanza. (1990). *African naturalism.* Columbus, OH: Pan African Publications.

National Association of Social Workers (NASW). (2007a). *Code of ethics.* Retrieved August 13, 2007 from http://www.socialworkers.org/pubs/code/code.asp

National Association of Social Workers (NASW). (2007b). *Issue fact sheets: Diversity and cultural competence.* Retrieved April 6, 2007, from http://www.naswdc.org/pressroom/features/issue/diversity.asp

National Council for the Accreditation of Teacher Education. (2002). *Professional standards for the accreditation of schools, colleges, and departments of education.* Washington, DC: Author. Retrieved August 12, 2005, from http://www.ncate.org/documents/unit_stnds_2002.pdf

Navarre, S. (1998). Salvador Minuchin's structural family therapy and its application to multicultural family systems. *Issues in Mental Health Nursing, 19*(6), 557–575.

Nelson, M.K. (2002). The challenge of self-sufficiency: Women on welfare redefining independence. *Journal of Contemporary Ethnography, 31*(5), 582–614.

Nesdale, D., & Lambert, A. (2007). Effects of experimentally manipulated peer rejection on children's negative affect, self-esteem, and maladaptive social behavior. *International Journal of Behavioral Development, 31*(2), 115-122.

Nevis, E.C. (1983). Evocative and provocative modes of influence in the implementation of change. *Gestalt Journal, 6*(2), 5–12.

New York State Judicial Committee on Women in the Courts. (2004). *Immigration and domestic violence: A short guide for New York State judges.* Retrieved June 23, 2005, from http://www.courts.state.ny.us/ip/womeninthecourts/Immigrationand DomesticViolence.pdf

Nezu, A.M. (2005). Beyond cultural competence: Human diversity and the appositeness of assertive goals. *Clinical Psychology, 12*(1), 19–24.

Nicoll, W.G., Bitter, J.R., Christensen, O.C., & Hawes, C. (2000). Adlerian brief therapy: Strategies and tactics. In J. Carlson & L. Sprery (Eds.), *Brief therapy with individuals and couples* (pp. 220–247). Phoenix: Zeig, Tucker & Theisen.

NIDA. (2007). *Drugs of abuse.* Retrieved August 27, 2007, at http://www.nida.nih.gov/

Niec, L.N., Hemme, J.M., & Yopp, J.M. (2005). Parent–child interaction therapy: The rewards and challenges of a group format. *Cognitive & Behavioral* Practice, *12*(1), 113–125.

Nimmagadda, J., & Cowger, C. (1999). Cross-cultural practice: Social worker ingenuity in the indigenization of practice knowledge. *International Social Work, 42*(3), 261–276.

Nybell, L.M., & Gray, S.S. (2004). Race, place, space: Meanings of cultural competence in three child welfare agencies. *Social Work, 49(1),* 17–26.

O'Brien, K.M., & Zamostny, K.P. (2003). Understanding adoptive families: An integrative review of empirical research and future directions for counseling psychology. *The Counseling Psychologist, 31*(6), 679–710.

O'Leary, E., Sheedy, G., O'Sullivan, K., & Thoresen, C. (2003). Cork older adult intervention project: Outcomes of Gestalt therapy group with older adults. *Counseling Psychology Quarterly, 16*(2), 131–144.

Office of Management and Budget. (1978). *Poverty measurement studies and alternative measures (Statistical policy directive 14).* Retrieved September 22, 2007, from http://www.census.gov/hhes/www/povmeas/ombdir14.html

Oliver, R. (1982). "Empty nest" or relationship restructuring? A rational-emotive approach to a mid-life transition. *Women and Therapy, 1*(2), 67–83.

Olson, D.H., McCubbin, H.I., Barnes, H.L., Larsen, A., Muxen, M.J., & Wilson, M. (1983). *Families: What makes them work.* Beverly Hills, CA: Sage.

Ozen, D. S. (2003). The impact of interparental divorce on adult attachment styles and perceived parenting styles of adolescents. *Journal of Divorce & Remarriage, 40*(1–2), 129-149.

Padilla-Walker, L.M., &Thompson, R.A. (2005). Combating conflicting messages of values: A closer look at parental strategies. *Social Development, 14*(2), 305–323.

Parents Without Partners, International. (2005). *Facts about single-parent families.* Retrieved October 13, 2005, from http://www.parentswithoutpartners.org/Support1.htm

Parents Without Partners. (2007). *Facts about single parent families.* Retrieved April 19, 2007, from http://www.parentswithoutpartners.org/Support1.htm

Patterson, C. (2000). Family relationships of lesbians and gay men. *Journal of Marriage & Family, 62*(4), 1052–1070.

Payne, M. (2005). *Modern social work theory.* Chicago: Lyceum.

Pedersen, P. (2000). *A handbook for developing multicultural awareness* (3rd ed.). Alexandria, VA: American Counseling Association.

Pederson, P.B. (1997). *Culture-centered counseling interventions: Striving for accuracy.* Thousand Oaks, CA: Sage.

Pena, E. (2003). Reconfiguring epistemological pacts: Creating a dialogue between psychoanalysis and Chicano/a subjectivity, a cosmopolitan perspective 1. *Journal for the Psychoanalysis of Culture & Society, 8*(2), 308–320.

Perls, F. (1969a). *Gestalt therapy verbatim.* Moab, UT: Real People Press.

Perls, F. (1969b). *In and out of the garbage pail.* Moab, UT: Real People Press.

Perls, F., Hefferline, R., & Goodman, R. (1951). *Gestalt therapy integrated: Excitement and growth in the human personality.* New York: Dell.

Person, E. (2004). Something borrowed: How mutual influences among gays, lesbians, bisexuals, and straights changed women's lives and psychoanalytic theory. *Annual of Psychoanalysis, 32,* 81–100.

Pettifor, J.L. (2001). Are professional codes of ethics relevant for multicultural counselling? *Canadian Journal of Counselling, 35*(1), 26–35.

Phinney, J.S. (1996). When we talk about American ethnic groups, what do we mean? *American Psychologist, 51*(9), 918–927.

Pichot, T., & Dolan, Y. M. (2003). *Solution-focused brief therapy: Its effective use in agency settings.* Binghamton, NY: Haworth Clinical Practice Press.

Plunkett, S.W., Henry, C. S., & Knaub, P.K. (1999). Family stressor events, family coping, and adolescent adaptation in farm and ranch families. *Adolescence, 34*(133), 147–168.

Ponterotto, J.G., Gretchen, D., Utsey, S., Reiger, B., & Austin, R. (2002). A revision of the multicultural counseling awareness scale. *Journal of Multicultural Counseling and Development, 30*(3), 153–180.

Population Reference Bureau. (2004). *Human population: Fundamentals of growth effect of migration on population growth.* Retrieved March 21, 2005, from http://www.prb.org/Content/NavigationMenu/PRB/Educators/Human_Population/Migration2/Migration1.htm

Porter, K. (2007). *Globalization: What is it?* Retrieved on March 21, 2007, from http://globalization.about.com/cs/whatisit/a/whatisit.htm

Portes, P., & Zady, M. (2002). Self-esteem in the adaptation of Spanish-speaking adolescents: The role of immigration, family conflict, and depression. *Hispanic Journal of Behavioral Sciences, 24*(3), 296–318.

Price, J. A. (1994). The Tao in family therapy. *Journal of Systemic Therapies, 13*(3), 53–63.

Quigley, T. (1998). *A brief outline of psychoanalytic theory: Freudian, Lacanian, and object relations theory.* Retrieved June 3, 2005, from http://homepage.newschool.edu/~quigleyt/vcs/psychoanalysis.html

Ramirez, R.R., & de la Cruz, P.G. (2003). *The Hispanic population in the United States: March 2002* (Current Population Reports, 20-545). Washington, DC: U.S. Census Bureau.

Raup, J. L., & Myers, J. E. (1989). The empty nest syndrome: Myth or reality? *Journal of Counseling & Development, 68*, 180–183.

Reeves, T., & Bennett, C. (2003). *The Asian and Pacific Islander population in the United States: March 2002 (Current Population Reports, 20-540).* Washington, DC: U.S. Census Bureau.

Reilly, S., & Schachtman, T.R. (2005). Pavlovian conditioning requires ruling out nonassociative factors to claim conditioning occurred. *International Journal of Comparative Psychology, 18*(1), 34–37.

Renik, O., & Spillius, E.B. (2004). Intersubjectivity in psychoanalysis. *International Journal of Psychoanalysis, 85*(5), 1053–1056.

Rhyne, J. (1990). Gestalt psychology/Gestalt therapy: Forms/contexts. *Journal of Art Therapy, 29*(1), 2–9.

Riley, S., & Malchiodi, C.A. (2003). Solution-focused and narrative approaches. In C.A. Malchiodi (Ed.), *Handbook of art therapy* (pp. 82–92). New York: Guilford Press.

Roberts, A.R., & Yeager, K.R. (2004). *Evidence-based practice manual: Research and outcome measures in health and human services.* Oxford: Oxford University Press.

Robinson, J. (1989). Clinical treatment of black families: Issues and strategies. *Social Work, 34*, 323–329.

Root, M.P.P. (Ed.) (1996). *The multiracial experience: Racial borders as the new frontier.* Thousand Oaks, CA: Sage.

Rothbaum, F., Rosen, K., Ujiite, T., & Uchida, N. (2002). Family systems theory, attachment theory, and culture. *Family Process, 41*(3), 328–356.

Running Wolf, P., & Rickard, J.A. (2003). Talking circles: A Native American approach to experiential learning. *Journal of* Multicultural *Counseling & Development, 31*(1), 39–43.

Russell, G. (1998). *American Indian facts of life: A profile of today's tribes and reservations.* Phoenix, AZ: Russell.

Ryan, D., & Martin, A. (2000). Lesbian, gay, bisexual, and transgender parents in the school systems. *School Psychology Review, 29*(2), 207–216.

Salzman, M. B. (2002). A culturally congruent consultation at a Bureau of Indian Affairs boarding school. *Journal of Individual Psychology, 58*(2), 132–147.

SAMHSA. (2007). *Drug free communities support program.* Retrieved September 19, 2007, at http://drugfreecommunities.samhsa.gov/

Sandhu, D.S., Leung, S.A., & Tang, M. (2003). Counseling approaches with Asian Americans and Pacific Islander Americans. In F.D. Harper & J. McFadden (Eds.), *Culture and counseling: New approaches* (pp. 99–114). Boston: Pearson.

Santisteban, D., Coatsworth, D., Perez-Vidal, A., Mitrani, V., Jean-Gilles, M., & Szapocznik, J. (1997). Brief structural/strategic family therapy with African and Hispanic high-risk youth. *Journal of Community Psychology, 25*(5), 453–468.

Satir, V. (1972). *People making.* Palo Alto, CA: Science and Behavior Books.

Savin-Williams, R. (1996). Self-labeling and disclosure among gay, lesbian, and bisexual youths. In J. Laird & R. Green (Eds.), *Lesbians and gays in couples and families: A handbook for therapists* (pp. 153–182): San Francisco: Jossey-Bass.

Scott, C., & Michele, A. (2003). The social construction of the divorce "problem": Morality, child victims, and the politics of gender. *Family Relations, 52*(4), 363–372.

Second Harvest Network. (1997). *Hunger 1997: The faces and facts.* Retrieved October 13, 2005, from http://www.secondharvest.org/more_files/clients_single_parent.pdf

Semmler, P.L., & Williams, C.B. (2000). Narrative therapy: A storied context for multicultural counseling. *Journal of Multicultural Counseling & Development, 28*(1), 51–62.

Sharps, M. J., Price-Sharps, J. L., & Day, S. S. (2005). Cognition at risk: Gestalt/feature-intensive processing, attention deficit, and substance abuse. *Current Psychology: Developmental, Learning, Personality, Social, 24*(2), 91-101.

Simmons, T., & O'Connell, M. (2003). *Married-couple and unmarried-partner households: 2000* (Census 2000 Special Reports). Washington, DC: U.S. Census Bureau.

Skinner, B.F. (1969). *Contingencies of reinforcement: A theoretical analysis.* New York: Appleton-Century-Crofts.

Skinner, H., Steinhauer, P., & Sitarenios, G. (1983). The family assessment measure. *Canadian Journal of Community Mental Health, 2,* 91–105.

Skinner, H., Steinhauer, P., & Sitarenios, G. (2000). Family assessment measure (FAM) and process model of family functioning. *Journal of Family Therapy, 22,* 190–210.

Slater, S. (1995). *The lesbian family life cycle.* New York: Free Press.

Slater, S., & Mencher, J. (1991). The lesbian family life cycle: A contextual approach. *American Journal of Orthopsychiatry, 61*(3), 372–382.

Smith, T. (Ed.). (2004). *Practicing multiculturalism: Affirming diversity in counseling and psychology.* Boston: Pearson.

Smith, D. M., & Elander, J. (2006). Effects of area and family deprivation on risk factors for teenage pregnancy among 13–15-year-old girls. *Psychology, Health & Medicine, 11*(4), 399-410.

Smucker Barnwell, S., Earleywine, M., & Gordis, E. B. (2005). Alcohol consumption moderates the link between cannabis use and cannabis dependence in an internet survey. *Psychology of Addictive Behaviors, 19*(2), 212–216.

Snowden, L.R. (2005). Racial, cultural and ethnic disparities in health and mental health: Toward theory and research at community levels. *American Journal of Community Psychology, 35*(1–2), 1–8.

Sodowsky, G.R. (1996). The Multicultural Counseling Inventory: Validity and applications in multicultural training. In G.R. Sodowsky & J.C. Impara (Eds.), *Multicultural assessment in counseling and clinical psychology* (pp. 283–324). Lincoln, NE: Buros Institute of Mental Measurements.

Sommer, R. (1994). *Male and female perpetrated abuse: Testing a diathesis-stress model*. Retrieved May 25, 2005, from http://www.fathersforlife.org/reena_sommer_DV_2c.htm

Spangler, D., & Brandl, B. (2007). Abuse in later life: Power and control dynamics and a victim-centered response. *Journal of the American Psychiatric Nurses Association, 12*(6), 322-331.

Spark, G. (1974). Grandparents and intergenerational family therapy. *Family Process, 13*, 225–238.

Spencer, M.B., Swanson, D.P., & Cunningham, M. (1991). Ethnicity, ethnic identity, and competence formation: Adolescent transition and cultural transformation. *Journal of Negro Education, 60*(3), 366–387.

Speziale, B., & Gopalakrishna, V. (2004). Social support and functioning of nuclear families headed by lesbian couples. *Affilia: Journal of Women & Social Work, 19*(2), 174–184.

Spiegler, M.D., & Guevremont, D.C. (2003). *Contemporary behavior therapy* (4th ed.). Pacific Grove, CA: Brooks/Cole.

Spruijt, E., DeGoede, M., & Vandervalk, I. (2001). The well-being of youngsters coming from six different family types. *Patient Education & Counseling, 45*(4), 285–294.

Stanhope, V., Solomon, P., Pernell-Arnold, A., Sands, R.G., Bourjolly, J.N. (2005). Evaluating cultural competence among behavioral health professionals. *Psychiatric Rehabilitation Journal 28*(3), 225–233.

Stedman, J.M. (1977). Behavior therapy strategies as applied to family therapy. *Family Therapy, 4*(3), 217–224.

Steinglass, P. (1987). A systems view of family interaction and psychopathology. In T. Jacob (Ed.), *Family interaction and psychopathology: Theories, methods, and findings* (pp. 25–65). New York: Plenum Press.

Stolley, K.S. (1993). Statistics on adoption in the United States. *The Future of Children: Adoption, 3*(1), 26–42.

Strand, P.S. (1997). Toward a developmentally informed narrative therapy. *Family Process, 36*(4), 325–339.

Strong, S., & Callahan, C.J. (2001). Professional responsibility to gay, lesbian, bisexual, and transgendered (GLBT) youths and families. In D.S. Sandhu (Ed.), *Elementary school counseling in the new millennium* (pp. 249–258). Alexandria, VA: American Counseling Association.

Substance Abuse and Mental Health Services Administration. (2004). *Results from the 2003 National Survey on Drug Use and Health: National Findings*. Rockville, MD: Office of Applied Studies.

Sue, D.W., & Sue, D. (2003). *Counseling the culturally diverse: Theory and practice* (4th ed.). New York: Wiley.

Sue, D.W., Ivey, A.E., & Pederson, P.B. (1996). *A theory of multicultural counseling and therapy*. Pacific Grove, CA: Brooks/Cole.

Suinn, R., Khoo, G., & Ahuna, G. (1995). The Suinn-Lew Asian Self-Identity Acculturation Scale: Cross-cultural information. *Journal of Multicultural Counseling & Development, 23*(3), 139–151.

Sutton, P.D. (2003). Births, marriages, divorces, and deaths: Provisional data for October-December 2002. *National vital statistics reports, 51*(10). Hyattsville, MD: National Center for Health Statistics.

Sutton, P. D. (2007). Births, marriages, divorces, and deaths: Provisional data for October 2006. *National vital statistics reports, 55*(17). Hyattsville, MD: National Center for Health Statistics.

Thornton, S., & Garrett, K. (1995). Ethnography as a bridge to multicultural practice. *Journal of Social Work Education, 31(1),* 67–74.

Tolman, R., & Raphael, J. (2000). A review of the research on welfare and domestic violence. *Journal of Social Issues, 56*(4), 655–682.

Torres-Rivera, E., Phan, L., Maddux, C., Wilber, M., & Garrett, M. (2001). Process versus content: Integrating personal awareness and counseling skills to meet the multicultural challenge of the twenty-first century. *Counselor Education & Supervision, 41,* 28–40.

Turner, F. J. (1996). *Social work treatment: Interlocking theoretical approaches* (4th ed.). New York: Free Press.

Turner, J. H. (1982). *The structure of sociological theory.* Homewood, IL: The Dorsey Press.\ United Nations. (2002). *International migration 2002.* Retrieved May 16, 2005, from http://www.un.org/esa/population/publications/ittmig2002/Migration 2002.pdf

United Nations Educational, Scientific and Cultural Organization. (UNESCO, 2005). *Culture and development.* Retrieved April 5, 2005, from http://portal.unesco.org/culture/en/ev.php-URL_ID=13031&URL_DO=DO_TOPIC&URL_SECTION=201.html

United Nations. (2002). *International migration 2002.* Retrieved May 16, 2005, from http://www.un.org/esa/population/publications/ittmig2002/Migration2002.pdf

University of Kentucky. (1989). *Collaboration for competency: Examining social work curriculum in the perspective of current practice with children and families.* Lexington, KY: University of Kentucky College of Social Work.

U.S. Census Bureau. (2001). *Census 2000 shows America's diversity.* Retrieved June 25, 2007, from http://www.census.gov/Press-Release/www/2001/cb01cn61.html

U. S. Census Bureau. (2001). *Profiles of general demographic characteristics 2000: 2000 Census of population and housing: United States.* Washington, DC: Department of Commerce.

U. S. Census Bureau. (2004a). *U.S. interim projections by age, sex, race, and Hispanic origin.* Retrieved March 5, 2005, from http://www.census.gov/ipc/www/usinterim proj/

U. S. Census Bureau. (2004b). *The black population in the United States: March 2004 (PPL-186).* Retrieved May 29, 2007, from http://www.census.gov/population/www/socdemo/race/ppl-186.html

U. S. Census Bureau. (2004c). *The Asian alone population in the United States: March 2004 (PPL-184).* Retrieved May 29, 2007, from http://www.census.gov/population/www/socdemo/race/ppl-184.html

U. S. Census Bureau. (2004d). *The Hispanic population in the United States: 2004.* Retrieved May 29, 2007, from http://www.census.gov/population/www/socdemo/hispanic/cps2004.html

U.S. Census Bureau. (2005a). *Living arrangements of black children under 18 years old: 1960 to present.* Retrieved August 17, 2005, from http://www.census.gov/population/socdemo/hh-fam/ch3.pdf

U.S. Census Bureau. (2005b). *Poverty status of people by family relationship, race, and Hispanic origin: 1959 to 2003.* Retrieved August 17, 2005, from http://www.census.gov/hhes/www/poverty/histpov/hstpov2.html

U.S. Census Bureau. (2006). *We the people: American Indians and Alaska Natives in the United States: Census 2000 special report.* Washington, DC: U.S. Department of Commerce.

U.S. Citizenship and Immigration Services. (2006). *Persons obtaining legal permanent resident status by broad class of admission and region and country of last residence: fiscal year 2006.* Retrieved August 30, 2007, from http://www.dhs.gov/xlibrary/assets/statistics/yearbook/2006/table11d.xls

U. S. Department of Health and Human Services (2001). *A guide to understanding female adolescents' substance abuse: Gender and ethnic considerations for prevention and treatment policy.* Retrieved on May 25, 2005, from http://www.girlpower.gov/press/research/FemaleAdolescentsGuideBacker110201.pdf

U.S. Department of Health and Human Services. (2004). *How many children were adopted in 2000 and 2001?* Washington, DC: National Adoption Information Clearinghouse.

U.S. Department of Justice (1991). *Bureau of Justice Statistics: Female victims of violent crime.* Retrieved May 29, 2005, from http://www.ojp.usdoj.gov/bjs/pub/pdf/fvvc.pdf

U.S. Department of Justice (1994). *Bureau of Justice Statistics selected findings: Violence between intimates.* Retrieved May 29, 2005, from http://www.ojp.usdoj.gov/bjs/pub/pdf/vbi.pdf

U.S. Department of Justice (1995). *Bureau of Justice Statistics special report: Violence against women: Estimates from the redesigned survey.* Retrieved May 29, 2005, from http://www.ojp.usdoj.gov/bjs/pub/pdf/femvied.pdf

U.S. Department of Justice (1998). *Violence by intimates: Analysis of data on crimes by current or former spouses, boyfriends, and girlfriends.* Retrieved May 29, 2005, from http://www.ojp.usdoj.gov/bjs/pub/pdf/vi.pdf

U.S. Department of Justice (2003). *Bureau of Justice Statistics crime data brief: Intimate partner violence, 1993–2001.* Retrieved May 29, 2005, from http://www.ojp.usdoj.gov/bjs/pub/pdf/ipv01.pdf

Valentan, L. (2002). *Where are the tribes?* Retrieved March 30, 2005, from http://eprentice.sdsu.edu/F02X1/lvalentan/del.htm

Viramontez Anguiano, R. P., & Harrison, S.M. (2002). Teaching cultural diversity to college students majoring in helping professions: The use of an eco-strengths perspective. *College Student Journal, 36*(1), 152–156.

Vontress, C., & Jackson, M. (2004). Reactions to multicultural counseling debate. *Journal of Mental Health Counseling, 26(1),* 74–80.

Wagner-Moore, L. E. (2004). Gestalt therapy: Past, present, theory, and research. *Psychotherapy: Theory, Research, Practice, Training, 41*(2), 180–189.

Waldron, H., & Kaminer, Y. (2004). On the learning curve: The emerging evidence supporting cognitive-behavioral therapies for adolescent substance abuse. *Addiction, 99*(2), 93–106.

Walsh, W. M. (1993). Gender and strategic marital therapy. *Family Journal: Counseling and Therapy for Couples and Families, 1*(2), 160-161.

Walsh, F. (1998). *Strengthening family resilience.* New York: Guilford Press.

Walsh, F., & McGoldrick, M. (1991). *Living beyond loss: Death in the family.* New York: Norton.

Wardle, F. (2001). *Supporting multiracial and multiethnic children and their families.* Retrieved May 24, 2005, from http://www.webcom.com/~intvoice/wardle2.html

Weinrach, S.G. (2003). A person-centered perspective to welfare-to-work services: In pursuit of the elusive and the unattainable. *Career Development Quarterly, 52*, 153–161.

Weston, K. (1991). *Families we choose: Lesbians, gays, kinship*. New York: Columbia University Press.

Wetter, M. G., & Wetter, J. (2006). Effective understanding and dealing with manipulation. In W. O'Donohue, N. A. Cummings, & J. L. Cummings (Eds.), *Clinical strategies for becoming a master psychotherapist* (pp. 87-93). Amsterdam: Elsevier.

Wheeler, G. (2005). Culture, self, and field: A Gestalt guide to the age of complexity. *Gestalt Review, 9*(1), 91–128.

White, L. (1999). Contagion in family affection: Mothers, fathers, and young adult children. *Journal of Marriage and Family, 61*(2), 284–295.

White, M. (1993). Deconstruction and therapy. In S.G. Gilligan & R. Price, *Therapeutic Conversations* (pp. 22–61). New York: W.W. Norton.

Wood, B., & Talmon, M. (1983). Family boundaries in transition: A search for alternatives. *Family Process, 22*(3), 347–357.

Worden, A.P. (2000). The changing boundaries of the criminal justice system: Redefining for older women. *Violence Against Women, 4*, 559–571.

Wuest, J., Ford-Gilboe, M., Merritt-Gray, M., & Berman, H. (2003). Intrusion: The central problem for family health promotion among children and single mothers after leaving an abusive partner. *Quarterly Health Research, 13*(5), 595–622.

Wulf, R. (1996). The historical roots of Gestalt therapy theory. Retrieved August 27, 2007, from http://www.gestalt.org/wulf.htm

Yamazaki, Y. (2004). An experiential approach to cross-cultural adaptation: A study of Japanese expatriates' learning styles, learning skills, and job satisfaction in the United States. *Dissertation Abstracts International Section A: Humanities & Social Sciences, 64*(12-A), 4526.

Yang, K. (2003). Cross-cultural differences in perspectives on the self. In V. Murphy-Berman & J. J. Berman (Eds.), *Beyond Maslow's culture-bound linear theory: A preliminary statement of the double-y model of basic human needs* (pp. 192–272). Lincoln: University of Nebraska Press.

Yeung, A., Neault, N., & Sonawalla, S. (2002). Screening for major depression in Asian-Americans: A comparison of the Beck and the Chinese Depression Inventory. *Acta Psychiatrica Scandinavica, 105*(4), 252–257.

Ying, Y., & Tracy, L. (2004). Psychometric properties of the Intergenerational Congruence in Immigrant Families—Parent Scale in Chinese Americans. *Social Work Research, 28*(1), 56–62.

Ying, Y., Lee, P.A., & Tsai, J.L. (2004). Psychometric properties of the Intergenerational Congruence in Immigrant Families: Child Scale in Chinese Americans. *Journal of Comparative Family Studies, 35*(1), 91–103.

Zamostny, K.P., Wiley, M.O., O'Brien, K.M., Lee, R.M., & Baden, A.L. (2003). Breaking the silence: Advancing knowledge about adoption for counseling psychologists. *The Counseling Psychologist, 31*(6), 647–650.

Zane, N., Morton, T., Chu, J., & Lin, N. (1999). Counseling and psychotherapy with Asian American clients. In T. Smith (Ed.), *Practicing multiculturalism: Affirming diversity in counseling and psychology* (pp. 190–214). Boston: Pearson.

Zlotnik, J., & Galambos, C. (2004). Evidence based practices in health care: Social work possibilities. *Health and Social Work, 29*(4), 259–261.

NAME INDEX

SUBJECT INDEX